The Pageant of Literature

GOETHE
TO
IBSEN

Sister M. Judine, I.H.M.

Marian High School, Birmingham, Michigan

CATHOLIC EDUCATION DIVISION
CED

New York   THE MACMILLAN COMPANY

A Division of The Crowell-Collier Publishing Company

Nihil obstat

EDWARD J. MONTANO, S.T.D.
CENSOR LIBRORUM

Imprimatur

✠ FRANCIS CARDINAL SPELLMAN
ARCHBISHOP OF NEW YORK

4E

ACKNOWLEDGMENTS

For permission to use material in this book grateful acknowledgment is made to the following:

Bantam Books, Inc.: For "God Sees the Truth, but Waits" and "Where Love Is, There God Is Also," from *The Short Stories of Leo Tolstoy* translated by Arthur Mendel and Barbara Makanowitzky. © Copyright 1960 by Bantam Books, Inc. and reprinted by permission of the publisher. All Rights Reserved.

The Bobbs-Merrill Company, Inc.: For selections from *Faust* by Johann Wolfgang von Goethe, translated by Bayard Quincy Morgan, Copyright © 1954, 1957 by The Liberal Arts Press, Inc. Reprinted by permission of The Liberal Arts Press Division of the Bobbs-Merrill Company, Inc.

Albert Bonnier Publishers: For "Autumn" by August Strindberg, translated by Erik Lidforss, published by Albert Bonnier, 1961.

The Citadel Press: For "The Two Grenadiers," "The Lorelei," "The Light Goes Out," "Twilight," "Journey by Water" and Sonnets to My Mother, B. Heine," from *The Prose and Poetry of Heinrich Heine*, edited by Frederic Ewen, published by The Citadel Press, 1948.

Babette Deutsch: For "The Prophet," "Autumn," "Grapes," and "To Chaadayev" by Alexander Pushkin, translated by Babette Deutsch, from A *Treasury of Russian Verse*. Reprinted by permission of Babette Deutsch.

The Macmillan Company, New York
Brett-Macmillan, Ltd., Galt, Ontario
Printed in the United States of America

Fawcett Publications, Inc.: For a selection from Victor Hugo's *Les Misérables*, translated by Charles E. Wilbour and abridged by James K. Robinson. Reprinted by permission of Premium World Classics, Fawcett Publications, Inc.

Kate Flores: For "Correspondences," "The Swan," and "Landscape" by Charles Baudelaire; for "The Drunken Boat" and "Morning" by Arthur Rimbaud; for "God Said . . ." and "The Sky Above the Roof" by Paul Verlaine. All translated by Kate Flores.

Samuel French, Inc.: For "The Boor" by Anton Chekhov, translated by Hilmar Baukhage.

Application for the right to perform or reproduce this play in any manner in the Dominion of Canada must be made to Samuel French (Canada) Ltd., 27 Grenville St., Toronto, Ont., Canada; in all other countries of the World outside the United States of America, to Samuel French, Ltd., 26 Southampton Street, Strand, London, W.C. 2, England.

William Heinemann Ltd.: For "An Honest Thief" translated by Constance Garnett from *An Honest Thief* by Fyodor Dostoyevsky. Reprinted by permission of William Heinemann Ltd. and The Macmillan Company. For "Mumu" from *Torrents of Spring* by Ivan Turgenev, translated by Constance Garnett. Reprinted by permission of William Heinemann Ltd.

The Macmillan Company: For "Grapes" and "To Chaadayev" by Alexander Pushkin, translated by Babette Deutsch, from *A Treasury of Russian Verse*, copyright 1949 by The Macmillan Company. Reprinted by permission of The Macmillan Company, Babette Deutsch, and Avrahm Yarmolinsky. For "An Honest Thief" from *An Honest Thief and Other Stories* by Fyodor Dostoyevsky, translated by Constance Garnett. Reprinted by permission of The Macmillan Company.

Random House, Inc.: For "The Bet" from *The Short Stories of Anton Chekhov* (ML-50). Copyright 1932 and renewed 1959 by The Modern Library, Inc. Published by Random House, Inc.

University of California Press: For "Moonlight" and "The Art of Poetry" by Paul Verlaine, translated by C. F. MacIntyre, from *French Symbolist Poetry*.

Louise Varèse: For "My Bohemia" by Arthur Rimbaud, translated by Louise Varèse.

CONTENTS

v

PRONUNCIATION KEY

The pronunciation of those authors' names which are difficult to pronounce will be found on the pages where the names first appear. The diacritical marks used are those found in *Webster's New World Dictionary*. The key to these diacritical marks follows.

a	*as in*	fat, lap
ā	*as in*	ape, date
â	*as in*	bare, care
ä	*as in*	car, father
à	*as in*	French *bal*; intermediate between **a** and **ä**
e	*as in*	ten, let
ē	*as in*	even, meet
ê	*as in*	here, dear
ẽr	*as in*	over, under
ë	*as in*	French *leur*
i	*as in*	is, hit
ī	*as in*	bite, mile
o	*as in*	lot, top
ō	*as in*	go, tone
ô	*as in*	horn, fork
ōō	*as in*	tool, troop
oo	*as in*	book, moor
ö	*as in*	French *feu*; round the lips for **ō** and try to pronounce **ā**
ô̂	*as in*	French *coq* and German *doch*
u	*as in*	up, cut
ū	*as in*	use, cute
ü	*as in*	French *duc* and German *grün*
ə	*as in*	*a*go, umbrell*a*
n		This symbol indicates that the vowel sound immediately preceding it is nasalized, as in French *en, mon*.
th	*as in*	thin, truth
th	*as in*	then, father

INTRODUCTION

𝒯HE nineteenth century, one of the most controversial and fluid of times in literature and art, was dominated from the first by writers imbued with the spirit of romanticism. Later in the century, realism, naturalism, and symbolism became predominant literary movements, which had far-reaching effects on writers of the twentieth century.

After 1770, the trend was away from the hard precision of neoclassicism. Literature was now marked by the democratic spirit prevailing in the social and political worlds, and by a fervent love of nature and of remote times, notably the medieval period. Where the neoclassical writers of the eighteenth century had emphasized reason, impersonality, factuality, and a strict adherence to the theories and rules of the classical writers, the romantics emphasized emotion, imagination, individuality, and the use of literary forms that allowed them to express their personal feelings more freely.

Among the foremost writers of the new romantic school was the great German poet and playwright, Johann Wolfgang von Goethe, whose poetic drama, *Faust*, set in the Middle Ages, remains one of the great plays of the Western world, with its sense of mystery and the preternatural, and its underlying protest against the materialism of Goethe's day.

The works of two poets, Heinrich Heine and Alexander Pushkin, reveal that the romantic writers could seem characteristically self-centered, even as they were dedicated to bettering the lot of the poor, the underprivileged, and their country, in general. While they upheld the dignity of the common man, contradictorily, they held themselves aloof from the "common herd," remembering their specific calling as persons apart. Their poetry, nevertheless, abounds in the rich, sensuous images of color and sound typical of the poets of their time.

While Goethe and Heine in Germany, Pushkin in Russia, and Leopardi in Italy were startling the literary world with the beauty of verse and freedom of forms hitherto untried, both Victor Hugo and Honoré de Balzac in France, working in the genres of the novel and short story, were providing achievements in fiction of the first magnitude. Hugo, though primarily a lyric poet, stirred the reading public of his day with such exciting novels as *Notre Dame de Paris* and *Les Misérables.* However, while Hugo remained a romanticist to the end, Balzac turned from the dreams and ideals of his contemporaries to a realistic interpretation of life. In more than a hundred novels and short stories, he exposed life in contemporary French society in the most detailed manner, thereby establishing a model for the new school of realism, which became the dominant literary movement in the second half of the nineteenth century and which has had a major influence on many modern writers.

In the world of science and technology, there was a growing interest in man in relation to his environment. In literature, this was reflected in the new trend toward naturalism—a preoccupation with the "scientific" or "case-history" type of fiction. The pioneer in this field was Gustave Flaubert, the French writer whose tales abound in minute observations of the most realistic kind so that, even when employing a romantic, medieval background, as in "The Legend of Saint Julian the Hospitaler," he succeeds in shocking the reader with brutal though finely drawn details. Hence, it is not surprising to find that his pupils, Emile Zola and Guy de Maupassant, going beyond their teacher's artistic attempts, revel in picturing the sordid and seamier side of life. Maupassant, in particular, delights in satire and a cynical fatalism, though his concern for perfection of technique is above reproach. Thus, naturalism degenerated, at times, into a depressing and brutal portrayal of man as a mere cog in a machine, with the author studying man's behavior as a chemist studies compounds and their reactions in a test tube. It was a sort of ultra-realism from which many modern writers have drawn their philosophy of life.

In Russia, on the other hand, both Leo Tolstoy and Feodor Dostoyevsky, while employing a strongly realistic style, were concerned primarily with man's inner, spiritual life and his relationship to the eternal values. If, as has been said, Dostoyevsky's characters are often drawn from the lowest levels of society, he delineates the base, the vile and the gross, not for their own sakes, nor to shock the sensibilities of a society he despised—as with Maupassant—but in the spirit of suffering and compassion for his fellow human beings.

Eventually there had to be a revolt against the crass naturalistic type of writing of the times. One of the most prominent was that of the French symbolist poets, such as Charles Baudelaire, Paul Verlaine, and Arthur Rimbaud, who rejected both the bourgeois mentality and the writing which reflected it. Sometimes called "romantics of indirection," the symbolists asserted a deep faith in the personal, the eternal, and the emotional, rather than the impersonal, the external, and the factual. Unlike the early romantics, however, they sought to capture in poetry not the precise and clear picture of what had affected them in nature and the world about them, but the "vagueness and elusiveness" of that experience; hence, not the thing itself, but only the *symbol* of the thing—what Baudelaire called the "color and sound and perfume" of the inner qualities of that thing. And the qualities were always to be brought out by metaphor—never directly.

In the field of the drama, too, the famous Norwegian, Henrik Ibsen, succeeded in employing the power and force of symbolism. Some of his greatest themes, such as the freedom of each individual to achieve his ideals in life, the universal conflict between illusion and reality, the narrowness of the society of his day, are powerfully projected through functional symbols operating within the most realistic of situations. For the fact remains that Ibsen, at times poetic and intensely mystical, was a realist of the first rank, presenting on the stage for the first time, ideas and problems, techniques and methods which revolutionized the theater and its art.

Amid all the varieties of innovation and reform of the nineteenth century, however, the romantic-realist temper dominated the age. For even the symbolist was but a romantic at heart, and the naturalist a realist gone to extremes. And if, as did happen, the "isms" of our own time—the impressionism of Joseph Conrad and Henry James, and the expressionism of James Joyce and T. S. Eliot—seem baffling reverses of the same process, they are, in the final analyses, offshoots respectively, of the intellectual romanticists and the psychological realists.

Thus, while the literature of Western Europe during the nineteenth century was marked by a revolution and a shifting of moods and attitudes as far-reaching in its effects as the political, industrial, and scientific upheavals, its temper was the one common to people of all times and places, and its plea, likewise universal, has ever been that of social awareness—"man's inhumanity to man."

GOETHE
TO
IBSEN

Johann Wolfgang von Goethe

Faust

Johann Wolfgang von Goethe * (1749–1832) was the most famous German novelist, poet, and playwright of his time. He has also been classified with the "giants of literature," Homer, Dante, and Shakespeare. Writing at a period when the transition from classicism to romanticism was in process, Goethe wrote his early works in the purely romantic fashion of his contemporaries. His two years of study in Italy, however, convinced him that the most perfect form of art could be achieved by blending the beauty of classicism with that of romanticism. He illustrated this ideal in his masterpiece, *Faust*, by having his German hero fall in love with Helen of ancient Greece.

Goethe was not only one of the major writers of Europe during his lifetime, he was also a lawyer and state adviser to the Duke of Weimar. He encouraged the latest scientific methods, and became a biologist of great repute. All of these phases of his remarkably versatile genius are reflected in *Faust*, notably in Part II, where the hero learns that true greatness is attained only by selfless devotion to the commonwealth.

From your study of English literature, you will recall the play *Dr. Faustus* by Christopher Marlowe. It is on this drama and the medieval morality play, *Everyman*, that Goethe based his great drama. In Marlowe's play, however, the devil wins his bargain with Faustus; in Goethe's version, the hero saves his immortal soul. After spending his life attempting to achieve supreme happiness through book learning, sensual pleasures, and the attainment of power through art, science, and politics, Faust rejects all of these as representing the vanity of earthly things. His dying words are:

> He only earns his freedom and existence
> Who daily conquers them anew.

One of Goethe's best-known translators, Bayard Taylor, summarized *Faust* succinctly: "*Faust* is, in the most comprehensive sense, a drama of the life of man." As a picture of man's struggle with the forces of good and evil within him, Goethe's play remains one of the great works in the literature of the Western world. As an allegory of the human soul, it is valid for all time.

* yō'hän vôlf'gän fôn gö'tə

1

The Prologue is the beginning of the play proper; it suggests the middle and states the end. Mephistopheles has his own views about men. He is concerned with the frightful predicament into which men have forced themselves by their abuse of Reason. He believes that man is enduring a perverted, animal existence, and hence, thinks that he can tempt Faust to *absolute* evil. From the Prologue you learn, then, that the drama will try to solve the eternal question: is man a successful creation? Will man, in the face of grave temptation, still acknowledge the distinction between good and evil? Mephistopheles, of course, thinks that he won't.

PROLOGUE IN HEAVEN

(THE LORD. THE HEAVENLY HOST. *Later* MEPHISTOPHELES. THE THREE ARCHANGELS *step forward.*)

RAPHAEL. As of old the sun intones his song in rivalry with brother spheres and completes his prescribed course with thunderous march. The sight of him gives strength to the angels, though none can fathom him; and the inconceivably lofty works are glorious as on the first day.

GABRIEL. And swiftly, and with inconceivable speed, the splendor of earth revolves; a brilliance as of paradise alternates with deep and dreadful night. The ocean foams up in broad currents at the deep base of the rocks, and sea and rocks are swept onward in the eternal, rapid course of the spheres.

MICHAEL. And tempests rage in rivalry from sea to land, from land to sea, forming in their fury a chain of the profoundest effect on every hand. There flames a flashing devastation before the path of the thunderclap. But Thy heralds, Lord, revere the gentle footfalls of Thy day.

ALL THREE. These sights give strength to the angels, while none can fathom Thee, and all Thy lofty works are glorious as on the first day.

MEPHISTOPHELES. Since you approach again, O Lord, asking after the state of things here with us, and since you used to be glad to see me, you find me too among the retinue. Forgive me, but I can't make up lofty phrases, not even if this whole company scoffs at me; my emotion would surely provoke·you to laughter, had you not forsworn laughing. Of sun and worlds I have nothing to say; all I see is the trouble men have. The little god of the world continues to be of the same old stamp and is as odd as on the first day. He would lead a somewhat better life had you not granted him the semblance of heavenly light; he calls it "reason," and merely uses it to be more beastly than any beast. He seems to me, by leave of Your Grace, to resemble one of the long-legged crickets which keeps on trying to fly and merely hops, and then lies there in the grass singing the same old song. Ah, and if he would only keep on lying in the grass! But he sticks his nose into every mess there is.

THE LORD. Have you nothing further to tell me? Do you come only to make accusations? Is there nothing on earth, to all eternity, to suit you?

MEPHISTOPHELES. No, Lord! I find things thoroughly bad there, as always. Men arouse my pity in their misery; even *I* am loath to torment the poor things.

THE LORD. Do you know Faust?

MEPHISTOPHELES. The doctor?

THE LORD. My servant!

MEPHISTOPHELES. I must say, he serves you in peculiar fashion. Not earthly is the food and drink of this madcap. His ferment drives him far, and he is half aware of his folly; from heaven he demands the fairest stars, and from earth every highest pleasure; and yet nothing, whether near or far, satisfies his deeply turbulent breast.

THE LORD. Even though he serves me but confusedly at present, I shall soon lead him into the light. Certainly the gardener knows, when the sapling turns green, that flower and fruit will adorn its future years.

MEPHISTOPHELES. What will you bet? You shall lose him yet, if you grant me permission to lead him without interference down my road!

THE LORD. So long as he lives on earth there shall be no prohibition upon you, for man errs as long as he strives.

MEPHISTOPHELES. I thank you for this, for I've never liked to have dealings with the dead. What I like most is full, fresh cheeks. I'm not at home to any corpse; my way is that of a cat with a mouse.

THE LORD. Very well, be it granted you! Draw this spirit away from his primal source and lead him, if you can get hold of him, along the downward way with you. Then stand abashed, when you must confess that a good man, for all the obscurity of his impulses, is well aware of the one right way.

MEPHISTOPHELES. Fair enough! but it won't be long! I'm not at all afraid of losing my bet. And if I achieve my purpose, you'll allow me to triumph with all my heart. He shall eat dust, and with a zest, like my cousin, the celebrated serpent.

THE LORD. In that respect too you may have fullest freedom, for I have never hated the like of you. Of all the spirits that deny, the roguish knave burdens me least. Man's activity can flag only too easily, and soon he gets to liking absolute passivity; hence I like to give him an associate who prods and pushes and must act as a devil.

But you archangels, true sons of the divine, may you delight in the rich and living beauty of the world! May the developing power which forever works and lives encompass you within the gracious confines of love; and let your enduring thoughts lend permanence to all that floats about in the form of unstable phenomena.

(*The heavens close,* THE ARCHANGELS *go their several ways.*)

MEPHISTOPHELES. I like to see the Chief from time to time, and take pains not to break with him. It's a pretty trait in a great lord to talk so humanly with the Devil himself.

PART I

Night

(FAUST *in a narrow, high-vaulted Gothic chamber, sitting uneasily at the desk in his armchair.*)

FAUST. Ah me! I've now studied thoroughly and with ardent effort philosophy, law, medicine, and even, alas! theology. And here I stand, poor fool, and am no wiser than before. I've the title of Master, even Doctor, and for ten years now I've been leading my pupils by the nose, up and down and back and forth—and realize that we can't know anything! And that is eating my heart out. True, I'm smarter than all these fops of Doctors, Masters, clerks, and preachers; nor am I tormented by scruple or doubt, or any

fear of hell or devil. In return, I'm deprived of all joy. For I
don't pretend to know anything worth knowing, or to be able to
teach anything that might improve men or convert them. Then
too, I've neither goods nor gold, nor is any worldly honor or
glory mine. No dog would lead such a life as this! And so I've
devoted myself to magic, hoping that through the power and
speech of the spirit many a secret might become known to me;
so that no longer, in a bitter sweat, I'll need to say things that I
don't know to be true; and so that I may discern what holds the
universe together in its deepest center, view all the working and
germinal forces, and be done with this traffic in words.

O light of the full moon, would that you were gazing for the
last time upon my pain, you whom I have seen, as I sat awake
at this desk, rise through so many a midnight hour. Then, as
now, it was over books and papers, mournful friend, that you appeared to me. Ah! could I but walk on mountain heights in your
beloved radiance, hover with spirits about mountain caverns,
rove over meadows in your dimness, and, unburdened of all this
fog of learning, find health by bathing in your dew!

Woe! still stuck in this dungeon here? Accursed, musty hole-
in-the-wall, where even the blessed light of heaven breaks but
dimly through the painted panes! Hemmed in by this pile of
books, which is gnawed by worms and covered with dust, and into
which smoke-blackened papers are thrust all the way up to the
vaulted ceiling; cluttered everywhere with flasks and jars, the place
stuffed full of old instruments, and the junk of generations on
top of that—that's your world! Men call that a world!

And still you ask why your heart is cramped with fear? Why
an inexplicable pain inhibits every stir of life within you? Instead
of living Nature, into which God put man at his creation, what
surrounds you in smoke and mold is nothing but animal bones and
human skeletons.

Up! flee! out into the open country! And this mysterious book,
from the hand of Nostradamus [1] himself, is it not guide enough
for you? Then you will come to know the course of the stars, and
with Nature instructing you the spirit power will dawn on you
that tells you how spirit speaks with spirit. In vain does arid specu-

[1] **Nostradamus:** Michel de Notre-Dame (1503-1566), who published a collec-
tion of prophecies

lation try to explain the sacred symbols to you: Spirits, you are hovering near me: answer me, if you hear me! (*He opens the volume, and his glance falls on the sign of the Macrocosm.[2]*) Ha! what rapture, at this sight, floods all my senses at once! I feel a youthful, holy joy of life coursing like a new fire through my nerves and veins. Was it a god that wrote these symbols which still the turmoil within me, fill my poor heart with joy, and with a mysterious force unveil the powers of Nature round about me? Am I a god? Such brightness grows in me! In these pure lines I see before me creative Nature at work. Only now do I grasp the meaning of the Sage's [3] word, "The spirit world is not barred; it is your mind that is closed, your heart that is dead! Up, neophyte, and bathe your earthly breast tirelessly in the glow of morning!" (*He studies the sign.*) How all things interweave to form the whole, each one working and living in the other, as if the heavenly forces were ascending and descending, passing the golden buckets from hand to hand, and pressing forward from heaven through the earth, their wings fragrant with blessings, until the entire universe resounds in one great harmony!

What a spectacle! But alas, no more than a spectacle. Where can I grasp you, infinite Nature? You breasts, where? Fountains of all life, to which both earth and heaven cling, toward which my languishing breast is straining—you swell, you give suck, and must I pine for you in vain? (*He turns the pages impatiently and perceives the sign of the Earth-Spirit.*)

How differently I am affected by this symbol! You, Spirit of Earth, are closer to me; already I feel my powers rising, already I am aglow as after drinking new wine. I feel courage to venture forth into the world, to bear the woe and the weal of earth, to wrestle with storms, and even in the crash of shipwreck not to despond.

Clouds are massing over me—the moon hides its light—the lamp goes out! Vapors rise!—Red rays are flashing about my head —A shudder breathes down from the vault above and lays hold on me! I feel that you are hovering about me, Spirit whom I invoke. Reveal yourself! Ah! how my heart is rent! All my senses are seething with new emotions. I feel my heart wholly surrendered

[2] **Macrocosm:** a medieval term for the universe
[3] **Sage:** a wise man

to you! You must, you must! and even if it should cost my life! (*He clutches the book and utters mysteriously the symbol of the Spirit. A reddish flame flashes;* THE SPIRIT *appears in the flame.*)

SPIRIT. Who calls to me?

FAUST (*with face averted*). Fearful apparition!

SPIRIT. Mightily have you drawn me on, long have you sucked at my sphere, and now—

FAUST. O dread! I can't bear the sight of you!

SPIRIT. In breathless impatience you implore to behold me, to hear my voice, to see my countenance; I am moved by the mighty entreaty of your soul, and here I am!—What contemptible terror takes you, superman! Where is the summons of your soul? Where is the breast which created a world within itself and sustained and cherished it, and which swelled, quivering with joy, at the prospect of lifting itself up to equal us, the Spirits? Where are you, Faust, whose voice rang out to me, who pressed forward to me with all your powers? Are you the one who, now that my breath thunders about you, quake to all the depths of your being, squirming away from me like a timorous worm?

FAUST. Shall I shrink from you, form of flame? I am he, I am Faust, I am your peer!

SPIRIT. In the floods of life, in the tempest of deeds, I surge up and down, weave to and fro! Birth and the grave, an eternal sea, a fluctuant weaving, a life aglow: so I work at the whirring loom of time and create the living garment of the deity.

FAUST. You who sweep about the wide world, busy Spirit, how near I feel myself to you!

SPIRIT. You are like the spirit whom you comprehend, not me! (*Disappears.*)

FAUST (*collapsing*). Not you? Whom then? I, the image of the deity! And not even like you! (*There is a knock.*) Curses! I know that knock—it's my assistant—there goes this supreme chance! Why must this plodding pedant interrupt the wealth of these visions? (WAGNER *enters in dressing gown and nightcap, lamp in hand.* FAUST *turns impatiently.*)

WAGNER. Pardon my intrusion! I heard you declaiming; no doubt you were reciting a Greek tragedy? It's an art from which I should like to benefit, for nowadays that's a way of getting ahead.

I've often heard it claimed that a preacher could learn from a comedian.

FAUST. Yes, if the preacher himself is a comedian, as may be the case now and then.

WAGNER. Ah me, when you're confined like this to your workshop, and hardly ever see the outside world even on a holiday, hardly through a spyglass, always only from afar, how shall you guide it by persuasion?

FAUST. If you don't *feel* it, you'll never achieve it—if it doesn't well forth out of your soul and conquer the hearts of all listeners with its genuine gusto. Aye, keep on sitting! Paste your borrowings together, make yourselves a ragout from others' banquets, and blow on your own handful of cinders to get a few paltry flames! Admiration of children and fools, if that's what your palate craves —but you'll never bring hearts together with anything that doesn't issue from your own heart.

WAGNER. But it's the delivery that makes the orator's fortune; I feel keenly that I still have a long way to go.

FAUST. Seek honestly for your advantage! Don't be a noisy, jingling fool! Good sense and a true message will deliver themselves without much art; and if you're in earnest about saying something, do you need to hunt for words? I know those glittering speeches you men make, in which you treat mankind to snippets artfully curled, as unrefreshing as the noisy wind that sets up an autumn rustle in the withered leaves.

WAGNER. O dear! Art is so long, and our life so short. In the very midst of my critical studies, my head and heart are often gripped by fear. How hard it is to attain the means whereby you work your way up to the sources! And before a poor devil has gone only half the way, like as not he'll be dead.

FAUST. The ancient parchment, is that the holy fount at which you hope to quench your thirst forever? You'll never get refreshment if it doesn't spring from your own soul.

WAGNER. Pardon me, but it's a great delight to get into the spirit of past times: to see how a wise man thought before our day, and how gloriously far we have advanced at last.

FAUST. O yes, advanced to the very stars! My friend, the ages of the past are to us a book with seven seals. What you call the spirit of the past is at bottom only the spirit of the historians, in which the past is reflected. And that reflection, truly, is often a sad affair! The public takes one look at it and runs away: it's a trash barrel and a junk room, and at best we get a pompous political play, with admirable pragmatic [4] maxims such as are fitly spoken by player-puppets.

WAGNER. But there's the world, the heart and soul of man! Surely everyone would like to have some knowledge of that.

FAUST. Yes, I know, what men are wont to call knowledge. Who will dare to call the child by its right name? The few who did acquire some true knowledge, and who were so foolish as not to keep their full hearts from spilling, who revealed their feelings and their visions to the rabble—from the beginning of time they have been crucified and burned.—I beg you, friend, the night is far advanced; we must break off for now.

WAGNER. I should have been glad to stay awake indefinitely, to talk so learnedly with you. But tomorrow, as it is Easter Sunday, you'll allow me another question or two. I've applied myself to my studies with zeal; it's true that I know a lot, but I'd like to know everything. (*Exit.*)

FAUST (*alone*). Strange that though this man's head continually clings to all that is shallow, he never loses hope, digging for treasure with a greedy hand and rejoicing if an angleworm turns up!

Has such a human voice the right to speak here, where spiritual abundance surrounded me? And yet, alas! for this once I thank you, sorriest of all sons of earth. You snatched me from the clutches of a despair which was on the point of destroying my mind. Ah, that apparition was so gigantic that I was bound to feel myself a veritable dwarf.

I, image of the deity, deeming myself already close to the mirror of eternal truth, exulting in the thought of myself amid heavenly glory and light, having sloughed off the son of earth; I, more than heavenly cherub, whose untrammeled force already dared presume that it flowed through the veins of Nature and by creative action enjoyed the life of gods, what punishment now is mine! One thundering word swept me off my feet.

I may not presume to liken myself to you. Though I possessed the power to draw you to me, I had no power to hold you. In

[4] **pragmatic:** an idea having validity only if it produces practical results

that blissful instant I felt so small, so great; you thrust me back, cruelly, into the uncertain lot of man. Who will teach me? What am I to avoid? Shall I obey that urge? Ah, our very deeds, as well as our sufferings, impede the course of our life.

Substances of more and more alien character intrude upon even the most glorious conceptions of the mind; when we attain to the good of this world, then anything better is termed fraud and illusion. And the glorious feelings which gave us life, they fade away in the earthly turmoil.

(*Faust now turns his attention to a long-necked alchemist's bottle or phial on the shelf nearby.*)

I salute you, unique phial, which I now fetch down with reverence. In you I venerate human wit and skill. You quintessence of blessed sleep-inducing herbs, you extract of all refined lethal powers, show your master your favor! I see you, and my pain is allayed; I grasp you, and my straining is lessened, as the flooding torrent of my mind ebbs little by little. Out into the high seas I am directed, the mirroring flood gleams at my feet, and a new day entices to new shores.

A fiery chariot comes floating toward me. I feel ready to penetrate the ether on a new course, leading to new spheres of unhampered activity. This exalted life, this divine rapture! And you, who were a worm but a moment ago, do you deserve it? Aye, turn your back resolutely upon the benign earthly sun! Have the temerity to snatch open the portals past which every man is fain to steal. Now is the time to prove by deeds that the dignity of man does not yield to the sublimity of the gods, by not shrinking back from that dark cavern in which imagination condemns itself to its own torment; time to press forward toward that passageway around whose narrow mouth all hell is aflame; time to resolve cheerfully upon this step, and were it at the risk of flowing out into nothingness.

Come down now, pure goblet of crystal! Out from your case, you of whom I have not thought these many years. You sparkled at my forefathers' joyous feasts, and cheered the serious-minded guests when one of them used you to toast the other. The many figures with their ingenious and opulent splendor, the drinker's obligation to explain them in rhyme or in a single draught to empty the entire bowl, this reminds me of many a night of my youth. Now I shall not hand you to any neighbor, nor shall your art make me display my wit. Here is a juice which swiftly intoxicates; with brown liquid it fills your hollow to the brim. That which I prepared, that which I choose, let this final draught be drunk with all my soul as a festive and lofty greeting to the morn! (*He puts the goblet to his lips.*)

Chime of Bells and Choral Song.

CHOIR OF ANGELS. Christ is risen! Joy to the mortal, whom his destructive, insidious, inherited shortcomings held in their toils.

FAUST. What deep-toned hum, what brightsome sound draws mightily the glass from my lips? You muted chimes, are you already proclaiming the first solemn hour of the Easter festival? You choirs, are you already singing the comforting song which once rang out from angels' lips around the night of a grave, assurance of a new covenant?

CHORUS OF WOMEN. With spices we had cared for him, we his faithful ones had laid him down; cloths and wrappings we neatly wound around him—ah! and now we find Christ no longer here.

CHOIR OF ANGELS. Christ is risen! Blessed the loving one who withstood the sad but saving, the strenuous test.

FAUST. You heavenly tones, mighty and yet gentle, why do you seek me here in the dust? Rather resound where soft men dwell. I hear your message, indeed, but it is faith I lack; miracle is the dearest child of faith. I dare not aspire to those spheres whence the lovely tidings ring out; and yet, accustomed to this sound as I have been from youth onward, even now it calls me back into life. In other days the kiss of heavenly love descended upon me in solemn sabbath stillness; so full of promise was the amplitude of the bell tones, and a prayer was fervent delight; then an inconceivably sweet yearning impelled me to rove through wood and meadow, and amid a thousand burning tears I felt a world come into being for me. This chant proclaimed the merry games of youth, the untroubled joy of the festival of spring; recollection with its childlike feeling restrains me now from taking that last solemn step. O sweet and heavenly songs, ring on! My tears well up, earth claims me once again.

CHOIR OF DISCIPLES. If the buried one has already gloriously raised himself on high, exalted while yet living; if in the rapture of becoming he is close to the joy of creating; we, alas, on the breast of earth, we are born to suffer. Seeing he has left us, his own, languishing here behind, ah, Master, we bewail Thy good fortune!

CHOIR OF ANGELS. Christ is risen, out of the lap of corruption: joyously free yourselves from your fetters! As by your deeds you praise him, demonstrating your love, feeding the hungry as brothers, journeying to preach the gospel, promising the rapture to come, to you the Master is near, for you he is here!

Outside the City Gates

(*The next day Faust finds some consolation in the Spring Festival. In this scene, the peasants are loud in their praises of Dr. Faust. Now the doctor and Wagner have left the gaiety and are walking outside the city gates.*)

FAUST. Just a few more paces up to yonder rock; let us rest here from our stroll. Here I have often sat alone, deep in thought, and tortured myself with praying and fasting. Rich in hope, firm in faith, with tears and sighs and wringing of hands I thought to wrest from the Lord of Heaven the end of that plague. Today the applause of the crowd sounds to me like mockery. O, if you could read in my soul, and see how little father and son were worthy of such fame. My father was a good man groping in the dark, who brooded with capricious zeal upon Nature and her sacred spheres, in honesty yet in his own peculiar fashion; and who, in the company of other adepts, locked himself into the black kitchen of necromancy [1] and, following interminable recipes, mixed the mutually incompatible. There a "Red Lion," a bold wooer, was married to the "Lily" in a tepid bath, and the two were then tortured over an open flame from one "bridal chamber" into another. When thereupon the "Young Queen" appeared in bright colors in the retort, this was the medicine: the patients died, and

---

[1] **necromancy**: black magic

nobody asked who had recovered.[2] And so with hellish concoctions we devastated these hills and dales far worse than the pestilence itself. I myself have given the poison to thousands; they withered away, and I must live to hear men praise the shameless murderers.

WAGNER. How can you distress yourself on that account? Does not an honest man do enough when he practices conscientiously and punctiliously the skill which has been transmitted to him? If you as stripling honor your father, then you will be glad to accept his learning; if you as man enlarge the bounds of science, then your son can attain to a higher goal.

FAUST. O happy he who can still cherish the hope of emerging from this ocean of error! . . . Alas, two souls dwell in my breast, each striving to detach itself from the other: the one, in earthy desire for love, holds fast to earth with clinging organs; the other lifts itself imperiously out of the dust toward the realms of exalted forebears. O, if there are spirits in the air, who rule and hover between earth and heaven, then come down to me out of your golden haze and lead me forth to a new and motley life! Or if I only had a magic cloak, to bear me into countries yet unknown! I'd not exchange it for the costliest robes, not even for the mantle of a king.

WAGNER. Don't summon the well-known troop of demons which flood the vaporous sphere above us and which prepare for man a host of dangers from every quarter. From the north the sharp spirit-tooth rushes upon you, with tongues like pointed darts; from the east they advance with desiccating breath and feed upon your lungs; if the south wind sends them from the desert, heaping fire upon fire around your head, the west brings up the swarm which first refreshes, only to drown you with all your fields and meadows. They like to eavesdrop because they delight in mischief, and they like to obey because they like to deceive us; they act as if sent from heaven, and lisp with angel tongues the lies they utter. But let us go! the world has turned to gray, the air is chilled, the mist is falling. It's when evening comes that one really appreciates one's home.—Why do you stand there like that, looking so amazed? What can excite you so in the dim light?

[2] the terms in this passage refer to the blending of various chemicals and the resulting precipitate

FAUST. Do you see that black dog coursing through grain and stubble?

WAGNER. I noticed it quite a while ago; it didn't seem important to me.

FAUST. Observe it closely! What do you take it to be?

WAGNER. A poodle which, like others, has a hard time finding its master's track.

FAUST. Do you notice how it is racing around us in a wide spiral, getting closer and closer? And if I'm not mistaken, a swirl of fire trails after it.

WAGNER. I see nothing but a black poodle. It may be an optical illusion with you.

FAUST. It seems to me that it is drawing with magical subtlety coils about our feet, to form some future fetter.

WAGNER. I see it leaping about us, uncertain and fearful, because it sees two strangers instead of its master.

FAUST. The circle is narrowing; already it's near!

WAGNER. You see! It's just a dog, no spirit. It growls and hesitates, lays itself on its belly. It wags its tail. All doggish ways.

FAUST. Join us! Come here!

WAGNER. It's only a silly poodle. If you stand still, it waits on you; speak to it, and it climbs up on you; drop something, and it will fetch it, or leap into the water after your cane.

FAUST. I suppose you're right; I find no trace of any spirit, and it's all a matter of training.

WAGNER. When a dog's well trained, even a wise man takes a liking to it. Indeed, this one, the students' excellent scholar, thoroughly deserves your favor. (*They go into the city gate.*)

Faust's Study I

(FAUST *enter with the poodle.*)

FAUST. I have forsaken fields and meadows, which a deep night covers, awakening the better soul in us with holy, foreboding awe. Wild impulses are now put to sleep, along with all unbridled action; the love for man stirs in us now, and the love for God. . . . We learn to prize the spiritual, we yearn for revelation, which flames nowhere with more dignity and beauty than in the New

Testament. I feel impelled to open up the original text and with sincere feeling to translate that sacred original into my beloved German.

(*Faust sets about his evening of study. The poodle, which he has placed on a cushion behind the stove, begins to growl and then to snarl loudly as Faust reads aloud to himself from the New Testament.*)

FAUST. It is written, "In the beginning was the *word!*" Already I stop short! Who will help me? I can't possibly give the *word* so high a value, and I must translate differently if I'm truly illumined by the spirit. It is written, "In the beginning was the *sense.*" Consider well this first line, lest your pen outrun itself! Is it *sense* which creates and works everything? It ought to read, "In the beginning was the *force!*" And yet, even while I write this down, something warns me that I shall not abide by it. The spirit comes to my aid! All at once I see the solution, and I write down confidently, "In the beginning was the *deed!*"

If I'm to share this room with you, poodle, then stop your howling, stop your barking!

(*Rebuked sharply by Faust, the animal suddenly is transformed before his eyes into a huge beast. Faust, undaunted, threatens it in the name of the Blessed Trinity.*)

FAUST. I do not threaten in vain. I will singe you with holy fire! Wait not to see the thrice glowing light! Await not the mightiest of my spells!

MEPHISTOPHELES (*as the mist falls, steps forth from behind the stove, dressed like a goliard*).[1] Why all this noise? How can I serve my lord?

FAUST. So this was the poodle's kernel! A journeying scholar? This case makes me laugh.

MEPHISTOPHELES. I salute the learned gentleman! You made me sweat with a vengeance.

FAUST. How do you call yourself?

MEPHISTOPHELES. The question seems to me petty in one who despises

---

[1] **goliard**: one of a class of wandering students in Europe, chiefly in the 12th and 13th centuries, noted for their rioting and intemperance

the *word* so greatly and who, far beyond caring for mere appearances, strives only toward the essence of things.

FAUST. With you gentlemen the essence can usually be read from the name you bear, in which it is revealed only too plainly when they call you Beelzebub or God-of-Flies, Destroyer, Liar. Very well, then, who *are* you?

MEPHISTOPHELES. A part of that force which always wills the bad and always works the good.

FAUST. What is the meaning of this riddle?

MEPHISTOPHELES. I am the spirit which always denies! And justly so; for everything that is born deserves to be destroyed; hence it would be better if nothing were born. And therefore all that you men call sin, destruction, or, in short, evil, is my proper element.

FAUST. You call yourself a part, and yet stand as a whole before me?

MEPHISTOPHELES. It is a modest truth I tell you. Though man, that little world of folly, usually deems himself to be an entirety—I'm a part of the part which was originally everything, a part of the darkness which chose to give birth to light, the proud light which now competes with its mother night for her old rank and for all of space; and yet without success, since, however it may strive, it remains chained and fastened to bodies. From bodies it streams out, it makes bodies beautiful, a body checks it on its course, and so, I hope, it won't be long until it meets destruction along with all the bodies.

FAUST. Now I'm acquainted with your estimable duties! You can't annihilate anything on a large scale, and so you're making a start on a small one.

MEPHISTOPHELES. And I must confess that little is achieved in that way. That which opposes itself to Nothing, this Something, this clumsy world, much as I've undertaken against it, never have I managed to get at it with all my floods, gales, quakes, and fire— unshaken, in the end, are sea and land. And that damned stuff, that brood of beasts and men, you can't do a thing to them: how many I have buried up to now! And always a new, fresh blood is in circulation. And so it goes on, enough to drive you mad! From air, from water, and from earth a thousand germs creep out, in the dry, the wet, the warm, the cold! If I hadn't reserved the flame for myself, I'd have nothing I could call my own.

FAUST. And so you oppose the ever active, beneficent, and creative force with the cold fist of the devil, which is maliciously clenched in vain! Try to launch out on something else, you queer son of chaos!

MEPHISTOPHELES. We really must put our minds to it; more of that on future occasions. May I for this time take my leave?

FAUST. I don't see why you ask. I've made your acquaintance now, and you may call on me as you like. Here's the window, there the door, and you can count on a chimney as well.

MEPHISTOPHELES. Let me confess: a small obstacle forbids my strolling out of here, namely, the witch's foot on your threshold—

FAUST. Does that pentagram [2] make trouble for you? Then tell me, you son of Hell, if that holds you in ban, how did you get in? How was such an intellect deluded?

MEPHISTOPHELES. Inspect it closely! It's not well drawn; the one angle which points outward is slightly open, as you see.

FAUST. That was a good chance hit! And so you're my prisoner? A bit of accidental luck.

MEPHISTOPHELES. The poodle noticed nothing when he ran in, but now the thing looks quite different; the Devil can't get out of the house.

FAUST. But why don't you go through the window?

MEPHISTOPHELES. It's a law for devils and ghosts that they must exit where they slipped in. The first is our choice, but in the second case we're bound by the law.

FAUST. Does Hell itself have its laws? I find that capital, for then a contract could be made with you gentlemen, and no doubt a binding one?

MEPHISTOPHELES. Whatever is promised you shall enjoy to the full, not be cheated out of any of it. But that can't be settled so quickly, and we'll discuss it presently; right now I beg you with the utmost urgency to release me for this once.

FAUST. Do stay a moment longer, and give me some good news before you go.

MEPHISTOPHELES. Let me go now! I'll soon come back, and then you may ask what you will.

FAUST. I didn't set a trap for you, did I? It was you who went into the snare yourself. Let him who holds the Devil keep on holding! He won't so easily catch him a second time.

[2] **pentagram:** a five-pointed star, a religious symbol

MEPHISTOPHELES. If it's your pleasure, then I am also ready to remain here and keep you company; but on condition that my arts
may offer you a worthy pastime.

FAUST. I like that, and you're at liberty to do so; but see to it that
the art be pleasing.

MEPHISTOPHELES. My friend, you'll gain more for your senses in this
hour than in the monotony of a whole year. What the tender
spirits sing to you, the lovely visions they bring, these are no empty
sorcery. Your sense of smell, too, will be entranced; then you will
titillate your palate; and then your sense of touch will be en-
raptured. No previous preparation is required: we are together,
now begin!

SPIRITS. Vanish, dark arches overhead! Let the blue sky look in more
charmingly, amiably. If only the dark clouds were dissipated!
Starlets twinkle, milder suns shine among them. The spirit beauty
of sons of heaven floats by in swaying inclination. Yearning affection follows on; and the fluttering ribbons of their robes cover the
lands, cover the arbors where lovers, deep in thought, give themselves to each other for life. Arbor on arbor! Sprouting vines!
Heavy the grapes tumble into the hopper of the impatient wine-
press, foaming wines shoot down in streams, ripple through pure
precious stones, leave the heights lying behind them, expand
into lakes around the abundance of green-clad hills. And the wild
fowl sip their rapture, fly toward the sun, fly toward the bright
islands which stir and rock upon the waves, where we hear those
who exult in chorus and see those who dance over the meads, all
of whom disport themselves in the open. Some clamber over the
heights, others swim across the waters, others float in the air—all
toward life, all toward the distance of loving stars, toward bliss-
fullest love.

MEPHISTOPHELES. He's asleep! Well done, airy, dainty lads! Faithfully you have sung him to sleep. For this concert I am in your
debt.—Faust, you are not yet the man to hold the Devil fast!
Invest him with sweet, frolicking dream figures, immerse him in
a sea of illusion. But to shatter the magic of this threshold I
require a rat's tooth. Not long do I need to conjure, already one
is rustling nearby and will hear me immediately.

The lord of rats and mice, of flies and frogs, of bedbugs and
lice commands you to venture forth and gnaw at this threshold,

just where he has dotted it with oil— There you come hopping! Now quickly to work! The tip which banned me is right there in front of the edge. One more bite, and the work is done.—Now, Faust, dream on until we meet again.

FAUST (*awaking*). Then am I cheated once again? Is this the outcome of that spirit throng, that a dream lied to me about the Devil, and that a poodle ran away from me?

Faust's Study II

(FAUST. MEPHISTOPHELES.)

FAUST. A knock? Come in! Who would bother me now?

MEPHISTOPHELES. 'Tis I.

FAUST. Come in!

MEPHISTOPHELES. Three times you have to say it.

FAUST. Come in, then!

MEPHISTOPHELES. That's the way I like you. I hope we shall get along. For to chase away your silly notions I am here as a noble squire, in a red suit with gold graid, a mantelet of heavy silk, the cock's feather on my hat, and a long, pointed rapier at my side; and my brief and friendly advice to you is to clothe yourself in like fashion, in order that you, being unfettered and free, may learn what life is.

FAUST. In any dress, I think, I shall feel the torment of this cramped earthly life. I'm too old to do nothing but play, too young to be without a desire. What can the world afford me? Renounce, renounce! that's the eternal song which rings in the ears of everyone, and which, throughout all our life, every hour hoarsely sings to us. Only with horror do I waken every morning, and I could weep bitter tears to see the day, which in all its course will not fulfill for me one wish, not *one*, but will diminish even the faint promise of any pleasure with obstinate fault-finding, and hinder the creativity of my spirit with life's countless distortions. What's more, when night descends I must stretch out upon my couch in anxiety; there too no rest is given me, for wild dreams will terrify me. The god who dwells in my breast can stir my soul to its depths, but though he sits enthroned over all my powers, he can move nothing in the world without; and so, existence is a burden to me, death desired, life hated.

MEPHISTOPHELES. And yet death is never a wholly welcome guest.

FAUST. O, happy is the man about whose temples death twines the bloody laurel in the splendor of victory, or the one whom, after the completion of a mad dance, death finds in the arms of a girl. O that I had dropped lifeless for sheer rapture at the power of that exalted spirit!

MEPHISTOPHELES. And yet somebody failed, in a certain night, to drain a cup of brown juice.

FAUST. Spying, it appears, is your sport.

MEPHISTOPHELES. I'm not omniscient; but I know a good many things.

FAUST. Even though a sweetly familiar strain drew me out of the fearful turmoil, deluding the remnant of my childlike feeling with the echo of a happy time, now I curse everything which invests the soul with lure and trickery, and which bans it in this mournful fleshly cavern with deceiving and flattering forces. Cursed first of all be the exalted opinion with which the spirit envelops itself! Cursed be the dazzling of phenomena which crowd in upon our senses! Cursed what is feigned in false dreams of fame, the delusion of an enduring name! Cursed what flatters us as possession, as wife and child, as hireling and plow! Cursed be Mammon, when with his gold he spurs us on to bold deeds, or when he adjusts the cushions for our idle diversion! Cursed be the balm-bringing juice of the grape! Cursed be that supreme gift of love! A curse on hope! A curse on faith! And a curse on patience most of all!

CHORUS OF SPIRITS (*invisible*). Woe! Woe! You have destroyed the lovely world with mighty fist; it tumbles and falls apart! A demigod has shattered it! We bear the ruins over into the void, and bewail the beauty lost. Mighty one among the sons of earth, build it more splendidly again, rebuild it in your bosom! Begin a new life course with a clear mind, and let new songs ring out in response!

MEPHISTOPHELES. These are the little ones who serve me. Hear how sagely they urge you on to pleasure and action! Far out into the world they want to lure you, out of the solitude in which senses and saps stand still.

Desist from playing with your grief, which eats at your life like a vulture; even the poorest company will make you realize that you are a human being among others. Yet it's not my intention to thrust you into the midst of rabble. I'm not one of the great; but if united with me you'll walk your way through life, then I'll gladly submit to be yours from this moment. I'll be your companion, and, if I suit you, I'll be your servant, yours to command.

FAUST. And what am I to do for you in return?

MEPHISTOPHELES. You've got plenty of time for that.

FAUST. No, no! the Devil is an egotist, and is not likely to do for God's sake what will be useful to anyone but himself. Speak the conditions plainly; such a servant brings danger into the house.

MEPHISTOPHELES. I'll bind myself to your service *here*, and will be at your beck and call without rest or relaxation; when we meet again over *yonder*, you shall do the like for me.

FAUST. Your "yonder" can't greatly disturb me. Once you've knocked this world to pieces, then let the other come into being. From this earth my joys spring up, and this sun shines down upon my sufferings; once I'm able to part from them, then let come what will and can. I want to hear no further talk as to whether there will be hate and love hereafter, and whether in those spheres too there is high and low.

MEPHISTOPHELES. With such an attitude you can risk it. Bind yourself; you shall promptly see my arts with joy, for I shall give you what no man has yet seen.

FAUST. What do you think to give, you poor Devil? Was the mind of a man, in its lofty striving, ever grasped by the like of you? But have you food which does not satisfy, red gold which without ceasing, like quicksilver, melts away in the hand, a game at which nobody ever wins, a girl who while on my breast is already ogling and flirting with my neighbor, or the lovely, divine rapture of an honor which disappears like a meteor? Show me the fruit that rots before you pick it, and trees which daily cover themselves with new green.

MEPHISTOPHELES. Such an assignment doesn't terrify me, and I can serve you with such treasures. But, good friend, there will also come a time when we shall want to feast upon something good in tranquillity.

FAUST. If ever I lay myself tranquilly upon a bed of ease, then let that be my immediate end! If ever you can so delude me with flattery that I'm pleased with myself, if you can deceive me with enjoyment, let that be my last day. This bet I offer!

MEPHISTOPHELES. Done!

FAUST. And done again! If ever I shall say to any moment: Do stay with me, you are so good! then you may put fetters upon me, then I will gladly perish! Then may the death knell ring, then you are free of your service, the clock may stop, its hands may fall—then let time be done for me!

MEPHISTOPHELES. Think this over carefully: we shall not forget it.

FAUST. That's your good right; I haven't rashly overestimated myself. As soon as I stagnate, I'm a slave, and I don't care whether I'm yours or whose.

MEPHISTOPHELES. This very day, at the doctors' banquet, I shall do my duty as your servant. But one thing more! For all contingencies of life or death, give me a few lines in writing.

FAUST. You demand something written, too, you pedant? Have you never known a man, or a man's word? Isn't it enough that my spoken word is to dispose of all my days, to eternity? Doesn't the world rush forward in all its streams, and shall a promise hold me? But this delusion is imbedded in our hearts, and who will willingly free himself of it? Happy is he who bears unsullied loyalty in his bosom: no sacrifice will ever cause him regret! But a parchment, written up and stamped, is a specter from which all men shrink. The word dies in the very pen that writes it, and wax and leather remain sovereign. What do you want of me, evil spirit? Bronze, marble, parchment, paper? Shall I write with stylus, chisel, pen? I give you freedom of choice.

MEPHISTOPHELES. Why so overdo your heated oratory? You know that any slip of paper will do. Just sign your name with a drop of blood.

FAUST. If this gives you complete satisfaction, then let's abide by the old farce.

MEPHISTOPHELES. Blood is a very special juice.

FAUST. Only have no fear of my breaking this contract. To strive with all my might is precisely what I am promising. I had inflated myself too high, and it is only to your level that I belong. The great spirit has scorned me, and Nature closes her gates against me. The thread of thinking has snapped, and I've long had a loathing for all knowledge. Let us quench glowing passions in the deeps of sensuality. Let every marvel you have, wrapped in un-penetrated magic veils, be made ready for me. Let us plunge into the rush of time, into the whirl of events. And so pain and enjoyment, success and chagrin, may alternate as best they can; it is only in ceaseless activity that man is himself.

MEPHISTOPHELES. For you no measure or mark is set. If it please you to nibble at everything, to snatch something on the wing, may that which delights you agree with you. Only I want you to take hold and not be bashful!

FAUST. But you heard me say that it's not a question of joy. I devote myself to delirium, to the most painful enjoyment, to enamored hate, stimulating discontent. My breast, which is cured of the will to knowledge, shall hereafter not be sealed against any pain; and whatever is allotted to the whole of mankind, that I wish to experience in my inner self, grasp with my mind the highest and deepest there is, heap upon my bosom all man's weal and woe, and thus expand my own self to be one with mankind, and, like it, in the end meet shipwreck and perish.

MEPHISTOPHELES. O believe me, who for many a thousand year have been chewing on this tough meat: no man, from the cradle to the grave, ever digests this ancient leaven! Take it from one of us, this entirety is made only for a god. *He* finds himself in an eternal glory, he has thrown *us* into darkness, and for *you* the only fitting thing is day *and* night.

FAUST. But I will!

MEPHISTOPHELES. Well said! But there's just one thing I'm afraid of: time is short and art is long. It seems to me that you should let yourself be instructed. Associate yourself with some poet, and let that gentleman's thoughts go roving: have him heap all noble qualities upon your honored pate, the lion's courage, the stag's fleetness, the Italian's fiery blood, the northerner's steadfastness. Let him find for you the secret of combining magnanimity and cunning, and show you how, with warm youthful desires, you can fall in love in accordance with a plan. I'd like myself to make the acquaintance of such a gentleman; I'd call him Sir Microcosm.[1]

FAUST. Well, what am I, if it's not possible to gain the crown of mankind, toward which all my senses drive?

MEPHISTOPHELES. Ultimately you are what you are. Put on a wig

---

[1] **Microcosm:** a world in miniature; man viewed as an epitome of the universe

with millions of curls, set your feet on buskins half a yard high, and still you'll always remain what you are.

FAUST. In vain, I feel, I have heaped upon myself all the treasures of the human mind: when I finally sit down, there's no new force that wells up from within. I'm not taller by a hair's breadth, and I'm no closer to the Infinite.

MEPHISTOPHELES. My good friend, you're seeing things just as people are mostly wont to see them; we must be smarter than that, before the joy of life flees from us. What the deuce! it's true that hands and feet and head and heart are yours; but all that I heartily enjoy, is that any the less mine? If I can pay for six stallions, isn't their strength mine? I race along, and what a man I am, as if I had twenty-four legs. So, look alive! Let all brooding go hang, and come with me out into the world.

(Mephistopheles promises to give Faust a taste of life in the world of passion, Part I, and the pleasure of power exercised in public business and art, Part II. First he views sensuous pleasure in Auerbach's wine cellar. Afterwards, Mephistopheles takes him to the witches' kitchen where he sees in a mirror a beautiful woman representing ideal beauty. Enamored of this vision, he consents to drink the love potion prepared by the witches, and, as a consequence, feels a renewed youth. Soon afterwards he meets an innocent peasant girl, Margaret, with whom he falls passionately in love.)

Street

*(*FAUST. MARGARET *passing by.)*

FAUST. Fair young lady, may I venture to offer you my arm and escort?

MARGARET. I'm neither a lady nor fair, and I can go home unescorted.

(She frees herself; exit.)

FAUST. By heaven, that's a beautiful girl! I've never seen anything like her. She's so chaste and virtuous, and yet at the same time a little saucy. The red of her lips, the sheen of her cheek—I'll not forget them as long as I live. The way she cast down her eyes impressed itself deeply on my heart; and how brusquely she spoke —simply enchanting!

(MEPHISTOPHELES *enters.*)

FAUST. Listen, you must get me that girl!

MEPHISTOPHELES. Why, which one?

FAUST. She just went by.

MEPHISTOPHELES. O, that one? She was coming from her confessor, who absolved her of all sin; I stole close by the confessional. She's only an innocent young girl who went to confession for nothing at all; I've got no power over her.

FAUST. She's over fourteen, isn't she?

MEPHISTOPHELES. Why, you talk like Jack the Rake, who craves every pretty flower for his own and flatters himself that there's no honor nor favor that can't be gathered in; but that's not always possible.

(*Faust seduces Margaret and kills Valentine, her outraged brother. Margaret becomes insane and kills her new-born child. Margaret is imprisoned and is about to be executed. Faust, unaware of her trials, enters into the magical orgies of a Walpurgis Night on the Harz Mountains. Anger at Mephistopheles floods his soul, however, when he realizes the torture Margaret is enduring.*)

Gloomy Day. A Field

(FAUST. MEPHISTOPHELES.)

FAUST. In misery! Despairing! Long and pitifully astray on the earth, and now imprisoned! That lovely, unhappy creature locked up in a dungeon as evildoer, to suffer horrible torments! So far things have gone! so far!—Treacherous, abominable spirit, and you have kept this a secret from me!—Aye, stand there, stand! roll your devilish eyes fiercely around in your head! Stand and defy me with your unendurable presence! Imprisoned! In irretrievable misery! Given over to evil spirits and to the judgment of heartless humanity! And all this while you've been lulling me with silly diversions, concealing from me her growing affliction, and letting her go helpless to destruction!

MEPHISTOPHELES. She's not the first.

FAUST. Hound! detestable monster!—Transform him, Infinite Spirit! transform this reptile back into his dog shape, in which it was often his pleasure to trot along before me at night, to roll over before the feet of the unsuspecting stroller, and to fasten upon his shoulders when he fell. Change him back into his favorite shape, that he may cringe on his belly before me in the sand, for me to kick him, the outcast of God!—Not the first!—Woe! Woe! not to be grasped by any human soul, that more than one creature has sunk into the depths of this misery, that the first one did not atone for the guilt of all the others in her writhing death agony before the eyes of the eternally pardoning God! The wretchedness of this one victim stirs me to the very marrow of my life—and you grin calmly across the doom of thousands!

MEPHISTOPHELES. And now here we are again, already at our wits' end, at the point where the minds of you men give way. Why do you make common cause with us if you can't see it through? You want to fly and you're not safe from dizziness? Did we intrude on you, or you on us?

FAUST. Don't bare your greedy teeth so at me! It disgusts me!—Great and glorious Spirit, who deemed me worthy of your appearance and who know my heart and soul, why chain me to this scoundrel, who gloats over harm and delights in destruction?

MEPHISTOPHELES. Will you never have done?

FAUST. Save her, or woe to you! The most horrible curses upon you for thousands of years!

MEPHISTOPHELES. I can't loose the fetters of the avenger, nor thrust back his bolts.—"Save her!"—Who was it that plunged her into ruin? I or you?

(FAUST *looks wildly about him.*)

(*After further arguing, Mephistopheles finally agrees to take Faust to Margaret's place of imprisonment.*)

Dungeon

FAUST (*with a bunch of keys and a lantern, before a small iron door*). A long unwonted awe grips me, and the whole misery of mankind. Here she dwells, behind this dank wall, and yet her crime was a fond delusion! You hesitate to go to her! You fear to see her again! Onward! Your timid lingering hastens her death. (*He takes hold of the lock. A voice sings within.*) "My mother,

who slew me! My father, the rogue who ate me! My little sister
saved up my bones in a cool spot; then I became a pretty bird of
the woods: fly away, fly away!"

FAUST (*unlocking*). She doesn't dream that her beloved is listening,
hearing her chains rattle, the straw rustle. (*He enters.*)

MARGARET (*hiding on her straw*). Woe! Woe! They're coming.
Bitter death!

FAUST (*softly*). Hush! Hush! I come to set you free.

MARGARET (*rolling over to face him*). If you're human, then feel
the misery I feel.

FAUST. You'll scream the guards out of their sleep! (*He takes hold
of her chains to unlock them.*)

MARGARET (*on her knees*). Who gave you, hangman, this power
over me? You're fetching me now, and it's only midnight. Have
mercy and let me live! Isn't tomorrow morning early enough?
(*She rises.*) After all, I'm still so young, so young! And already
I have to die! I was beautiful, too, and that was my ruin. My
lover was near, but now he's far; my wreath lies torn, the flowers
scattered. Don't seize me so roughly! Spare me! What have I done
to you? Don't let me plead in vain; why, I never saw you in all
my life!

FAUST. How can I stand this agony?

(*Faust discovers, as the conversation continues, that Margaret is hope-
lessly insane. She speaks constantly of her dead child and mother, and
he begins, at last, to realize the extent of his crime. The scene ends with
Margaret's obstinate refusal to leave the dungeon and her plea for salvation.*)

MARGARET. We shall see each other again; but not at the dance.
The throng is crowding in, but no sound is heard. The square, the
streets can't hold them all. The death bell tolls, the wand is
broken. How they seize and bind me! Already they've moved me
to the block. Already at every neck the sharp blade is flashing
which is aimed at mine. The world is silent as the grave!

FAUST. O would I had never been born!

MEPHISTOPHELES (*appears outside*). Come, or you're lost! Futile
hesitation! Lagging and babbling! My horses shiver, the dawnlight
grows.

MARGARET. What's that rising up out of the ground? He! He! Send
him away! What does he want in this holy place? He wants me!
FAUST. You shall live!
MARGARET. Judgment of God, I have given myself up to you!
MEPHISTOPHELES (to FAUST). Come! Come! Or I'll leave you in the
lurch with her.
MARGARET. I am Thine, Father! Save me! Angels! Heavenly hosts,
cluster around to protect me! Henry,[1] you make me shudder!
MEPHISTOPHELES. She is doomed!
VOICE (from above). She is saved!
MEPHISTOPHELES (to FAUST). Come to me! (Vanishes with FAUST.)
VOICE (from within, dying away). Henry! Henry!

End of Part I

PART II

(Part II opens with Faust forgetting his former suffering through the
delights of nature. Mephistopheles then introduces him to the world of
public affairs and the world of aesthetic beauty in classical and romantic
art.

Faust is transplanted to the palace of the Emperor whom he saves
from bankruptcy with the aid of Mephistopheles. During a magnificent
pageant, the devil conjures up, as a brilliant spectacle, the forms of Helen
and Paris, the world-famous Greek lovers. Faust falls in love with Helen,
representing the ideal of classical art, but is unable to realize his love.
Faust's one desire now is to be united with this ideal beauty. In Act III,
Faust rescues Helen from Menelaus with the aid of Mephistopheles.
From the union of Helen and Faust emerges the spirit of poetry, Euphorion, symbolic of the union of the classical with the romantic.
Euphorion and Helen disappear, but Faust, ennobled by his union with
Helen, realizes that the enjoyment of transitory beauty is no more endur-
ing than is other experience.

Faust's next desire is to subdue nature and to use it in the service of
man. In Act IV, he defeats an uprising against the Emperor, and receives,
in return, a long stretch of half-submerged seacoast. He determines to
reclaim the land and to make it the home of a happy and contented
people. His purpose is a social and humanitarian one, in contrast to his
earlier selfish purposes.

[1] **Henry:** Margaret's name for her lover

At the opening of Act V, *Faust*, now very old, has almost completed his great task, but he has met a difficulty. The land has been reclaimed, the country is now completely his, but for the cottage of a poor and aged couple who refuse to move.)

Palace

MEPHISTOPHELES (*to* FAUST). With serious brow and gloomy glance you learn of your exalted fortune. Lofty wisdom is crowned, for shore and sea are reconciled; from the shore the sea willingly receives your ships for their swift course; you may say, then, that from here, from this palace, your arm embraces the entire world. From this spot the start was made, and here stood the first house of boards; down to the sea a tiny ditch was scratched, where today the oar splashes lustily. Your lofty design, and the industry of your men, won the victory over earth and sea. From here—

FAUST. That cursèd *here!* Just that weighs on me painfully. To you, resourceful as you are, I have to say it: in my heart I feel stab after stab, it's impossible for me to bear it! And I'm ashamed to say it. The old folks up there should leave, for I'd like to sit under those lindens: those few trees, which are not mine, spoil my worldwide possessions. I should like, in order to look far around, to build platforms there from bough to bough, thus opening wide courses to my gaze, thus to behold all that I have done, to survey with one glance this masterpiece of the human mind, which shrewdly planned the realization of a great gain: creating habitable lands for many peoples.

Thus we are tormented worst by the feeling of what we lack despite our wealth. The ringing of the bell, the scent of the lindens, they hold me fast as in a church or a tomb. The option of an all-powerful will is frustrated by that sand. How shall I get this out of my soul? The bell tinkles, and I boil with rage.

MEPHISTOPHELES. Naturally! Some prime annoyance is bound to embitter your life. Who'll deny it? That jingling seems repulsive to any refined ear. And that accursed ding-dong-dinging, beclouding a clear evening sky, intrudes upon every happening in life, from man's first bath down to his burial, as if between ding and dong all life were a dream that's forgotten.

FAUST. That couple's opposition and obstinacy are embittering my most glorious gains, so that, to my own deep and fierce pain, I cannot but weary of being just.

MEPHISTOPHELES. Well, why be so timid about this? Shouldn't you have relocated them long ago?

FAUST. Then go and take them out of my way!—You know the pretty little property which I picked out for the old couple.

MEPHISTOPHELES. They'll be carried away and set down, and before you can look around they'll be on their feet again; after violence has been lived down, a fine abode will reconcile them.

Black Night

LYNCEUS THE TOWERMAN (*singing at his lookout*). Born for seeing, appointed for looking, sworn keeper of the tower, I like the world. I gaze into the distance, and I see from here the moon and the stars, the woods and the deer. So I see the everlasting beauty in all things, and as I have always liked them, so I like myself, too. You fortunate eyes, whatever you may have beheld, no matter how things were, yet surely all was very beautiful. (*Pause.*)

Not merely for enjoyment have I been posted here on high; what a fearful horror threatens me from the darkling world! I see flashes of sparks scattering through the double darkness of the lindens; a red glow is in motion, steadily fanned to greater size by the growing draft. Oh! the hut is aflame inside, though it stood there moss-covered and damp; swift aid is required, no deliverance at hand. Alas! the good old couple, wont to move so carefully around their fire, will become the prey of this smoking blaze! What a terrible happening! Flame is flaming, glowing red stands the black, moss-grown structure; if only the good people would escape from the hell of that wild conflagration! Bright flashes are licking upward through leaves and boughs; dry branches, flickering as they flare, quickly turn red and crash down. Eyes of mine, should you see that happen? Must I be so farsighted? The little chapel collapses under the weight of the falling boughs. Already the treetops are caught by the darting, serpentining flames. Down to their roots the hollow trunks are aglow, dark red in their glowing. (A *long pause, followed by singing.*) What used to appeal to the gaze, the growth of centuries, is gone.

FAUST (*on the balcony, facing the dunes*). What is that wailing song from above? The words are in my ear, but the tones are too late. My towerman laments; and I, in my soul, am vexed by my act of impatience. Yet, though the stand of lindens is destroyed, their half-charred trunks a dreadful sight, it won't take long to erect a lookout for gazing into infinity. And I visualize as well the new dwelling which will encompass that old couple, who, feeling that they have been magnanimously spared, will happily spend their latter days there.

MEPHISTOPHELES (*below with* THREE MEN). Here we come on the run; your pardon, but the affair didn't go off nicely. We rapped at the door, we knocked on the door, and still nobody opened; we rattled the door, we went on knocking, and now the rotten door lay flat; we called aloud and uttered grave threats, but we found no hearing. And, as things go in such a case, they didn't listen, and they weren't willing; but we didn't dally, and briskly we removed them for you. The old couple didn't struggle much; they fell in a faint for fright. A stranger, who had concealed himself there and wanted to fight, was laid low. In the brief time of our wild conflict straw took fire from coals which got scattered about. Now it is all aflame, a funeral pyre of those three.

FAUST. Were you deaf to my words? I wanted an exchange, wanted no robbery. This ill-considered, mad trick has my curse: divide it among you!

CHORUS. The old saw rings out: give ready obedience to power! And if you are bold, and see it through, then risk your house and home and—you. (*Exeunt.*)

FAUST (*on the balcony*). The stars are hiding their glance and gleam, the fire's dying down, with lessened flame; a quivering breeze quickens it again and brings smoke and fume up here to me. Swiftly ordered, too swiftly done!—What shadowy forms come floating this way?

Midnight

(FOUR GRAY WOMEN *enter*.)

FIRST WOMAN. My name is Dearth.

SECOND WOMAN. My name is Debt.

THIRD WOMAN. My name is Care.

FOURTH WOMAN. My name is Trouble.

CHORUS OF THREE. The door is locked, we can't get in; a rich man lives there, and we don't care to enter.

DEARTH. Then I become a shadow.

DEBT. Then I become nothing.

TROUBLE. A spoiled man turns his face away from me.

CARE. Sisters, you cannot and may not enter. Care steals in through the keyhole. (CARE *disappears*.)

DEARTH. Gray sisters, withdraw from here.

DEBT. I will join you, keeping close by your side.

TROUBLE. Trouble will escort you, close upon your heels.

ALL THREE. The clouds are on the move, the stars disappear! Back yonder, back yonder! from far, far away, he is coming, our brother, see, there he comes—Death.

(*As Care [worry or anxiety] enters the palace, Faust commands her to withdraw. Instead of obeying, Care curses Faust with blindness because he has refused to acknowledge her power.*)

FAUST (*blinded*). The night seems to crowd in deep and deeper still, yet here within shines a bright light. What I have planned I will hasten to complete; it is only the master's word that carries weight. Up from your beds, servants, to a man! Let us see my bold conception reach success. Seize your tools, bestir shovels and spades! The task staked out must be promptly achieved. My strict orders and your swift diligence will result in the very finest reward; for the completion of the greatest of works, *one* mind suffices for a thousand pairs of hands.

Great Forecourt of the Palace—Torches

MEPHISTOPHELES (*leading as overseer*). This way, this way! Come in, come in, you rickety lemures,[1] half-creatures patched together out of ligaments, sinews, and bones!

LEMURES (*in chorus*). At once we come to serve you, and as we half understood it, a spacious land seems to be involved which we are to get. We have sharpened stakes, and a long chain for measuring; but we've forgotten why we were the ones to be called.

MEPHISTOPHELES. What is involved here is no artistic endeavor; just follow your own measurements. Let the tallest of you lay himself down at full length, and the rest of you lift the turf round about him; then dig out an oblong hole, as was done for our forefathers. Out of the palace into the narrow housing, that's the stupid end it comes down to, after all.

LEMURES (*digging with roguish gestures*). When I was young and lived and loved, I thought that life was sweet; where sounds were gay, and merriment reigned, 'twas there I stirred my feet. Now malicious old age has hit me with its crutch. I stumbled over the entrance to a grave; well, why did it chance to be open?

FAUST (*issuing from the palace, groping along the doorposts*). How the clink of the spades delights me! It is the gang which is working for me, reconciling the land with itself, setting bounds to the waves, and investing the sea with a firm barrier.

MEPHISTOPHELES (*aside*). You are working for *us*, after all, with your dams and dikes; for already you are preparing a great feast for Neptune, the water-devil. You men are lost in any event—the elements are in league with us, and destruction is what it will come to in the end.

FAUST. Overseer!

MEPHISTOPHELES. Here!

FAUST. Utilize every possible means of procuring gang upon gang of workmen: encourage them with satisfactions and severity, pay them, entice them, impress them! Every day I wish to have a report on the lengthening of the canal we have planned.

MEPHISTOPHELES (*in an undertone*). According to the report I have, no canal is mentioned, only a grave.

---

[1] **lemures:** the spirits of the departed

FAUST. A marsh extends along the mountains, infecting all we have gained so far; to drain that foul pit, too, would be supreme as well as final achievement. I'll create room for millions to dwell, not in security, to be sure, but in a free activity. Green and fruitful fields; men and flocks immediately contented on this latest ground, swiftly settled under protection of the lofty dike piled up by a bold and busy populace. Here in the interior, a land like paradise. Then let the flood outside rage up to the crest: as soon as the waters nibble at it in order to rush in with might, a communal impulse will make haste to close the gap.

Yes! to this purpose I am wholly devoted, and this is wisdom's final conclusion: he alone deserves freedom as well as life who has to win them by conquest every day. And thus, surrounded by peril, child, man, and graybeard will spend their productive years. Such a throng I should like to see, and stand on free ground with a people free. To that moment I'd have a right to say, "Do stay with me, you are so good!" Not in aeons can the traces of my earthly days disappear.—In the anticipation of such exalted happiness I now enjoy the supreme moment. (FAUST *falls backward*; THE LEMURES *catch him and lay him on the ground.*)

MEPHISTOPHELES. No pleasure satiated, no bliss contented him, and so he went on courting shifting forms; this last poor, empty moment is the one the poor fellow wished to hold fast. He who withstood me so powerfully is mastered by time, and this old man lies dead on the sand. The clock has stopped—

CHORUS. Has stopped! It's as mute as midnight. The hand drops.

MEPHISTOPHELES. It drops, and all is accomplished.

CHORUS. All is past.

MEPHISTOPHELES. Past! A stupid word. Why "past"? Past and pure Not, wholly identical. Of what meaning for us is eternal creating, just to snatch away created things and make them nothing? "Then it is past." What is to be read out of that? It's just as if it had never been, and yet it goes around in a circle as if it did exist. I'd prefer to that the Eternally Void.

Interment

LEMURE. SOLO. Who built this house so badly with shovels and spades?

LEMURES. CHORUS. It's been made too well for you, dull fellow in hempen dress.

LEMURE. SOLO. Who made such poor provision for the hall? Where are table and chairs?

LEMURES. CHORUS. All was lent for a brief time; there are so many claimants.

MEPHISTOPHELES. The body is prone, and if the soul tries to escape, I'll quickly show it the item written with blood—but unfortunately they now have so many means of wresting souls from the devil. Our old methods are offensive, but for new ones we lack recommendations; formerly I'd have managed this alone, but now I must call in accomplices.

We are badly off in everything! Traditional customs, old privileges—you can no longer put your trust in anything. In former days the soul slipped out with the last breath; I would watch for it and like a cat with the quickest mouse, snap! I would hold it in tightly clenched claws. Now it hesitates and will not forsake the gloomy spot, the vile corpse's loathsome house; only the elements, which hate each other, ultimately drive it out ignominiously. And if I torment myself for hours and days, the painful question is, When? How? Where? Death grown old has lost his swift force, and even Whether? long remains dubious; often I would look greedily at limbs grown rigid—it was only illusion, and they would stir, would move again. (*Fantastic gestures of conjuration, aping the file-leader.*) Come forward briskly, double your pace, you gentlemen of the straight and of the crooked horn, you of the old tried and true brand of devils, and bring the mouth of hell right along with you. True, hell has many, many mouths, and it swallows in keeping with rank and dignity; but hereafter people will not be so particular, even in this final game of life. (*The horrible mouth of hell opens on the left.*)

Canine teeth are bared; from the vaulted gullet streams the raging flood of fire, and in the boiling reek of the background I see the city of flame eternally aglow. The red surf dashes forward up to the teeth, and the damned, hoping for rescue, swim up; but the hyena chews them up in colossal style, and they anxiously renew their hot course. In the nooks there is still much to be revealed, so much of unequaled terror in the tiniest space. You do well to frighten sinners: but still they'll take it to be lies and fraud and dream.

(*To the fat devils with short, straight horns.*) Now then, pot-bellied rascals with cheeks of fire! You are mightily aglow and puffed up with hellish sulfur; short, chunky, eternally stiff necks! Lie in wait down here, watch for a phosphorescent gleam; that's the tiny soul—Psyche with wings which you are to pluck out of her, turning her into a filthy worm; I'll put my brand on her, then away with her in a whirlwind of fire!

(*To the gaunt devils with long, crooked horns.*) You gangling clowns, file-leading giants, reach up into the air, keep trying without stopping! Arms outstretched, sharp claws showing, so as to catch the fluttering, fleeing one. Undoubtedly she's unhappy in her old house, and genius always heads for the height.

(GLORY *from above, at right.*)

THE HEAVENLY HOST. Follow, emissaries, kindred of Heaven, in leisurely flight: to forgive sinners and bid the dust live; make pleasant paths for all beings, as your tarrying train floats on its way!

MEPHISTOPHELES. I hear cacophonies, a repulsive jingling, coming from above with unwelcome light. It's that knavish botchery, such as just suits a sanctimonious taste. You know how, in hours of deep depravity, we planned the annihilation of the human race; the worst atrocities we could think up are the favorite objects of their devotion. They come hypocritically, these dandies, and that's how they have snatched many a soul away from us, fighting us with our own weapons; for they are devils, too, but disguised. To lose out in this case would be an eternal disgrace for you; close up on the grave and hold its rim tight!

CHOIR OF ANGELS (*strewing roses*). Resplendent roses, shedding balm! Fluttering, floating, mysteriously giving life: each winged twig unseals its buds and hastens to bloom. Let springtime sprout in purple and green, carrying paradise to him now at rest.

MEPHISTOPHELES (*to* THE SATANS). Why duck and twitch? Is that our way in hell? Stand your ground and let them strew. Take your places, all you idiots! I suppose they think they can snow in the red hot devils with such flowery fluff; but it will melt and shrivel as you blow on it. Now blow, you blowhards!—Stop, that's enough!—Your exhalation is turning the whole flight pale.—Not so violent! Shut your mouths and nostrils! On my word, you blew too strongly. That you can never learn proper moderation! The stuff's not only shriveling, it's turning brown, drying up, now it's burning! Already it's floating this way with bright and poisonous flames; brace yourselves against it, form a dense crowd!—Their force is extinguished, all their courage is gone! The devils are sniffing an unfamiliar and seductive fire.

CHOIR OF ANGELS. Blessed blossoms, frolicsome flames, disseminate love, readying rapture, as hearts may desire. Words of truth, unclouded skies: for eternal hosts there is day everywhere!

MEPHISTOPHELES. O curses! O shame upon such drips! Satans are standing on their heads, and the clumsy chumps turn cartwheel upon cartwheel and plunge rump first into hell. My blessing on your well-deserved hot bath! But I'll stay at my post. (*Flailing at the hovering roses.*) Begone, will-o'-the-wisps! You there! Shine as bright as you will, but if I catch you, all you are is a disgusting bit of cheesy slime. What are you fluttering about for? Get out, will you?—Something like pitch and sulfur is nipping my neck.

CHOIR OF ANGELS. You must give up what does not belong to you; you must not endure what disturbs your soul. If it intrudes with violence, we must show our mettle. Love brings in only those who love. . . . Turn back to the light, loving flames! Let the truth save those who wreak their own damnation, that they may joyously free themselves from evil, to be among the blest in the communion of souls.

MEPHISTOPHELES (*getting control of himself*). What is happening to me?—Like Job, the whole fellow is one boil after another, shuddering at himself and yet at the same time triumphant as he sees through himself completely, and puts his faith in himself and his ancient race; for the noble devilish parts are saved, and the love-witchery is merely attacking the skin. The cursed flames have now burned themselves out, and, as is wholly proper for me, I curse you one and all!

CHOIR OF ANGELS. Sacred fires! He whom they invest feels himself blest in life with those who are good. Now all arise as one and utter praise! The air is cleansed, let the spirit draw breath! (*They rise aloft, bearing away* FAUST's *immortal part.*)

MEPHISTOPHELES (*looking about*). But how is this—where have they gone to?—You gang of minors, you took me by surprise.—And they've escaped with their booty in flight toward heaven; that's why they were nibbling at this grave! I've been robbed of a great, unique treasure: they have cunningly cozened me out of that lofty soul which had pledged itself to me.

With whom shall I now lodge my complaint? Who will procure for me the rights I have won?—You're deceived in your old age, and serves you right; you're in a very bad way.—I have mismanaged disgracefully, and a great expediture has been shamefully wasted; a common lust, a silly flirtatiousness, attacked the case-hardened devil. And if it was a bit of mad childishness with which the experienced old fox occupied himself, then certainly it was no slight folly that got possession of him at the end.

(*In the closing scene, Angels, bearing Faust's "immortal part," explain why he was saved.*)

THE NOBLE MEMBER OF THE SPIRIT WORLD IS SAVED FROM EVIL. WE CAN REDEEM ANYONE WHO KEEPS ON STRIVING AND STRUGGLING. AND IF, BESIDES, LOVE FROM ON HIGH HAS TAKEN AN INTEREST IN HIM, THE BLESSED HOST WILL MEET HIM WITH A HEARTFELT WELCOME.

For Discussion

Prologue

1. What was the attitude of the three angels toward the universe as revealed in their opening speeches? How would you describe the tone of the speeches? What relation do you see between the angels' description of nature and the action that is to follow?
2. What did Mephistopheles think would be the outcome of his "bet" with God? How did his opinion of man support this opinion? What eternal question is this play going to attempt to answer?
3. Point out the satirical quality in Mephistopheles' opening speech. What evidence of his pride is revealed? From the prologue, what is your opinion of Mephistopheles' attitude toward the Almighty?
4. How does the prologue serve as an exposition of the play as a whole? Show its likeness to the medieval morality play. Which story in the Old Testament does the prologue resemble? Explain.

5. A popular trend in Goethe's day was the use of anthropomorphism; that is, the representing of spiritual beings as having human characteristics. Point out evidence of anthropomorphism in this opening scene.

6. What is your personal judgment of the devil's attitude toward the Almighty as Goethe presented it?

PART I

Night

1. In the long opening soliloquy, what did Goethe reveal about Faust's state of mind and his attitude toward the world? What did Faust mean when he said that he had studied "even, alas! theology"?

2. To what did Faust turn in desperation? Why? What was the significance of the Spirit's final words to Faust?

3. Why was Wagner's entrance at this point dramatically effective? What did you find out about Faust from his conversation with his assistant? Why was he grateful to Wagner?

4. Point out lines which reveal that Faust despaired of grasping true knowledge. How does Goethe also show the Renaissance interest in man as man?

5. How did Faust plan to escape his present miserable state? What reasons do you have for believing this plan will, or will not, prove effective?

6. Explain why the music of the Easter choirs has implicit in it the virtue of hope.

7. In this scene, as throughout the play, Faust often speaks in a way which is both poetic and romantic in tone. Select passages from this scene which most effectively reveal these two qualities. What do they contribute to the characterization of Faust?

Outside the City Gates

1. From whom did Faust inherit his skill in the "black art"? What would this "art" be called today? Why was Faust so bitter about the acclaim he was receiving?

2. Contrast the attitudes of Wagner and Faust in this scene. Did Wagner's reasoning follow a logical pattern? Why or why not?

3. Describe Faust's "two souls." In your opinion, was this peculiar to Faust, or is it applicable to human beings in general? Explain.

4. What power did Faust desire to come to his aid? What was Wagner's response to this? Do you think the dog was, or was not, the first intimation of the presence of this power? Explain.

Faust's Study I

1. Analyze Faust's preoccupation with the New Testament passage. What foreshadowing do you find here, of his possible destiny? Discuss.
2. Why did Mephistopheles call himself "the spirit which always denies"; that is, the one who denies truth or thinks of it as nonexistent?
3. Mephistopheles confessed various weaknesses to Faust. Why was he unable to destroy "this clumsy world" which opposes itself to Nothing? Why couldn't he leave Faust's study?
4. How did Mephistopheles reveal his power to Faust in this scene?
5. In your opinion, if Mephistopheles, representing evil, was aware of weaknesses in himself, why was he so formidable an adversary?
6. Point out the humor in this scene. How did Mephistopheles mingle the strange and the everyday in the way he spoke with Faust?

Faust's Study II

1. Why was Faust dissatisfied with life? Which things did he consider curses on mankind? Do you agree with his list? Why or why not? Why did Faust think that Mephistopheles would be unable to rescue him from despair?
2. In his quest for the answers to the great mysteries of life and death, Faust typified the ideal Renaissance man of his day. He was not satisfied with surface answers, but wanted to know the *how* and *why* of things. He was also intent upon self-perfectibility in every area— physical, moral, and spiritual. Point out indications in this scene of these traits in Faust.
3. In his contract with the devil, what condition did Faust make? (This is important for an appreciation of the play's ending.) Point out sentences in this scene that reveal that Faust had completely delivered himself up to despair. Why did he feel that all his intellectual knowledge had been useless?
4. Do you agree with Faust that "it is only in ceaseless activity that man is himself"? Why or why not?
5. Mephistopheles believed that Faust's ruin was certain. On what did he base this belief?

Street

1. In the way Faust talked about Margaret, would you say that his passion for her was in any way idealized? Explain.
2. Why did Mephistopheles have no power over Margaret?

Gloomy Day. A Field

1. What evidence in this scene revealed that Faust was beginning to realize his mistake?
2. Explain the logic of Mephistopheles' answer to Faust (page 26), beginning "Why do you make common cause with us if you can't see it through? . . ."
3. Do you agree or disagree with Mephistopheles that it was Faust who was to blame for Margaret's fall? Explain.

Dungeon

1. Why did Faust refer to Margaret's crime as a "fond delusion"? What was Margaret referring to when she cried out that her "wreath lies torn, the flowers scattered"?
2. What did Faust's reaction to Margaret's sad state reveal about him? What was Mephistopheles' reaction to what was occurring? Explain how the emotional state of each of the three characters in this scene showed Goethe's sense of dramatic contrast.
3. Although it seemed heartless that Faust left Margaret to a terrible fate, what good, if any, would have resulted from his staying? In your opinion, did Faust's leaving make the incident more realistic? Why or why not? How was it related to the pact Faust had with the devil?

PART II

Palace

1. Faust is now at the height of his power, yet, he is unhappy. Why? What was his attitude toward the old couple? Point out the lines which reveal how he is typical of a man greedy for power.
2. In this same speech, Faust expresses one of his noblest aspirations: "creating habitable lands for many peoples." How does he contradict, in a sense, both the ugliness of his greed brought out a few lines before, and, without his being aware of it, Mephistopheles' aim to make him hardened to all good?
3. What is the meaning of Mephistopheles' speech on page 29, beginning, "Naturally! Some prime annoyance is bound to embitter your life. . . ." To which "bells" in man's existence is he referring? Do you think the imagery in this speech is effective? Why or why not?

Black Night and Midnight

1. Point out and discuss the effectiveness of the visual images Goethe employed to describe the fire.

2. Using evidence from the preceding scene, do you think Faust was, or was not, to blame for the old couples' death? Explain. What did this scene reveal about Faust's character? Did he remind you in any way of Macbeth? Explain.

3. In the brief scene that follows (Midnight), why do you think Care was the only one of the gray women who could enter the palace? What was Faust's attitude toward his great project after he was struck blind? What was the bright light that he still had within him?

4. Discuss the change in Faust from a wrong-headed, aimless, yearning romanticist of the Middle Ages into what he is now: an energetic organizer.

Great Forecourt of the Palace

1. Irony is a mode of expression in which the author says one thing but means the opposite. In this scene there is a great stress on irony. Faust failed to understand the meaning of the lemures' digging, while Mephistopheles believed Faust to be irrevocably his. Reread Faust's speech in Part I, beginning, "If ever I shall say to any moment . . ." (page 22). Which is the precise *moment* as it is pictured to be in this scene at the close of Faust's life?

2. A second reading of Faust's "supreme moment" speech reveals that Faust, in reality, was expressing his satisfaction only with some future moment which can be enjoyed only in anticipation; but it is a choice of good, not evil. Discuss.

3. What was revealed about Mephistopheles' attitude toward Faust in the devil's speech beginning, "No pleasure satiated, no bliss contented him . . ."? Explain the meaning of "He who withstood me so power- fully is mastered by time." Do you think Mephistopheles was satis- fied with the bargain he made with Faust? Why or why not?

Interment

1. Point out lines that reveal that Mephistopheles was unaware of Faust's salvation. How does this scene comment on Faust's scornful remark to Mephistopheles early in the play: "Was the mind of man, in its lofty striving, ever grasped by the likes of you?" In your opinion, did Mephistopheles ever truly understand Faust's soul? Point out passages throughout the play to support your answer.

2. In Mephistopheles' first long speech in this scene, he prepared to grab Faust's soul. Point out the mingling of seriousness and humor in this speech. Have you found Mephistopheles' account of the terrors of the damned in any authentic sources? If so, where? Discuss the theological rightness of his account.

3. Mephistopheles needed assistance for the final claiming of Faust's soul. What does this imply about the devil's claim to power? What does it imply regarding man's innate dignity? Explain Mephistopheles' final sentence in his speech to the "gaunt devils with long, crooked horns" (page 36).
4. Explain how Goethe's description of the final "battle" over Faust's soul was human in essence though it dealt only with preternatural and angelic powers.
5. Faust, without deliberately trying to do so, outwitted Mephistopheles. What hints did Goethe give the reader which pointed to this ending? Why did Mephistopheles miss the point so often?
6. What was your reaction to the play as a whole? Do you think Goethe's characterization of Faust was an accurate picture of man? Give reasons to support your answer.

For Composition

1. Write a composition in which you defend or oppose Goethe's view of man. Refer to specific passages where his ideas are clearly stated. Be sure to include Goethe's emphasis on the power of human activity over evil.
2. Write an essay in which you explain the meaning of Faust's conviction that "he alone deserves freedom as well as life who has to win them by conquest every day." How did Faust, himself, prove the meaning and worth of these words in his life? What men in modern times have put the meaning of these words into use?
3. In a short composition, show through specific examples how Goethe's understanding of the "human comedy" goes hand in hand with a sense of humor.
4. In his famous essay, "What Is a Classic?" the French critic, Saint-Beuve (1804–1869), wrote that the author of a true classic is one who has:

> enriched the human mind, increased its treasure, and caused it to advance a step; who has discovered some moral and not equivocal truth, or revealed some external passion in that heart where all seemed known and discovered; who has expressed his thought, observation or intention, in no matter what form, only provided that it be broad and great, refined and sensible, sane and beautiful in itself; who has spoken to all in his own peculiar style, a style which is to be also that of the whole world, . . . a style new and old, easily contemporary with all time. . . .

Using several points from this quotation, develop an essay in which you show that *Faust* is a true classic.

Friedrich von Schiller

Friedrich von Schiller (1759–1805) was one of Goethe's intimate friends and a major figure in the Romantic Movement in Germany. A poet, dramatist, literary critic, and historian, he was a fervent advocate of moral and spiritual freedom. Influenced by the "Storm and Stress" literary movement of his day, he aimed at destroying social injustices and tyranny wherever he saw it. As a result of his play, *The Robbers*, which dealt with political tyranny, Schiller was imprisoned for a short time in 1782, and was forbidden to write any more plays. He fled from his native duchy and lived in Dresden, Weimar, and Jena. It was during these years that he became a close friend of Goethe and other important literary men, such as Johann Gottfried von Heider and Christoph Martin Wieland.

Schiller is perhaps best known for his poetic dramas, a form which best suited his mind and temperament, and which eventually won him the title of Germany's greatest dramatist. His most famous plays, such as *Don Carlos*, *Wallenstein*, *Marie Stuart*, and *William Tell*, are written in blank verse and in a melodious language which reflects his lofty ideals. The lyrics which follow reveal Schiller's sensitive and poetic imagination and his deep faith in the triumph of the good, the true, and the beautiful, values which he sought to realize in his own inner life.

Thekla's Song

THE cloud doth gather, the green wood roar,
The damsel paces along the shore;
The billows they tumble with might, with might;
And she flings out her voice to the darksome night;
    Her bosom is swelling with sorrow;   5
The world it is empty, the heart will die,
There's nothing to wish for beneath the sky:
Thou Holy One, call thy child away!
I've lived and loved, and that was today—
    Make ready my grave-clothes tomorrow.   10

(*tr. Samuel Taylor Coleridge*)

The Maid of Orleans

AT thee *the Mocker* sneers in cold derision,
  Through thee he seeks to desecrate and dim
Glory for which he hath no soul or vision,
  For "God" and "Angel" are but sounds with him.
He makes the jewels of the heart his booty,   5
And scoffs at Man's Belief and Woman's Beauty.

Yet thou—a lowly shepherdess!—descended
  Not from a kingly but a godly race,
Art crowned by Poësy! Amid the splendid
  Of Heaven's high stars she builds thy dwellingplace,   10
Garlands thy temples with a wreath of glory,
And swathes thy memory in eternal Story.

The Base of this weak world exult at seeing
  The Fair defaced, the Lofty in the dust;
Yet grieve not! There are godlike hearts in being   15
  Which worship still the Beautiful and Just.
Let Momus [1] and his mummers please the crowd,
Of nobleness alone a noble mind is proud.

               (*tr. James Clarence Mangan*)

To My Friends

Belovèd friends! More glorious times than ours
Of old existed: men of loftier powers
  Than we can boast have flourished:—who shall doubt it?
A million stones dug from the depths of Earth
Will bear this witness for the ancient worth,   5
  If History's chronicles be mute about it.
     But, all are gone—those richly-gifted souls—
      That constellation of illustrious names:
     For Us, for Us, the current moment rolls,
      And We, We live, and have our claims.   10

[1] **Momus:** in Greek mythology, the god of censure and ridicule

My friends! The wanderer tells us—and we own—
That Earth shows many a more luxuriant zone
    Than that whereunder we sedately live;
But, if denied a paradise, our hearts
Are still the home of science and the arts,   15
    And glow and gladden in the light they give;
        And if beneath our skies the laurel pines,
            And winter desolates our myrtle boughs,
        The curling tendrils of our joyous vines
            Shed freshest greenness round our brows.   20

May burn more feverish life, more maddening pleasures,
Where four assembled worlds exchange their treasures,
    At London, in the world's Commercial Hall;
A thousand stately vessels come and go,
And costly sights are there, and pomp and show,   25
    And Gold is lord and idolgod of all!
        But will the sun be mirrored in the stream
            Sullied and darkened by the flooding rains?
        No! On the still smooth lake alone his beam
            Is brightly imaged, and remains.   30

The beggar at St. Angelo's might gaze
With scorn upon our North, for he surveys
    The one, lone, only, everliving Rome—
All shapes of beauty fascinate his eye;
He sees a brilliant heaven below the sky   35
    Shine in Saint Peter's wonderwaking dome.
        But, even while beaming with celestial glory,
            Rome is the grave of long-departed years;
        It is the green young plant and not the hoary
            And time-worn trunk that blooms and cheers.   40

Prouder achievements may perchance appear
Elsewhere than signalize our humble sphere,
    But never nowhere underneath the sun.
We see in pettier outlines on our stage,
Which miniatures the world of every age,   45
    The storied feats of bypassed eras done.

All things are but redone, reshown, retold,
Fancy alone is ever young and new;
Man and the universe shall both grow old,
But not the forms her pencil drew!   50

(*tr. James Clarence Mangan*)

For Discussion

"Thekla's Song"

1. This short lyric is from one of Schiller's plays, *The Piccolemini*, and is typically romantic. What romantic attitude toward the world does the poem reveal? Explain the last two lines.

2. What romantic elements are present in the imagery of the poem?

3. Samuel Taylor Coleridge, who translated this poem, cunningly mingled two different meters to produce the melodious effects in this poem. Point out these two meters. In your opinion, why might this poem of Schiller's have had a strong appeal for Coleridge?

"The Maid of Orleans"

1. This poem, like his poetic drama, *The Maid of Orleans*, reveals Schiller's devotion to St. Joan. Whom did "the Mocker" represent? According to the poet, of what was Joan a victim?

2. Explain how stanza 3 repeats the basic image of stanza 1. What universal idea is expressed in these two stanzas?

3. Point out lines which show Schiller's idealism and his admiration for St. Joan's life of integrity. Why do some critics speak of Schiller's admiration as an indication of his strong "Platonism"? Look up the meaning of this term in an encyclopedia before discussing the question.

4. Do you think that some of the lines are overly sentimental? Why or why not? In your opinion, is the poem more a tribute to beauty than to St. Joan? Give reasons for your answer.

"To My Friends"

1. What is the theme of this poem? Explain why Schiller's message is more meaningful when you realize that his friends were the leading intellectuals of the time—the dramatist and poet, Goethe; the philosophers, Fichte and Schelling; and the poets, Herder and Wieland.

2. Explain the last four lines of the poem. Do you agree or disagree with the idea expressed? Why?

3. In what way is the poem an encouragement to young people? Point out lines to support your answer.
4. What is the mood of this poem? How do the imagery and diction reflect this mood?
5. Point out examples of metaphors in "To My Friends." Do you think they add to or detract from the effectiveness of the poem? Why?

For Composition

Schiller is perhaps best known in literature for his poetic dramas. Read one of his plays, *Don Carlos, Marie Stuart, The Maid of Orleans,* or *William Tell.* Write a critical review of the play, pointing out its theme, its romantic qualities, and your opinion of the effectiveness of the drama.

Heinrich Heine

Heinrich Heine * (1797–1856), one of the great German lyric poets, has been called the poet of love and freedom and the "greatest wit of his century." Because of his views on the brotherhood of all men and his advocacy of love and tolerance, he has also been called "cosmopolitan and international." Although he was born in Germany, Heine lived the greater part of his life in Paris. During the last eight years of his life, he was bedridden with a spinal disease, but despite his great suffering, his mind remained clear and alert, and he wrote some of his finest poetry during this period.

Although Heine also wrote dramas, essays, and political satires, he has been acclaimed chiefly for his lyrics. These short poems, with their simple verse forms eloquently reflect the romantic spirit of the nineteenth century. The musical and rhythmical charm of his poetry is second only to that of Goethe, and the works of few poets have been set to music as often as those of Heine.

The Two Grenadiers

Toward France there journeyed two grenadiers:
In Russia they had been bound;
And when they crossed the German frontiers
They bowed their heads to the ground.

For here they heard the tidings of woe: 5
That the glory of France was drained—
Her great host vanquished and crushed by the foe—
And the emperor, the emperor chained.

The grenadiers together cried
At the sorrowful news of the war.   10
Said the first: "I'm all one ache inside;
How my wound flares up once more!"

* hīn′rikh hī′nə

49

The other said: "The song is done;
I'd die with you today—
But I've a wife and a little one   15
Who'd starve with me away."

"What matters child, what matters wife?
There's a loftier pulse in my veins;
If they hunger, let them go begging through life—
My emperor, my emperor's in chains!   20

"There's one thing, brother, you must do:
Promise that when I die
You'll carry my corpse to France with you;
In French earth let me lie.

"The honor-cross on its scarlet band   25
You must lay upon my breast,
Gird on my sword, and in my hand
Allow my gun to rest.

"So, like a sentry, I'll lie in my tomb
And silently take heed   30
Till at last I hear a cannon-boom
And the trot of a neighing steed.

"Then will the Emperor ride over my grave,
While sabres flash and rattle:
Then will I rise up armed from the grave—   35
For the Emperor, the Emperor to battle!"

(tr. Aaron Kramer)

Twilight

I sat on the pale sea-sand
Grieved by my thoughts and lonely.
The sun sank ever lower, and threw
Red hot streaks upon the water,
And the white, the far-away billows,   5

Urged on by the flood,
Sparkled and murmured nearer and nearer—
A singular noise, a whispering and piping,
A laughing and murmuring, sighing and whistling,
Through all a mysterious cradle-song humming—   10
I thought I was hearing forgotten legends,
Ancient, lovely fables,
That I once, as a boy,
Learned from the neighbors' children,
When on a summer's evening,   15
On the steps before the street-door,
We squatted down to the quiet telling,
With little, hearkening hearts
And curious-clever eyes;—
While, opposite us at the window,   20
By fragrant flower-pots,
The grown-up girls were sitting,
Rosy-faced,
Smiling and lit by the moon.

(tr. Aaron Kramer)

Journey by Water

Counting the waves as they roll by
I lean against the mast.
Goodbye, my lovely fatherland!
My ship is sailing fast.

I pass my pretty sweetheart's house   5
And see the windows shine.
I stare until my eyes pop out,
But no one makes a sign.

You blinding teardrops, leave my eyes,
That I may clearly see.   10
Sick heart of mine, don't break beneath
This giant agony.

(tr. Aaron Kramer)

2 Sonnets: To My Mother, B. Heine

1

It's been my way to walk with head held high;
I've got a pretty tough and stubborn mind;
And if the king himself should pass, he'd find
That I'm a lad who'll look him in the eye.

And yet, dear mother, this I'll frankly say: 5
No matter how puffed up my pride may be,
When I am near your sweet serenity
My haughtiness begins to melt away.

Is it your soul that strangely holds my flight?
Your towering soul, that bravely pierces all   10
And soars up flashing toward the heavenly light?
Or am I tortured now when I recall
My many wrongs, that filled your heart with woe?
Your beautiful, big heart that loved me so?

2

I left you once in wild insanity—
To travel through the world from end to end,
To see if love were hiding in some land,
That I might lift and clasp it lovingly.

I looked for love on all the streets; I'd wait   5
With arms outstretched in front of every door—
For little alms of passion I'd implore—
But, laughing, all they gave me was cold hate.

And ever did I stray toward love; forever
Toward love; and yet I came upon it never—   10
And turned back home, in sickness and despair.
But here you were—I saw you drawing nigh—
And ah! the thing that swam within your eye—
That sweet, that long-desired love, was there.

(tr. Aaron Kramer)

The Light Goes Out

The curtain falls upon the play,
And lords and ladies drive away.
But did they seem to like the show?
I think I heard: *"Bravissimo!"*
A prominent assembly cheered   5
Its poet to the highest rafter.
But now the house has hushed its laughter,
And all the lights have disappeared.

But wait! What could that sound have been?
Close by the empty stage?—perhaps   10
It is a feeble string that snaps—
The string of an old violin.
Some peevish rats morosely flit
Backward and forward through the pit.
The whole place smells of rancid oil.   15
The final lamp goes pale, and sighs,
And hisses bitterly, and dies.
The wretched fire—it was my soul.

(*tr. Aaron Kramer*)

The Lorelei

I cannot explain the sadness
That's fallen on my breast.
An old, old fable haunts me,
And will not let me rest.

The air grows cool in the twilight,   5
And softly the Rhine flows on;
The peak of a mountain sparkles
Beneath the setting sun.

More lovely than a vision,
A girl sits high up there;   10

Her golden jewelry glistens,
She combs her golden hair.

With a comb of gold she combs it,
And sings an evensong;
The wonderful melody reaches   15
A boat, as it sails along.

The boatman hears, with an anguish
More wild than was ever known;
He's blind to the rocks around him,
His eyes are for her alone.   20

—At last the waves devoured
The boat, and the boatman's cry;
And this she did with her singing,
The golden Lorelei.

> (*tr. Aaron Kramer*)

For Discussion

"The Two Grenadiers"

1. In this brief but clearly defined picture of two soldiers in Napoleon's army, the reader glimpses the history of an entire people—a people divided by two opposing attitudes or "loves." What are these two "loves"? According to human values, which is the greater "love"?
2. Which of the soldiers was the idealist? Which was the realist? With whom did you agree? Give reasons to support your answer. Do you think that the first grenadier tended to sentimentalize his attitude toward Napoleon? Why or why not?
3. In reading this poem, it is necessary to take into account the almost fanatical allegiance of Napoleon's men. How would a modern soldier look upon such an attachment to a general? Do you think that the grenadier's insistence that life was meaningless now that his country's leader was defeated, detracted from his devotion to France itself? Explain. In your opinion, what is true patriotism?
4. A study of the craft of this poem reveals a splendid use of economy. What situation was swiftly presented in the first eight lines? Explain the effectiveness of the simile in lines 29-30. In the closing four lines,

what dramatic contrast was implied in the first grenadier's personal life and for all of France?

"Twilight"

1. In this lyric, Heine reveals his ability to paint vivid pictures with words. In the poet's description of the waves, which words seem surprising? Do you think these descriptive words are justified? Why or why not?
2. How did the waves evoke memories in Heine of a summer evening? Would you say that this scene, remembered from the poet's childhood, was just personal to Heine or did it also have universality? Explain.
3. Point out examples of images in the poem which appeal to the senses.
4. This poem illustrates Heine's fine sense of the value of simple, melodious words. How does his diction compare, for example, with Wordsworth's or with other romantic poets of his time?
5. Explain how this poem is an excellent example of Wordsworth's definition of poetry as "emotion recollected in tranquillity."

"Journey by Water"

1. Heine was forced, in a sense, into exile by the German Nationalists who accused him of disloyalty when he showed strong opposition to the autocracy then in force. This poem gives voice to the millions, in Heine's time and later, who have been forced under similar circumstances to leave their home and fatherland. In your opinion, is the simplicity and compactness of this poem more effective than a long, angry invective against his persecutors might be? Why or why not?
2. What is the mood of this poem? How do the images contribute to this mood?
3. In what way does the poem reflect the romantic spirit of the times? How might a poem written today on the same subject differ in mood and tone?

"To My Mother, B. Heine"

1. In sonnet 1, point out the presence of both pride and humility in the son. Which of the two reasons presented by the poet do you think best explains why his "haughtiness begins to melt away"? Explain.
2. In sonnet 2, what is the universal truth expressed? What was the poet seeking and where did he finally find it?
3. In your opinion, are these two sonnets excessively sentimental? Why or why not? While these poems are seemingly very personal, do you think Heine also saw his mother as representing something impersonal? If so, what might she have represented to him?

4. Show how the forms of these poems, though they are called sonnets, do not follow the regular sonnet patterns.
5. Heine's poetry is noted for its simplicity. Do you think that this simplicity adds to the effectiveness of these poems? Why or why not? Point out figures of speech in the poems. Do they add or detract from the simplicity? Why?

"The Light Goes Out"

1. What, precisely, was the light referred to in the poem? Did it necessarily refer to Heine's sight which he lost almost completely near the end of his life, or could it refer to the loss of inspiration? If it was both, did the metaphors used convey both ideas effectively? Why or why not?
2. Describe the empty theater, its sights, sounds, and general atmosphere. Explain the figures of speech in stanza 2.
3. In the play *Macbeth*, the tragic hero, sensing his downfall, called life "a poor player that struts and frets his hour upon the stage and then is heard no more." Compare Heine's idea with Shakespeare's. Are these sentiments true of all earthly fame? Explain.

"The Lorelei"

1. This is, perhaps, Heine's most famous poem that has been set to music. It is based on the German legend of the enchantress who, by her singing, caused sailors to wreck their boats on her rock in the Rhine River. What do you think the Lorelei represents? Why do you think this poem has been so popular throughout the world?
2. Point out images that appeal to the senses and contribute to the ideas presented.

For Composition

1. Write a critical evaluation of Heine's poetry. Give your opinion of his subject matter, style, diction, and value for the reader. Quote lines from the poems you have read to support your ideas.
2. Heine, like Schiller, was a representative of the Romantic Movement in Germany. In several well-organized paragraphs, compare and contrast the work of these two poets. Refer specifically to poems you have read.

Victor Hugo

Jean Valjean and the Bishop's Candlesticks

Perhaps the greatest champion of the Romantic Movement opposed to the neoclassic tradition of the eighteenth century was Victor Hugo (1802–1885). One of the great creative energies in literature, Hugo dominated the literary scene in France throughout much of the nineteenth century with his poems, novels, plays, and various prose writings.

Hugo first achieved success through the publication of two volumes of romantic poems in the 1820's. In the 1830's, he wrote several plays, notably *Hernani*, which, while it is no longer considered a work of the first rank, caused a revolution at the time among French dramatists. The opening night of the play resulted in an actual riot in the theater between the partisans and opponents of this new type of drama. From then on, Hugo was seen as the undisputed leader of romanticism.

Hugo is not only one of the most prolific writers of all time, he is also one of the most original and vivid. Though his poetry is acknowledged today as his greatest achievement, two of his novels have continued to be popular with modern readers: *Notre Dame de Paris* (popularly known as *The Hunchback of Notre Dame*) and *Les Misérables*, one of the outstanding works of fiction of the nineteenth century. In the chapter from this novel which follows, you will glimpse Hugo's power to depict unforgettable characters and incidents filled with suspense, as well as his deep understanding of human beings caught in their environment.

ONE evening, after his walk in the town, the Bishop of D—— remained quite late in his room. He was busy with his great work on Duty, which unfortunately is left incomplete. He carefully dissected all that the Fathers and Doctors have said on this serious topic. He collated with much labor these injunctions into a harmonious whole, which he wished to offer to souls.

At eight o'clock he was still at work, writing with some inconvenience on little slips of paper, with a large book open on his knees, when Madame Magloire, as usual, came in to take the silver from the panel near the bed. A moment after, the bishop, knowing that the table was laid, and that his sister was perhaps waiting, closed his book and went into the dining room.

Madame Magloire had just finished placing the plates.

While she was arranging the table, she was talking with Mademoiselle Baptistine.

The lamp was on the table, which was near the fireplace, where a good fire was burning.

Mademoiselle Baptistine has so often related what occurred at the bishop's house that evening, that many persons are still living who can recall the minutest details.

Just as the bishop entered, Madame Magloire was speaking with some warmth. She was talking to *Mademoiselle* upon a familiar subject, and one to which the bishop was quite accustomed. It was a discussion on the means of fastening the front door.

It seems that while Madame Magloire was out making provision for supper, she had heard the news in sundry places. There was talk that an ill-favored runaway, a suspicious vagabond, had arrived and was lurking somewhere in the town, and that some unpleasant adventures might befall those who should come home late that night; besides, that the police was very bad, as the prefect and the mayor did not like one another, and were hoping to injure each other by untoward events; that it was the part of wise people to be their own police, and to protect their own persons; and that everyone ought to be careful to shut up, bolt, and bar his house properly, and *secure his door thoroughly*.

Madame Magloire dwelt upon these last words; but the bishop having come from a cold room, seated himself before the fire and began to warm himself, and then, he was thinking of something else. He did not hear a word of what was let fall by Madame Magloire, and she repeated it. Then Mademoiselle Baptistine, endeavoring to satisfy Madame Magloire without displeasing her brother, ventured to say timidly:

"Brother, do you hear what Madame Magloire says?"

"I heard something of it indistinctly," said the bishop. Then turning his chair half round, putting his hands on his knees, and raising towards the old servant his cordial and good-humored face, which the firelight shone upon, he said: "Well, well! what is the matter? Are we in any great danger?"

This readiness to question her encouraged Madame Magloire; it seemed to indicate that the bishop was really well-nigh alarmed. She continued triumphantly: "Yes, monseigneur; it is true. There will something happen tonight in the town: everybody says so. The police are so badly organized" (a convenient repetition). "To live in this mountainous country, and not even to have street lamps! If one goes out, it is dark as a pocket. And I say, monseigneur, and mademoiselle says also—"

"Me?" interrupted the sister; "I say nothing. Whatever my brother does is well done."

Madame Magloire went on as if she had not heard this protestation:

"We say that this house is not safe at all; and if monseigneur will permit me, I will go and tell Paulin Musebois, the locksmith, to come and put the old bolts in the door again; they are there, and it will take but a minute. I say we must have bolts, were it only for tonight; for I say that a door which opens by a latch on the outside to the first comer, nothing could be more horrible: and then monseigneur has the habit of always saying 'Come in,' even at midnight. But, my goodness! there is no need even to ask leave—"

At this moment there was a violent knock on the door.

"Come in!" said the bishop.

The door opened.

It opened quickly, quite wide, as if pushed by someone boldly and with energy.

A man entered.

He came in, took one step, and paused, leaving the door open behind him. He had his knapsack on his back, his stick in his hand, and a rough, hard, tired, and fierce look in his eyes, as seen by the firelight. He was hideous. It was an apparition of ill omen.

Madame Magloire had not even the strength to scream. She stood trembling with her mouth open.

Mademoiselle Baptistine turned, saw the man enter, and started up half alarmed; then, slowly turning back again towards the fire she looked at her brother, and her face resumed its usual calmness and serenity.

The bishop looked upon the man with a tranquil eye.

As he was opening his mouth to speak, doubtless to ask the stranger what he wanted, the man, leaning with both hands on his club, glanced from one to another in turn, and without waiting for the bishop to speak, said in a loud voice:

"See here! My name is Jean Valjean.* I am a convict; I have been nineteen years in the galleys. Four days ago I was set free, and started for Pontarlier, which is my destination; during those four days I have walked from Toulon. Today I have walked twelve leagues. When I reached this place this evening I went to an inn, and they sent me away on account of my yellow passport, which I had shown at the mayor's office, as was necessary. I went to another inn; they said: 'Get out!' It was the same with one as with another; nobody would have me. I went to the prison, and the turnkey would not let me in. I crept into a dog-kennel, the dog bit me, and drove me away as if he had been a man; you would have said that he knew who I was. I went into the fields to sleep beneath the stars: there were no stars; I thought it would rain, and there was no good God to stop the drops, so I came back to the town to get the shelter of some doorway. There in the square I lay down upon a stone; a good woman showed me your house, and said: 'Knock there!' I have knocked. What is this place? Are you an inn? I have money; my savings, one hundred and nine francs and fifteen sous which I have earned in the galleys by my work for nineteen years. I will pay. What do I care? I have money. I am very tired—twelve leagues on foot, and I am so hungry. Can I stay?"

"Madame Magloire," said the bishop, "put on another plate."

The man took three steps, and came near the lamp which stood on the table. "Stop," he exclaimed; as if he had not been understood, "not that, did you understand me? I am a galley-slave—a convict—I am just from the galleys." He drew from his pocket a large sheet of yellow paper, which he unfolded. "There is my passport, yellow as you see. That is enough to have me kicked out wherever I go. Will you read it? I know how to read, I do. I learned in the galleys. There is a school there for those who care for it. See, here is what they have put in the passport: 'Jean Valjean, a liberated convict, native of ——,' you don't care for that, 'has been nineteen years in the galleys; five years for burglary; fourteen years for having attempted four times to escape. This man is very dangerous.' There you have it! Everybody has thrust me out; will you receive me? Is this

* jhän val jhän'

an inn? Can you give me something to eat, and a place to sleep? Have you a stable?"

"Madame Magloire," said the bishop, "put some sheets on the bed in the alcove."

Madame Magloire went out to fulfil her orders.

The bishop turned to the man:

"Monsieur, sit down and warm yourself: we are going to take supper presently, and your bed will be made ready while you sup."

At last the man quite understood; his face, the expression of which till then had been gloomy and hard, now expressed stupefaction, doubt, and joy, and became absolutely wonderful. He began to stutter like a madman.

"True? What! You will keep me? you won't drive me away? a convict! You call me *Monsieur* and don't say 'Get out, dog!' as everybody else does. I thought that you would send me away, so I told first off who I am. Oh! the fine woman who sent me here! I shall have a supper! a bed like other people with mattress and sheets —a bed! It is nineteen years that I have not slept on a bed. You are really willing that I should stay? You are good people! Besides I have money: I will pay well. I beg your pardon, Monsieur Innkeeper, what is your name? I will pay all you say. You are a fine man. You are an innkeeper, an't you?"

"I am a priest who lives here," said the bishop.

"A priest," said the man. "Oh, noble priest! Then you do not ask any money? You are the curé, an't you? the curé of this big church? Yes, that's it. How stupid I am; I didn't notice your cap."

While speaking, he had deposited his knapsack and stick in the corner, replaced his passport in his pocket, and sat down. Mademoiselle Baptistine looked at him pleasantly. He continued:

"You are humane, Monsieur Curé; you don't despise me. A good priest is a good thing. Then you don't want me to pay?"

"No," said the bishop, "keep your money. How much have you? You said a hundred and nine francs, I think."

"And fifteen sous," added the man.

"One hundred and nine francs and fifteen sous. And how long did it take you to earn that?"

"Nineteen years."

"Nineteen years!"

The bishop sighed deeply.

Madame Magloire brought in a plate and set it on the table.

"Madame Magloire," said the bishop, "put this plate as near the fire as you can." Then turning towards his guest, he added: "The night wind is raw in the Alps; you must be cold, monsieur."

Every time he said this word monsieur, with his gently solemn, and heartily hospitable voice, the man's countenance lighted up. *Monsieur* to a convict is a glass of water to a man dying of thirst at sea. Ignominy thirsts for respect.

"The lamp," said the bishop, "gives a very poor light."

Madame Magloire understood him, and going to his bedchamber, took from the mantel the two silver candlesticks, lighted the candles, and placed them on the table.

"Monsieur Curé," said the man, "you are good; you don't despise me. You take me into your house; you light your candles for me, and I hav'n't hid from you where I come from, and how miserable I am."

The bishop, who was sitting near him, touched his hand gently and said: "You need not tell me who you are. This is not my house; it is the house of Christ. It does not ask any comer whether he has a name, but whether he has an affliction. You are suffering; you are hungry and thirsty; be welcome. And do not thank me; do not tell me that I take you into my house. This is the home of no man, except him who needs an asylum. I tell you, who are a traveller, that you are more at home here than I; whatever is here is yours. What need have I to know your name? Besides, before you told me, I knew it."

The man opened his eyes in astonishment:

"Really? You knew my name?"

"Yes," answered the bishop, "your name is my brother."

"Stop, stop, Monsieur Curé," exclaimed the man. "I was famished when I came in, but you are so kind that now I don't know what I am; that is all gone."

The bishop looked at him again and said:

"You have seen much suffering?"

"Oh, the red blouse, the ball and chain, the plank to sleep on, the heat, the cold, the galley's crew, the lash, the double chain for nothing, the dungeon for a word,—even when sick in bed, the chain. The dogs, the dogs are happier! nineteen years! and I am forty-six, and now a yellow passport. That is all."

"Yes," answered the bishop, "you have left a place of suffering. But listen, there will be more joy in heaven over the tears of a repentant sinner than over the white robes of a hundred good men. If you are leaving that sorrowful place with hate and anger against men, you are worthy of compassion; if you leave it with goodwill, gentleness, and peace, you are better than any of us."

Meantime Madame Magloire had served up supper; it consisted of soup made of water, oil, bread, and salt, a little pork, a scrap of mutton, a few figs, a green cheese, and a large loaf of rye bread. She had, without asking, added to the usual dinner of the bishop a bottle of fine old Mauves wine.

The bishop's countenance was lighted up with this expression of pleasure, peculiar to hospitable natures. "To supper!" he said briskly, as was his habit when he had a guest. He seated the man at his right. Mademoiselle Baptistine, perfectly quiet and natural, took her place at his left.

The bishop said the blessing, and then served the soup himself, according to his usual custom. The man fell to, eating greedily.

After having said good night to his sister, Monseigneur Bienvenu took one of the silver candlesticks from the table, handed the other to his guest, and said to him:

"Monsieur, I will show you to your room."

The man followed him.

The house was so arranged that one could reach the alcove in the oratory only by passing through the bishop's sleeping chamber. Just as they were passing through this room Madame Magloire was putting up the silver in the cupboard at the head of the bed. It was the last thing she did every night before going to bed.

The bishop left his guest in the alcove, before a clean white bed. The man set down the candlestick upon a small table.

"Come," said the bishop, "a good night's rest to you: tomorrow morning, before you go, you shall have a cup of warm milk from our cows."

"Thank you, Monsieur l'Abbé," said the man.

Scarcely had he pronounced these words of peace, when suddenly he made a singular motion which would have chilled the two good women of the house with horror, had they witnessed it. Even now it is hard for us to understand what impulse he obeyed at that moment. Did he intend to give a warning or to throw out a menace? Or was he simply obeying a sort of instinctive impulse, obscure even to himself? He turned abruptly towards the old man, crossed his arms, and casting a wild look upon his host, exclaimed in a harsh voice:

"Ah, now, indeed! You lodge me in your house, as near you as that!"

He checked himself, and added, with a laugh, in which there was something horrible:

"Have you reflected upon it? Who tells you that I am not a murderer?"

The bishop responded:

"God will take care of that."

Then with gravity, moving his lips like one praying or talking to himself, he raised two fingers of his right hand and blessed the man, who, however, did not bow; and without turning his head or looking behind him, went into his chamber.

When the alcove was occupied, a heavy serge curtain was drawn in the oratory, concealing the altar. Before this curtain the bishop knelt as he passed out, and offered a short prayer.

As to the man, he was so completely exhausted that he did not even avail himself of the clean white sheets; he blew out the candle with his nostril, after the manner of convicts, and fell on the bed, dressed as he was, into a sound sleep.

Midnight struck as the bishop came back to his chamber.

A few moments afterwards all in the little house slept.

As the cathedral clock struck two, Jean Valjean awoke.

What awakened him was too good a bed. For nearly twenty years he had not slept in a bed, and, although he had not undressed, the sensation was too novel not to disturb his sleep.

Many thoughts came to him, but there was one which continually presented itself, and which drove away all others. What that thought was, we shall tell directly. He had noticed the six silver plates and the large ladle that Madame Magloire had put on the table.

His mind wavered a whole hour, and a long one, in fluctuation and in struggle. The clock struck three. He opened his eyes, rose up hastily in bed, reached out his arm and felt his haversack, which he had put into the corner of the alcove, then he thrust out his legs and placed his feet on the ground, and found himself, he knew not how, seated on his bed.

He continued in this situation, and would perhaps have remained there until daybreak, if the clock had not struck the quarter or the half-hour. The clock seemed to say to him: "Come along!"

He rose to his feet, hesitated for a moment longer, and listened; all was still in the house: he walked straight and cautiously towards the window, which he could discern. The night was not very dark; there was a full moon, across which large clouds were driving before the wind. This produced alternations of light and shade, out-of-doors eclipses and illuminations, and indoors a kind of glimmer. This glimmer, enough to enable him to find his way, changing with the passing clouds, resembled that sort of livid light, which falls through the window of a dungeon before which men are passing and repassing. On reaching the window, Jean Valjean examined it. It had no bars, opened into the garden, and was fastened, according to the fashion of the country, with a little wedge only. He opened it; but as the cold, keen air rushed into the room, he closed it again immediately. He looked into the garden with that absorbed look which studies rather than sees. The garden was enclosed with a white wall, quite low, and readily scaled. Beyond, against the sky, he distinguished the tops of trees at equal distances apart, which showed that this wall separated the garden from an avenue or a lane planted with trees.

When he had taken this observation, he turned like a man whose mind is made up, went to his alcove, took his haversack, opened it, fumbled in it, took out something which he laid upon the bed, put his shoes into one of his pockets, tied up his bundle, swung it upon his shoulders, put on his cap, and pulled the visor down over his eyes, felt for his stick, and went and put it in the corner of the window, then returned to the bed, and resolutely took up the object which he had laid on it. It looked like a short iron bar, pointed at one end like a spear.

It would have been hard to distinguish in the darkness for what use this piece of iron had been made. Could it be a lever? Could it be a club?

In the daytime, it would have been seen to be nothing but a miner's drill. At that time, the convicts were sometimes employed in quarrying stone on the high hills that surround Toulon, and they often had miners' tools in their possession. Miners' drills are of solid iron, terminating at the lower end in a point, by means of which they are sunk into the rock.

He took the drill in his right hand and, holding his breath, with stealthy steps, he moved towards the door of the next room, which was the bishop's, as we know. On reaching the door, he found it unlatched. The bishop had not closed it.

Jean Valjean listened. Not a sound. He pushed the door.

He pushed it lightly with the end of his finger, with the stealthy and timorous carefulness of a cat. The door yielded to the pressure with a silent, imperceptible movement, which made the opening a little wider.

He waited a moment, and then pushed the door again more boldly.

It yielded gradually and silently. The opening was now wide enough for him to pass through; but there was a small table near the door which with it formed a troublesome angle, and which barred the entrance.

Jean Valjean saw the obstacle. At all hazards the opening must be made still wider.

He so determined, and pushed the door a third time, harder than before. This time a rusty hinge suddenly sent out into the darkness a harsh and prolonged creak.

Jean Valjean shivered. The noise of this hinge sounded in his ears as clear and terrible as the trumpet of the Judgment Day.

He stood still, petrified like the pillar of salt, not daring to stir. Some minutes passed. The door was wide open; he ventured a look into the room. Nothing had moved. He listened. Nothing was stirring in the house. The noise of the rusty hinge had wakened nobody.

Suddenly he stopped: he was near the bed, he had reached it sooner than he thought.

Nature sometimes joins her effects and her appearances to our acts with a sort of serious and intelligent appropriateness, as if she would compel us to reflect. For nearly a half hour a great cloud had darkened the sky. At the moment when Jean Valjean paused before the bed the cloud broke as if purposely, and a ray of moonlight crossing the high window, suddenly lighted up the bishop's pale face. He slept tranquilly. He was almost entirely dressed, though in bed, on account of the cold nights of the lower Alps, with a dark woolen garment which covered his arms to the wrists. His head had fallen on the pillow in the unstudied attitude of slumber; over the side of the bed hung his hand, ornamented with the pastoral ring, and which had done so many good deeds, so many pious acts. His entire countenance was lit up with a vague expression of content, hope, and happiness. It was more than a smile and almost a radiance.

Jean Valjean was in the shadow with the iron drill in his hand, erect, motionless, terrified, at this radiant figure. He had never seen anything comparable to it. This confidence filled him with fear. The moral world has no greater spectacle than this; a troubled and restless conscience on the verge of committing an evil deed, contemplating the sleep of a good man.

He did not remove his eyes from the old man. The only thing which was plain from his attitude and his countenance was a strange indecision. You would have said he was hesitating between two realms, that of the doomed and that of the saved. He appeared ready either to cleave this skull, or kiss this hand.

In a few moments he raised his left hand slowly to his forehead and took off his hat: then, letting his hand fall with the same slowness, Jean Valjean resumed his contemplations, his cap in his left hand, his club in his right, and his hair bristling on his fierce-looking head.

Under this frightful gaze the bishop still slept in profoundest peace.

The crucifix above the mantelpiece was dimly visible in the moonlight, apparently extending its arms towards both, with a benediction for one and a pardon for the other.

Suddenly Jean Valjean put on his cap, then passed quickly, without looking at the bishop, along the bed, straight to the cupboard which he perceived near its head; he raised the drill to force the lock; the key was in it; he opened it; the first thing he saw was the basket of silver, he took it, crossed the room with hasty stride, careless of noise, reached the door, entered the oratory, took his stick, stepped out, put the silver in his knapsack, threw away the basket, ran across the garden, leaped over the wall like a tiger, and fled.

The next day at sunrise, Monseigneur Bienvenu was walking in the garden. Madame Magloire ran towards him quite beside herself.

"Monseigneur, monseigneur," cried she, "does your greatness know where the silver basket is?"

"Yes," said the bishop.

"God be praised" said she, "I did not know what had become of it."

The bishop had just found the basket on a flowerbed. He gave it to Madame Magloire and said: "There it is."

"Yes," said she, "but there is nothing in it. The silver?"

"Ah!" said the bishop, "it is the silver then that troubles you. I do not know where that is."

"Good heavens! it is stolen. That man who came last night stole it."

And in the twinkling of an eye, with all the agility of which her age was capable, Madame Magloire ran to the oratory, went into the alcove, and came back to the bishop. The bishop was bending with some sadness over a cochlearia des Guillons, which the basket had broken in falling. He looked up at Madame Magloire's cry:

"Monseigneur, the man has gone! the silver is stolen!"

While she was uttering this exclamation her eyes fell on an angle of the garden where she saw traces of an escalade.[1] A capstone of the wall had been thrown down.

"See, there is where he got out; he jumped into Cochefilet lane. The abominable fellow! he has stolen our silver!"

The bishop was silent for a moment, then raising his serious eyes, he said mildly to Madame Magloire:

"Now first, did this silver belong to us?"

Madame Magloire did not answer; after a moment the bishop continued:

"Madame Magloire, I have for a long time wrongfully withheld this silver; it belonged to the poor. Who was this man? A poor man evidently."

In a few minutes he was breakfasting at the same table at which Jean Valjean sat the night before. While breakfasting, Monseigneur Bienvenu pleasantly remarked to his sister who said nothing, and Madame Magloire who was grumbling to herself, that there was really no need even of a wooden spoon or fork to dip a piece of bread into a cup of milk.

---

[1] **escalade:** the act of scaling a high wall by means of a ladder

Just as the brother and sister were rising from the table, there was a knock at the door.

"Come in," said the bishop.

The door opened. A strange, fierce group appeared on the threshold. Three men were holding a fourth by the collar. The three men were gendarmes; the fourth Jean Valjean.

A brigadier of gendarmes, who appeared to head the group, was near the door. He advanced towards the bishop, giving a military salute.

"Monseigneur," said he—

At this word Jean Valjean, who was sullen and seemed entirely cast down, raised his head with a stupefied air—

"Monseigneur!" he murmured, "then it is not the curé!"

"Silence!" said a gendarme, "it is monseigneur, the bishop."

In the meantime Monseigneur Bienvenu had approached as quickly as his great age permitted:

"Ah, there you are!" said he, looking towards Jean Valjean, "I am glad to see you. But! I gave you the candlesticks also, which are silver like the rest, and would bring two hundred francs. Why did you not take them along with your plates?"

Jean Valjean opened his eyes and looked at the bishop with an expression which no human tongue could describe.

"Monseigneur," said the brigadier, "then what this man said was true? We met him. He was going like a man who was running away, and we arrested him in order to see. He had this silver."

"And he told you," interrupted the bishop, with a smile, "that it had been given him by a good old priest with whom he had passed the night. I see it all. And you brought him back here? It is all a mistake."

"If that is so," said the brigadier, "we can let him go."

"Certainly," replied the bishop.

The gendarmes released Jean Valjean, who shrank back—

"Is it true that they let me go?" he said in a voice almost inarticulate, as if he were speaking in his sleep.

"Yes! you can go. Do you not understand?" said a gendarme.

"My friend," said the bishop, "before you go away, here are your candlesticks; take them."

He went to the mantelpiece, took the two candlesticks, and brought them to Jean Valjean. The two women beheld the action without a word, or gesture, or look, that might disturb the bishop.

Jean Valjean was trembling in every limb. He took the two candlesticks mechanically, and with a wild appearance.

"Now," said the bishop, "go in peace. By the way, my friend, when you come again, you need not come through the garden. You can always come in and go out by the front door. It is closed only with a latch, day or night."

Then turning to the gendarmes, he said:

"Messieurs, you can retire." The gendarmes withdrew.

Jean Valjean felt like a man who is just about to faint.

The bishop approached him, and said, in a low voice:

"Forget not, never forget that you have promised me to use this silver to become an honest man."

Jean Valjean, who had no recollection of this promise, stood confounded. The bishop had laid much stress upon these words as he uttered them. He continued, solemnly:

"Jean Valjean, my brother: you belong no longer to evil, but to good. It is your soul that I am buying for you. I withdraw it from dark thoughts and from the spirit of perdition, and I give it to God!"

For Discussion

1. What was your emotional reaction at the end of this chapter, both toward the bishop and the thief? In your opinion, did the bishop's compassion and love equal or outweigh Jean's ingratitude? Explain. How did the author prepare you for this ending? Point out passages to support your answer.
2. What did you learn about the character of the bishop before Jean Valjean's entry? Which incidents later proved the bishop to be a sincerely holy person?
3. After the bishop's great kindness to him, did Jean's theft of the silver seem unbelievable to you? Why or why not? In your discussion, remember what he had confessed about himself earlier, and what he revealed about his attitude toward society. Was his evil deed performed without a struggle? Point out details which prove your answer.
4. Hugo reveals a characteristic of the nineteenth-century novelist to describe settings which are strongly in keeping with the hero's actions and moods. Point out instances where the elements in nature add to the tone and mood of this selection. How do they contribute, also, to the element of suspense?

5. What do you consider the theme of the story? Show how this theme is the direct antithesis of everything Jean believed after his long term in prison. Point out passages which reveal the author's attitude toward the society of his day. In particular, prove that Hugo is showing that Jean Valjean is the product of a society whose values no longer harmonize with truth.

6. Both the bishop and Jean were confronted with choices that involved a risk which could result in tragedy. In the bishop's case, a soul weighed in the balance. How strongly did the bishop sense this? To what extremes did he go to prove it? What promise did he finally extract from Jean, although Jean never expressed it in words?

7. At which point in the chapter did Jean make his greatest choice? How do you know this? Prove that his choices could also result in tragedy.

8. The author's artistry is shown at the end of the chapter by leaving both Jean and the reader astonished. How does the ability to leave the obvious unsaid add to the chapter's interest? Did it also make you enter more fully into the experience of the character? Explain.

The Poor Children

Take heed of this small child of earth;
   He is great; he hath in him God most high.
Children before their fleshly birth
   Are lights alive in the blue sky.

In our light bitter world of wrong   5
   They come; God gives us them awhile.
His speech is in their stammering tongue,
   And his forgiveness in their smile.

Their sweet light rests upon our eyes.
   Alas! their right to joy is plain.   10
If they are hungry Paradise
   Weeps, and, if cold, Heaven thrills with pain.

The want that saps their sinless flower
   Speaks judgment on sin's ministers.
Man holds an angel in his power.   15
   Ah! deep in Heaven what thunder stirs,

When God seeks out these tender things
   Whom in the shadow where we sleep
He sends us clothed about with wings,
   And finds them ragged babes that weep!   20

                (*tr. Algernon Charles Swinburne*)

The Grave and the Rose

The Grave said to the Rose,
   "What of the dews of dawn,
Love's flower, what end is theirs?"
   "And what of spirits flown,
The souls whereon doth close   5
   The tomb's mouth unawares?"
The Rose said to the Grave.

The Rose said, "In the shade
   From the dawn's tears is made
A perfume faint and strange,   10
   Amber and honey sweet."
   "And all the spirits fleet
Do suffer a sky-change,
   More strangely than the dew,
   To God's own angels new,"   15
The Grave said to the Rose.

          (*tr. Andrew Lang*)

More Strong Than Time

Since I have set my lips to your full cup, my sweet,
Since I my pallid face between your hands have laid,
Since I have known your soul, and all the bloom of it,
And all the perfume rare, now buried in the shade;
Since it was given to me to hear one happy while,   5
The words wherein your heart spoke all its mysteries,
Since I have seen you weep, and since I have seen you smile,
Your lips upon my lips, and your eyes upon my eyes;

Since I have known above my forehead glance and gleam,
A ray, a single ray, of your star, veiled always,   10
Since I have felt the fall, upon my lifetime's stream,
Of one rose petal plucked from the roses of your days;

I now am bold to say to the swift changing hours,
Pass, pass upon your way, for I grow never old,
Fleet to the dark abysm with all your fading flowers,   15
One rose that none may pluck, within my heart I hold.

Your flying wings may smite, but they can never spill
The cup fulfilled of love, from which my lips are wet;
My heart has far more fire than you can frost to chill,
My soul more love than you can make my soul forget.   20

          (*tr. Andrew Lang*)

The Genesis of Butterflies

The dawn is smiling on the dew that covers
The tearful roses; lo, the little lovers
That kiss the buds, and all the flutterings
In jasmine bloom, and privet, of white wings,
That go and come, and fly, and peep and hide,   5
With muffled music, murmured far and wide.
Ah, the Springtime, when we think of all the lays
That dreamy lovers send to dreamy Mays,
Of the fond hearts within a billet bound,
Of all the soft silk paper that pens wound,   10
The messages of love that mortals write
Filled with intoxication of delight,
Written in April and before the Maytime
Shredded and flown, playthings for the wind's playtime,
We dream that all white butterflies above,   15
Who seek through clouds or waters souls to love,
And leave their lady mistress in despair,
To flit to flowers, as kinder and more fair,
Are but torn love-letters, that through the skies
Flutter, and float, and change to butterflies.   20

(tr. Andrew Lang)

A Sunset

I love the evenings, passionless and fair, I love the evens,
Whether old manor-fronts their ray with golden fulgence leavens,
   In numerous leafage bosomed close;
Whether the mist in reefs of fire extend its reaches sheer,
Or a hundred sunbeams splinter in an azure atmosphere   5
   On cloudy archipelagos.

Oh, gaze ye on the firmament! a hundred clouds in motion,
Up-piled in the immense sublime beneath the winds' commotion,
   Their unimagined shapes accord:
Under their waves at intervals flame a pale levin [1] through,   10
[1] **levin:** lightning

As if some giant of the air amid the vapors drew
  A sudden elemental sword.

The sun at bay with splendid thrusts still keeps the sullen fold;
And momently at distance sets, as a cupola of gold,
  The thatched roof of a cot a-glance;   15
Or on the blurred horizon joins his battle with the haze;
Or pools the glooming fields about with inter-isolate blaze,
  Great moveless meres of radiance.

Then mark you how there hangs athwart the firmament's
    swept track,
Yonder, a mighty crocodile with vast irradiant back,   20
  A triple row of pointed teeth?
Under its burnished belly slips a ray of eventide,
The flickerings of a hundred glowing clouds its tenebrous side
  With scales of golden mail ensheathe.

Then mounts a palace, then the air vibrates—the vision flees.   25
Confounded to its base, the fearful cloudy edifice
  Ruins immense in mounded wrack;
Afar the fragments strew the sky, and each envermeiled [2] cone
Hangeth, peak downward, overhead, like mountains overthrown
  When the earthquake heaves its hugy back.   30

These vapors, with their leaden, golden, iron, bronzèd glows,
Where the hurricane, the waterspout, thunder, and hell repose,
  Muttering hoarse dreams of destined harms,—
'Tis God who hangs their multitude amid the skiey deep,
As a warrior that suspendeth from the roof-tree of his keep   35
  His dreadful and resounding arms!

All vanishes! The Sun, from topmost heaven precipitated,
Like a globe of iron which is tossed back fiery red
  Into the furnace stirred to fume,
Shocking the cloudy surges, plashed from its impetuous ire,   40
Even to the zenith spattereth in a flecking scud of fire
  The vaporous and inflamèd spaume.[3]

[2] **envermeiled**: colored as if with vermilion
[3] **spaume**: archaic form of *spume*; froth, foam

O contemplate the heavens! Whenas the vein-drawn day dies pale,
In every season, every place, gaze through their every veil,
   With love that has not speech for need!   45
Beneath their solemn beauty is a mystery infinite:
If winter hue them like a pall, or if the summer night
   Fantasy them starry brede.⁴

(tr. Francis Thompson)

For Discussion

"The Poor Children"

1. What was the poet lamenting in this poem? In your opinion, did Hugo's "message" interfere with, or add to, the emotional impact of the poem? Explain.
2. Point out lines which reveal the great dignity which Hugo saw in children. Do you find the poet's picture of children too sentimental? Why or why not?
3. How does the *abba* rhyme scheme of each stanza affect the "message" of the poem? In other words, do you think that the form fits the thought? Explain.

"The Grave and the Rose"

1. This poem is an excellent example of poetic economy. It deals with two popular themes: the transitoriness of the beauty in things of nature and the real beauty—new even to God's angels—of the soul, when, transformed at death, it enters eternity. The theme is brought out entirely through direct questions and replies. What question did the Grave ask the Rose? What did the Rose, in turn, ask the Grave?
2. Point out the irony in both questions.
3. Explain in your own words the reply of the Grave and the Rose.
4. Note that the conversation is between two objects which symbolize two opposite notions. Explain each. What paradox do you see here?

"More Strong Than Time"

1. To what did Hugo compare love? Do you think this metaphor was justified? Why or why not?
2. What was the rose within the poet's heart "that none may pluck"? Point out other images that conveyed Hugo's emotion.
3. What is the theme of the poem? Compare and contrast it with Shakespeare's sonnet 116.

⁴ **brede:** embroidery

"The Genesis of Butterflies"

1. According to Hugo, what was the genesis of butterflies? What did he believe happened to most love-letters written in springtime? Do you think that his ideas are effective? Why or why not?
2. Is the mood of this poem serious and cynical, or is it merely humorous and light? Explain.
3. How did the imagery contribute to the mood of the poem? Point out lines to support your answer.

"A Sunset"

1. In this poem, the poet saw several different images created by the setting sun. In stanza 2, for instance, he imagined the sun lancing the piled-up clouds "As if some giant . . . drew/ A sudden elemental sword." How is this image borne out in the third stanza?
2. In the fourth stanza, the poet pictured a mighty crocodile. Describe it in prose as the author saw it. How does it resemble or contrast with any images you have seen in looking at the clouds in the setting sun? Discuss.
3. In the final stanza, what did the poet imply about the mystery of the "heavens" at any season? How did his convictions about the beauties of nature contrast with the beliefs of the English romantic poets, such as Shelley, Wordsworth, and Byron? In your opinion, who had the truer concept, Hugo or the English poets? Explain.
4. Hugo's poetry frequently reveals how the sounds of words support both the meaning and mood of a poem; for example, *archipelago* in line 6, means "a large body of water with many scattered islands, such as the Aegean Sea." How does the sound of *archipelago* support the meaning of the word? Select other words, including some of the archaic or obsolete words in the poem, and explain how they illustrate this point.
5. What is the dominant mood of the poem? How might it differ from the mood of a modern poem written on the same subject?

For Composition

In fiction, it is usually more difficult to present a "good" character convincingly than it is to present a "bad" character. The bishop in *Les Misérables* is a good character. Write a short composition in which you give your reasons for thinking he is, or is not, as convincing a character as Jean Valjean. Refer to passages from the selection to support your opinion.

Giacomo Leopardi

The Italian poet Giacomo Leopardi (1798–1837), like his German contemporary, Arthur Schopenhauer,[1] was a profound pessimist who believed that evil predominated over good and that misery was man's common lot. During most of his short lifetime, Leopardi was afflicted with ill health and with periods of partial blindness, which contributed to his gloomy outlook on life. Nevertheless, he ranks among the masters of Italian lyric poetry. His verse, marked by great beauty of imagery, clearly reflects the romantic tendencies of the period—a mood of melancholy, a strong distaste for the world of men and a desire for solitude, an intense patriotism for his country, and a deep feeling for nature. Like Wordsworth, he saw nature as a means of lightening man's burden and bringing him serenity. For Leopardi, however, this serenity was only temporary. Both the lyrical beauty of his verse and his deep pessimism can be seen in the poems that follow.

To Himself

Now shalt thou rest for aye,
My weary heart. The final error dies
Wherewith I nourished my divinest dreams.
'Tis gone. I feel in me for sweet delusions
Not merely hope, but even desire, is dead.   5
Rest for all time. Enough
Hath been thine agitation. There is nought
So precious, thou shouldst seek it; and the earth
Deserveth not a sigh. But weary bitterness
Is life, nought else, and ashes is the world.   10
Be now at peace. Despair
For the last time. Unto our race did Fate
Give nought, save death. Now hold in scorn and hate
Thyself and Nature and the Power Unknown,
That reigns supreme unto the grief of all,   15
And the vast vanity of this terrestrial ball.

(*tr. Francis H. Cliffe*)

[1] **Arthur Schopenhauer** (1788-1860): German philosopher who saw the world as made up of unsatisfied wants and pain

The Lonely Bird

Upon the summit of the ancient tower
Unto the land around, thou, lonely bird,
Carollest sweetly till the evening hour,
And through the vale thy melody is heard.
Spring makes the gentle air   5
Fragrant and bright, and animates the fields,
Bidding the gazer in his heart rejoice.
Hark to the lowing herds, the flocks that bleat,
The other birds that full of joyaunce sing
And in the air in happy circles meet,   10
As though they homage to their fair time bring.
Thou, full of thought, beholdest all aside,
Nor carest to take wing
With thy companions, scorning their delight.
Thou singest, and the flower   15
Of spring thus fadeth with thy life's sweet hour.
    Ah me! how like to thine
My habit doth appear! Pleasure and mirth,
The happy offspring of our earlier age,
And thou, Youth's brother, Love,   20
Thou bitter sigh of our advancing years,
I heed not; why, I cannot tell; but far
From them I take my way;
And like a hermit lone,
Nor to my birthplace known,   25
I see the spring of my existence die.
This day that now is yielding to the night,
Was in our hamlet ever festive held.
Upon the air serene the bells resound
And frequent firing of the distant guns,   30
Arousing the deep echoes far and wide.
In festival attire
The youths and maidens go,
Leaving their homes, upon the country paths,
Rejoicing to be seen and to admire.   35
I to this tower, remote
From sight of men, repairing all alone,

All joy and mirth postpone
For other times; and as I gaze on high,
The sun doth strike mine eye;   40
Beyond the summit of yon mountain far,
After the day serene,
He sinketh to his rest, and seems to say
That happy youth is leaving me for aye.

    Thou, lonely warbler, coming to the close   45
Of what the stars have granted thee to live,
In truth of these thy ways
Shalt not complain, for Nature on thee lays
Thy fondness of repose.
To me, if of old age   50
The dreaded terrors stern
I cannot from me turn,
When to no heart this soul of mine can yearn,
When void the earth will be, the future day
More than the present, wearisome and gray: 55
How will this lone mood seem?
What shall I of myself in past years deem?
Ah me! repent too late,
And often gaze behind disconsolate.

                          (*tr. Francis H. Cliffe*)

For Discussion

"To Himself"

1. This poem has been called the "very triumph of negation." Which lines particularly conveyed the feeling of despair? Would you say that the actual act of writing this poem, which gave form to the author's feelings, supported or opposed the despair? Explain.
2. Point out the use of metaphors in this poem. Do you think they intensified the mood of the poem or weakened it? Explain. What is the "final error" in line 2?
3. Contrast Leopardi's attitude to life with the true Christian concept of life. Why is despair out of place in a redeemed world? What causes for rejoicing had the poet lost sight of?

"The Lonely Bird"

1. In what ways did the poet compare himself to the bird? Point out lines to support your answer. What mood was created through this comparison?
2. What things natural to man gave Leopardi no pleasure? What was his reaction to the youths and maidens on this annual festive day? Why might he have reacted as he did?
3. What symbolic meaning did the poet find in the setting sun and the close of day?
4. Point out the use of personification in this poem. Indicate other figures of speech used by the poet. In your opinion, did they add to the effectiveness of this poem? Why or why not?

For Composition

1. Write an essay in which you present evidence of Leopardi's strong romantic tendencies. Quote lines from the poems you have read.
2. Leopardi's poetry reflects a deep pessimism. Heine's poetry often reflects a quiet sadness. Write a short paper in which you point out this difference between the two poets, as revealed in their work.

Alexander Pushkin

Alexander Pushkin (1799–1837), the most brilliant poet of the romantic period in Russia, excelled not only in the field of lyric and narrative poetry, but also in the fields of the novel, the drama, and the short story. His play *Boris Godunov*, his verse-novel *Eugene Onegin*, and his tale *The Queen of Spades* have all been made into operas by outstanding Russian composers, such as Moussorgsky and Tschaikovsky. Other works by Pushkin have been the basis for musical compositions by Glinka and Rimsky-Korsakov. Pushkin's first poems were published in 1814, and he began to participate in the literary life of St. Petersburg.

An individualist and a revolutionary, Pushkin worked at an early age in civil service which he heartily disliked, but where he saw political injustice at close range. His siding with political rebels twice brought about unofficial exile for him, during which times he produced some of his best writings. His personal life, much like Byron's, was hectic and undisciplined, and he was finally killed in a duel at the age of thirty-eight.

Pushkin's influence on Russian literature has been great and his lyrics are among the finest in the language. His versatility in mood and subject matter is reflected in the poems that follow. His romanticism is apparent in his care for nature, his energetic love of life and freedom, and his feeling that the role of the poet was a holy calling.

Grapes

I shall not miss the roses, fading
When springtime's hurrying days are done;
I love the grapes whose clusters ripen
Upon the hillsides in the sun—
The glory of my fertile valley,   5
They hang, each lustrous as a pearl,
Gold autumn's joy, oblong, transparent,
Like the slim fingers of a girl.

(*tr. Babette Deutsch*)

To Chaadayev[1]

Not long we basked in the illusions
Of love, of hope, of tranquil fame;
Like morning mist, like dreams' delusions,
Youth's pastimes vanished as they came.
But still, with strong desires burning,   5
Beneath oppression's fearful hand,
The bidding of the fatherland
We are impatiently discerning;
In hope, in torment, we are turning
Toward freedom, wishing she were near,   10
As a young lover waits his dear
And looks and longs, consumed with yearning.
While freedom fires the blood, and now
While honor summons us—O hear it!
Friend, to our country let us vow   15
The noble strivings of the spirit.
Comrade, believe: joy's star will leap
Upon our sight, a radiant token;
Russia will rouse from her long sleep;
And where autocracy lies, broken,   20
Our names shall yet be graven deep.

                              (*tr. Babette Deutsch*)

Message to Siberia

Deep in the Siberian mine,
Keep your patience proud;
The bitter toil shall not be lost,
The rebel thought unbowed.

The sister of misfortune, Hope,   5
In the under-darkness dumb
Speaks joyful courage to your heart:
The day desired will come.

[1] Pyotr Chaadayev was a friend of Pushkin whom he met at school. He was an elegant officer of the Hussars and at one time a liberal.

And love and friendship pour to you
Across the darkened doors, 10
Even as round your galley-beds
My free music pours.

The heavy-hanging chains will fall,
The walls will crumble at a word;
And Freedom greet you in the light, 15
And brothers give you back the sword.

(tr. Max Eastman)

The Prophet

Athirst in spirit, through the gloom
Of an unpeopled waste I blundered,
And saw a six-winged Seraph loom
Where the two pathways met and sundered.
He laid his fingers on my eyes: 5
His touch lay soft as slumber lies,—
And like an eagle's, scared and shaken,
Did my prophetic eyes awaken.
He touched my ears, and lo! they rang
With a reverberating clang: 10
I heard the spheres revolving, chiming,
The angels in their soaring sweep,
The monsters moving in the deep,
The green vine in the valley climbing.
And from my mouth the Seraph wrung 15
Forth by its roots my sinful tongue;
The idle tongue that slyly babbled,
The vain, malicious, the unchaste,
And the wise serpent's tongue he placed
In my numb mouth with hand blood-dabbled; 20
And with a sword he clove my breast,
Drew forth the heart that shook with dread
And in my gaping bosom pressed
A glowing coal of fire instead.

Upon the wastes, a lifeless clod,   25
I lay, and heard the voice of God:
"Arise, oh, prophet, look and ponder:
Arise, charged with my will and spurred,
The roadways and the seaways wander,
Kindling men's hearts with this, my Word."   30

(*tr. Babette Deutsch*)

Autumn (a fragment)

"What does not then pass through my drowsy mind?"—DERZHAVIN

1

October has arrived. The grove is shaking
The last reluctant leaves from naked boughs.
A breath of autumn cold—the road is freezing;
The millpond, glazed with ice, is in a drowse,
Though the brook babbles; with his pack my neighbor   5
Makes for the distant field—his hounds will rouse
The woods with barking, and his horse's feet
Will trample cruelly the winter wheat.

2

This is my time! What is the spring to me?
Thaw is a bore: mud running thick and stinking;   10
Spring makes me ill: my mind is never free
From dizzy dreams, my blood's in constant ferment.
Give me instead winter's austerity,
The snows under the moon—and what is gayer
Than to glide lightly in a sleigh with her   15
Whose fingers are like fire beneath the fur?

3

And oh, how jolly, on the placid river
To glide steel-shod, swiftly, with easy grace!

The shining stir of festivals in winter!
But there's a limit—nobody could face   20
Six months of snow—even that cave dweller,
The bear, would growl "enough" in such a case.
Sleigh rides with young Armidas pall, by Jove,
And you turn sour with loafing by the stove.

4

Oh, darling summer, I could cherish you,   25
If heat and dust and gnats and flies were banished.
You dull the mind, the heart grows weary, too.
We, like the meadows, suffer drought and wither.
Drink is our only thought, and how we rue
Old woman Winter, at whose funeral banquet   30
Pancakes and wine were served, but now we hold
Memorial feasts of ices, sweet and cold.

5

They say ill things of the last days of autumn:
But I, friend reader, not a one will hear;
Her quiet beauty touches me as surely   35
As does a wistful child, to no one dear.
She can rejoice me more, I tell you frankly,
Than all the other seasons of the year.
I am a humble lover, so I should
Find singularly much in her that's good.   40

6

How shall I make it clear? I find her pleasing
As you, perhaps, may like a sickly girl,
Condemned to die, poor creature, who is drooping
And without one word of reproach to hurl
At life, forsaking her. Upon her pallid   45
Young lips a little smile is seen to curl.
She does not hear the grave's abysmal yawn.
Today she lives—tomorrow she is gone.

7

Oh, mournful season that delights the eyes,
Your farewell beauty captivates my spirit. 50
I love the pomp of Nature's fading dyes,
The forests, garmented in gold and purple,
The rush of noisy wind, and the pale skies
Half-hidden by the clouds in darkling billows,
The early frost, the sun's infrequent ray, 55
And threats of grizzled Winter far away.

8

Each time that autumn comes I bloom afresh;
For me, I find, the Russian cold is good;
Again I go through life's routine with relish;
Sleep comes in season, and the need for food; 60
Desire seethes—and I am young and merry,
My heart beats fast with lightly leaping blood.
I'm full of life—such is my organism
(If you will please excuse the prosaism).

9

My horse is brought; far out onto the plain 65
He carries me; the frozen valley echoes
To his bright hooves with resonant refrain;
The ice creaks under him and as he gallops
In the keen wind he waves his streaming mane.
But day soon flickers out. At the forgotten 70
Hearth, where the fire purrs low or leaps like wind,
I read, or nourish long thoughts in my mind.

10

And I forget the world in the sweet silence,
Imagination lulls me, and once more
The soul oppressed by the old lyric fever 75
Trembles, reverberates, and seeks to pour

Its burden freely forth, and as though dreaming
I watch the children that my fancy bore,
And I am host to the invisible throngs
Who fill my reveries and build my songs.   80

11

And thoughts stir bravely in my head, and rhymes
Run forth to meet them on light feet, and fingers
Reach for the pen, and the good quill betimes
Asks for the foolscap. Wait: the verses follow.
Thus a still ship sleeps on still seas. Hark: Chimes!   85
And swiftly all hands leap to man the rigging,
The sails are filled, they belly in the wind—
The monster moves—a foaming track behind.

12

It sails. But whither shall we sail? . . .

(*tr. Babette Deutsch*)

For Discussion

"Grapes"

1. Simplicity is the keynote in these eight lines, yet the poem is rich in imagery and sound. Show specifically how Pushkin achieved this richness within simplicity.
2. Point out the two similes in the poem. Do you think they are accurate and effective? Why or why not?
3. What mood has the poet created in this brief poem? Do you think he has revealed the wonder to be found in an ordinary object? Explain. Do you think the wonder was implicit in the object or was it imposed by the poet? Discuss.

"To Chaadayev"

1. What is the theme of this poem? In what way is it typically romantic?
2. Do you agree with the idea expressed in the first four lines? Why or why not?
3. This poem communicates a sense of energy and unrest. Point out words which convey this feeling.

4. Despite the restlessness in the poem, there is also a feeling of order and composure. How do the meter and rhymes contribute to this?

"Message to Siberia"

1. How does this poem reveal Pushkin's political sentiments?
2. Describe the conditions of the people to whom this poem was addressed. In what sense is the poet's message a universal one?
3. Do you think that the rhythm of this poem is appropriate to the thought? Why or why not?

"The Prophet"

1. Like the Old Testament account of Isaiah's preparation for his important mission as God's prophet, this poem describes the poet's rigorous preparation for his "holy calling." What line in the poem describes his purpose as a "prophet"? Explain the line.
2. In your own words, describe the poet's experience in meeting the Seraph. Why were the Seraph's acts so violent? How are these acts related to the statement that "the Spirit can fulfill itself only in body"?
3. What was remarkable about the things the poet heard? If he had described the things he *saw*, what things might he have listed?
4. Lines 15-24 portray the agony experienced by the poet, the *afflatus* spoken of by Virgil and the early philosophers. Do you think the images in these lines are too violent? Why or why not?
5. In the Bible, "The Word" is Christ, the Word of God. Has the term in line 30 the same meaning? Explain.

"Autumn"

1. What reasons did Pushkin give for his love of autumn? What made him dislike spring and summer? How did he feel about winter? Explain.
2. To what did the poet compare autumn? Do you think this comparison is justified? Why or why not?
3. Point out the appeal to the various senses in stanzas 7-9. What dramatic contrast is presented in stanza 9? Do you think these stanzas reveal Pushkin's ability to observe the fleeting emotions of man accurately? Point out lines to support your answer.
4. In stanzas 10-11, Pushkin revealed another reason for loving autumn. What was it? Do you think this reason was more significant to the poet than his earlier reasons? Why or why not?
5. What figures of speech are used to describe poetic inspiration? What metaphor describes poetic creation? Do you think it is fitting? Explain. What is the meaning of the last line?

6. Point out lines in this poem which reveal both Pushkin's sensitivity to nature and his sense of humor.

7. To prove that Pushkin was a master both of diction and mood, quote lines or passages where, through an accurate choice of words, a mood was created to suit the season being described. Point out examples of alliteration.

For Composition

1. In her book, *Poetry*, Elizabeth Drew writes, "The impulse behind all art is to give a personal form to some part of the raw material presented by life. Living is both raw and confused, but in giving it a design the artist does not want to lose all its rawness, for that is the intensity with which it has been felt." Using this quotation as a basis, write a paper in which you show how "Autumn" illustrates the truth of this statement. What was the "raw material" Pushkin used in this poem? How did he give it "design"? Where did he preserve the "rawness" of life?

2. In "Autumn," Pushkin praised this season for its effect on his poetic creativity. Write a composition in which you show why you agree or disagree with this viewpoint. Would the "austerity" of winter be a better time of year for a poet to gather his thoughts and write? Explain why or why not.

3. There is an interesting relation between Pushkin's "The Prophet" and lines 29-82 of Edna St. Vincent Millay's "Renascence." Write an essay in which you compare and contrast these two poems.

4. Every season has been praised in poetry—and criticized. Choose one season that you particularly like or dislike. Write a composition in which you present the reasons for your attitude toward this season.

Honoré de Balzac

A Passion in the Desert

Even as Victor Hugo was being hailed as the leader of the Romantic Movement in France, Honoré de Balzac (1799–1850) was emerging on the literary scene, representing the new realistic movement which was to dominate European literature in the second half of the nineteenth century. The leading French realist of his time, Balzac worked incessantly and with tremendous energy, producing in twenty years nearly one hundred novels. His principal works, such as *Père Goriot*, *Eugénie Grandet*, and *Caesar Birrotteau*, were part of a grandiose plan he conceived called the *Comédie Humaine*. This vast group of novels presented a complete picture of modern French civilization, and showed not only the effect of environment on people, but revealed every type of human being with all his vices and virtues. With scrupulous care, Balzac analyzed and recorded the thoughts, motives, and actions of each of his characters, and his settings were described with an astonishing attention to realistic detail. It has been said that "he paid attention to streets in the manner of a topographer, to dwellings and shops like an archaeologist, to rooms and furniture as would an antiquarian, to clothes and personal mannerisms with the flair of a detective."

Although Balzac was a realist and wished to present life as it was, he also had in him a strain of the romantic, which is apparent in the following story. "A Passion in the Desert" contains some of the realistic description for which Balzac is famous, but it also tells a story which is strange and even mystical. As one critic has put it "Balzac followed the soul and the senses faithfully on their strongest errands. . . . He realized, as the Greeks did, that human life is made up of elemental passions and necessity."

*T*HE whole show is dreadful," she cried, coming out of the menagerie of M. Martin. She had just been looking at that daring speculator "working with his hyena"—to speak in the style of the program.

"By what means," she continued, "can he have tamed these animals to such a point as to be certain of their affection for——."

"What seems to you a problem," said I, interrupting, "is really quite natural."

"Oh!" she cried, letting an incredulous smile wander over her lips.

"You think that beasts are wholly without passions?" I asked her. "Quite the reverse; we can communicate to them all the vices arising in our own state of civilization."

She looked at me with an air of astonishment.

"Nevertheless," I continued, "the first time I saw M. Martin, I admit, like you, I did give vent to an exclamation of surprise. I found myself next to an old soldier with the right leg amputated, who had come in with me. His face had struck me. He had one of those intrepid heads, stamped with the seal of warfare, and on which the battles of Napoleon are written. Besides, he had that frank good-humored expression which always impresses me favorably. He was without doubt one of those troopers who are surprised at nothing, who find matter for laughter in the contortions of a dying comrade, who bury or plunder him quite light-heartedly, who stand intrepidly in the way of bullets; in fact, one of those men who waste no time in deliberation, and would not hesitate to make friends with the devil himself. After looking very attentively at the proprietor of the menagerie getting out of his box, my companion pursed up his lips with an air of mockery and contempt, with that peculiar and expressive twist which superior people assume to show they are not taken in. Then when I was expatiating on the courage of M. Martin, he smiled, shook his head knowingly, and said, 'Well known.'

"How 'well known'?" I said. "If you would only explain to me the mystery I should be vastly obliged."

"After a few minutes, during which we made acquaintance, we went to dine at the first *restaurateur's* whose shop caught our eye. At dessert a bottle of champagne completely refreshed and brightened up the memories of this odd old soldier. He told me his story, and I said he had every reason to exclaim, 'Well known.' "

When she got home, she teased me to that extent and made so many promises, that I consented to communicate to her the old soldier's confidences. Next day she received the following episode of an epic which one might call "The Frenchman in Egypt."

During the expedition in Upper Egypt under General Desaix, a

Provencal soldier fell into the hands of the Mangrabins, and was taken by these Arabs into the deserts beyond the falls of the Nile.

In order to place a sufficient distance between themselves and the French army, the Mangrabins made forced marches, and only rested during the night. They camped round a well overshadowed by palm trees under which they had previously concealed a store of provisions. Not surmising that the notion of flight would occur to their prisoner, they contented themselves with binding his hands, and after eating a few dates, and giving provender to their horses, went to sleep.

When the brave Provençal saw that his enemies were no longer watching him, he made use of his teeth to steal a scimitar, fixed the blade between his knees, and cut the cords which prevented using his hands; in a moment he was free. He at once seized a rifle and dagger; then, taking the precaution to provide himself with a sack of dried dates, oats, and powder and shot, and to fasten a scimitar to his waist, he leaped into a horse, and spurred on vigorously in the direction where he thought to find the French army. So impatient was he to see a bivouac again that he pressed on the already tired courser at such speed that its flanks were lacerated with his spurs, and at last the poor animal died, leaving the Frenchman alone in the desert. After walking some time in the sand with all the courage of an escaped convict, the soldier was obliged to stop, as the day had already ended. In spite of the beauty of an oriental sky at night, he felt he had not strength enough to go on. Fortunately he had been able to find a small hill, on the summit of which a few palm trees shot up into the air; it was their verdure seen from afar which had brought hope and consolation to his heart. His fatigue was so great that he lay down upon a rock of granite, capriciously cut out like a camp-bed; there he fell asleep without taking any precaution to defend himself while he slept. He had made the sacrifice of his life. His last thought was one of regret. He repented having left the Mangrabins, whose nomad life seemed to smile on him now that he was afar from them and without help. He was awakened by the sun, whose pitiless rays fell with all their force on the granite and produced an intolerable heat—for he had had the stupidity to place himself inversely to the shadow thrown by the verdant majestic heads of the palm trees. He looked at the solitary trees and shuddered—they reminded him of the graceful shafts crowned with foliage which characterize the Saracen columns in the cathedral of Arles.

But when, after counting the palm trees, he cast his eye around him, the most horrible despair was infused into his soul. Before him stretched an ocean without limit. The dark sand of the desert spread farther than sight could reach in every direction, and glittered like steel struck with a bright light. It might have been a sea of looking-glass, or lakes melted together in a mirror. A fiery vapor carried up in streaks made a perpetual whirlwind over the quivering land. The sky was lit with an oriental splendor of insupportable purity, leaving naught for the imagination to desire. Heaven and earth were on fire.

The silence was awful in its wild and terrible majesty. Infinity, immensity, closed in upon the soul from every side. Not a cloud in the sky, not a breath in the air, not a flaw on the bosom of the sand, ever moving in diminutive waves; the horizon ended as at sea on a clear day, with one line of light, definite as the cut of a sword.

The Provençal threw his arms around the trunk of one of the palm trees, as though it were the body of a friend, and then in the shelter of the thin straight shadow that the palm cast upon the granite, he wept. Then sitting down he remained as he was, contemplating with profound sadness the implacable scene, which was all he had to look upon. He cried aloud, to measure the solitude. His voice, lost in the hollows of the hill, sounded faintly, and aroused no echo—the echo was in his own heart. The Provençal was twenty-two years old;—he loaded his carbine.

"There'll be time enough," he said to himself, laying on the ground the weapon which alone could bring him deliverance.

Looking by turns at the black expanse and the blue expanse, the soldier dreamed of France—he smelt with delight the gutters of Paris—he remembered the towns through which he had passed, the faces of his fellow-soldiers, the most minute details of his life. His southern fancy soon showed him the stones of his beloved Provence, in the play of the heat which waved over the spread sheet of the desert. Fearing the danger of this cruel mirage, he went down the opposite side of the hill to that by which he had come up the day before. The remains of a rug showed that this place of refuge had at one time been inhabited; at a short distance he saw some palm trees full of dates. Then the instinct which binds us to life awoke again in his heart. He hoped to live long enough to await the passing of some Arabs, or perhaps he might hear the sound of cannon; for at this time Bonaparte was traversing Egypt.

This thought gave him new life. The palm tree seemed to bend with the weight of the ripe fruit. He shook some of it down. When he tasted this unhoped-for manna, he felt sure that the palms had been cultivated by a former inhabitant—the savory, fresh meat of the dates was proof of the care of his predecessor. He passed suddenly from dark despair to an almost insane joy. He went up again to the top of the hill, and spent the rest of the day in cutting down one of the sterile palm trees, which the night before had served him for shelter. A vague memory made him think of the animals of the desert; and in case they might come to drink at the spring, visible from the base of the rocks but lost farther down, he resolved to guard himself from their visits by placing a barrier at the entrance of his hermitage.

In spite of his diligence, and the strength which the fear of being devoured asleep gave him, he was unable to cut the palm in pieces, though he succeeded in cutting it down. At eventide the king of the desert fell; the sound of its fall resounded far and wide, like a sign in the solitude; the soldier shuddered as though he had heard some voice predicting woe.

But like an heir who does not long bewail a deceased parent, he tore off from this beautiful tree the tall broad green leaves which are its poetic adornment, and used them to mend the mat on which he was to sleep.

Fatigued by the heat and his work, he feel asleep under the red curtains of his wet cave.

In the middle of the night his sleep was troubled by an extraordinary noise; he sat up, and the deep silence around him allowed him to distinguish the alternative accents of a respiration whose savage energy could not belong to a human creature.

A profound terror, increased still further by the darkness, the silence, and his waking images, froze his heart within him. He almost felt his hair stand on end, when by straining his eyes to their utmost he perceived through the shadows two faint yellow lights. At first he attributed these lights to the reflection of his own pupils, but soon the vivid brilliance of the night aided him gradually to distinguish the objects around him in the cave, and he beheld a huge animal lying but two steps from him. Was it a lion, a tiger, or a crocodile?

The Provençal was not educated enough to know under what species his enemy ought to be classed; but his fright was all the greater, as his ignorance led him to imagine all terrors at once; he endured a cruel torture, noting every variation of the breathing close to him without daring to make the slightest movement. An odor, pungent like that of a fox, but more penetrating, profounder —so to speak—filled the cave, and when the Provençal became sensible of this, his terror reached its height, for he would no longer doubt the proximity of a terrible companion, whose royal dwelling served him for shelter.

Presently the reflection of the moon, descending on the horizon, lit up the den, rendering gradually visible and resplendent the spotted skin of a panther.

The lion of Egypt slept, curled up like a big dog, the peaceful possessor of a sumptuous niche at the gate of a hotel; its eyes opened for a moment and closed again; its face was turned toward the man. A thousand confused thoughts passed through the Frenchman's mind; first he thought of killing it with a bullet from his gun, but he saw there was not enough distance between them for him to take proper aim—the shot would miss the mark. And if it were to wake!—the thought made his limbs rigid. He listened to his own heart beating in the midst of the silence, and cursed the too violent pulsations which the flow of blood brought on, fearing to disturb that sleep which allowed him time to think of some means of escape.

Twice he placed his hand on his scimitar, intending to cut off the head of his enemy; but the difficulty of cutting the stiff, short hair compelled him to abandon this daring project. To miss would be to die for *certain*, he thought; he preferred the chances of fair fight, and made up his mind to wait till morning; the morning did not leave him long to wait.

He could now examine the panther at ease; its muzzle was smeared with blood.

"She's had a good dinner," he thought, without troubling himself as to whether her feast might have been on human flesh. "She won't be hungry when she gets up."

It was a female. The fur on her belly and flanks was glistening white; many small marks like velvet formed beautiful bracelets round her feet; her sinuous tail was also white, ending with black rings; the overpart of her dress, yellow like unburnished gold, very lissom and soft, had the characteristic blotches in the form of rosettes, which distinguish the panther from every other feline species.

This tranquil and formidable hostess snored in an attitude as graceful as that of a cat lying on a cushion. Her bloodstained paws, nervous and well-armed, were stretched out before her face, which rested upon them, and from which radiated her straight, slender whiskers, like threads of silver.

If she had been like that in a cage, the Provençal would doubtless have admired the grace of the animal, and the vigorous contrasts of vivid color which gave her robe an imperial splendor; but just then his sight was troubled by her sinister appearance.

The presence of the panther, even asleep, could not fail to produce the effect which the magnetic eyes of the serpent are said to have on the nightingale.

For a moment the courage of the soldier began to fail before this danger, though no doubt it would have risen at the mouth of a cannon charged with shell. Nevertheless, a bold thought brought daylight to his soul and sealed up the source of the cold sweat which sprang forth on his brow. Like men driven to bay who defy death and offer their body to the smiter, so he, seeing in this merely a tragic episode, resolved to play his part with honor to the last.

"The day before yesterday the Arabs would have killed me perhaps," he said; so considering himself as good as dead already, he waited bravely, with excited curiosity, his enemy's awakening.

When the sun appeared, the panther suddenly opened her eyes; then she put out her paws with energy, as if to stretch them and get rid of cramp. At last she yawned, showing the formidable apparatus of her teeth and pointed tongue, rough as a file.

"A regular *petite maîtresse*," thought the Frenchman, seeing her roll herself about so softly and coquettishly. She licked off the blood which stained her paws and muzzle, and scratched her head with reiterated gestures full of prettiness. "All right, make a little toilet," the Frenchman said to himself, beginning to recover his gaiety with his courage; "we'll say good morning to each other presently," and he seized the small, short dagger which he had taken from the

Mangrabins. At this moment the panther turned her head toward the man and looked at him fixedly without moving.

The rigidity of her metallic eyes and their insupportable luster made him shudder, especially when the animal walked toward him. But he looked at her caressingly, staring into her eyes in order to magnetize her, and let her come quite close to him; then with a movement both gentle and amorous, as though he were caressing the most beautiful of women, he passed his hand over her whole body, from the head to the tail, scratching the flexible vertebrae which divided the panther's yellow back. The animal waved her tail voluptuously, and her eyes grew gentle; and when for the third time the Frenchman accomplished this interesting flattery, she gave forth one of those purrings by which our cats express their pleasure; but this murmur issued from a throat so powerful and so deep, that it resounded through the cave like the last vibrations of an organ in a church. The man, understanding the importance of his caresses, redoubled them in such a way as to surprise and stupefy his imperious courtesan. When he felt sure of having extinguished the ferocity of his capricious companion, whose hunger had so fortunately been satisfied the day before, he got up to go out of the cave; the panther let him go out, but when he had reached the summit of the hill she sprang with the lightness of a sparrow hopping from twig to twig, and rubbed herself against his legs, putting up her back after the manner of all the race of cats. Then regarding her guest with eyes whose glare had softened a little, she gave vent to that wild cry which naturalists compare to the grating of a saw.

"She is exacting," said the Frenchman, smilingly.

He was bold enough to play with her ears; he caressed her belly and scratched her head as hard as he could.

When he saw that he was successful, he tickled her skull with the point of his dagger, watching for the right moment to kill her, but the hardness of her bones made him tremble for his success.

The sultana of the desert showed herself gracious to her slave; she lifted her head, stretched out her neck, and manifested her delight by the tranquillity of her attitude. It suddenly occurred to the soldier that to kill this savage princess with one blow he must poignard her in the throat.

He raised the blade, when the panther, satisfied no doubt, laid herself gracefully at his feet, and cast up at him glances in which, in spite of their natural fierceness, was mingled confusedly a kind of good-will. The poor Provençal ate his dates, leaning against one of the palm trees, and casting his eyes alternately on the desert in quest of some liberator and on his terrible companion to watch her uncertain clemency.

The panther looked at the place where the date stones fell, and every time that he threw one down her eyes expressd an incredible mistrust.

She examined the man with an almost commercial prudence. However, this examination was favorable to him, for when he had finished his meager meal she licked his boots with her powerful rough tongue, brushing off with marvelous skill the dust gathered in the creases.

"Ah, but when she's really hungry!" thought the Frenchman. In spite of the shudder this thought caused him, the soldier began to measure curiously the proportions of the panther, certainly one of the most splendid specimens of its race. She was three feet high and four feet long without counting her tail; this powerful weapon, rounded like a cudgel, was nearly three feet long. The head, large as that of a lioness, was distinguished by a rare expression of refinement. The cold cruelty of a tiger was dominant, it was true, but there was also a vague resemblance to face of a sensual woman. Indeed, the face of this solitary queen had something of the gaiety of a drunken Nero: she had satiated herself with blood, and she wanted to play.

The soldier tried if he might walk up and down, and the panther left him free, contenting herself with following him with her eyes, less like a faithful dog than a big Angora cat, observing everything, and every movement of her master.

When he looked around, he saw, by the spring, the remains of his horse; the panther had dragged the carcass all that way; about two-thirds of it had been devoured already. The sight reassured him.

It was easy to explain the panther's absence, and the respect she had had for him while he slept. The first piece of good luck emboldened him to tempt the future, and he conceived the wild hope of continuing on good terms with the panther during the entire day, neglecting no means of taming her, and remaining in her good graces.

He returned to her, and had the unspeakable joy of seeing her wag her tail with an almost imperceptible movement at his approach. He sat down then, without fear, by her side, and they began to play together; he took her paws and muzzle, pulled her ears, rolled her over on her back, stroked her warm, delicate flanks. She let him do whatever he liked, and when he began to stroke the hair on her feet she drew her claws in carefully.

The man, keeping the dagger in one hand, thought to plunge it into the belly of the too-confiding panther, but he was afraid that he would be immediately strangled in her last convulsive struggle; besides, he felt in his heart a sort of remorse which bid him respect a creature that had done him no harm. He seemed to have found a friend, in a boundless desert; half unconsciously he thought of his first sweetheart, whom he had nicknamed "Mignonne" by way of contrast, because she was so atrociously jealous that all the time of their love he was in fear of the knife with which she had always threatened him.

This memory of his early days suggested to him the idea of making the young panther answer to this name, now that he began to admire with less terror her swiftness, suppleness, and softness. Toward the end of the day he had familiarized himself with his perilous position; he now almost liked the painfulness of it. At last his companion had got into the habit of looking up at him whenever he cried in a falsetto voice, "Mignonne."

At the setting of the sun Mignonne gave, several times running, a profound melancholy cry. "She's been well brought up," said the light-hearted soldier; "she says her prayers." But this mental joke only occurred to him when he noticed what a pacific attitude his companion remained in. "Come, *ma petite blonde*, I'll let you go to bed first," he said to her, counting on the activity of his own legs to run away as quickly as possible, directly she was asleep, and seek another shelter for the night.

The soldier waited with impatience the hour of his flight, and when it had arrived he walked vigorously in the direction of the Nile; but hardly had he made a quarter of a league in the sand when he heard the panther bounding after him crying with that saw-like cry more dreadful even than the sound of her leaping.

"Ah!" he said, "then she's taken a fancy to me; she has never met any one before, and it is really quite flattering to have her first love." That instant the man fell into one of those movable quicksands so terrible to travellers and from which it is impossible to save oneself. Feeling himself caught, he gave a shriek of alarm; the panther seized him with her teeth by the collar, and, springing vigorously backward, drew him as if by magic out of the whirling sand.

"Ah, Mignonne!" cried the soldier, caressing her enthusiastically; "we're bound together for life and death—but no jokes, mind!" and he retraced his steps.

From that time the desert seemed inhabited. It contained a being to whom the man could talk, and whose ferocity was rendered gentle by him, though he could not explain to himself the reason for their strange friendship. Great as was the soldier's desire to stay upon guard, he slept.

On awakening he could not find Mignonne; he mounted the hill, and in the distance saw her springing toward him after the habit of these animals, who cannot run on account of the extreme flexibility of the vertebral column. Mignonne arrived, her jaws covered with blood; she received the wonted caress of her companion, showing with much purring how happy it made her. Her eyes, full of languor, turned still more gently than the day before toward the Provençal who talked to her as one would to a tame animal.

"Ah! Mademoiselle, you are a nice girl, aren't you? Just look at that! so we like to be made much of, don't we? Aren't you ashamed of yourself? So you have been eating some Arab or other, have you? that doesn't matter. They're animals just the same as you are; but don't you take to eating Frenchmen, or I shan't like you any longer."

She played like a dog with its master, letting herself be rolled over, knocked about, and stroked, alternately; sometimes she herself would provoke the soldier, putting up her paw with a soliciting gesture.

Some days passed in this manner. This companionship permitted the Provençal to appreciate the sublime beauty of the desert; now that he had a living thing to think about, alternations of fear and quiet, and plenty to eat, his mind became filled with contrast and his life began to be diversified.

Solitude revealed to him all her secrets, and enveloped him in her delights. He discovered in the rising and setting of the sun sights unknown to the world. He knew what it was to tremble when he heard over his head the hiss of a bird's wing, so rarely did they pass, or when he saw the clouds, changing and many-colored travelers, melt one into another. He studied in the nighttime the effect of the moon upon the ocean of sand, where the simoom made waves swift of movement and rapid in their change. He lived the life of the Eastern day, marveling at its wonderful pomp; then, after having reveled in the sight of a hurricane over the plain where the whirling sands made red, dry mists and death-bearing clouds, he would welcome the night with joy, for then fell the healthful freshness of the stars, and he listened to imaginary music in the skies. Then solitude taught him to unroll the treasures of dreams. He passed whole hours in remembering mere nothings, and comparing his present life with his past.

At last he grew passionately fond of the panther; for some sort of affection was a necessity.

Whether it was that his will powerfully projected had modified the character of his companion, or whether, because she found abundant food in her predatory excursions in the desert, she respected the man's life, he began to fear for it no longer, seeing her so well tamed.

He devoted the greater part of his time to sleep, but he was obliged to watch like a spider in its web that the moment of his deliverance might not escape him, if any one should pass the line marked by the horizon. He had sacrificed his shirt to make a flag with, which he hung at the top of a palm tree, whose foliage he had torn off. Taught by necessity, he found the means of keeping it spread out, by fastening it with little sticks; for the wind might not be blowing at the moment when the passing traveler was looking through the desert.

It was during the long hours, when he had abandoned hope, that he amused himself with the panther. He had come to learn the different inflections of her voice, the expressions of her eyes; he had studied the capricious patterns of all the rosettes which marked the gold of her robe. Mignonne was not even angry when he took hold of the tuft at the end of her tail to count her rings, those graceful ornaments which glittered in the sun like jewelry. It gave him pleasure to contemplate the supple, fine outlines of her form, the whiteness of her belly, the graceful pose of her head. But it was especially when she was playing that he felt most pleasure in looking at her; the agility and youthful lightness of her movements were a continual surprise to him; he wondered at the supple way in which she jumped and climbed, washed herself and arranged her fur, crouched down and prepared to spring. However rapid her spring might be, however slippery the stone she was on, she would always stop short at the word "Mignonne."

One day, in a bright midday sun, an enormous bird coursed through the air. The man left his panther to look at this new guest; but after waiting a moment the deserted sultana growled deeply.

"My goodness! I do believe she's jealous," he cried, seeing her eyes become hard again; "the soul of Virginie has passed into her body; that's certain."

The eagle disappeared into the air, while the soldier admired the curved contour of the panther.

But there was such youth and grace in her form! she was beautiful as a woman! the blond fur of her robe mingled well with the delicate tints of faint white which marked her flanks.

The profuse light cast down by the sun made this living gold, these russet markings, to burn in a way to give them an indefinable attraction.

The man and the panther looked at one another with a look full of meaning; the coquette quivered when she felt her friend stroke her head; her eyes flashed like lightning—then she shut them tightly.

"She has a soul," he said, looking at the stillness of this queen of the sands, golden like them, white like them, solitary and burning like them.

"Well," she said, "I have read your plea in favor of beasts; but how did two so well adapted to understand each other end?"

"Ah, well! you see, they ended as all great passions do end—by a misunderstanding. For some reason *one* suspects the other of treason; they don't come to an explanation through pride, and quarrel and part from sheer obstinacy."

"Yet sometimes at the best moments a single word or a look is enough—but anyhow go on with your story."

"It's horribly difficult, but you will understand, after what the old villain told me over his champagne.

"He said—'I don't know if I hurt her, but she turned round, as if enraged, and with her sharp teeth caught hold of my leg—gently, I daresay; but I, thinking she would devour me, plunged my dagger into her throat. She rolled over, giving a cry that froze my heart;

and I saw her dying, still looking at me without anger. I would have given all the world—my cross even, which I had not got then—to have brought her to life again. It was as though I had murdered a real person; and the soldiers who had seen my flag, and were come to my assistance, found me in tears.'

" 'Well sir,' he said, after a moment of silence, 'since then I have been in war in Germany, in Spain, in Russia, in France; I've certainly carried my carcass about a good deal, but never have I seen anything like the desert. Ah! yes, it is very beautiful!'

" 'What did you feel there?' I asked him.

" 'Oh! that can't be described, young man. Besides, I am not always regretting my palm trees and my panther. I should have to be very melancholy for that. In the desert, you see, there is everything, and nothing.'

" 'Yes, but explain——'

" 'Well,' he said, with an impatient gesture, 'it is God without mankind.' "

For Discussion

1. The point that the narrator in this story set out to make is contained in the third paragraph on page 92. Restate the idea in your own words. Indicate the passage near the end of the story where the "communicated vice" disrupted the friendship between the panther and the man. Do you agree or disagree with this viewpoint about the relation of men and beasts? Explain.

2. Do you think that Balzac was an accurate observer of human nature in the paragraph on page 103, beginning, "Ah, well! you see, they ended as all great passions do end—by a misunderstanding. . . ."? Why or why not? What comment on life do you think the author was making? How does it differ from a similar comment Hugo might make?

3. Did you find the friendship between the man and the panther believable or unbelievable? Why? In your opinion, was the ending inevitable? Why or why not? What reasons do you have for believing that Balzac's purpose was not simply to tell a fantastic story?

4. In relation to the story, explain the meaning of, "In the desert, you see, there is everything and nothing . . . it is God without mankind." What general meaning do you see in this statement?

5. Judging from this story, would you say that Balzac believed in evolution and pantheism? Explain.

6. Although this story is not typical of Balzac's realistic fiction, it does contain many realistic elements. Point out examples of this. Do you think that these passages make the story more believable? Why or why not?

7. Balzac is noted for the detailed observations he makes of his characters. Show through specific examples how this is revealed in his characterizations of the man and the panther.

For Composition

1. Write a composition in which you compare and contrast the way Balzac, the realist, saw people in this story and the way Hugo, the romantic, saw people in "Jean Valjean and the Bishop's Candlesticks."

2. Animals often give the appearance of having qualities akin to those of human beings, while retaining their animal characteristics. Write a short narrative based on an experience of your own, or of someone you know, which supports or contradicts this statement.

$\mathcal{I}van$ $\mathcal{T}urgenev$

Mumu

About the middle of the nineteenth century in Russia, there began a great creative period which produced the mighty novelists, Tolstoy and Dostoyevsky, and the playwright and short-story writer, Chekhov. This productive time in Russian literature also produced another writer of stature, the novelist and short-story writer, Ivan Turgenev * (1818–1883).

Like many of his literary contemporaries, Turgenev was a sincere humanitarian and liberal, deeply concerned with the social and political problems of his country. His first book of short stories, *Notes of a Sportsman* (1852), were sketches of Russian country life permeated with a sympathy for the impoverished peasants. His best-known novel, *Fathers and Sons*, about the conflict between the old and the new, was vehemently attacked by both conservatives and liberals, after which Turgenev left Russia. He lived the last twenty years of his life in Paris among the leading French writers of the period.

Although Turgenev, like many of the other Russian writers of his time, was a realist, he was more romantic than they. He was acclaimed the one writer who most perfectly portrayed the "soul of the Russian of his century." His work has a lyrical quality, particularly in his descriptive passages of landscape. He combined a clarity and precision with an emotional suggestiveness which gives his style great charm. In his stories and novels, he worked painstakingly to present the exact atmosphere and setting, to capture the precise mood and tone, and to arouse the emotions of the reader by detailed descriptions which are often poetical. In "Mumu," Turgenev reveals his sympathy with the serfs and his strong opposition to the injustice of their lot under the old regime. He also shows his keen observations of human beings and his ability to create characters who are alive and universal.

$\mathcal{I}$N one of the outlying streets of Moscow, in a gray house with white columns and a balcony, warped all askew, there was once living a lady, a widow, surrounded by a numerous household of serfs. Her sons were in the government service at Petersburg; her

* ē-vän toor-gā'nyef

106

daughters were married; she went out very little, and in solitude lived through the last years of her miserly and dreary old age. Her day, a joyless and gloomy day, had long been over; but the evening of her life was blacker than night.

Of all her servants, the most remarkable personage was the porter, Gerasim, a man full twelve inches over the normal height, of heroic build, and deaf and dumb from his birth. The lady, his owner, had brought him up from the village where he lived alone in a little hut, apart from his brothers, and was reckoned about the most punctual of her peasants in the payment of the seignorial dues. Endowed with extraordinary strength, he did the work of four men; work flew apace under his hands, and it was a pleasant sight to see him when he was plowing, while, with his huge palms pressing hard upon the plow, he seemed alone, unaided by its poor horse, to cleave the yielding bosom of the earth, or when, about St. Peter's Day, he plied his scythe with a furious energy that might have mown a young birch copse up by the roots, or swiftly and untiringly wielded a flail over two yards long; while the hard oblong muscles of his shoulders rose and fell like a lever. His perpetual silence lent a solemn dignity to his unwearying labor. He was a splendid peasant, and, except for his affliction, any girl would have been glad to marry him. . . . But now they had taken Gerasim to Moscow, bought him boots, had him made a full-skirted coat for summer, a sheepskin for winter, put into his hand a broom and a spade, and appointed him porter.

At first he intensely disliked his new mode of life. From his childhood he had been used to field labor, to village life. Shut off by his affliction from the society of men, he had grown up, dumb and mighty, as a tree grows on a fruitful soil. When he was transported to the town, he could not understand what was being done with him; he was miserable and stupefied, with the stupefaction of some strong young bull, taken straight from the meadow, where the rich grass stood up to his belly, taken and put in the truck of a railway train, and there, while smoke and sparks and gusts of steam puff out upon the sturdy beast, he is whirled onwards, whirled along with loud roar and whistle, whither—God knows!

What Gerasim had to do in his new duties seemed a mere trifle to him after his hard toil as a peasant; in half-an-hour, all his work was done, and he would once more stand stock-still in the middle of the courtyard, staring open-mouthed at all the passers-by, as though trying to wrest from them the explanation of his perplexing position; or he would suddenly go off into some corner, and flinging a long way off the broom or the spade, throw himself on his face on the ground, and lie for hours together without stirring, like a caged beast. But man gets used to anything, and Gerasim got used at last to living in town. He had little work to do; his whole duty consisted in keeping the courtyard clean, bringing in a barrel of water twice a day, splitting and dragging in wood for the kitchen and the house, keeping out strangers, and watching at night. And it must be said he did his duty zealously. In his courtyard there was never a shaving lying about, never a speck of dust; if sometimes, in the muddy season, the wretched nag, put under his charge for fetching water, got stuck in the road, he would simply give it a shove with his shoulder, and set not only the cart but the horse itself moving. If he set to chopping wood, the ax fairly rang like glass, and chips and chunks flew in all directions. And as for strangers, after he had one night caught two thieves and knocked their heads together—knocked them so that there was not the slightest need to take them to the police-station afterwards—every one in the neighborhood began to feel a great respect for him; even those who came in the daytime, by no means robbers, but simply unknown persons, at the sight of the terrible porter, waved and shouted to him as though he could hear their shouts. With all the rest of the servants, Gerasim was on terms, hardly friendly—they were afraid of him—but familiar; he regarded them as his fellows. They explained themselves to him by signs, and he understood them, and exactly carried out all orders, but knew his own rights too, and soon no one dared to take his seat at the table. Gerasim was altogether of a strict and serious temper; he liked order in everything; even the cocks did not dare to fight in his presence, or woe betide them! directly he caught sight of them, he would seize them by the legs, swing them ten times round in the air like a wheel, and throw them in different directions. There were geese, too, kept in the yard; but the goose, as is well known, is a dignified and reasonable bird; Gerasim felt a respect for them, looked after them, and fed them; he was himself not unlike a gander of the steppes. He was assigned a little garret over the kitchen; he arranged it himself to his own liking, made a bedstead in it of oak boards on four stumps of wood for legs—a truly Titanic bedstead;

one might have put a ton or two on it—it would not have bent under the load; under the bed was a solid chest; in a corner stood a little table of the same strong kind, and near the table a three-legged stool, so solid and squat that Gerasim himself would sometimes pick it up and drop it again with a smile of delight. The garret was locked up by means of a padlock that looked like a kalatch or basket-shaped loaf, only black; the key of this padlock Gerasim always carried about him in his girdle. He did not like people to come to his garret.

So passed a year, at the end of which a little incident befell Gerasim.

The old lady, in whose service he lived as porter, adhered in everything to the ancient ways, and kept a large number of servants. In her house were not only laundresses, sempstresses, carpenters, tailors and tailoresses, there was even a harness-maker—he was reckoned as a veterinary surgeon, too—and a doctor for the servants; there was a household doctor for the mistress; there was, lastly, a shoemaker, by name Kapiton Klimov, a sad drunkard. Klimov regarded himself as an injured creature, whose merits were unappreciated, a cultivated man from Petersburg, who ought not to be living in Moscow without occupation—in the wilds, so to speak; and if he drank, as he himself expressed it emphatically, with a blow on his chest, it was sorrow drove him to it. So one day his mistress had a conversation about him with her head steward, Gavrila, a man whom, judging solely from his little yellow eyes and nose like a duck's beak, fate itself, it seemed, had marked out as a person in authority. The lady expressed her regret at the corruption of the morals of Kapiton, who had, only the evening before, been picked up somewhere in the street.

"Now, Gavrila," she observed, all of a sudden, "now, if we were to marry him, what do you think, perhaps he would be steadier?"

"Why not marry him, indeed, 'm? He could be married, 'm," answered Gavrila, "and it would be a very good thing, to be sure, 'm."

"Yes; only who is to marry him?"

"Ay, 'm. But that's at your pleasure, 'm. He may, anyway, so to say, be wanted for something; he can't be turned adrift altogether."

"I fancy he likes Tatiana."

Gavrila was on the point of making some reply, but he shut his lips tightly.

"Yes! . . . let him marry Tatiana," the lady decided, taking a pinch of snuff complacently. "Do you hear?"

"Yes, 'm," Gavrila articulated, and he withdrew.

Returning to his own room (it was in a little lodge, and was almost filled up with metal-bound trunks), Gavrila first sent his wife away, and then sat down at the window and pondered. His mistress's unexpected arrangement had clearly put him in a difficulty. At last he got up and sent to call Kapiton. Kapiton made his appearance. . . . But before reporting their conversation to the reader, we consider it not out of place to relate in few words who was this Tatiana, whom it was to be Kapiton's lot to marry, and why the great lady's order had disturbed the steward.

Tatiana, one of the laundresses referred to above (as a trained and skillful laundress she was in charge of the fine linen only), was a woman of twenty-eight, thin, fair-haired, with moles on her left cheek. Moles on the left cheek are regarded as of evil omen in Russia—a token of unhappy life. . . . Tatiana could not boast of her good luck. From her earliest youth she had been badly treated; she had done the work of two, and had never known affection; she had been poorly clothed and had received the smallest wages. Relations she had practically none; an uncle she had once had, a butler, left behind in the country as useless, and other uncles of hers were peasants—that was all. At one time she had passed for a beauty, but her good looks were very soon over. In disposition, she was very meek, or, rather, scared; towards herself, she felt perfect indifference; of others, she stood in mortal dread; she thought of nothing but how to get her work done in good time, never talked to any one, and trembled at the very name of her mistress, though the latter scarcely knew her by sight. When Gerasim was brought from the country, she was ready to die with fear on seeing his huge figure, tried all she could to avoid meeting him, even dropped her eyelids when sometimes she chanced to run past him, hurrying from the house to the laundry. Gerasim at first paid no special attention to her, then he used to smile when she came his way, then he began even to stare admiringly at her, and at last he never took his eyes off her. She took his fancy, whether by the mild expression of her face or the timidity of her movements, who can tell? So one day she was stealing across the yard, with a starched dressing-jacket of her mistress's carefully poised on her outspread fingers . . . some one suddenly grasped her vigorously by the elbow; she turned round and fairly screamed; behind her stood Gerasim. With a foolish smile, making inarticulate caressing grunts, he held out to her a ginger-bread cock with gold tinsel on his tail and wings. She was about to refuse it, but he thrust it forcibly into her hand, shook his head, walked away, and turning round, once more grunted something very affectionately to her. From that day forward he gave her no peace; wherever she went, he was on the spot at once, coming to meet her, smiling, grunting, waving his hands; all at once he would pull a ribbon out of the bosom of his smock and put it in her hand, or would sweep the dust out of her way. The poor girl simply did not know how to behave or what to do. Soon the whole household knew of the dumb porter's wiles; jeers, jokes, sly hints were showered upon Tatiana. At Gerasim, however, it was not every one who would dare to scoff; he did not like jokes; indeed, in his presence, she, too, was left in peace. Whether she liked it or not, the girl found herself to be under his protection. Like all deaf-mutes, he was very suspicious, and very readily perceived when they were laughing at him or at her. One day, at dinner, the wardrobe-keeper, Tatiana's superior, fell to nagging, as it is called, at her, and brought the poor thing to such a state that she did not know where to look, and was almost crying with vexation. Gerasim got up all of a sudden, stretched out his gigantic hand, laid it on the wardrobe-maid's head, and looked into her face with such grim ferocity that her head positively flopped upon the table. Every one was still. Gerasim took up his spoon again and went on with his cabbage-soup. "Look at him, the dumb devil, the wood-demon!" they all muttered in undertones, while the wardrobe-maid got up and went out into the maids' room. Another time, noticing that Kapiton—the same Kapiton who was the subject of the conversation reported above—was gossiping somewhat too attentively with Tatiana, Gerasim beckoned him to him, led him into the cartshed, and taking up a shaft that was standing in a corner by one end, lightly, but most significantly, menaced him with it. Since then no one addressed a word to Tatiana. And all this cost him nothing. It is true the wardrobe-maid, as soon as she reached the maids' room, promptly fell into a fainting-fit, and behaved altogether so skillfully that Gerasim's rough action reached his mistress's knowledge the same day. But the capricious old lady only laughed, and several times, to the great offense of the wardrobe-maid, forced her to repeat "how he bent your head down with his heavy hand," and next day she sent Gerasim a ruble. She looked on him with favor as a strong and faithful watchman. Gerasim stood in considerable awe of her, but, all the same, he had hopes of her favor, and was preparing to go to her with a petition for leave to marry Tatiana. He was only waiting for a new coat, promised him by the steward, to present a proper appearance before his mistress, when this same mistress suddenly took it into her head to marry Tatiana to Kapiton.

The reader will now readily understand the perturbation of mind that overtook the steward Gavrila after his conversation with his mistress. "My lady," he thought, as he sat at the window, "favors Gerasim, to be sure"—(Gavrila was well aware of this, and that was why he himself looked on him with an indulgent eye)—"still he is a speechless creature. I could not, indeed, put it before the mistress that Gerasim's courting Tatiana. But, after all, it's true enough; he's a queer sort of husband. But on the other hand, that devil, God forgive me, has only got to find out they're marrying Tatiana to Kapiton, he'll smash up everything in the house, 'pon my soul! There's no reasoning with him; why, he's such a devil, God forgive my sins, there's no getting over him nohow . . . 'pon my soul!"

Kapiton's entrance broke the thread of Gavrila's reflections. The dissipated shoemaker came in, his hands behind him, and lounging carelessly against a projecting angle of the wall, near the door, crossed his right foot in front of his left, and tossed his head, as much as to say, "What do you want?"

Gavrila looked at Kapiton, and drummed with his fingers on the windowframe. Kapiton merely screwed up his leaden eyes a little, but he did not look down, he even grinned slightly, and passed his hand over his whitish locks which were sticking up in all directions. "Well, here I am. What is it?"

"You're a pretty fellow," said Gavrila, and paused. "A pretty fellow you are, there's no denying!"

Kapiton only twitched his little shoulders. "Are you any better, pray?" he thought to himself.

"Just look at yourself, now, look at yourself," Gavrila went on reproachfully; "now, whatever do you look like?"

Kapiton serenely surveyed his shabby tattered coat, and his patched trousers, and with special attention stared at his burst boots, especially the one on the tip-toe of which his right foot so gracefully poised, and he fixed his eyes again on the steward.

"Well?"

"Well?" repeated Gavrila. "Well? And then you say well? You look like old Nick himself, God forgive my saying so, that's what you look like."

Kapiton blinked rapidly.

"Go on abusing me, go on, if you like, Gavrila Andreitch," he thought to himself again.

"Here, you've been drunk again," Gavrila began, "drunk again, haven't you? Eh? Come, answer me!"

"Owing to the weakness of my health, I have exposed myself to spirituous beverages, certainly," replied Kapiton.

"Owing to the weakness of your health! . . . They let you off too easy, that's what it is; and you've been apprenticed in Petersburg. . . . Much you learned in your apprenticeship! You simply eat your bread in idleness."

"In that matter, Gavrila Andreitch, there is one to judge me, the Lord God Himself, and no one else. He also knows what manner of man I be in this world, and whether I eat my bread in idleness. And as concerning your contention regarding drunkenness, in that matter, too, I am not to blame, but rather a friend; he led me into temptation, but was diplomatic and got away, while I . . ."

"While you were left, like a goose, in the street. Ah, you're a dissolute fellow! But that's not the point," the steward went on. "I've something to tell you. Our lady . . ." here he paused a minute, "it's our lady's pleasure that you should be married. Do you hear? She imagines you may be steadier when you're married. Do you understand?"

"To be sure I do."

"Well, then. For my part I think it would be better to give you a good hiding. But there—it's her business. Well? are you agreeable?"

Kapiton grinned.

"Matrimony is an excellent thing for any one, Gavrila Andreitch; and, as far as I am concerned, I shall be quite agreeable."

"Very well, then," replied Gavrila, while he reflected to himself: "There's no denying the man expresses himself very properly. Only there's one thing," he pursued aloud: "the wife our lady's picked out for you is an unlucky choice."

"Why, who is she, permit me to inquire?"

"Tatiana."

"Tatiana?"

And Kapiton opened his eyes, and moved a little away from the wall.

"Well, what are you so alarmed about? . . . Isn't she to your taste, hey?"

"Not to my taste, do you say, Gavrila Andreitch! She's right enough, a hardworking steady girl. . . . But you know very well yourself, Gavrila Andreitch, why that fellow, that wild man of the woods, that monster of the steppes, he's after her, you know. . . ."

"I know, mate, I know all about it," the butler cut him short in a tone of annoyance: "but there, you see . . ."

"But upon my soul, Gavrila Andreitch! why, he'll kill me, by God, he will, he'll crush me like some fly; why, he's got a fist—why, you kindly look yourself what a fist he's got; why, he's simply got a fist like Minin Pozharsky's. You see he's deaf; he beats and does not hear how he's beating! He swings his great fists, as if he's asleep. And there's no possibility of pacifying him; and for why? Why, because, as you know yourself, Gavrila Andreitch, he's deaf, and what's more, has no more wit than the heel of my foot. Why, he's a sort of beast, a heathen idol, Gavrila Andreitch, and worse . . . a block of wood; what have I done that I should have to suffer from him now? Sure it is, it's all over with me now; I've knocked about, I've had enough to put up with, I've been battered like an earthenware pot, but still I'm a man, after all, and not a worthless pot."

"I know, I know, don't go talking away. . . ."

"Lord, my God!" the shoemaker continued warmly, "when is the end? when, O Lord! A poor wretch I am, a poor wretch whose sufferings are endless! What a life, what a life mine's been, come to think of it! In my young days, I was beaten by a German I was 'prentice to; in the prime of life beaten by my own countrymen, and last of all, in ripe years, see what I have been brought to. . . ."

"Ugh, you flabby soul!" said Gavrila Andreitch. "Why do you make so many words about it?"

"Why, do you say, Gavrila Andreitch? It's not a beating I'm afraid of, Gavrila Andreitch. A gentleman may chastise me in private, but give me a civil word before folks, and I'm a man still; but see now, whom I've to do with. . . ."

"Come, get along," Gavrila interposed impatiently. Kapiton turned away and staggered off.

"But, if it were not for him," the steward shouted after him, "you would consent for your part?"

"I signify my acquiescence," retorted Kapiton as he disappeared. His fine language did not desert him, even in the most trying positions.

The steward walked several times up and down the room.

"Well, call Tatiana now," he said at last.

A few instants later, Tatiana had come up almost noiselessly, and was standing in the doorway.

"What are your orders, Gavrila Andreitch?" she said in a soft voice.

The steward looked at her intently.

"Well, Taniusha," he said, "would you like to be married? Our lady has chosen a husband for you."

"Yes, Gavrila Andreitch. And whom has she deigned to name as a husband for me?" she added falteringly.

"Kapiton, the shoemaker."

"Yes, sir."

"He's a feather-brained fellow, that's certain. But it's just for that the mistress reckons upon you."

"Yes, sir."

"There's one difficulty . . . you know the deaf man, Gerasim, he's courting you, you see. How did you come to bewitch such a bear? But you see, he'll kill you, very like, he's such a bear. . . ."

"He'll kill me, Gavrila Andreitch, he'll kill me, and no mistake."

"Kill you. . . . Well, we shall see about that. What do you mean by saying he'll kill you? Has he any right to kill you? Tell me yourself."

"I don't know, Gavrila Andreitch, about his having any right or not."

"What a woman! why, you've made him no promise, I suppose. . . ."

"What are you pleased to ask of me?"

The steward was silent for a little, thinking, "You're a meek soul!" "Well, that's right," he said aloud; "we'll have another talk with you later; now you can go, Taniusha; I see you're not unruly, certainly."

Tatiana turned, steadied herself a little against the doorpost, and went away.

"And, perhaps, our lady will forget all about this wedding by tomorrow," thought the steward; "and here am I worrying myself for nothing! As for that insolent fellow, we must tie him down, if it comes to that, we must let the police know . . ." "Ustinya Fyedorovna!" he shouted in a loud voice to his wife, "heat the samovar, my good soul. . . ." All that day Tatiana hardly went out of the laundry. At first she had started crying, then she wiped away her tears, and set to work as before. Kapiton stayed till late at night at the ginshop with a friend of his, a man of gloomy appearance, to whom he related in detail how he used to live in Petersburg with a gentleman, who would have been all right, except he was a bit too strict, and he had a slight weakness besides, he was too fond of drink; and, as to the fair sex, he didn't stick at anything. His gloomy companion merely said yes; but when Kapiton announced at last that, in a certain event, he would have to lay hands on himself to-morrow, his gloomy companion remarked that it was bedtime. And they parted in surly silence.

Meanwhile, the steward's anticipations were not fulfilled. The old lady was so much taken up with the idea of Kapiton's wedding, that even in the night she talked of nothing else to one of her companions, who was kept in her house solely to entertain her in case of sleeplessness, and, like a night cabman, slept in the day. When Gavrila came to her after morning tea with his report, her first question was: "And how about our wedding—is it getting on all right?" He replied, of course, that it was getting on first rate, and that Kapiton would appear before her to pay his reverence to her that day. The old lady was not quite well; she did not give much time to business. The steward went back to his own room, and called a council. The matter certainly called for serious consideration. Tatiana would make no difficulty, of course; but Kapiton had declared in the hearing of all that he had but one head to lose, not two or three. . . . Gerasim turned rapid sullen looks on every one, would not budge from the steps of the maids' quarters, and seemed to guess that some mischief was being hatched against him. They met together. Among them was an old sideboard waiter, nicknamed Uncle Tail, to whom every one looked respectfully for counsel, though all they got out of him was, "Here's a pretty pass! to be sure, to be sure, to be sure!" As a preliminary measure of security, to provide against contingencies, they locked Kapiton up in the lumber-room where the filter was kept; then considered the question with

the gravest deliberation. It would, to be sure, be easy to have recourse
to force. But Heaven save us! there would be an uproar, the mistress
would be put out—it would be awful! What should they do? They
thought and thought, and at last thought out a solution. It had many
a time been observed that Gerasim could not bear drunkards. . . .
As he sat at the gates, he would always turn away with disgust when
some one passed by intoxicated, with unsteady steps and his cap on
one side of his ear. They resolved that Tatiana should be instructed
to pretend to be tipsy, and should pass by Gerasim staggering and
reeling about. The poor girl refused for a long while to agree to
this, but they persuaded her at last; she saw, too, that it was the
only possible way of getting rid of her adorer. She went out. Kapiton
was released from the lumber-room; for, after all, he had an interest
in the affair. Gerasim was sitting on the curb-stone at the gates,
scraping the ground with a spade. . . . From behind every corner,
from behind every window-blind, the others were watching him. . . .
The trick succeeded beyond all expectations. On seeing Tatiana, at
first, he nodded as usual, making caressing, inarticulate sounds; then
he looked carefully at her, dropped his spade, jumped up, went up
to her, brought his face close to her face. . . . In her fright she staggered more than ever, and shut her eyes. . . . He took her by the
arm, whirled her right across the yard, and going into the room
where the council had been sitting, pushed her straight at Kapiton.
Tatiana fairly swooned away. . . . Gerasim stood, looked at her,
waved his hand, laughed, and went off, stepping heavily, to his
garret. . . . For the next twenty-four hours, he did not come out of
it. The postilion Antipka said afterwards that he saw Gerasim
through a crack in the wall, sitting on his bedstead, his face in his
hand. From time to time he uttered soft regular sounds; he was
wailing a dirge, that is, swaying backwards and forwards with his
eyes shut, and shaking his head as drivers or bargemen do when
they chant their melancholy songs. Antipka could not bear it, and
he came away from the crack. When Gerasim came out of the
garret next day, no particular change could be observed in him.
He only seemed, as it were, more morose, and took not the slightest
notice of Tatiana or Kapiton. The same evening, they both had to
appear before their mistress with geese under their arms, and in
a week's time they were married. Even on the day of the wedding
Gerasim showed no change of any sort in his behavior. Only, he

came back from the river without water, he had somehow broken the barrel on the road; and at night, in the stable, he washed and rubbed down his horse so vigorously, that it swayed like a blade of grass in the wind, and staggered from one leg to the other under his fists of iron.

All this had taken place in the spring. Another year passed by, during which Kapiton became a hopeless drunkard, and as being absolutely of no use for anything, was sent away with the store wagons to a distant village with his wife. On the day of his departure, he put a very good face on it at first, and declared that he would always be at home, send him where they would, even to the other end of the world; but later on he lost heart, began grumbling that he was being taken to uneducated people, and collapsed so completely at last that he could not even put his own hat on. Some charitable soul stuck it on his forehead, set the peak straight in front, and thrust it on with a slap from above. When everything was quite ready, and the peasants already held the reins in their hands, and were only waiting for the words "With God's blessing!" to start, Gerasim came out of his garret, went up to Tatiana, and gave her as a parting present a red cotton handkerchief he had bought for her a year ago. Tatiana, who had up to that instant borne all the revolting details of her life with great indifference, could not control herself upon that; she burst into tears, and as she took her seat in the cart, she kissed Gerasim three times like a good Christian. He meant to accompany her as far as the town-barrier, and did walk beside her cart for a while, but he stopped suddenly at the Crimean ford, waved his hand, and walked away along the riverside.

It was getting towards evening. He walked slowly, watching the water. All of a sudden he fancied something was floundering in the mud close to the bank. He stooped over, and saw a little white-and-black puppy, who, in spite of all its efforts, could not get out of the water; it was struggling, slipping back, and trembling all over its thin wet little body. Gerasim looked at the unlucky little dog, picked it up with one hand, put it into the bosom of his coat, and hurried with long steps homewards. He went into his garret, put the rescued puppy on his bed, covered it with his thick overcoat, ran first to the stable for straw, and then to the kitchen for a cup of milk. Carefully folding back the overcoat, and spreading out the straw, he set the milk on the bedstead. The poor little puppy was not more than three weeks old, its eyes were only just open—one eye still seemed rather larger than the other; it did not know how to lap out of a cup, and did nothing but shiver and blink. Gerasim took hold of its head softly with two fingers, and dipped its little nose into the milk. The pup suddenly began lapping greedily, sniffing, shaking itself, and choking. Gerasim watched and watched it, and all at once he laughed outright. . . . All night long he was waiting on it, keeping it covered, and rubbing it dry. He fell asleep himself at last, and slept quietly and happily by its side.

No mother could have looked after her baby as Gerasim looked after his little nursling. At first, she—for the pup turned out to be a bitch—was very weak, feeble, and ugly, but by degrees she grew stronger and improved in looks, and thanks to the unflagging care of her preserver, in eight months' time she was transformed into a very pretty dog of the spaniel breed, with long ears, a bushy spiral tail, and large expressive eyes. She was devotedly attached to Gerasim, and was never a yard from his side; she always followed him about wagging her tail. He had even given her a name—the dumb know that their inarticulate noises call the attention of others. He called her Mumu. All the servants in the house liked her, and called her Mumu, too. She was very intelligent, she was friendly with every one, but was only fond of Gerasim. Gerasim, on his side, loved her passionately, and he did not like it when other people stroked her; whether he was afraid for her, or jealous—God knows! She used to wake him in the morning, pulling at his coat; she used to take the reins in her mouth, and bring him up the old horse that carried the water, with whom she was on very friendly terms. With a face of great importance, she used to go with him to the river; she used to watch his brooms and spades, and never allowed any one to go into his garret. He cut a little hole in his door on purpose for her, and she seemed to feel that only in Gerasim's garret she was completely mistress and at home; and directly she went in, she used to jump with a satisfied air upon the bed. At night she did not sleep at all, but she never barked without sufficient cause, like some stupid house-dog, who, sitting on its hind-legs, blinking, with its nose in the air, barks simply from dullness, at the stars, usually three times in succession. No! Mumu's delicate little voice was never raised without good reason; either some stranger was passing close to the fence, or there was some suspicious sound or rustle somewhere. . . . In fact, she was an excellent watchdog. It is true that there was another dog in the yard, a tawny old dog with brown spots, called Wolf, but he was never, even at night, let off the chain; and, indeed, he was so decrepit that he did not even wish for freedom. He used to lie curled up in his kennel, and only rarely uttered a sleepy, almost noiseless bark, which broke off at once, as though he were himself aware of its uselessness. Mumu never went into the mistress's house; and when Gerasim carried wood into the rooms, she always stayed behind, impatiently waiting for him at the steps, pricking up her ears and turning her head to right and to left at the slightest creak of the door. . . .

So passed another year. Gerasim went on performing his duties as house-porter, and was very well content with his lot, when suddenly an unexpected incident occurred. . . . One fine summer day the old lady was walking up and down the drawing-room with her dependants. She was in high spirits; she laughed and made jokes. Her servile companions laughed and joked too, but they did not feel particularly mirthful; the household did not much like it, when their mistress was in a lively mood, for, to begin with, she expected from every one prompt and complete participation in her merriment, and was furious if any one showed a face that did not beam with delight, and secondly, these outbursts never lasted long with her, and were usually followed by a sour and gloomy mood. That day she had got up in a lucky hour; at cards she took the four knaves, which means the fulfillment of one's wishes (she used to try her fortune on the cards every morning), and her tea struck her as particularly delicious, for which her maid was rewarded by words of praise, and by twopence in money. With a sweet smile on her wrinkled lips, the lady walked about the drawing-room and went up to the window. A flower-garden had been laid out before the window, and in the very middle bed, under a rose-bush, lay Mumu busily gnawing a bone. The lady caught sight of her.

"Mercy on us!" she cried suddenly; "what dog is that?"

The companion, addressed by the old lady, hesitated, poor thing, in that wretched state of uneasiness which is common in any person in a dependent position who doesn't know very well what significance to give to the exclamation of a superior.

"I d . . . d . . . don't know," she faltered: "I fancy it's the dumb man's dog."

"Mercy!" the lady cut her short: "but it's a charming little dog! order it to be brought in. Has he had it long? How is it I've never seen it before? . . . Order it to be brought in."

The companion flew at once into the hall.

"Boy, boy!" she shouted: "bring Mumu in at once! She's in the flower-garden."

"Her name's Mumu then," observed the lady: "a very nice name."

"Oh, very, indeed!" chimed in the companion. "Make haste, Stepan!"

Stepan, a sturdily-built young fellow, whose duties were those of a footman, rushed head-long into the flower-garden, and tried to capture Mumu, but she cleverly slipped from his fingers, and with her tail in the air, fled full speed to Gerasim, who was at that instant in the kitchen, knocking out and cleaning a barrel, turning it upside down in his hands like a child's drum. Stepan ran after her, and tried to catch her just at her master's feet; but the sensible dog would not let a stranger touch her, and with a bound, she got away. Gerasim looked on with a smile at all this ado; at last, Stepan got up, much amazed, and hurriedly explained to him by signs that the mistress wanted the dog brought in to her. Gerasim was a little astonished; he called Mumu, however, picked her up, and handed her over to Stepan. Stepan carried her into the drawing-room, and put her down on the parquette floor. The old lady began calling the dog to her in a coaxing voice. Mumu, who had never in her life been in such magnificent apartments, was very much frightened, and made a rush for the door, but, being driven back by the obsequious Stepan, she began trembling, and huddled close up against the wall.

"Mumu, Mumu, come to me, come to your mistress," said the lady; "come, silly thing . . . don't be afraid."

"Come, Mumu, come to the mistress," repeated the companions. "Come along!"

But Mumu looked round her uneasily, and did not stir.

"Bring her something to eat," said the old lady. "How stupid she is! she won't come to her mistress. What's she afraid of?"

"She's not used to your honor yet," ventured one of the companions in a timid and conciliatory voice.

Stepan brought in a saucer of milk, and set it down before Mumu, but Mumu would not even sniff at the milk, and still shivered, and looked round as before.

"Ah, what a silly you are!" said the lady, and going up to her, she stooped down, and was about to stroke her, but Mumu turned her head abruptly, and showed her teeth. The lady hurriedly drew back her hand. . . .

A momentary silence followed. Mumu gave a faint whine, as though she would complain and apologise. . . . The old lady moved back, scowling. The dog's sudden movement had frightened her.

"Ah!" shrieked all the companions at once, "she's not bitten you, has she? Heaven forbid! (Mumu had never bitten any one in her life.) Ah! ah!"

"Take her away," said the old lady in a changed voice. "Wretched little dog! What a spiteful creature!"

And, turning round deliberately, she went towards her boudoir. Her companions looked timidly at one another, and were about to follow her, but she stopped, stared coldly at them, and said, "What's that for, pray? I've not called you," and went out.

The companions waved their hands to Stepan in despair. He picked up Mumu, and flung her promptly outside the door, just at Gerasim's feet, and half-an-hour later a profound stillness reigned in the house, and the old lady sat on her sofa looking blacker than a thunder-cloud.

What trifles, if you think of it, will sometimes disturb any one!

Till evening the lady was out of humor; she did not talk to any one, did not play cards, and passed a bad night. She fancied the eau-de-Cologne they gave her was not the same as she usually had, and that her pillow smelt of soap, and she made the wardrobe-maid smell all the bed linen—in fact she was very upset and cross altogether. Next morning she ordered Gavrila to be summoned an hour earlier than usual.

"Tell me, please," she began, directly the latter, not without some inward trepidation, crossed the threshold of her boudoir, "what dog was that barking all night in our yard? It wouldn't let me sleep!"

"A dog, 'm . . . what dog, 'm . . . may be, the dumb man's dog, 'm," he brought out in a rather unsteady voice.

"I don't know whether it was the dumb man's or whose, but it wouldn't let me sleep. And I wonder what we have such a lot of dogs for! I wish to know. We have a yard dog, haven't we?"

"Oh yes, 'm, we have, 'm. Wolf, 'm."

"Well, why more, what do we want more dogs for? It's simply

introducing disorder. There's no one in control in the house—that's what it is. And what does the dumb man want with a dog? Who gave him leave to keep dogs in my yard? Yesterday I went to the window, and there it was lying in the flower-garden; it had dragged in some nastiness it was gnawing, and my roses are planted there. . . ."

The lady ceased.

"Let her be gone from today . . . do you hear?"

"Yes, 'm."

"Today. Now go. I will send for you later for the report."

Gavrila went away.

As he went through the drawing-room, the steward by way of maintaining order moved a bell from one table to another; he stealthily blew his duck-like nose in the hall, and went into the outer-hall. In the outer-hall, on a locker was Stepan asleep in the attitude of a slain warrior in a battalion picture, his bare legs thrust out below the coat which served him for a blanket. The steward gave him a shove, and whispered some instructions to him, to which Stepan responded with something between a yawn and a laugh. The steward went away, and Stepan got up, put on his coat and his boots, went out and stood on the steps. Five minutes had not passed before Gerasim made his appearance with a huge bundle of hewn logs on his back, accompanied by the inseparable Mumu. (The lady had given orders that her bedroom and boudoir should be heated at times even in the summer.) Gerasim turned sideways before the door, shoved it open with his shoulder, and staggered into the house with his load. Mumu, as usual, stayed behind to wait for him. Then Stepan, seizing his chance, suddenly pounced on her, like a kite on a chicken, held her down to the ground, gathered her up in his arms, and without even putting on his cap, ran out of the yard with her, got into the first fly he met, and galloped off to a market-place. There he soon found a purchaser, to whom he sold her for a shilling, on condition that he would keep her for at least a week tied up; then he returned at once. But before he got home, he got off the fly, and going right round the yard, jumped over the fence into the yard from a back street. He was afraid to go in at the gate for fear of meeting Gerasim.

His anxiety was unnecessary, however; Gerasim was no longer in the yard. On coming out of the house he had at once missed Mumu.

He never remembered her failing to wait for his return, and began
running up and down, looking for her, and calling her in his own
way. . . . He rushed up to his garret, up to the hay-loft, ran out into
the street, this way and that. . . . She was lost! He turned to the
other serfs, with the most despairing signs, questioned them about
her, pointing to her height from the ground, describing her with his
hands. . . . Some of them really did not know what had become of
Mumu, and merely shook their heads; others did know, and smiled
to him for all response, while the steward assumed an important air,
and began scolding the coachmen. Then Gerasim ran right away out
of the yard.

It was dark by the time he came back. From his worn-out look,
his unsteady walk, and his dusty clothes, it might be surmised that
he had been running over half Moscow. He stood still opposite the
windows of the mistress' house, took a searching look at the steps
where a group of house-serfs were crowded together, turned away,
and uttered once more his inarticulate "Mumu." Mumu did not answer. He went away. Every one looked after him, but no one smiled
or said a word, and the inquisitive postilion Antipka reported next
morning in the kitchen that the dumb man had been groaning all
night.

All the next day Gerasim did not show himself, so that they were
obliged to send the coachman Potap for water instead of him, at
which the coachman Potap was anything but pleased. The lady asked
Gavrila if her orders had been carried out. Gavrila replied that they
had. The next morning Gerasim came out of his garret, and went
about his work. He came in to his dinner, ate it, and went out again,
without a greeting to any one. His face, which had always been
lifeless, as with all deaf-mutes, seemed now to be turned to stone.
After dinner he went out of the yard again, but not for long; he
came back, and went straight up to the hay-loft. Night came on,
a clear moonlight night. Gerasim lay breathing heavily, and incessantly turning from side to side. Suddenly he felt something pull at
the skirt of his coat. He started, but did not raise his head, and even
shut his eyes tighter. But again there was a pull, stronger than before; he jumped up . . . before him, with an end of string round her
neck, was Mumu, twisting and turning. A prolonged cry of delight
broke from his speechless breast; he caught up Mumu, and hugged
her tight in his arms, she licked his nose and eyes, and beard and

moustache, all in one instant. . . . He stood a little, thought a minute, crept cautiously down from the hay-loft, looked round, and having satisfied himself that no one could see him, made his way successfully to his garret. Gerasim had guessed before that his dog had not got lost by her own doing, that she must have been taken away by the mistress' orders; the servants had explained to him by signs that his Mumu had snapped at her, and he determined to take his own measures. First he fed Mumu with a bit of bread, fondled her, and put her to bed, then he fell to meditating, and spent the whole night long in meditating how he could best conceal her. At last he decided to leave her all day in the garret, and only to come in now and then to see her, and to take her out at night. The hole in the door he stopped up effectually with his old overcoat, and almost before it was light he was already in the yard, as though nothing had happened, even—innocent guile!—the same expression of melancholy on his face. It did not even occur to the poor deaf man that Mumu would betray herself by her whining; in reality, every one in the house was soon aware that the dumb man's dog had come back, and was locked up in his garret, but from sympathy with him and with her, and partly, perhaps, from dread of him, they did not let him know that they had found out his secret. The steward scratched his head, and gave a despairing wave of his hand, as much as to say, "Well, well, God have mercy on him! If only it doesn't come to the mistress' ears!"

But the dumb man had never shown such energy as on that day; he cleaned and scraped the whole courtyard, pulled up every single weed with his own hand, tugged up every stake in the fence of the flower-garden, to satisfy himself that they were strong enough, and unaided drove them in again; in fact, he toiled and labored so that even the old lady noticed his zeal. Twice in the course of the day Gerasim went stealthily in to see his prisoner; when night came on, he lay down to sleep with her in the garret, not in the hay-loft, and only at two o'clock in the night he went out to take her a turn in the fresh air. After walking about the courtyard a good while with her, he was just turning back, when suddenly a rustle was heard behind the fence on the side of the back street. Mumu pricked up her ears, growled—went up to the fence, sniffed, and gave vent to a loud shrill bark. Some drunkard had thought fit to take refuge under the fence for the night. At that very time the old lady had just fallen asleep after a prolonged fit of "nervous agitation"; these fits of agitation always overtook her after too hearty a supper. The sudden bark waked her up: her heart palpitated, and she felt faint. "Girls, girls!" she moaned. "Girls!" The terrified maids ran into her bedroom. "Oh, oh, I am dying!" she said, flinging her arms about in her agitation. "Again, that dog again! . . . Oh, send for the doctor. They mean to be the death of me. . . . The dog, the dog again! Oh!" And she let her head fall back, which always signified a swoon. They rushed for the doctor, that is, for the household physician, Hariton. This doctor, whose whole qualification consisted in wearing soft-soled boots, knew how to feel the pulse delicately. He used to sleep fourteen hours out of the twenty-four, but the rest of the time he was always sighing, and continually dosing the old lady with cherrybay drops. This doctor ran up at once, fumigated the room with burnt feathers, and when the old lady opened her eyes, promptly offered her a wineglass of the hallowed drops on a silver tray. The old lady took them, but began again at once in a tearful voice complaining of the dog, of Gavrila, and of her fate, declaring that she was a poor old woman, and that every one had forsaken her, no one pitied her, everyone wished her dead. Meanwhile the luckless Mumu had gone on barking, while Gerasim tried in vain to call her away from the fence. "There . . . there . . . again," groaned the old lady, and once more she turned up the whites of her eyes. The doctor whispered to a maid, she rushed into the outer-hall, and shook Stepan, he ran to wake Gavrila, Gavrila in a fury ordered the whole household to get up.

Gerasim turned round, saw lights and shadows moving in the windows, and with an instinct of coming trouble in his heart, put Mumu under his arm, ran into his garret, and locked himself in. A few minutes later five men were banging at his door, but feeling the resistance of the bolt, they stopped. Gavrila ran up in a fearful state of mind, and ordered them all to wait there and watch till morning. Then he flew off himself to the maids' quarter, and through an old companion, Liubov Liubimovna, with whose assistance he used to steal tea, sugar, and other groceries and to falsify the accounts, sent word to the mistress that the dog had unhappily run back from somewhere, but that tomorrow she should be killed, and would the mistress be so gracious as not to be angry and to overlook it. The old lady would probably not have been so soon appeased, but the doctor had in his haste given her fully forty drops instead of twelve. The strong dose of narcotic acted; in a quarter of an hour the old lady was in a sound and peaceful sleep; while Gerasim was lying with a white face on his bed, holding Mumu's mouth tightly shut.

Next morning the lady woke up rather late. Gavrila was waiting till she should be awake, to give the order for a final assault on Gerasim's stronghold, while he prepared himself to face a fearful storm. But the storm did not come off. The old lady lay in bed and sent for the eldest of her dependent companions.

"Liubov Liubimovna," she began in a subdued weak voice—she was fond of playing the part of an oppressed and forsaken victim; needless to say, every one in the house was made extremely uncomfortable at such times—"Liubov Liubimovna, you see my position; go, my love, to Gavrila Andreitch, and talk to him a little. Can he really prize some wretched cur above the repose—the very life—of his mistress? I could not bear to think so," she added, with an expression of deep feeling. "Go, my love; be so good as to go to Gavrila Andreitch for me."

Liubov Liubimovna went to Gavrila's room. What conversation passed between them is not known, but a short time after, a whole crowd of people was moving across the yard in the direction of Gerasim's garret. Gavrila walked in front, holding his cap on with his hand, though there was no wind. The footmen and cooks were close behind him; Uncle Tail was looking out of a window, giving instructions, that is to say, simply waving his hands. At the rear there was a crowd of small boys skipping and hopping along; half of them were outsiders who had run up. On the narrow staircase leading to the garret sat one guard; at the door were standing two more with sticks. They began to mount the stairs, which they entirely blocked up. Gavrila went up to the door, knocked with his fist, shouting, "Open the door!"

A stifled bark was audible, but there was no answer.

"Open the door, I tell you," he repeated.

"But, Gavrila Andreitch," Stepan observed from below, "he's deaf, you know—he doesn't hear."

They all laughed.

"What are we to do?" Gavrila rejoined from above.

"Why, there's a hole there in the door," answered Stepan, "so you shake the stick in there."

Gavrila bent down.

"He's stuffed it up with a coat or something."

"Well, you just push the coat in."

At this moment a smothered bark was heard again.

"See, see—she speaks for herself," was remarked in the crowd, and again they laughed.

Gavrila scratched his ear.

"No, mate," he responded at last, "you can poke the coat in yourself, if you like."

"All right, let me."

And Stepan scrambled up, took the stick, pushed in the coat, and began waving the stick about in the opening, saying, "Come out, come out!" as he did so. He was still waving the stick, when suddenly the door of the garret was flung open; all the crowd flew pell-mell down the stairs instantly, Gavrila first of all. Uncle Tail locked the window.

"Come, come, come," shouted Gavrila from the yard, "mind what you're about."

Gerasim stood without stirring in his doorway. The crowd gathered at the foot of the stairs. Gerasim, with his arms akimbo, looked down at all these poor creatures in German coats; in his red peasant's shirt he looked like a giant before them. Gavrila took a step forward.

"Mind, mate," said he, "don't be insolent."

And he began to explain to him by signs that the mistress insisted on having his dog; that he must hand it over at once, or it would be the worse for him.

Gerasim looked at him, pointed to the dog, made a motion with his hand round his neck, as though he were pulling a noose tight, and glanced with a face of inquiry at the steward.

"Yes, yes," the latter assented, nodding; "yes, just so."

Gerasim dropped his eyes, then all of a sudden roused himself and pointed to Mumu, who was all the while standing beside him, innocently wagging her tail and pricking up her ears inquisitively. Then he repeated the strangling action round his neck and significantly struck himself on the breast, as though announcing he would take upon himself the task of killing Mumu.

"But you'll deceive us," Gavrila waved back in response.

Gerasim looked at him, smiled scornfully, struck himself again on the breast, and slammed-to the door.

They all looked at one another in silence.

"What does that mean?" Gavrila began. "He's locked himself in."

"Let him be, Gavrila Andreitch," Stepan advised; "he'll do it if he's promised. He's like that, you know. . . . If he makes a promise, it's a certain thing. He's not like us others in that. The truth's the truth with him. Yes, indeed."

"Yes," they all repeated, nodding their heads, "yes—that's so—yes."

Uncle Tail opened his window, and he too said, "Yes."

"Well, maybe, we shall see," responded Gavrila; "anyway, we won't take off the guard. Here you, Eroshka!" he added, addressing a poor fellow in a yellow nankeen coat, who considered himself to be a gardener, "what have you to do? Take a stick and sit here, and if anything happens, run to me at once!"

Eroshka took a stick, and sat down on the bottom stair. The crowd dispersed, all except a few inquisitive small boys, while Gavrila went home and sent word through Liubov Liubimovna to the mistress, that everything had been done, while he sent a postilion for a policeman in case of need. The old lady tied a knot in her handkerchief, sprinkled some eau-de-Cologne on it, sniffed at it, and rubbed her temples with it, drank some tea, and, being still under the influence of the cherrybay drops, fell asleep again.

An hour after all this hubbub the garret door opened, and Gerasim showed himself. He had on his best coat; he was leading Mumu by a string. Eroshka moved aside and let him pass. Gerasim went to the gates. All the small boys in the yard stared at him in silence. He did not even turn round; he only put his cap on in the street. Gavrila sent the same Eroshka to follow him and keep watch on him as a spy. Eroshka, seeing from a distance that he had gone into a cookshop with his dog, waited for him to come out again.

Gerasim was well known at the cookshop, and his signs were understood. He asked for cabbage soup with meat in it, and sat down with his arms on the table. Mumu stood beside his chair, looking calmly at him with her intelligent eyes. Her coat was glossy; one could see she had just been combed down. They brought Gerasim the soup. He crumbled some bread into it, cut the meat up small, and put the plate on the ground. Mumu began eating in her usual refined way, her little muzzle daintily held so as scarcely to touch her food. Gerasim gazed a long while at her; two big tears suddenly rolled from his eyes; one fell on the dog's brow, the other into the soup. He shaded his face with his hand. Mumu ate up half the plateful, and came away from it, licking her lips. Gerasim got up, paid for the soup, and went out, followed by the rather perplexed glances of the waiter. Eroshka, seeing Gerasim, hid round a corner, and letting him get in front, followed him again.

Gerasim walked without haste, still holding Mumu by a string. When he got to the corner of the street, he stood still as though reflecting, and suddenly set off with rapid steps to the Crimean Ford. On the way he went into the yard of a house, where a lodge was being built, and carried away two bricks under his arm. At the Crimean Ford, he turned along the bank, went to a place where there were two little rowing-boats fastened to stakes (he had noticed them there before), and jumped into one of them with Mumu. A lame old man came out of a shed in the corner of a kitchen-garden and shouted after him; but Gerasim only nodded, and began rowing so vigorously, though against stream, that in an instant he had darted two hundred yards away. The old man stood for a while, scratched his back first with the left and then with the right hand, and went back hobbling to the shed.

Gerasim rowed on and on. Moscow was soon left behind. Meadows stretched each side of the bank, market gardens, fields, and copses; peasants' huts began to make their appearance. There was the fragrance of the country. He threw down his oars, bent his head down to Mumu, who was sitting facing him on a dry cross seat—the bottom of the boat was full of water—and stayed motionless, his mighty hands clasped upon her back, while the boat was gradually carried back by the current towards the town. At last Gerasim drew himself up hurriedly, with a sort of sick anger in his face, he tied up the bricks he had taken with string, made a running noose, put it round Mumu's neck, lifted her up over the river, and for the last time looked at her . . . she watched him confidingly and without any fear, faintly wagging her tail. He turned away, frowned, and wrung his hands. . . . Gerasim heard nothing, neither the quick shrill whine of Mumu as she fell, nor the heavy splash of the water; for him the noisiest day was soundless and silent as even the stillest night is not silent to us. When he opened his eyes again, little wavelets were hurrying over the river, chasing one another; as before they broke against the boat's side, and only far away behind wide circles moved widening to the bank.

Directly Gerasim had vanished from Eroshka's sight, the latter returned home and reported what he had seen.

"Well, then," observed Stepan, "he'll drown her. Now we can feel easy about it. If he once promises a thing. . . ."

No one saw Gerasim during the day. He did not have dinner at home. Evening came on; they were all gathered together to supper, except him.

"What a strange creature that Gerasim is!" piped a fat laundry-maid; "fancy, upsetting himself like that over a dog. . . . Upon my word!"

"But Gerasim has been here," Stepan cried all at once, scraping up his porridge with a spoon.

"How? when?"

"Why, a couple of hours ago. Yes, indeed! I ran against him at the gate; he was going out again from here; he was coming out of the yard. I tried to ask him about his dog, but he wasn't in the best of humors, I could see. Well, he gave me a shove; I suppose he only meant to put me out of his way, as if he'd say, 'Let me go, do!' but he fetched me such a crack on my neck, so seriously, that—oh! oh!" And Stepan, who could not help laughing, shrugged up and rubbed the back of his head. "Yes," he added; "he has got a fist; it's something like a fist, there's no denying that!"

They all laughed at Stepan, and after supper they separated to go to bed.

Meanwhile, at that very time, a gigantic figure with a bag on his shoulders and a stick in his hand was eagerly and persistently stepping out along the T—— highroad. It was Gerasim. He was hurrying on without looking round; hurrying homewards, to his own village, to his own country. After drowning poor Mumu, he had run back to his garret, hurriedly packed a few things together in an old horse-cloth, tied it up in a bundle, tossed it on his shoulder, and so was ready. He had noticed the road carefully when he was brought to Moscow; the village his mistress had taken him from lay only about twenty miles off the highroad. He walked along it with a sort of invincible purpose, a desperate and at the same time joyous determination. He walked, his shoulders thrown back and his chest expanded; his eyes were fixed greedily straight before him. He hastened as though his old mother were waiting for him at home, as though she were calling him to her after long wanderings in strange parts, among strangers. The summer night, that was just drawing in, was still and warm; on one side, where the sun had set, the horizon was still light and faintly flushed with the last glow of the vanished day; on the other side a blue-grey twilight had already risen up. The night was coming up from that quarter. Quails were in hundreds around; corncrakes were calling to one another in the thickets. . . . Gerasim could not hear them; he could not hear the delicate night-whispering of the trees, by which his strong legs carried him, but he smelt the familiar scent of the ripening rye, which was wafted from the dark fields; he felt the wind, flying to meet him—the wind from home— beat caressingly upon his face, and play with his hair and his beard. He saw before him the whitening road homewards, straight as an arrow. He saw in the sky stars innumerable, lighting up his way, and stepped out, strong and bold as a lion, so that when the rising sun shed its moist rosy light upon the still fresh and unwearied traveler, already thirty miles lay between him and Moscow.

In a couple of days he was at home, in his little hut, to the great astonishment of the soldier's wife who had been put in there. After praying before the holy pictures, he set off at once to the village elder. The village elder was at first surprised; but the hay-cutting had just begun; Gerasim was a first-rate mower, and they put a scythe into his hand on the spot, and he went to mow in his old way, mowing so that the peasants were fairly astounded as they watched his wide sweeping strokes and the heaps he raked together. . . .

In Moscow the day after Gerasim's flight they missed him. They went to his garret, rummaged about in it, and spoke to Gavrila. He came, looked, shrugged his shoulders, and decided that the dumb man had either run away or had drowned himself with his stupid dog. They gave information to the police, and informed the lady. The old lady was furious, burst into tears, gave orders that he was to be found whatever happened, declared she had never ordered the dog to be destroyed, and, in fact, gave Gavrila such a rating that he could do nothing all day but shake his head and murmur, "Well!" until Uncle Tail checked him at last, sympathetically echoing "We-ell!" At last the news came from the country of Gerasim's being there. The old lady was somewhat pacified; at first she issued a mandate for him to be brought back without delay to Moscow; afterwards, however, she declared that such an ungrateful creature was absolutely of no use to her. Soon after this she died herself; and her heirs had no thought to spare for Gerasim; they let their mother's other servants redeem their freedom on payment of an annual rent.

And Gerasim is living still, a lonely man in his lonely hut; he is strong and healthy as before, and does the work of four men as before, and as before is serious and steady. But his neighbors have observed that ever since his return from Moscow he has quite given up the society of women; he will not even look at them, and does not keep even a single dog. "It's his good luck, though," the peasants reason; "that he can get on without female folk; and as for a dog—what need has he of a dog? you wouldn't get a thief to go into his yard for any money!" Such is the fame of the dumb man's Titanic strength.

For Discussion

1. Despite Gerasim's affliction and his state of isolation, he had an unmistakable dignity and human depth. Point out details which indicate that he was no run-of-the-mill servant. What qualities and virtues made him a sympathetic character? Show how the author revealed these qualities through Gerasim's actions and through what others said about him.

2. In tracing the chain of events which led to Gerasim's final, lonely state, Turgenev employed irony; that is, an outcome of events contrary to what would naturally be hoped for or expected. What, for example, became of Tatiana, the only girl to whom Gerasim ever showed affection? Do you see an ironic reversal of values in the behavior or manners of Mumu as compared with that of Tatiana? Explain.

3. In the case of Tatiana, how did the author reveal the lack of freedom in the lives of the serfs? How did he show evidence of class distinction even among the servants in the rich lady's household? How, for example, did Kapiton speak of Gerasim in his conversation with the steward?

4. Describe the rich old lady. Point out details which made clear her whims and moods. What did you find out about her from her attitude toward the servants?

5. Why do you think none of the servants opposed her treatment of them? In your opinion, were they completely devoid of self-respect and the ability to think for themselves? Explain. What did their action prior to Kapiton's wedding reveal about them?

6. Twice, the object of Gerasim's affection was taken away from him. How do you account for the fact that his fellow-servants, instead of standing by him, set out, by common consent, to deprive him of what he wanted?
7. Reread the last paragraph of the story. Show how the peasants completely missed the significance of Gerasim's way of living. Explain the irony of the last sentence.
8. There are several conflicts—external and internal—in this story. One external conflict is between the Russian nobility and the serfs. Explain. Describe other external conflicts you found in the story.
9. What was the main internal conflict which Gerasim had to resolve? What was the climax of the story? Was this also the resolution of the conflict? Explain.
10. Point out passages which reveal the lyrical quality in Turgenev's descriptions.

For Composition

1. In a short composition, explain why you think Turgenev called this story "Mumu" rather than "Gerasim." Do you think he was correct in naming the story after the dog? Why or why not?
2. With specific references to the story, write a critical essay in which you show how Turgenev reveals his mastery of characterization. Include the way he creates a sympathetic character like Gerasim, and the way he deals with those who are incapable of great love or great desires.
3. Gerasim, in the end, defied the forces of his environment and set out for the place of his birth. In a short theme, show that his action proved him a man apart, a truly integrated personality with an inate sense of freedom—a symbol, indeed, that if the spirit is free, no earthly chains can really bind a man.

Gustave Flaubert

The Legend of Saint Julian the Hospitaler

In France, the realistic tradition in fiction begun by Balzac was carried on by Gustave Flaubert * (1821–1880). His most famous novel,
Madame Bovary, was a carefully documented and pitiless view of middle-
class French life and romantic notions of love. When it appeared in 1857,
it caused a great controversy in France, but it established Flaubert as the
chief realist of his time.

Flaubert's work reveals his desire for absolute objectivity and accuracy
of description, as a means of presenting a realistic picture of life. For him
perfection of style was primary. It is said that he sometimes pondered a
whole day in search of the right word and a month in looking for the
exact phrase. He was also concerned with portraying characters and
situations as they were. To this end, he searched for the smallest
incidents, the slightest gesture of a character, the most minute details of
a setting which would make his story come alive. Even when he wrote
of a romantic, far-off time and place, as in "The Legend of Saint Julian the
Hospitaler," his characters were real and convincing. For all his realism,
however, Flaubert reveals in this story an awareness that man is not just a
product of his environment, that beyond the senses there is the world
of the spirit.

1

*J*ULIAN'S father and mother dwelt in a castle built on the slope
of a hill, in the heart of the woods.

The towers at its four corners had pointed roofs covered with
leaden tiles, and the foundation rested upon solid rocks, which
descended abruptly to the bottom of the moat.

In the courtyard, the stone flagging was as immaculate as the
floor of a church. Long rainspouts, representing dragons with yawning jaws, directed the water towards the cistern, and on each windowsill of the castle a basil or a heliotrope bush bloomed, in painted
flowerpots.

* güs tȧv′ flō bȧr′

A second enclosure, surrounded by a fence, comprised a fruit orchard, a garden decorated with figures wrought in bright-hued flowers, an arbor with several bowers, and a mall for the diversion of the pages. On the other side were the kennel, the stables, the bakery, the wine press and the barns. Around these spread a pasture, also enclosed by a strong hedge.

Peace had reigned so long that the portcullis was never lowered; the moats were filled with water; swallows built their nests in the cracks of the battlements, and as soon as the sun shone too strongly, the archer who all day long paced to and fro on the curtain, withdrew to the watchtower and slept soundly.

Inside the castle, the locks on the door shone brightly; costly tapestries hung in the apartments to keep out the cold; the closets overflowed with linen, the cellar was filled with casks of wine, and the oak chests fairly groaned under the weight of moneybags.

In the armory could be seen, between banners and the heads of wild beasts, weapons of all nations and of all ages, from the slings of the Amalekites and the javelins of the Garamantes, to the broadswords of the Saracens and the coats of mail of the Normans.

The largest spit in the kitchen could hold an ox; the chapel was as gorgeous as a king's oratory. There was even a Roman bath in a secluded part of the castle, though the good lord of the manor refrained from using it, as he deemed it a heathenish practice.

Wrapped always in cape made of fox-skins, he wandered about the castle, rendered justice among his vassals and settled his neighbors' quarrels. In the winter, he gazed dreamily at the falling snow, or had stories read aloud to him. But as soon as the fine weather returned, he would mount his mule and sally forth into the country roads, edged with ripening wheat, to talk with the peasants to whom he distributed advice. After a number of adventures he took unto himself a wife of high lineage.

She was pale and serious, and a trifle haughty. The horns of her headdress touched the top of the doors and the hem of her gown trailed far behind her. She conducted her household like a cloister. Every morning she distributed work to the maids, supervised the making of preserves and unguents, and afterwards passed her time in spinning, or in embroidering altar-cloths. In response to her fervent prayers, God granted her a son!

Then there was great rejoicing; and they gave a feast which lasted three days and four nights, with illuminations and soft music. Chickens as large as sheep, and the rarest spices were served; for the entertainment of the guests, a dwarf crept out of a pie; and when the bowls were too few, for the crowd swelled continuously, the wine was drunk from helmets and hunting horns.

The young mother did not appear at the feast. She was quietly resting in bed. One night she awoke, and beheld in a moonbeam that crept through the window something that looked like a moving shadow. It was an old man clad in sackcloth, who resembled a hermit. A rosary dangled at his side and he carried a beggar's sack on his shoulder. He approached the foot of the bed, and without opening his lips said: "Rejoice, O Mother! Thy son shall be a saint."

She would have cried out, but the old man, gliding along the moonbeam, rose through the air and disappeared. The songs of the banqueters grew louder. She could hear angels' voices, and her head sank back on the pillow, which was surmounted by the bone of a martyr, framed in precious stones.

The following day, the servants, upon being questioned, declared, to a man, that they had seen no hermit. Then, whether dream or fact, this must certainly have been a communication from heaven; but she took care not to speak of it, lest she should be accused of presumption.

The guests departed at daybreak, and Julian's father stood at the castle gate, where he had just bidden farewell to the last one, when a beggar suddenly emerged from the mist and confronted him. He was a gipsy—for he had a braided beard and wore silver bracelets on each arm. His eyes burned and, in an inspired way, he muttered some disconnected words: "Ah! Ah! thy son!—great bloodshed—great glory—happy always—an emperor's family."

Then he stopped to pick up the alms thrown to him, and disappeared in the tall grass.

The lord of the manor looked up and down the road and called as loudly as he could. But no one answered him! The wind only howled and the morning mists were fast dissolving.

He attributed his vision to a dullness of the brain resulting from too much sleep. "If I should speak of it," quoth he, "people would laugh at me." Still, the glory that was to be his son's dazzled him, albeit the meaning of the prophecy was not clear to him, and he even doubted that he had heard it.

The parents kept their secret from each other. But both cherished the child with equal devotion, and as they considered him marked by God, they had great regard for his person. His cradle was lined with the softest feathers, and a lamp representing a dove burned continually over it; three nurses rocked him night and day, and with his pink cheeks and blue eyes, brocaded cloak and embroidered cap, he looked like a little Jesus. He cut all his teeth without even a whimper.

When he was seven years old his mother taught him to sing, and his father lifted him upon a tall horse, to inspire him with courage. The child smiled with delight, and soon became familiar with everything pertaining to chargers. An old and very learned monk taught him the Gospel, the Arabic numerals, the Latin letters, and the art of painting delicate designs on vellum. They worked in the top of a tower, away from all noise and disturbance.

When the lesson was over, they would go down into the garden and study the flowers.

Sometimes a herd of cattle passed through the valley below, in charge of a man in Oriental dress. The lord of the manor, recognizing him as a merchant, would despatch a servant after him. The stranger, becoming confident, would stop on his way and after being ushered into the castle hall, would display pieces of velvet and silk, trinkets and strange objects whose use was unknown in those parts. Then, in due time, he would take leave, without having been molested and with a handsome profit.

At other times, a band of pilgrims would knock at the door. Their wet garments would be hung in front of the hearth and after they had been refreshed by food they would relate their travels, and discuss the uncertainty of vessels on the high seas, their long journeys across burning sands, the ferocity of the infidels, the caves of Syria, the Manger and the Holy Sepulchre. They made presents to the young heir of beautiful shells, which they carried in their cloaks.

The lord of the manor very often feasted his brothers-at-arms, and over the wine the old warriors would talk of battles and attacks, of war-machines and of the frightful wounds they had received, so that Julian, who was a listener, would scream with excitement; then his father felt convinced that some day he would be a conqueror. But in the evening, after the Angelus, when he passed through the crowd of beggars who clustered about the church door, he distributed his alms with so much modesty and nobility that his mother fully expected to see him become an archbishop in time.

His seat in the chapel was next to his parents, and no matter how long the services lasted, he remained kneeling on his *prie-dieu*, with folded hands and his velvet cap lying close beside him on the floor.

One day, during mass, he raised his head and beheld a little white mouse crawling out of a hole in the wall. It scrambled to the first altar step and then, after a few gambols, ran back in the same direction. On the following Sunday, the idea of seeing the mouse again worried him. It returned; and every Sunday after that he watched for it; and it annoyed him so much that he grew to hate it and resolved to do away with it.

So, having closed the door and strewn some crumbs on the steps of the altar, he placed himself in front of the hole with a stick. After a long while a pink snout appeared, and then the whole mouse crept out. He struck it lightly with his stick and stood stunned at the sight of the little, lifeless body. A drop of blood stained the floor. He wiped it away hastily with his sleeve, and picking up the mouse, threw it away, without saying a word about it to anyone.

All sorts of birds pecked at the seeds in the garden. He put some peas in a hollow reed, and when he heard birds chirping in a tree, he would approach cautiously, lift the tube and swell his cheeks; then, when the little creatures dropped about him in multitudes, he could not refrain from laughing and being delighted with his own cleverness.

One morning, as he was returning by way of the curtain, he beheld a fat pigeon sunning itself on the top of the wall. He paused to gaze at it; where he stood the rampart was cracked and a piece of stone was near at hand; he gave his arm a jerk and the well-aimed missile struck the bird squarely, sending it straight into the moat below.

He sprang after it, unmindful of the brambles, and ferreted around the bushes with the litheness of a young dog.

The pigeon hung with broken wings in the branches of a privet hedge.

The persistence of its life irritated the boy. He began to strangle it, and its convulsions made his heart beat quicker, and filled him with a wild, tumultuous voluptuousness, the last throb of its heart making him feel like fainting.

At supper that night, his father declared that at his age a boy should begin to hunt; and he arose and brought forth an old writing-book which contained, in questions and answers, everything pertaining to the pastime. In it, a master showed a supposed pupil how to train dogs and falcons, lay traps, recognize a stag by its fumets, and a fox or a wolf by footprints. He also taught the best way of discovering their tracks, how to start them, where their refuges are usually to be found, what winds are the most favorable, and further enumerated the various cries, and the rules of the quarry.

When Julian was able to recite all these things by heart, his father made up a pack of hounds for him. There were twenty-four greyhounds of Barbary, speedier than gazelles, but liable to get out of temper; seventeen couples of Breton dogs, great barkers, with broad chests and russet coats flecked with white. For wild-boar hunting and perilous doubling, there were forty boar-hounds as hairy as bears.

The red mastiffs of Tartary, almost as large as donkeys, with broad backs and straight legs, were destined for the pursuit of the wild bull. The black coats of the spaniels shone like satin; the barking of the setters equaled that of the beagles. In a special enclosure were eight growling bloodhounds that tugged at their chains and rolled their eyes, and these dogs leaped at men's throats and were not afraid even of lions.

All ate wheat bread, drank from marble troughs, and had high-sounding names.

Perhaps the falconry surpassed the pack; for the master of the castle, by paying great sums of money, had secured Caucasian hawks, Babylonian sakers, German gerfalcons, and pilgrim falcons captured on the cliffs edging the cold seas, in distant lands. They were housed in a thatched shed and were chained to the perch in the order of size. In front of them was a little grass-plot where, from time to time, they were allowed to disport themselves.

Bag-nets, baits, traps and all sorts of snares were manufactured.

Often they would take out pointers who would set almost immediately; then the whippers-in, advancing step by step, would cautiously spread a huge net over their motionless bodies. At the command, the dogs would bark and arouse the quails; and the ladies of the neighborhood, with their husbands, children and handmaids, would fall upon them and capture them with ease.

At other times they used a drum to start hares; and frequently foxes fell into the ditches prepared for them, while wolves caught their paws in the traps.

But Julian scorned these convenient contrivances; he preferred to hunt away from the crowd, alone with his steed and his falcon. It was almost always a large, snow-white, Scythian bird. His leather hood was ornamented with a plume, and on his blue feet were bells; and he perched firmly on his master's arm while they galloped across the plains. Then Julian would suddenly untie his tether and let him fly, and the bold bird would dart through the air like an arrow. One might perceive two spots circle around, unite, and then disappear in the blue heights. Presently the falcon would return with a mutilated bird, and perch again on his master's gauntlet with trembling wings.

Julian loved to sound his trumpet and follow his dogs over hills and streams, into the woods; and when the stag begin to moan under their teeth, he would kill it deftly, and delight in the fury of the brutes, which would devour the pieces spread out on the warm hide.

On foggy days, he would hide in the marshes to watch for wild geese, otters and wild ducks.

At daybreak, three equerries waited for him at the foot of the steps; and though the old monk leaned out of the dormer window and made signs to him to return, Julian would not look around.

He heeded neither the broiling sun, the rain nor the storm; he drank spring water and ate wild berries, and when he was tired, he lay down under a tree; and he would come home at night covered with earth and blood, with thistles in his hair and smelling of wild beasts. He grew to be like them. And when his mother kissed him, he responded coldly to her caress and seemed to be thinking of deep and serious things.

He killed bears with a knife, bulls with a hatchet, and wild boars with a spear; and once, with nothing but a stick, he defended himself against some wolves, which were gnawing corpses at the foot of a gibbet.

One winter morning he set out before daybreak, with a bow slung across his shoulder and a quiver of arrows attached to the pummel of his saddle. The hoofs of his steed beat the ground with regularity and his two beagles trotted close behind. The wind was blowing hard and icicles clung to his cloak. A part of the horizon cleared, and he beheld some rabbits playing around their burrows. In an instant, the two dogs were upon them, and seizing as many as they could, they broke their backs in the twinkling of an eye.

Soon he came to a forest. A woodcock, paralyzed by the cold, perched on a branch, with its head hidden under its wing. Julian, with a lunge of his sword, cut off its feet, and without stopping to pick it up, rode away.

Three hours later he found himself on the top of a mountain so high that the sky seemed almost black. In front of him, a long, flat rock hung over a precipice, and at the end, two wild goats stood gazing down into the abyss. As he had no arrows (for he had left his steed behind), he thought he would climb down to where they stood; and with bare feet and bent back he at last reached the first goat and thrust his dagger below its ribs. But the second animal, in its terror, leaped into the precipice. Julian threw himself forward to strike it, but his right foot slipped, and he fell, face downward and with outstretched arms, over the body of the first goat.

After he returned to the plains, he followed a stream bordered by willows. From time to time, some cranes, flying low, passed over his head. He killed them with his whip, never missing a bird. He beheld in the distance the gleam of a lake which appeared to be of lead, and in the middle of it was an animal he had never seen before, a beaver with a black muzzle. Notwithstanding the distance that separated them, an arrow ended its life and Julian only regretted that he was not able to carry the skin home with him.

Then he entered an avenue of tall trees, the tops of which formed a triumphal arch to the entrance of a forest. A deer sprang out of the thicket and a badger crawled out of its hole, a stag appeared in the road, and a peacock spread its fan-shape tail on the grass—and after he had slain them all, other deer, other stags, other badgers, other peacocks, and jays, blackbirds, foxes, porcupines, polecats, and lynxes, appeared; in fact, a host of beasts that grew more and more numerous with every step he took. Trembling, and with a look of appeal in their eyes, they gathered around Julian, but he did not stop slaying them; and so intent was he on stretching his bow, drawing his sword and whipping out his knife, that he had little thought for aught else. He knew that he was hunting in some country since an indefinite time, through the very fact of his existence, as everything seemed to occur with the ease one experiences in dreams. But presently an extraordinary sight made him pause.

He beheld a valley shaped like a circus and filled with stags which, huddled together, were warming one another with the vapor of their breaths that mingled with the early mist.

For a few minutes, he almost choked with pleasure at the prospect of so great a carnage. Then he sprang from his horse, rolled up his sleeves, and began to aim.

When the first arrow whizzed through the air, the stags turned their heads simultaneously. They huddled closer, uttered plaintive cries, and a great agitation seized the whole herd. The edge of the valley was too high to admit of flight; and the animals ran around the enclosure in their efforts to escape. Julian aimed, stretched his bow and his arrows fell as fast and thick as raindrops in a shower.

Maddened with terror, the stags fought and reared and climbed on top of one another; their antlers and bodies formed a moving mountain which tumbled to pieces whenever it displaced itself.

Finally the last one expired. Their bodies lay stretched out on the sand with foam gushing from the nostrils and the bowels protruding. The heaving of their bellies grew less and less noticeable, and presently all was still.

Night came, and behind the trees, through the branches, the sky appeared like a sheet of blood.

Julian leaned against a tree and gazed with dilated eyes at the enormous slaughter. He was now unable to comprehend how he had accomplished it.

On the opposite side of the valley, he suddenly beheld a large stag, with a doe and their fawn. The buck was black and of enormous size; he had a white beard and carried sixteen antlers. His mate was the color of dead leaves, and she browsed upon the grass, while the fawn, clinging to her udder, followed her step by step.

Again the bow was stretched, and instantly the fawn dropped dead, and seeing this, its mother raised her head and uttered a poignant, almost human wail of agony. Exasperated, Julian thrust his knife into her chest, and felled her to the ground.

The great stag had watched everything and suddenly he sprang forward. Julian aimed his last arrow at the beast. It struck him between his antlers and stuck there.

The stag did not appear to notice it; leaping over the bodies, he was coming nearer and nearer with the intention, Julian thought, of charging at him and ripping him open, and he recoiled with inexpressible horror. But presently the huge animal halted, and, with eyes aflame and the solemn air of a patriarch and a judge, repeated thrice, while a bell tolled in the distance:

"Accursed! Accursed! Accursed! some day, ferocious soul, thou wilt murder thy father and thy mother!"

Then he sank on his knees, gently closed his lids and expired.

At first Julian was stunned, and then a sudden lassitude and an immense sadness came over him. Holding his head between his hands, he wept for a long time.

His steed had wandered away; his dogs had forsaken him; the solitude seemed to threaten him with unknown perils. Impelled by a sense of sickening terror, he ran across the fields, and choosing a path at random, found himself almost immediately at the gates of the castle.

That night he could not rest, for, by the flickering light of the hanging lamp, he beheld again the huge black stag. He fought against the obsession of the prediction and kept repeating: "No! No! No! I cannot slay them!" and then he thought: "Still, supposing I desired to?—" and he feared that the devil might inspire him with this desire.

During three months, his distracted mother prayed at his bedside, and his father paced the halls of the castle in anguish. He consulted the most celebrated physicians, who prescribed quantities of medicines. Julian's illness, they declared, was due to some injurious wind or to amorous desire. But in reply to their questions, the young man only shook his head. After a time, his strength returned, and he was able to take a walk in the courtyard, supported by his father and the old monk.

But after he had completely recovered, he refused to hunt.

His father, hoping to please him, presented him with a large Saracen saber.

It was placed on a panoply that hung on a pillar, and a ladder was required to reach it. Julian climbed up to it one day, but the heavy weapon slipped from his grasp, and in falling grazed his father and tore his cloak. Julian, believing he had killed him, fell in a swoon.

After that, he carefully avoided weapons. The sight of a naked sword made him grow pale, and this weakness caused great distress to his family.

In the end, the old monk ordered him in the name of God, and of his forefathers, once more to indulge in the sports of a nobleman.

The equerries diverted themselves every day with javelins and Julian soon excelled in the practice.

He was able to send a javelin into bottles, to break the teeth of the weather-cocks on the castle and to strike doornails at a distance of one hundred feet.

One summer evening, at the hour when dusk renders objects indistinct, he was in the arbor in the garden, and thought he saw two white wings in the background hovering around the espalier. Not for a moment did he doubt that it was a stork, and so he threw his javelin at it.

A heart-rending scream pierced the air.

He had struck his mother, whose cap and long streamers remained nailed to the wall.

Julian fled from home and never returned.

2

He joined a horde of adventurers who were passing through the place.

He learned what it was to suffer hunger, thirst, sickness and filth. He grew accustomed to the din of battles and to the sight of dying men. The wind tanned his skin. His limbs became hardened through contact with armor, and as he was very strong and brave, temperate and of good counsel, he easily obtained command of a company.

At the outset of a battle, he would electrify his soldiers by a motion of his sword. He would climb the walls of a citadel with a knotted rope, at night, rocked by the storm, while sparks of fire clung to his cuirass, and molten lead and boiling tar poured from the battlements.

Often a stone would break his shield. Bridges crowded with men gave way under him. Once, by turning his mace, he rid himself of fourteen horsemen. He defeated all those who came forward to fight him on the field of honor, and more than a score of times it was believed that he had been killed.

However, thanks to Divine protection, he always escaped, for he shielded orphans, widows, and aged men. When he caught sight of one of the latter walking ahead of him, he would call to him to show his face, as if he feared that he might kill him by mistake.

All sorts of intrepid men gathered under his leadership, fugitive slaves, peasant rebels, and penniless rascals; he then organized an army which increased so much that he became famous and was in great demand.

He succored in turn the Dauphin of France, the King of England, the Templars of Jerusalem, the General of the Parths, the Negus of Abyssinia and the Emperor of Calicut. He fought against Scandinavians covered with fishscales, against Negroes mounted on red asses and armed with shields made of hippopotamus hide, against gold-colored Indians who wielded great, shining swords above their heads. He conquered the Troglodytes and the cannibals. He traveled through regions so torrid that the heat of the sun would set fire to the hair of one's head; he journeyed through countries so glacial that one's arms would fall from the body; and he passed through places where the fogs were so dense that it seemed like being surrounded by phantoms.

Republics in trouble consulted him; when he conferred with ambassadors, he always obtained unexpected concessions. Also, if a monarch behaved badly, he would arrive on the scene and rebuke him. He freed nations. He rescued queens sequestered in towers. It was he and no other that killed the serpent of Milan and the dragon of Oberbirbach.

Now, the Emperor of Occitania, having triumphed over the Spanish Mussulmans, had taken the sister of the Caliph of Cordova as a concubine, and had had one daughter by her, whom he brought up in the teachings of Christ. But the Caliph, feigning that he wished to become converted, made him a visit, and brought with him a numerous escort. He slaughtered the entire garrison and threw the Emperor into a dungeon, and treated him with great cruelty in order to obtain possession of his treasures.

Julian went to his assistance, destroyed the army of infidels, laid siege to the city, slew the Caliph, chopped off his head and threw it over the fortifications like a cannon ball.

As a reward for so great a service, the Emperor presented him with a large sum of money in baskets; but Julian declined it. Then the Emperor, thinking that the amount was not sufficiently large, offered him three quarters of his fortune, and on meeting a second refusal, proposed to share his kingdom with his benefactor. But Julian only thanked him for it, and the Emperor felt like weeping with vexation at not being able to show his gratitude, when he suddenly tapped his forehead and whispered a few words in the ear of one of his courtiers; the tapestry curtains parted and a young girl appeared.

Her large black eyes shone like two soft lights. A charming smile parted her lips. Her curls were caught in the jewels of her open-necked robe, and the grace of her youthful body could be divined under the transparency of her tunic.

She was dainty, round-cheeked, and slender-waisted.

Julian was absolutely dazzled, all the more since he had always led a chaste life.

So he married the Emperor's daughter, and received at the same time a castle she had inherited from her mother; and when the rejoicings were over, he departed with his bride, after many courtesies had been exchanged on both sides. . . .

(*Julian now remained at peace in the great castle, receiving daily the homage and affection of the people. At night, however, he dreamed of his former way of life and was still haunted by the notion of killing his parents. One evening he confessed his fear to his wife. She assured him that his fears were groundless and urged him to take up hunting again. He did so. During his absence, his beloved parents came on a surprise visit, and Julian's wife insisted that they sleep in her own bed. At dawn, Julian returned home, angry and frustrated after an unsuccessful night of hunting, unaware of his parents' presence in the castle.*)

The stained windows dimmed the pale light of dawn. Julian stumbled over some garments lying on the floor and a little further on, he knocked against a table covered with dishes. "She must have eaten," he thought; so he advanced cautiously towards the bed which was concealed by the darkness in the back of the room. When he reached the edge, he leaned over the pillow where the two heads were resting close together and stooped to kiss his wife. His mouth encountered a man's beard.

He fell back, thinking he had become crazed; then he approached the bed again and his searching fingers discovered some hair which seemed to be very long. In order to convince himself that he was mistaken, he once more passed his hand slowly over the pillow. But this time he was sure that it was a beard and that a man was there! a man lying beside his wife!

Flying into an ungovernable passion, he sprang upon them with his drawn dagger, foaming, stamping and howling like a wild beast. After a while he stopped.

The corpses, pierced through the heart, had not even moved. He listened attentively to the two death-rattles; they were almost alike, and as they grew fainter, another voice, coming from far away, seemed to continue them. Uncertain at first, this plaintive voice came nearer and nearer, grew louder and louder and presently he recognized, with a feeling of abject terror, the bellowing of the great black stag.

And as he turned around, he thought he saw the specter of his wife standing at the threshold with a light in her hand.

The sound of the murder had aroused her. In one glance she understood what had happened and fled in horror, letting the candle drop from her hand. Julian picked it up.

His father and mother lay before him, stretched on their backs, with gaping wounds in their breasts; and their faces, the expression of which was full of tender dignity, seemed to hide what might be an eternal secret.

Splashes and blotches of blood were on their white skin, on the bedclothes, on the floor, and on an ivory Christ which hung in the alcove. The scarlet reflection of the stained window, which just then was struck by the sun, lighted up the bloody spots and appeared to scatter them around the whole room. Julian walked toward the corpses, repeating to himself and trying to believe that he was mistaken, that it was not possible, that there are often inexplicable likenesses.

At last he bent over to look closely at the old man and he saw, between the half-closed lids, a dead pupil that scorched him like fire. Then he went over to the other side of the bed, where the other corpse lay, but the face was partly hidden by bands of white hair. Julian slipped his finger beneath them and raised the head, holding it at arm's length to study its features, while, with his other hand he lifted the torch. Drops of blood oozed from the mattress and fell one by one upon the floor.

At the close of the day, he appeared before his wife, and in a changed voice commanded her first not to answer him, not to approach him, not even to look at him, and to obey, under the penalty of eternal damnation, every one of his orders, which were irrevocable.

The funeral was to be held in accordance with the written in-structions he had left on a chair in the death-chamber.

He left her his castle, his vassals, all his worldly goods, without keeping even his clothes or his sandals, which would be found at the top of the stairs.

She had obeyed the will of God in bringing about his crime, and accordingly she must pray for his soul, since henceforth he should cease to exist.

The dead were buried sumptuously in the chapel of a monastery which it took three days to reach from the castle. A monk wearing a hood that covered his head followed the procession alone, for nobody dared to speak to him. And during the mass, he lay flat on the floor with his face downward and his arms stretched out at his sides.

After the burial, he was seen to take the road leading into the mountains. He looked back several times, and finally passed out of sight.

3

He left the country and begged his daily bread on his way.

He stretched out his hand to the horsemen he met in the roads, and humbly approached the harvesters in the fields; or else re-mained motionless in front of the gates of castles; and his face was so sad that he was never turned away.

Obeying a spirit of humility, he related his history to all men, and they would flee from him and cross themselves. In villages through which he had passed before, the good people bolted the doors, threatened him, and threw stones at him as soon as they recognized him. The more charitable ones placed a bowl on the windowsill and closed the shutters in order to avoid seeing him.

Repelled and shunned by everyone, he avoided his fellowmen and nourished himself with roots and plants, stray fruits and shells which he gathered along the shores.

Often, at the bend of a hill, he could perceive a mass of crowded roofs, stone spires, bridges, towers and narrow streets, from which arose a continual murmur of activity.

The desire to mingle with men impelled him to enter the city. But the gross and beastly expression of their faces, the noise of their industries and the indifference of their remarks, chilled his very heart. On holidays, when the cathedral bells rang out at daybreak and filled the people's hearts with gladness, he watched the inhabitants coming out of their dwellings, the dancers in the public squares, the fountains of ale, the damask hangings spread before the houses of princes; and then, when night came, he would peer through the windows at the long tables where families gathered and where grandparents held little children on their knees; then sobs would rise in his throat and he would turn away and go back to his haunts.

He gazed with yearning at the colts in the pastures, the birds in their nests, the insects on the flowers; but they all fled from him at his approach and hid or flew away. So he sought solitude. But the wind brought to his ears sounds resembling death-rattles; the tears of the dew reminded him of heavier drops, and every evening, the sun would spread blood in the sky, and every night, in his dreams, he lived over his parricide.

He made himself a hair-shirt lined with iron spikes. On his knees, he ascended every hill that was crowned with a chapel. But the unrelenting thought spoiled the splendor of the tabernacles and tortured him in the midst of his penances.

He did not rebel against God, who had inflicted his action, but he despaired at the thought that he had committed it.

He had such a horror of himself that he took all sorts of risks. He rescued paralytics from fire and children from the waves. But the ocean scorned him and the flames spared him. Time did not allay his torment, which became so intolerable that he resolved to die.

One day, while he was stooping over a fountain to judge of its depth, an old man appeared on the other side. He wore a white beard and his appearance was so lamentable that Julian could not keep back his tears. The old man also was weeping. Without recognizing him, Julian remembered confusedly a face that resembled his. He uttered a cry; for it was his father who stood before him; and he gave up all thought of taking his own life.

Thus weighted down by his recollections, he traveled through many countries and arrived at a river which was dangerous, because of its violence and the slime that covered its shores. Since a long time nobody had ventured to cross it.

The bow of an old boat, whose stern was buried in the mud,

showed among the reeds. Julian, on examining it closely, found a pair of oars and hit upon the idea of devoting his life to the service of his fellowmen.

He began by establishing on the bank of the river a sort of road which would enable people to approach the edge of the stream; he broke his nails in his efforts to lift enormous stones which he pressed against the pit of his stomach in order to transport them from one point to another; he slipped in the mud, he sank into it, and several times was on the very brink of death.

Then he took to repairing the boat with debris of vessels, and afterwards built himself a hut with putty and trunks of trees.

When it became known that a ferry had been established, passengers flocked to it. They hailed him from the opposite side by waving flags, and Julian would jump into the boat and row over. The craft was very heavy, and the people loaded it with all sorts of baggage, and beasts of burden, who reared with fright, thereby adding greatly to the confusion. He asked nothing for his trouble; some gave him left-over victuals which they took from their sacks or worn-out garments which they could no longer use.

The brutal ones hurled curses at him, and when he rebuked them gently they replied with insults, and he was content to bless them.

A little table, a stool, a bed made of dead leaves and three earthen bowls were all he possessed. Two holes in the wall served as windows. On one side, as far as the eye could see, stretched barren wastes studded here and there with pools of water; and in front of him flowed the greenish waters of the wide river. In the spring, a putrid odor arose from the damp sod. Then fierce gales lifted clouds of dust that blew everywhere, even settling in the water and in one's mouth. A little later swarms of mosquitoes appeared, whose buzzing and stinging continued night and day. After that, came frightful frosts which communicated a stone-like rigidity to everything and inspired one with an insane desire for meat. Months passed when Julian never saw a human being. He often closed his lids and endeavored to recall his youth;—he beheld the courtyard of a castle, with greyhounds stretched out on a terrace, an armory filled with valets, and under a bower of vines a youth with blond curls, sitting between an old man wrapped in furs and a lady with a high cap; presently the corpses rose before him, and then he would throw himself face downward on his cot and sob:

"Oh! poor father! poor mother! poor mother!" and would drop into a fitful slumber in which the terrible visions recurred.

One night he thought that some one was calling to him in his sleep. He listened intently, but could hear nothing save the roaring of the waters.

But the same voice repeated: "Julian!"

It proceeded from the opposite shore, a fact which appeared extraordinary to him, considering the breadth of the river.

The voice called a third time: "Julian!"

And the high-pitched tones sounded like the ringing of a church-bell.

Having lighted his lantern, he stepped out of his cabin. A frightful storm raged. The darkness was complete and was illuminated here and there only by the white waves leaping and tumbling.

After a moment's hesitation, he untied the rope. The water presently grew smooth and the boat glided easily to the opposite shore, where a man was waiting.

He was wrapped in a torn piece of linen; his face was like a chalk mask, and his eyes were redder than glowing coals. When Julian held up his lantern he noticed that the stranger was covered with hideous sores; but notwithstanding this, there was in his attitude something like the majesty of a king.

As soon as he stepped into the boat, it sank deep into the water, borne downward by his weight; then it rose again and Julian began to row.

With each stroke of the oars, the force of the waves raised the bow of the boat. The water, which was blacker than ink, ran furiously along the sides. It formed abysses and then mountains, over which the boat glided, then it fell into yawning depths where, buffeted by the wind, it whirled around and around.

Julian leaned far forward and, bracing himself with his feet, bent backwards so as to bring his whole strength into play. Hailstones cut his hands, the rain ran down his back, the velocity of the wind suffocated him. He stopped rowing and let the boat drift with the tide. But realizing that an important matter was at stake, a command which could not be disregarded, he picked up the oars again; and the rattling of the tholes mingled with the clamorings of the storm.

The little lantern burned in front of him. Sometimes birds

fluttered past it and obscured the light. But he could distinguish the eyes of the leper who stood at the stern, as motionless as a column.

And the trip lasted a long, long time.

When they reached the hut, Julian closed the door and saw the man sit down on the stool. The species of shroud that was wrapped around him had fallen below his loins, and his shoulders and chest and lean arms were hidden under blotches of scaly pustules. Enormous wrinkles crossed his forehead. Like a skeleton, he had a hole instead of a nose, and from his bluish lips came breath which was fetid and as thick as mist.

"I am hungry," he said.

Julian set before him what he had, a piece of pork and some crusts of coarse bread.

After he had devoured them, the table, the bowl, and the handle of the knife bore the same scales that covered his body.

Then he said: "I thirst!"

Julian fetched his jug of water and when he lifted it, he smelled an aroma that dilated his nostrils and filled his heart with gladness. It was wine; what a boon! but the leper stretched out his arm and emptied the jug at one draught.

Then he said: "I am cold!"

Julian ignited a bundle of ferns that lay in the middle of the hut. The leper approached the fire and, resting on his heels, began to warm himself; his whole frame shook and he was failing visibly; his eyes grew dull, his sores began to break, and in a faint voice he whispered:

"Thy bed!"

Julian helped him gently to it, and even laid the sail of his boat over him to keep him warm.

The leper tossed and moaned. The corners of his mouth were drawn up over his teeth; an accelerated death-rattle shook his chest and with each one of his aspirations, his stomach touched his spine. At last, he closed his eyes.

"I feel as if ice were in my bones! Lay thyself beside me!" he commanded. Julian took off his garments; and then, as naked as on the day he was born, he got into the bed; against his thigh he could feel the skin of the leper, and it was colder than a serpent and as rough as a file.

He tried to encourage the leper, but he only whispered:

"Oh! I am about to die! Come closer to me and warm me. Not with thy hands! No! with thy whole body."

So Julian stretched himself out upon the leper, lay on him, lips to lips, chest to chest.

Then the leper clasped him close and all at once his eyes shone like stars; his hair lengthened into sunbeams; the breath of his nostrils had the scent of roses; a cloud of incense rose from the hearth, and the waves outside began to murmur harmoniously. An abundance of bliss, a superhuman joy, filled the soul of the swooning Julian, while he who clasped him to his breast grew and grew until his head and his feet touched the opposite walls of the cabin. The roof flew off, disclosing the heavens, and Julian ascended into the blue, face to face with Our Lord Jesus Christ, who bore him straight to heaven.

And this is the story of Saint Julian the Hospitaler, as it is given on the stained-glass window of a church in my birthplace.

For Discussion

1. What signs early in the story hinted that Julian's life would be one of great beauty and great pain? To what two sharply contradictory ways of life did he seem attracted as a boy?

2. In what mood did Julian commit his first small act of slaughter? What significance did you find in the fact that he told no one about it? Point out evidence which revealed that, as a huntsman, Julian enjoyed killing for its own sake.

3. In Part 2, Julian was no longer interested in hunting. Why? What replaced this interest? In what way were his new activities different from his earlier pursuits? In what way were they akin? Do you think his conduct among men was consistent with his character? Why or why not?

4. How was Julian's wife the unwitting instrument of his undoing and also of his conversion?

5. In Part 3, did Julian's new mode of existence surprise you? Why or why not? From hints earlier in the story, show that this new way of life was not inconsistent for Julian.

6. Do you think that Julian's guilt came only from the specific crime he had committed, or from a general way of mind which this terrible

crime represented? Explain. What was the significance of Julian's self-imposed task of ferrying people across the dangerous river?

7. Julian's greatest task came in his encounter with the leper. Explain. What did Julian's actions reveal about him? What general meaning do you see in the ending of the story?

8. In some ways, Julian is a romantic character, though very different from the medieval, romantic hero in *Sir Gawain and the Green Knight,* which you read last year. Point out the differences between Gawain and Julian.

9. There are two high points in this story. The first comes at the end of Part 2; the second comes at the end of Part 3. In your opinion, which of these dramatic moments is the climax of the story? Explain.

10. Flaubert's objective style and careful attention to realistic details are evident in this story. Point out dramatic examples of this throughout the story. What is the effect of these realistic details?

11. Is Flaubert's style essentially simple or complex? Quote sentences to support your answer. Do you think this style is appropriate for the story that is being told? Why or why not?

12. A legend is a story that has come down from the past and which may have some historical basis. A second, though obsolete, meaning of the word is "the story of the life of a saint." In the light of these two definitions, show the appropriateness of the title of this story.

For Composition

1. Look up the meaning of the word *hospitaler* in a dictionary. Then write a composition in which you show how Julian's title is in sharp contrast to his earlier way of life.

2. Write an essay in which you compare Julian's services to others with those of St. Christopher.

3. One critic has described the story of St. Julian as meaning that "we find God only in absolute self-identification with the lowliest and most miserable of our brother-creatures." Write a composition in defense of this great truth.

Feodor Dostoyevsky

An Honest Thief

Feodor Dostoyevsky * (1821–1881), one of the great realistic novelists Russia has produced, is best known for his four major novels, *Crime and Punishment, The Idiot, The Brothers Karamazov,* and *The Possessed.* In these and other works, including his short stories, Dostoyevsky revealed a profound knowledge of human nature and of the deep struggle within man between good and evil, selfishness and altruism, arrogance and humility. His understanding of people's inner lives and of their subtle and often contradictory behavior has, perhaps, never been equaled in fiction.

Part of Dostoyevsky's own life is as dramatic as any story he wrote. At twenty-four, he was acclaimed for his first novel, *Poor Folk.* His triumph, however, was short-lived, for he was arrested in 1849, together with other young radicals opposed to the existing government, and was sentenced to death. At the very last moment, as he was facing the firing squad, the czar's courier brought a reprieve. He was sentenced, instead, to four years of hard labor in Siberia and to another four years as a common soldier. This period of great suffering explains, in part, the overwhelming pity for humanity expressed in his work.

In his novels and short stories, Dostoyevsky was primarily interested in the creation of character and mood. His characters are predominantly poor, wretched people, sometimes defiant and rebellious, sometimes meek; but in all their unhappiness they emerge as living human beings. The main character in "An Honest Thief" is a typical Dostoyevsky "hero," who arouses deep pity as he struggles toward "resurrection."

*O*NE morning, just as I was about to set off to my office, Agravena, my cook, washerwoman and housekeeper, came in to me and, to my surprise, entered into conversation.

She had always been such a silent, simple creature that, except for her daily inquiry about dinner, she had not uttered a word for the last six years. I, at least, had heard nothing else from her.

* fyô′dôr dôs tô-yef′ski

156

"Here I have come in to have a word with you, sir," she began abruptly; "you really ought to let the little room."

"Which little room?"

"Why, the one next the kitchen, to be sure."

"What for?"

"What for? Why, because folks do take in lodgers, to be sure."

"But who would take it?"

"Who would take it? Why, a lodger would take it, to be sure."

"But, my good woman, one could not put a bedstead in it; there wouldn't be room to move! Who could live in it?"

"Who wants to live there? As long as he has a place to sleep in. Why, he would live in the window."

"In what window?"

"In what window? As though you didn't know! The one in the passage, to be sure. He would sit there, sewing or doing anything else. Maybe he would sit on a chair, too. He's got a chair; and he has a table, too; he's got everything."

"Who is 'he,' then?"

"Oh, a good man, a man of experience. I will cook for him. And I'll ask him three rubles a month for his board and lodging."

After prolonged efforts I succeeded at last in learning from Agravena that an elderly man had somehow managed to persuade her to admit him into the kitchen as a lodger and boarder. Any notion Agravena took into her head had to be carried out; if not, I knew she would give me no peace. When anything was not to her liking, she at once began to brood, and sank into a deep dejection that would last for a fortnight or three weeks. During that period my dinners were spoiled, my linen was mislaid, my floors went unscrubbed; in short, I had a great deal to put up with. I had observed long ago that this inarticulate woman was incapable of conceiving a project, of originating an idea of her own. But if anything like a notion or a project was by some means put into her feeble brain, to prevent its being carried out meant, for a time, her moral assassination. And so, as I cared more for my peace of mind than for anything else, I forthwith consented.

"Has he a passport[1] anyway, or something of the sort?"

"To be sure, he has. He is a good man, a man of experience; three rubles he's promised to pay."

[1] A passport was required of natives as well as foreigners.

The very next day the new lodger made his appearance in my
modest bachelor quarters; but I was not put out by this, indeed I
was inwardly pleased. I lead as a rule a very lonely hermit's existence.
I have scarcely any friends; I hardly ever go anywhere. As I had
spent ten years never coming out of my shell, I had, of course,
grown used to solitude. But another ten or fifteen years or more of
the same solitary existence, with the same Agravena, in the same
bachelor quarters, was in truth a somewhat cheerless prospect. And
therefore a new inmate, if well-behaved, was a heaven-sent blessing.

Agravena had spoken truly: my lodger was certainly a man of experience. From his passport it appeared that he was an old soldier,
a fact which I should have known indeed from his face. An old
soldier is easily recognized. Astafy Ivanovitch was a favorable speci-
men of his class. We got on very well together. What was best of
all, Astafy Ivanovitch would sometimes tell a story, describing some
incident in his own life. In the perpetual boredom of my existence
such a story-teller was a veritable treasure. One day he told me one
of these stories. It made an impression on me. The following event
was what led to it.

I was left alone in the flat; both Astafy and Agravena were out
on business of their own. All of a sudden I heard from the inner
room somebody—I fancied a stranger—come in; I went out; there
actually was a stranger in the passage, a short fellow wearing no
overcoat in spite of the cold autumn weather.

"What do you want?"

"Does a clerk called Alexandrov live here?"

"Nobody of that name here, brother. Good-bye."

"Why, the dvornik[2] told me it was here," said my visitor, cautiously
retiring toward the door.

"Be off, be off, brother, get along."

Next day after dinner, while Astafy Ivanovitch was fitting on a
coat which he was altering for me, again some one came into the
passage. I half opened the door.

Before my very eyes my yesterday's visitor, with perfect composure,
took my wadded greatcoat from the peg and, stuffing it under his
arm, darted out of the flat. Agravena stood all the time staring at
him, agape with astonishment and doing nothing for the protection
of my property. Astafy Ivanovitch flew in pursuit of the thief and

[2] **dvornik:** lodge-keeper, concierge

ten minutes later came back out of breath and empty-handed. He had vanished completely.

"Well, there's a piece of luck, Astafy Ivanovitch!"

"It's a good job your cloak is left! Or he would have put you in a plight, the thief!"

But the whole incident had so impressed Astafy Ivanovitch that I forgot the theft as I looked at him. He could not get over it. Every minute or two he would drop the work upon which he was engaged, and would describe over again how it had all happened, how he had been standing, how the greatcoat had been taken down before his very eyes, not a yard away, and how it had come to pass that he could not catch the thief. Then he would sit down to his work again, then leave it once more, and at last I saw him go down to the dvornik to tell him all about it, and to upbraid him for letting such a thing happen in his domain. Then he came back again and began scolding Agravena. Then he sat down to his work again, and long afterwards he was still muttering to himself how it had all happened, how he stood there and I was here, how before our eyes, not a yard away, the thief took the coat off the peg, and so on. In short, though Astafy Ivanovitch understood his business, he was a terrible slow-coach and busybody.

"He's made fools of us, Astafy Ivanovitch," I said to him in the evening, as I gave him a glass of tea. I wanted to while away the time by recalling the story of the lost greatcoat, the frequent repetition of which, together with the great earnestness of the speaker, was beginning to become very amusing.

"Fools, indeed, sir! Even though it is no business of mine, I am put out. It makes me angry though it is not my coat that was lost. To my thinking there is no vermin in the world worse than a thief. Another takes what you can spare, but a thief steals the work of your hands, the sweat of your brow, your time ... Ugh, it's nasty! One can't speak of it! It's too vexing. How is it you don't feel the loss of your property, sir?"

"Yes, you are right, Astafy Ivanovitch, better if the thing had been burnt; it's annoying to let the thief have it, it's disagreeable."

"Disagreeable! I should think so! Yet, to be sure, there are thieves and thieves. And I have happened, sir, to come across an honest thief."

"An honest thief? But how can a thief be honest, Astafy Ivano-vitch?"

"There you are right indeed, sir. How can a thief be honest? There are none such. I only meant to say that he was an honest man, sure enough, and yet he stole. I was simply sorry for him."

"Why, how was that, Astafy Ivanovitch?"

"It was about two years ago, sir. I had been nearly a year out of a place, and just before I lost my place I made the acquaintance of a poor lost creature. We got acquainted in a public-house. He was a drunkard, a vagrant, a beggar, he had been in a situation of some sort, but from his drinking habits he had lost his work. Such a ne'er-do-well! God only knows what he had on! Often you wouldn't be sure if he'd a shirt under his coat; everything he could lay his hands upon he would drink away. But he was not one to quarrel; he was a quiet fellow. A soft, good-natured chap. And he'd never ask, he was ashamed; but you could see for yourself the poor fellow wanted a drink, and you would stand it for him. And so we got friendly, that's to say, he stuck to me ... It was all one to me. And what a man he was, to be sure! Like a little dog he would follow me; wherever I went there he would be; and all that after our first meeting, and he as thin as a thread-paper! At first it was 'let me stay the night'; well, I let him stay.

"I looked at his passport, too; the man was all right.

"Well, the next day it was all the same story, and then the third day he came again and sat all day in the window and stayed the night. Well, thinks I, he is sticking to me; give him food and drink and shelter at night, too—here am I, a poor man, and a hanger-on to keep as well! And before he came to me, he used to go in the same way to a government clerk's; he attached himself to him; they were always drinking together; but he, through trouble of some sort, drank himself into the grave. My man was called Emelyan Ilyitch. I pondered and pondered what I was to do with him. To drive him away I was ashamed. I was sorry for him; such a pitiful, God-forsaken creature I never did set eyes on. And not a word said, either; he does not ask, but just sits there and looks into your eyes like a dog. To think what drinking will bring a man down to!

"I keep asking myself how I am to say to him: 'You must be moving, Emelyanoushka, there's nothing for you here, you've come to the wrong place. I shall soon not have a bite for myself, how am I to keep you too?'

"I sat and wondered what he'd do when I said that to him. And I seemed to see how he'd stare at me, if he were to hear me say that, how long he would sit and not understand a word of it. And when it did get home to him at last, how he would get up from the window, would take up his bundle—I can see it now, the red-check handkerchief full of holes, with God knows what wrapped up in it, which he had always with him, and then how he would set his shabby old coat to rights, so that it would look decent and keep him warm, so that no holes would be seen—he was a man of delicate feelings! And how he'd open the door and go out with tears in his eyes. Well, there's no letting a man go to ruin like that ... One's sorry for him.

"And then, again, I think, how am I off myself? Wait a bit. Emelyanoushka, says I to myself, you've not long to feast with me: I shall soon be going away and then you will not find me.

"Well, sir, our family made a move; and Alexander Filimonovitch, my master (now deceased, God rest his soul!) said, 'I am thoroughly satisfied with you, Astafy Ivanovitch; when we come back from the country we will take you on again.' I had been butler with them; a nice gentleman he was, but he died that same year. Well, after seeing him off, I took my belongings, what little money I had, and I thought I'd have a rest for a time, so I went to an old woman I knew, and I took a corner in her room. There was only one corner free in it. She had been a nurse, so now she had a pension and a room of her own. Well, now good-bye, Emelyanoushka, thinks I, you won't find me now, my boy.

"And what do you think, sir? I had gone out to see a man I knew, and when I came back in the evening, the first thing I saw was Emelyanoushka! There he was, sitting on my box and his checked bundle beside him; he was sitting in his ragged old coat, waiting for me. And to while away the time he had borrowed a church book from the old lady, and was holding it wrong side upwards. He'd scented me out! My heart sank! Well, thinks I, there's no help for it—why didn't I turn him out at first? So I asked him straight off: 'Have you brought your passport, Emelyanoushka?'

"I sat down on the spot, sir, and began to ponder: will a vagabond like that be very much trouble to me? And on thinking it over it seemed he would not be much trouble. He must be fed, I thought. Well, a bit of bread in the morning, and to make it go down better I'll buy him an onion. At midday I should have to give him another bit of bread and an onion; and in the evening, onion again with kvass,[3] with some more bread if he wanted it. And if some cabbage soup were to come our way, then we should both have had our fill. I am no great eater myself, and a drinking man, as we all know, never eats; all he wants is herb-brandy or green vodka. He'll ruin me with his drinking, I thought, but then another idea came into my head, sir, and took great hold on me. So much so that if Emelyanoushka had gone away I should have felt that I had nothing to live for, I do believe ... I determined on the spot to be a father and guardian to him. I'll keep him from ruin, I thought, I'll wean him from the glass! You wait a bit, thought I; very well, Emelyanoushka, you may stay, only you must behave yourself; you must obey orders.

"Well, thinks I to myself, I'll begin by training him to work of some sort, but not all at once, let him enjoy himself a little first, and I'll look round and find something you are fit for, Emelyanoushka. For every sort of work a man needs a special ability, you know, sir. And I began to watch him on the quiet; I soon saw Emelyanoushka was a desperate character. I began, sir, with a word of advice: I said this and that to him. 'Emelyanoushka,' said I, 'you ought to take a thought and mend your ways. Have done with drinking! Just look what rags you go about in: that old coat of yours, if I may make bold to say so, is fit for nothing but a sieve. A pretty state of things! It's time to draw the line, sure enough.' Emelyanoushka sat and listened to me with his head hanging down. Would you believe it, sir? It had come to such a pass with him, he'd lost his tongue through drink and could not speak a word of sense. Talk to him of cucumbers and he'd answer back about beans! He would listen and listen to me and then heave such a sigh. 'What are you sighing for, Emelyan Ilyitch?' I asked him.

" 'Oh, nothing; don't you mind me, Astafy Ivanovitch. Do you know there were two women fighting in the street today, Astafy Ivanovitch? One upset the other woman's basket of cranberries by accident.'

" 'Well, what of that?'

[3] **kvass:** a non-intoxicating drink

" 'And the second one upset the other's cranberries on purpose and trampled them under foot, too.'

" 'Well, and what of it, Emelyan Ilyitch?'

" 'Why, nothing, Astafy Ivanovitch, I just mentioned it.'

" ' "Nothing, I just mentioned it!" ' Emelyanoushka, my boy, I thought, you've squandered and drunk away your brains!

" 'And do you know, a gentleman dropped a money-note on the pavement in Gorohovy Street; no, it was Sadovy Street. And a peasant saw it and said, "That's my luck"; and at the same time another man saw it and said, "No, it's my bit of luck. I saw it before you did." '

" 'Well, Emelyan Ilyitch?'

" 'And the fellows had a fight over it, Astafy Ivanovitch. But a policeman came up, took away the note, gave it back to the gentleman and threatened to take up both men.'

" 'Well, but what of that? What is there edifying about it, Emelyanoushka?'

" 'Why, nothing, to be sure. Folks laughed, Astafy Ivanovitch.'

" 'Ach, Emelyanoushka! What do the folks matter? You've sold your soul for a brass farthing! But do you know what I have to tell you, Emelyan Ilyitch?'

" 'What, Astafy Ivanovitch?'

" 'Take a job of some sort, that's what you must do. For the hundredth time I say to you, set to work, have some mercy on yourself!'

" 'What could I set to, Astafy Ivanovitch? I don't know what job I could set to, and there is no one who will take me on, Astafy Ivanovitch.'

" 'That's how you came to be turned off, Emelyanoushka, you drinking man!'

" 'And do you know Vlass, the waiter, was sent for to the office today, Astafy Ivanovitch?'

" 'Why did they send for him, Emelyanoushka?' I asked.

" 'I could not say why, Astafy Ivanovitch. I suppose they wanted him there, and that's why they sent for him.'

"A-ach, thought I, we are in a bad way, poor Emelyanoushka! The Lord is chastising us for our sins. Well, sir, what is one to do with such a man?

"But a cunning fellow he was, and no mistake. He'd listen and listen to me, but at last I suppose he got sick of it. As soon as he sees I am beginning to get angry, he's pick up his old coat and out he'd slip and leave no trace. He'd wander about all day and come back at night drunk. Where he got the money from, the Lord only knows; I had no hand in that.

" 'No,' said I, 'Emelyan Ilyitch, you'll come to a bad end. Give over drinking, mind what I say now, give it up! Next time you come home in liquor, you can spend the night on the stairs. I won't let you in!'

"After hearing that threat, Emelyanoushka sat at home that day and the next; but on the third he slipped off again. I waited and waited; he didn't come back. Well, at last, I don't mind owning, I was in a fright, and I felt for the man too. What have I done to him? I thought. I've scared him away. Where's the poor fellow gone to now? He'll get lost maybe. Lord have mercy upon us!

"Night came on; he did not come. In the morning I went out into the porch; I looked, and if he hadn't gone to sleep in the porch! There he was with his head on the step, and chilled to the marrow of his bones.

" 'What next, Emelyanoushka, God have mercy on you! Where will you get to next?'

" 'Why, you were—sort of—angry with me, Astafy Ivanovitch, the other day, you were vexed and promised to put me to sleep in the porch, so I didn't—sort of—venture to come in, Astafy Ivanovitch, and so I lay down here . . .'

"I did feel angry, and sorry too.

" 'Surely you might undertake some other duty, Emelyanoushka, instead of lying here guarding the steps,' I said.

" 'Why, what other duty, Astafy Ivanovitch?'

" 'You lost soul'—I was in such a rage, I called him that—'if you could but learn tailoring-work! Look at your old rag of a coat! It's not enough to have it in tatters, here you are sweeping the steps with it! You might take a needle and boggle up your rags, as decency demands. Ah, you drunken man!'

"What do you think, sir? He actually did take a needle. Of course I said it in jest, but he was so scared he set to work. He took off his coat and began threading the needle. I watched him; as you may well guess, his eyes were all red and bleary, and his hands were all of a shake. He kept shoving and shoving the thread and could not get it through the eye of the needle; he kept screwing his eyes up and wetting the thread and twisting it in his fingers—it was no good! He gave it up and looked at me.

" 'Well,' said I, 'this is a nice way to treat me! If there had been folks by to see, I don't know what I should have done! Why, you simple fellow, I said it to you in joke, as a reproach. Give over your nonsense. God bless you! Sit quiet and don't put me to shame, don't sleep on my stairs and make a laughing-stock of me.'

" 'Why, what am I to do, Astafy Ivanovitch? I know very well I am a drunkard and good for nothing! I can do nothing but vex you, my bene-benefactor. . . .'

"And at that his blue lips began all of a sudden to quiver, and a tear ran down his white cheeks and trembled on his stubbly chin, and then poor Emelyanoushka burst into a regular flood of tears. Mercy on us! I felt as though a knife were thrust into my heart! The sensitive creature! I'd never have expected it! Who could have guessed it? No, Emelyanoushka, thought I, I shall give you up altogether. You can go your way like the rubbish you are.

"Well, sir, why make a long story of it? And the whole affair is so trifling; it's not worth wasting words upon. Why, you, for instance, sir, would not have given a thought to it, but I would have given a great deal—if I had a great deal to give—that it never should have happened at all.

"I had a pair of riding breeches by me, sir, deuce take them, fine, first-rate riding breeches they were, too, blue with a check on it. They'd been ordered by a gentleman from the country, but he would not have them after all; said they were not full enough, so they were left on my hands. It struck me they were worth something. At the second-hand dealer's I ought to get five silver rubles for them, or if not I could turn them into two pairs of trousers for Petersburg gentlemen and have a piece over for a waistcoat for myself. Of course for poor people like us everything comes in. And it happened just then that Emelyanoushka was having a sad time of it. There he sat day after day; he did not drink, not a drop passed his lips, but he sat and moped like an owl. It was sad to see him—he just sat and brooded. Well, thought I, either you've not got a copper to spend, my lad, or else you're turning over a new leaf of yourself, you've given it up, you've listened to reason. Well, sir, that's how it was with us; and just then came a holiday. I went to vespers; when I came home I found Emelyanoushka sitting in the window, drunk and rocking to and fro.

"Ah! so that's what you've been up to, my lad! And I went to get something out of my chest. And when I looked in, the breeches were not there . . . I rummaged here and there; they'd vanished. When I'd ransacked everywhere and saw they were not there, something seemed to stab me to the heart. I ran first to the old dame and began accusing her; of Emelyanoushka I'd not the faintest suspicion, though there was cause for it in his sitting there drunk.

" 'No,' said the old body, 'God be with you, my fine gentleman, what good are riding breeches to me? Am I going to wear such things? Why, a skirt I had I lost the other day through a fellow of your sort . . . I know nothing; I can tell you nothing about it,' she said.

" 'Who has been here, who has been in?' I asked.

" 'Why, nobody has been, my good sir,' says she; 'I've been here all the while; Emelyan Ilyitch went out and came back again; there he sits, ask him.'

" 'Emelyanoushka,' said I, 'have you taken those new riding breeches for anything; you remember the pair I made for that gentleman from the country?'

" 'No, Astafy Ivanovitch,' said he; 'I've not—sort of—touched them.'

"I was in a state! I hunted high and low for them—they were nowhere to be found. And Emelyanoushka sits there rocking himself to and fro. I was squatting on my heels facing him and bending over the chest, and all at once I stole a glance at him . . . Alack, I thought; my heart suddenly grew hot within me and I felt myself flushing up too. And suddenly Emelyanoushka looked at me.

" 'No, Astafy Ivanovitch,' said he, 'those riding breeches of yours, maybe, you are thinking, maybe, I took them, but I never touched them.'

" 'But what can have become of them, Emelyan Ilyitch?'

" 'No, Astafy Ivanovitch,' said he, 'I've never seen them.'

" 'Why, Emelyan Ilyitch, I suppose they've run off themselves, eh?'

" 'Maybe they have, Astafy Ivanovitch.'

"When I heard him say that, I got up at once, went up to him, lighted the lamp and sat down to work to my sewing. I was altering a waistcoat for a clerk who lived below us. And wasn't there a burning pain and ache in my breast! I shouldn't have minded so much if I had put all the clothes I had in the fire. Emelyanoushka seemed to have an inkling of what a rage I was in. When a man is guilty, you know, sir, he scents trouble far off, like the birds of the air before a storm.

" 'Do you know what, Astafy Ivanovitch,' Emelyanoushka began, and his poor old voice was shaking as he said the words, 'Antip Prohoritch, the apothecary, married the coachman's wife this morning, who died the other day—'

"I did give him a look, sir, a nasty look it was; Emelyanoushka understood it too. I saw him get up, go to the bed, and begin to rummage there for something. I waited—he was busy there a long time and kept muttering all the while, 'No, not there, where can the blessed things have got to?' I waited to see what he'd do; I saw him creep under the bed on all fours. I couldn't bear it any longer. 'What are you crawling about under the bed for, Emelyan Ilyitch?' said I.

" 'Looking for the breeches, Astafy Ivanovitch. Maybe they've dropped down there somewhere.'

" 'Why should you try to help a poor simple man like me,' said I, 'crawling on your knees for nothing, sir?'—I called him that in my vexation.

" 'Oh, never mind, Astafy Ivanovitch, I'll just look. They'll turn up, maybe, somewhere.'

" 'H'm,' said I, 'look here, Emelyan Ilyitch!'

" 'What is it, Astafy Ivanovitch?' said he.

" 'Haven't you simply stolen them from me like a thief and a robber, in return for the bread and salt you've eaten here?' said I.

"I felt so angry, sir, at seeing him fooling about on his knees before me.

" 'No, Astafy Ivanovitch.'

"And he stayed lying as he was on his face under the bed. A long time he lay there and then at last he crept out. I looked at him, and the man was as white as a sheet. He stood up, and sat down near me in the window and sat so for some ten minutes.

" 'No, Astafy Ivanovitch,' he said, and all at once he stood up and came towards me, and I can see him now; he looked dreadful. 'No, Astafy Ivanovitch,' said he, 'I never—sort of—touched your breeches.'

"He was all of a shake, poking himself in the chest with a trembling finger, and his poor old voice shook so that I was frightened, sir, and sat as though I was rooted to the window-seat.

" 'Well, Emelyan Ilyitch,' said I, 'as you will, forgive me if I, in my foolishness, have accused you unjustly. As for the breeches, let them go hang; we can live without them. We've still our hands, thank God; we need not go thieving or begging from some other poor man; we'll earn our bread.'

"Emelyanoushka heard me out and went on standing there before me. I looked up, and he had sat down. And there he sat all evening without stirring. At last I lay down to sleep. Emelyanoushka went on sitting in the same place. When I looked out in the morning, he was lying curled up in his old coat on the bare floor; he felt too crushed even to come to bed. Well, sir, I felt no more liking for the fellow from that day, in fact for the first few days I hated him. I felt, as one may say, as though my own son had robbed me, and done me a deadly hurt. Ach, thought I, Emelyanoushka, Emelyanoushka! And Emelyanoushka, sir, went on drinking for a whole fortnight without stopping. He was drunk all the time, and regularly besotted. He went out in the morning and came back late at night, and for a whole fortnight I didn't get a word out of him. It was as though grief was gnawing at his heart, or as though he wanted to do for himself completely. At last he stopped; he must have come to the end of all he'd got, and then he sat in the window again. I remember he sat there without speaking for three days and three nights; all of a sudden I saw that he was crying. He was just sitting there, sir, and crying like anything; a perfect stream, as though he didn't know how his tears were flowing. And it's a sad thing, sir, to see a grown-up man and an old man, too, crying from woe and grief.

" 'What's the matter, Emelyanoushka?' said I.

"He began to tremble so that he shook all over. I spoke to him for the first time since that evening.

" 'Nothing, Astafy Ivanovitch.'

" 'God be with you, Emelyanoushka, what's lost is lost. Why are you moping about like this?' I felt sorry for him.

"Oh, nothing, Astafy Ivanovitch, it's no matter. I want to find some work to do, Astafy Ivanovitch.'

" 'And what sort of work, pray, Emelyanoushka?'

" 'Why, any sort; perhaps I could find a situation such as I used to have. I've been already to ask Fedosay Ivanitch. I don't like to be a burden on you, Astafy Ivanovitch. If I can find a situation, Astafy Ivanovitch, then I'll pay you it all back, and make you a return for all your hospitality.'

" 'Enough, Emelyanoushka, enough; let bygones be bygones— and no more to be said about it. Let us go on as we used to do before.'

" 'No, Astafy Ivanovitch, you, maybe, think—but I never touched your riding breeches.'

" 'Well, have it your own way, God be with you, Emelyanoushka.'

" 'No, Astafy Ivanovitch, I can't go on living with you, that's clear. You must excuse me, Astafy Ivanovitch.'

" 'Why, God bless you, Emelyan Ilyitch, who's offending you and driving you out of the place—am I doing it?'

" 'No, it's not the proper thing for me to live with you like this, Astafy Ivanovitch. I'd better be going.'

"He was so hurt, it seemed, he stuck to his point. I looked at him, and sure enough, up he got and pulled his old coat over his shoulders.

" 'But where are you going, Emelyan Ilyitch? Listen to reason: what are you about? Where are you off to?'

" 'No, good-bye, Astafy Ivanovitch, don't keep me now'—and he was blubbering again—'I'd better be going. You're not the same now.'

" 'Not the same as what? I am the same. But you'll be lost by yourself like a poor helpless babe, Emelyan Ilyitch.'

" 'No, Astafy Ivanovitch, when you go out now, you look at your chest and it makes me cry to see it, Astafy Ivanovitch. You'd better let me go, Astafy Ivanovitch, and forgive me all the trouble I've given you while I've been living with you.'

"Well, sir, the man went away. I waited for a day; I expected he'd be back in the evening—no. Next day no sign of him, nor the third day either. I began to get frightened; I was so worried, I couldn't drink, I couldn't eat, I couldn't sleep. The fellow had quite disarmed me. On the fourth day I went out to look for him; I peeped into all the taverns, to inquire for him—but no, Emelyanoushka was lost. 'Have you managed to keep yourself alive, Emelyanoushka?' I wondered. 'Perhaps he is lying dead under some hedge, poor drunkard, life a sodden log.' I went home more dead than alive. Next day I went out to look for him again. And I kept cursing myself that I'd been such a fool as to let the man go off by himself. On the fifth day it was a holiday—in the early morning I heard the door creak. I looked up and there was my Emelyanoushka coming in. His face was blue and his hair was covered with dirt as though he'd been sleeping in the street; he was as thin as a match. He took off his old coat, sat down on the chest, and looked at me. I was delighted to see him, but I felt overtaken in some sin, as true as I am here, sir, I'd have died like a dog before I'd have come back. But Emelyanoushka did come back. And a sad thing it was, sure enough, to see a man sunk so low. I began to look after him, to talk kindly to him, to comfort him.

" 'Well, Emelyanoushka,' said I, 'I am glad you've come back. Had you been away much longer I should have gone to look for you in the taverns again today, Are you hungry?'

" 'No, Astafy Ivanovitch.'

" 'Come, now, aren't you really? Here, brother, is some cabbage soup left over from yesterday; there was meat in it; it is good stuff. And here is some bread and onion. Come, eat it, it'll do you no harm.'

"I made him eat it, and I saw at once that the man had not tasted food for maybe three days—he was as hungry as a wolf. So it was hunger that had driven him to me. My heart was melted looking at the poor fellow. 'Let me run to the tavern,' thought I, 'I'll get something to ease his heart and then we'll make an end of it. I've no more anger in my heart against you, Emelyanoushka!' I brought him some vodka. 'Here, Emelyan Ilyitch, let us have a drink for the holiday. Like a drink? And it will do you good.' He held out his hand, held it out greedily; he was just taking it, and then he stopped himself. But a minute after, I saw him take it, and lift it to his mouth, spilling it on his sleeve. But though he got it to his lips, he set it down on the table again.

" 'What is it, Emelyanoushka?'

" 'Nothing, Astafy Ivanovitch, I—sort of—'

" 'Won't you drink it?'

" 'Well, Astafy Ivanovitch, I'm not—sort of —going to drink any more, Astafy Ivanovitch.'

" 'Do you mean you've given it up altogether, Emelyanoushka, or are you only not going to drink today?'

"He did not answer. A minute later I saw him rest his head on his hand.

" 'What's the matter, Emelyanoushka, are you ill?'

" 'Why, yes, Astafy Ivanovitch, I don't feel well.'

"I took him and laid him down on the bed. I saw that he really was ill: his head was burning hot and he was shivering with fever. I sat by him all day; towards night he was worse. I mixed him some oil and onion and kvass and bread broken up.

" 'Come, eat some of this,' said I, 'and perhaps you'll be better.' He shook his head. 'No,' said he, 'I won't have any dinner today, Astafy Ivanovitch.'

"I made some tea for him; I quite flustered our old woman—he was no better. Well, thinks I, it's a bad outlook! The third morning I went for a medical gentleman. There was one I knew living close by, Kostopravov by name. I'd made his acquaintance when I was in service with the Bosomyagins; he'd attended me. The doctor came and looked at him. 'He's in a bad way,' said he, 'it was no use sending for me. But if you like I can give him a powder.' Well, I didn't give him a powder. I thought that's just the doctor's little game; and then the fifth day came.

"He lay, sir, dying before my eyes. I sat in the window with my work in my hands. The old woman was heating the stove. We were all silent. My heart was simply breaking over him, the good-for-nothing fellow; I felt as if it were a son of my own I was losing. I knew that Emelyanoushka was looking at me. I'd seen the man all the day long making up his mind to say something and not daring to.

"At last I looked up at him; I saw such misery in the poor fellow's eyes. He had kept them fixed on me but when he saw that I was looking at him, he looked down at once.

" 'Astafy Ivanovitch.'

" 'What is it, Emelyanoushka?'

" 'If you were to take my old coat to a secondhand dealer's, how much do you think they'd give you for it, Astafy Ivanovitch?'

" 'There's no knowing how much they'd give. Maybe they would give me a ruble for it, Emelyan Ilyitch.'

"But if I had taken it, they wouldn't have given a farthing for it, but would have laughed in my face for bringing such a trumpery thing. I simply said that to comfort the poor fellow, knowing the simpleton he was.

" 'But I was thinking, Astafy Ivanovitch, they might give you three rubles for it; it's made of cloth, Astafy Ivanovitch. How could they give only one ruble for a cloth coat?'

" 'I don't know, Emelyan Ilyitch,' said I, 'if you are thinking of taking it you should certainly ask three rubles to begin with.'

"Emelyanoushka was silent for a time, and then he addressed me again—

" 'Astafy Ivanovitch.'

" 'What is it, Emelyanoushka?' I asked.

" 'Sell my coat when I die, and don't bury me in it. I can lie as well without it; and it's a thing of some value—it might come in useful.'

"I can't tell you how it made my heart ache to hear him. I saw that the death agony was coming on him. We were silent again for a bit. So an hour passed by. I looked at him again: he was still staring at me, and when he met my eyes he looked down again.

" 'Do you want some water to drink, Emelyan Ilyitch?' I asked.

" 'Give me some, God bless you, Astafy Ivanovitch.'

"I gave him a drink.

" 'Thank you, Astafy Ivanovitch,' said he.

" 'Is there anything else you would like, Emelyanoushka?'

" 'No, Astafy Ivanovitch, there's nothing I want, but I—sort of—'

" 'What?'

" 'I only—'

" 'What is it, Emelyanoushka?'

" 'Those riding breeches—it was—sort of—I who took them—Astafy Ivanovitch.'

" 'Well, God forgive you, Emelyanoushka,' said I, 'you poor, sorrowful creature. Depart in peace!'

"And I was choking myself, sir, and the tears were in my eyes. I turned aside for a moment.

" 'Astafy Ivanovitch—'

"I saw Emelyanoushka wanted to tell me something; he was trying to sit up, trying to speak, and mumbling something. He flushed red all over suddenly, looked at me . . . then I saw him turn white again, whiter and whiter, and he seemed to sink away all in a minute. His head fell back, he drew one breath, and gave up his soul to God."

For Discussion

1. What type of person did Astafy Ivanovitch represent in the beginning of the story? How did his reaction to the theft of the narrator's coat reveal his "moral superiority"? Did he show another side to his personality in his relationship with Emelyan? Explain.
2. What reason did Astafy Ivanovitch give himself for asking Emelyan to stay with him? Did Astafy Ivanovitch have any other reason for taking the man into his house? What do you think he meant by "It seemed as if life would be a burden to me if Emelyan went away"?
3. What made Astafy Ivanovitch suspect that Emelyan had stolen his breeches? Why do you think Astafy Ivanovitch was so upset when Emelyan disappeared and did not return?
4. Considering the type of man Astafy Ivanovitch was presented as at the beginning of the story, did you find the final scene with Emelyan inconsistent? Why or why not?
5. What did you feel about Emelyan at the end of the story? Despite all his defects, why is he not a villain? Was there anything about him that you liked?
6. Do you think Dostoyevsky was in sympathy with Astafy Ivanovitch, Emelyan, or both? Explain. What did this story reveal about Dostoyevsky's social beliefs?
7. Emelyan's life illustrates Dostoyevsky's pattern in dealing with his "criminal" characters: sin, punishment (suffering), repentance (resurrection) and forgiveness (love). How does this pattern reveal itself specifically in the story?
8. "An Honest Thief" has a complex structure with its two narrators. It also seems to ramble and take seemingly irrelevant by-paths until the reader gets to the main story about Emelyan. In your opinion, what did the first part of the narrative about the boarder, the taking of the narrator's coat, and the tailor's reaction to the theft contribute to the main story? Did this rambling in any way reflect the outward conduct and inner conflicts of Emelyan? Explain.

For Composition

1. Just before his death, Dostoyevsky delivered his famous address on the true meaning of Russian nationalism at the unveiling of Pushkin's

monument in Moscow. In this address, he summed up his own credo: "'To be a real Russian and to be wholly Russian means only this: to be a brother to all men, to be universally human." Write a composition in which you point out specifically the application of this statement to "An Honest Thief."

2. Although Dostoyevsky and Turgenev were both writing at the same period, their work is quite different in some respects. Write a paper in which you compare and contrast "Mumu" and "An Honest Thief." Point out where these stories are alike and different in mood, characterization, theme, and style.

Leo Tolstoy

God Sees the Truth, but Waits

Leo Tolstoy (1828–1910), one of the foremost novelists in Russian and world literature, devoted only part of his time to writing fiction. He was also an important social reformer and writer on ethics and religion. He lived most of his life on his estate, writing, tilling the land in close association with the peasants, and questioning the meaning of life and the part played by the human will in man's fulfillment of himself. As a friend and defender of the serfs, the lowest class of Russian society in the nineteenth century, he came to know the common man's worth—his dignity and capacity for happiness in the midst of poverty and suffering.

Tolstoy believed that every man had within him the power to understand what is good, and should strive to be just to himself and to others. Deeply troubled by his own wealth and success, as compared with the conditions of the Russian people, he renounced all of his property in 1890, and divided it among his wife and children. He lived the last years of his life in great simplicity, writing, preaching charity, and helping people.

Tolstoy's tireless search for truth is reflected in his novels and short stories, most notably in his two major works, *War and Peace* and *Anna Karenina*, which rank among the great realistic novels of the world. The two short stories that follow reveal Tolstoy's powerful yet simple style, and his belief that society would only be improved when men and women tried to become better human beings in their personal lives and learned to love each other.

*I*N the town of Vladimir there lived a young merchant named Aksenov. He owned two shops and his own house. A handsome fellow with fair curly hair, he was the life of the party and the first to strike up a song. When he was younger, Aksenov used to drink a lot, and when he had drunk too much would get into brawls; but since his marriage, he had given up drinking except for occasional lapses.

One summer day, Aksenov had to travel to a fair at Nizhni. When he began to say good-by to his family, his wife said to him:

175

"Ivan Dmitrievich, don't go today. I had a bad dream about you."

Aksenov chuckled and said:

"Are you afraid that I'll go off on a binge at the fair?"

"I don't know myself what I fear, but it was such a strange thing that I dreamed—you had come back from another town and had taken off your hat, and I saw that your hair had gone completely gray."

Aksenov laughed.

"That means there'll be profits! You'll see, I'll have good fortune and bring you rich gifts."

Then he said good-by and left.

When he had gone half the way, he met a merchant friend of his and they stopped for the night. They drank tea together and went to sleep in adjoining rooms. Aksenov did not like to sleep long. He awoke in the middle of the night and, since it was easier to travel while it was still cool he woke the coachman and told him to harness the horses. Then he went to the soot-covered cabin of the innkeeper, paid his bill, and left.

After he had gone forty versts, he stopped again, fed the horses, and rested on the front porch of the inn. At dinner time, he went out onto the back porch, asked for a samovar, took a guitar and began to play. Suddenly a troika with ringing bells drove up to the inn. An official and two soldiers got out of the carriage. The official went up to Aksenov and asked him who he was and where he was from. Aksenov told him what he wanted to know and asked if he would like to join him for tea. But the official continued to question him: "Where did you sleep last night? Were you alone or with a merchant? Did you see the merchant in the morning? Why did you leave the inn so early?" Aksenov wondered why he was being asked these things. He told him all that had occurred, then added, "But why are you questioning me like this? I'm not some kind of thief or bandit. I am traveling on my own business, and there's nothing for you to question me about."

Then the official called a soldier and said:

"I am the district police officer, and I am asking you these questions because the merchant you stayed with last night has been found with his throat cut. Show me your things. Search him!"

They went into the cabin, took out his suitcase and bag, untied them and began to search. Suddenly, the officer pulled out a knife from the bag and shouted:

"Whose knife is this?"

Aksenov loked. He saw that they had found a knife covered with blood in his bag, and he was frightened.

"And why is there blood on the knife?"

Aksenov wanted to answer, but could not speak.

"I . . . I don't know . . . I . . . knife . . . I, not mine . . ."

Then the officer said:

"In the morning they found a merchant with his throat cut. There is no one besides you who could have done it. The cabin was locked from the inside, and no one except you had been inside. You have in your bag a knife covered with blood, and, in fact, guilt is written all over your face. Now tell us, how did you kill him and how much money did you steal?"

Akensov swore that he did not do it, that he had not seen the merchant since they had drunk tea together, that the only money he had was his own eight thousand rubles, that the knife was not his. But his voice broke, his face was pale, and he shook with fear as though he were guilty.

The officer called a soldier and told him to bind Aksenov and take him out to a cart. When they bound his feet and lifted him onto the cart, Aksenov crossed himself and began to cry. They took away his bags and money and sent him to jail in a nearby town. Inquiries were made in Vladimir to find out what sort of man Aksenov was. All the merchants and inhabitants of Vladimir noted that when he was younger Aksenov drank and caroused, but that he was a good man.

Then he was brought to trial and charged with the murder of a merchant from Riazan and the theft of twenty thousand rubles.

His wife was grief-stricken and did not know what to think. Her children were young: one was still at the breast. She took them all and went to the town where her husband was imprisoned. At first they refused to let her in, but she implored the prison authorities, and they took her to her husband. When she saw him in prison clothes, chained, and with thieves, she collapsed and for a long time remained unconscious. Then she placed her children about her, sat beside him, and began to tell him about things at home and to ask about all that had happened to him. He told her everything.

"And what now?" she asked.

"We must petition the Tsar. They cannot let an innocent man perish!"

His wife said that she had already sent a petition to the Tsar but that it had not been allowed to reach him.

Aksenov was silent and only grew more despondent.

"It wasn't for nothing that, you remember, I dreamed of your turning gray," his wife said. "Look, you are already beginning to gray from grief. You should not have gone."

She began to run her fingers through his hair and said:

"Vanya, my dearest one, tell your wife the truth; didn't you do it?"

"And you too suspect me?" He covered his face with his hands and wept. A guard came in then and said that his wife and children had to leave. Aksenov said good-by to his family for the last time.

When his wife had left, Aksenov began to think about all that had been said. When he recalled that his wife too had suspected him and that she had asked if he killed the merchant, he said to himself:

"Clearly, only God can know the truth, and one must turn to God alone and from God alone await mercy." From that time on Aksenov ceased sending petitions, ceased hoping, and only prayed to God. He was sentenced to flogging and hard labor. The sentence was carried out. They flogged him with a knout, and when the knout wounds had closed, they herded him along with other convicts to Siberia.

For twenty-six years Aksenov lived in Siberian servitude. The hair of his head turned as white as snow and his beard grew long, thin and gray. All his joyfulness vanished. He grew hunched, moved along quietly, spoke little, never laughed and often prayed to God.

While in prison Aksenov learned to make boots. With the money he earned he bought the *Lives of the Saints* and read it when there was light enough in the prison. On holidays he went to the prison church where he read the Gospels and, since his voice was still good, sang in the choir. The prison officials liked Aksenov for his humility, and his fellow prisoners respected him and called him "Grandpa" and "Godly one." When there were any petitions concerning prison conditions, the other prisoners always sent Aksenov to present them to the officials; and when quarrels arose among them, the prisoners always went to him to judge the case.

No one from Aksenov's home wrote him, and he did not even know if his wife and children were still alive.

One day they brought some new convicts to the prison. In the evening all the old convicts gathered around the new ones and began to ask them what town or village they were from and why they had been exiled. Aksenov also sat down on one of the long, elevated shelf-bunks near the new inmates and dejectedly listened to what they said.

One of the new convicts was a tall, robust old man of about sixty with a clipped, gray beard. He was telling of his arrest.

"So, fellows, I was sent here for no reason at all. I unharnessed a horse from a coachman's sleigh. They grabbed me. 'Thief,' they said. I told them that I had only wanted to get where I was going faster and that I had let the horse go. In fact, the coachman was a friend of mine. 'All right?' I asked. 'No, you stole the horse,' they said. Now, I have stolen things, but they didn't know what or where. I've done things that should have landed me here long ago, although they never caught me. But there's no justice at all in their driving me here this time. Lies! I've been in Siberia before, although I didn't stay long."

"Where are you from?" one of the convicts asked.

"Our family comes from Vladimir, local tradespeople. My name is Makar, Makar Semenovich, in full."

Aksenov raised his head and asked:

"Semenych, have you ever heard anything about the Aksenov merchants in Vladimir? Are they alive?"

"Who hasn't heard of them! Rich merchants, although their father is in Siberia, a sinner like ourselves, no doubt. And you, Grandpa, what are you in for?"

Aksenov did not like to talk about his own misfortune. He sighed and said:

"For my sins I have spent these twenty-six years in hard labor."

"And what sort of sins?" Makar Semenov asked.

"Those worth this punishment," Aksenov said, and he wanted to say no more about it. But the other prisoners told the newcomer why Aksenov had been sent to Siberia. They told him how someone had killed a merchant and had planted a knife on Aksenov and that for this Aksenov had been falsely convicted.

When Makar Semenov heard this and looked at Aksenov, he slapped his knees with his hands and said:

"Well, that's something! That's really something! How you've aged, Grandpa!"

They asked him why he was so surprised and where he had seen Aksenov, but Makar Semenov did not answer and only said:

"It's a miracle, lads, the way people meet."

At these words Aksenov began to wonder if this man knew something about the murder of the merchant, and he asked:

"Have you heard of this affair before, Semenych, or have you seen me before?"

"Of course I've heard about it! News travels quickly. But it happened long ago, and you forget what you've heard."

"Did you ever hear, perhaps, who killed the merchant?" Aksenov then asked.

Makar Semenov laughed and said:

"The one whose knife they found in your bag probably did it. And if someone did plant a knife on you, well, a man's not a thief until he's caught, you know. But how could anyone have put a knife in your bag? Wasn't it right by your head? You would have heard something."

As soon as Aksenov heard these words he realized that it was this very man who had killed the merchant. He got up and walked off. All that night he could not fall asleep, but lay deeply depressed. He recalled the past. He saw his wife as she had been on that last day when he left for the fair. It was as though she stood there alive before him. He saw her face and her eyes. He heard her voice speak to him and laugh. He saw his children as they were then, little ones, one in a little coat, the other at the breast. And he remembered how he himself had been then—young and gay. He recalled how he had sat on the porch at the inn where they arrested him, how he had played the guitar and how happy he had been. And he remembered the place where they had whipped him, the executioner, the crowd gathered around, the chains, the convicts, the whole twenty-six years of prison life: and he remembered his age. So great a gloom came upon him that he wanted to kill himself.

"And all because of that scoundrel!" Aksenov thought.

He felt such fury toward Makar Semenov that he wanted to revenge himself even though it cost him his own life. He prayed all night, but could not calm down. The next day, he did not go near Makar Semenov and did not look at him.

This went on for two weeks. Aksenov could not sleep nights, and he was so forlorn he did not know where to turn.

One night while he was walking about the prison barracks he noticed handfuls of dirt being thrown from beneath one of the long shelf-bunks shared by the prisoners. He stopped to look. Suddenly, Makar Semenov jumped out from under the bunk and with a frightened expression looked at Aksenov. Aksenov wanted to move on in order not to face him, but Makar grabbed his arm and told him how he had been digging a passage beneath the wall and carrying dirt out in his boot tops and how he had been scattering the dirt in the street when the prisoners were sent off to work.

"Just be quiet about this, old fellow, and I'll take you along. If you talk, they'll whip me. But I won't let you get away—I'll kill you."

Looking at the scoundrel, Aksenov shook with rage. He jerked his arm away and said:

"There's no reason for me to leave here, and there's no need to kill me—you killed me long ago. And whether or not I tell about you depends on how God directs my soul."

The next day as they were leading the convicts off to work, a guard noticed Makar Semenov scattering dirt. They searched the barracks and found the hole. The warden came to the barracks and asked all of them: "Who dug this hole?" They all denied doing it. Those who knew the truth did not betray Makar Semenov because they knew that he would be whipped half to death. Then the warden turned to Aksenov. He knew that Aksenov was an honorable man and said:

"Old man, you are truthful—tell me before God, who did this?"

Makar Semenov stood as though nothing had happened, looking at the warden, but not turning to look at Aksenov. Aksenov's lips and hands trembled and for a long time he could not speak. He thought to himself: "Why should I protect him, why should I forgive him when he has ruined my life? Let him pay for my torments. But if I tell, they'll flog him. And what if I have been wrong about him? In any case will things be any easier for me?"

The warden asked him again:

"Well, old man, tell the truth, who dug the hole?"

Aksenov glanced at Makar Semenov and said:

"I cannot tell, your excellency. God has not directed me to do so. I will not tell. It is in your power to do what you want with me."

No matter how hard the warden tried to persuade him, Aksenov said nothing more. So, they did not discover who had dug the hole.

The next night, as Aksenov lay on his bed and had just about fallen asleep, he heard someone come up to him and sit on the bunk at his feet. He looked in the dark and recognized Makar.

"What more do you want of me? What are you doing here?" he asked.

Makar Semenov was silent. Aksenov raised himself and said:

"What do you want? Get out of here or I'll call the guard."

Makar Semenov bent close to Aksenov and in a whisper said:

"Ivan Dmitrich, forgive me!"

"For what shall I forgive you?"

"I killed the merchant and planted the knife on you. I wanted to kill you too, but I heard noises outside. I slipped the knife into your bag and climbed out the window."

Aksenov was silent and did not know what to say. Makar Semenov dropped from the bunk, bowed to the ground and said:

"Ivan Dmitrich, forgive me. For God's sake, forgive me. I'll confess that I killed the merchant. They'll pardon you, and you can go home."

"It's easy for you to talk," Aksenov said, "but how I have suffered! Where can I go now? . . . My wife is dead, my children have forgotten me. There's no place for me."

Makar Semenov did not rise, but beat his head on the ground and said:

"Ivan Dmitrich, forgive! When they whipped me with a knout it was easier for me than it is now to look at you. . . . But you pitied me before when you didn't betray me. Forgive me for Christ's sake! Forgive this accursed wretch." And he began to sob.

When Aksenov heard Makar Semenov weeping, he began to cry himself and said:

"God will forgive you. Perhaps I am a hundred times worse than you."

Suddenly, his soul grew calm. He ceased to yearn for his home and he no longer wanted to leave prison, but only thought of his final hour.

In spite of what Aksenov had said, Makar Semenov confessed his guilt. When they issued the order permitting Aksenov to return home, he was already dead.

For Discussion

1. Although Aksenov was innocent, how do you explain his behavior when he was accused by the police of the crime? What relation do you see between this and the end of the story when Aksenov said to Semenov, "Perhaps I am a hundred times worse than you"?
2. Why did the question Aksenov's wife asked him in prison affect him so deeply? How did it influence his behavior from then on? Do you think he was right to act as he did? Why or why not?
3. Describe the position Aksenov held among the prisoners in the Siberian camp. What did this reveal about his spiritual growth during his years of suffering?
4. What struggle took place in Aksenov when the warden asked him who had been digging under the wall? How did Aksenov resolve the conflict? Do you think he made the correct choice? Why or why not?
5. Why do you think Aksenov did not take advantage of Semenov's confession? Was this consistent with the development of Aksenov's character? Explain. In your own words, state the theme of this story.
6. Point out passages which show that Aksenov was not meek and passive, but dynamic and practical.
7. Foreshadowing is the dropping of important hints by an author to prepare the reader for what is to come. How was the tragedy that occurred to Aksenov foreshadowed early in the story?
8. Tolstoy had the problem of making this story, based on accidental circumstances, seem plausible. Do you think the story gave the appearance of being possible and true? Why or why not? Did the plausibility of the story depend essentially on characterization or on action? Explain.
9. This story has three distinct settings. How did the author succeed in unifying the diverse situations in the inn, the prison, and the Siberian camp? Observe how, with the increase of Aksenov's suffering, there is an increase in his spiritual growth.

Where Love Is, God Is

*I*N a certain town, there once lived a shoemaker named Martin Avdeich. He lived in a cellar in a tiny room with one window. The window looked out on the street, and through it one could watch the people passing by. Only their feet could be seen, but it was by their shoes that Martin Avdeich recognized people. Martin Avdeich had lived in the same place a long time and knew many people. It was a rare pair of shoes in the neighborhood that had not passed through his hands once or twice. Some he had resoled, some he had patched, others he had restitched, and for some he had even made new toes. And he often saw his work go by the window. Avdeich had a great deal of work because he worked honestly, used good material, did not overcharge, and kept his word. If he could finish a job on time, he took it; if he could not, he would say so in advance and not deceive people. Everyone knew Avdeich and he always had plenty of work.

He had always been a good man, and as he grew older, he began to give more thought to his soul and draw closer to God. His wife had died while he was still an apprentice, and had left him with only one son, three years of age; their older children had all died before. At first Martin wanted to send his little son to his sister in the country; then he felt remorse, thinking: "It would be hard for my little Kapitoshok to grow up in a strange family. I'll keep him myself." So Avdeich left his master and moved with his son into an apartment. But God granted Avdeich no luck with his children. As soon as the boy had grown up and begun to be a delight and a help to his father, he caught a disease, went to bed, had fever for a week, and died. Martin buried his son and became despondent, so despondent that he began grumbling at God. In his despair, he asked God for death more than once, and reproached Him for taking his beloved only son instead of an old man like himself. Avdeich stopped going to church. Then, one day, an old man from his native village, who had been on a pilgrimage for seven years, came by on his way from Troitsa. Avdeich talked with him and complained about his misfortunes.

"And I no longer want to live, Holy Man," he said; "if only I could die. That's all I ask of God. I've become a man without hope, now."

And the old man replied to him:

"What you are saying is not good, Martin; we must never judge God's doings. God's judgment decides them, not our minds. God judged that your son should die and you should live; which means it was best so. And what makes you miserable is that you want to live for your own pleasure."

"But what else does one live for?" asked Martin.

And the old man said to him:

"One must live for God, Martin. He gives you life, and you must live for Him. When you begin to live for Him, you will no longer grieve for anything, and everything will seem easy for you."

Martin was silent. Then he said:

"And how does one live for God?"

And the old man said:

"That's what Christ showed us: how to live for God. Can you read? Buy the Gospel and read it: there you'll learn how to live for God. Everything is to be found there."

These words made a deep impression on Avdeich's heart. And that very day he went and bought himself the New Testament in large print and began reading it.

Avdeich had meant to read only on holidays, but when he began reading, he felt so at peace in his soul, that he began to read every day. Once he became so absorbed in reading that he burned out all the kerosene in his lamp before he could tear himself away from the book. And the more he read, the more clearly he understood what God wanted of him and how one must live for God; and his heart grew lighter and lighter. Before, when he lay down to sleep, he used to moan and groan and keep remembering his Kapitoshok, but now he just repeated over and over: "Glory to Thee, glory to Thee, O Lord! Thy will be done." And from that time on, Avdeich's whole life was transformed. Before, he used to drink tea in the tavern on holidays, and, as a matter of fact, would not refuse a little vodka. After drinking a while with a friend, although not drunk, he would leave the inn tipsy and talking nonsense; and he sometimes shouted at people or abused them. Now all these habits left him of themselves, and his life became calm and happy. From early morning, he would sit at his work, and after the day's work he would take out his little lamp, put it on the table, get his book from the shelf, open it, and settle down to read. And the more he read, the more he understood; and the more he understood, the clearer and more joyful his heart became.

One evening, Martin had become absorbed and read late. He was reading the Gospel according to Luke. He read through the Sixth Chapter and the verses:

"If a man strikes thee on the cheek, offer him the other cheek too; if a man would take away thy cloak, do not begrudge him thy coat along with it. Give to every man who asks, and if a man takes what is thine, do not ask him to restore it. As you would have men treat you, you are to treat them; not otherwise."

Martin also read those verses in which the Lord says:

"How is it that you call me Master, Master, and will not do what I bid you? If anyone comes to me and listens to my commandments and carries them out, I will tell you what he is like; he is a man that would build a house, who dug, dug deep, and laid his foundation on rock. Then a flood came, and the river broke upon that house, but could not stir it; it was founded upon rock. But the man who listens to what I say and does not carry it out is like a man who built his house in the earth without foundation; when the river broke upon it, it fell at once, and great was that house's ruin."

As Avdeich read these words, his soul became happy. He took off his glasses, laid them on the book, leaned his elbows on the table, and became thoughtful. And he began to measure his life against these words. And he thought to himself:

"Is my house built on rock or on sand? If it's rock, it's good. It seems quite easy, sitting here alone; it's easy to think you've followed all God's commandments, but then you overstep—and sin again. Still, I'll keep trying. It's already better. Help me, O Lord!"

Thinking these thoughts, he was about to go to bed, but did not want to tear himself away from the book. He began reading the Seventh Chapter; he read about the centurion, about the widow's son, about the answer to John's disciples, and he came to the place in which the rich Pharisee invites the Lord to his house as a guest; and he read how the sinful woman anointed His feet and bathed them with her tears, and how He absolved her. And he came to the Forty-Fourth Verse and began reading:

"Then he turned toward the woman, and said to Simon, Dost thou see this woman? I came into thy house, and thou gavest me no water for my feet; she has washed my feet with her tears, and wiped them with her hair. Thou gavest me no kiss of greeting; she has never ceased to kiss my feet since I entered; thou didst not pour oil on my head; she has anointed my feet, and with ointment."

He read these verses and thought:

"Thou gavest no water, thou gavest no kiss, thou didst not pour oil on My head . . ." And again Avdeich took off his glasses, laid then on the book, and became thoughtful. "The Pharisee must have been just like me," he said to himself. "Like me, he thought only of himself. He would drink tea in warmth and comfort, but without giving a thought to his guest. He took care of himself, but no care of his guest. And who was his guest? The Lord Himself! If He had come to me, would I have done the same?"

And Avdeich put his head in his hands and fell asleep without realizing it.

"Martin!" A voice seemed to breathe in his ear, suddenly.

Martin roused himself, half-awake.

"Who's there?" He turned around, glanced toward the door—no one. He settled down again. Suddenly he heard distinctly:

"Martin! Oh, Martin! Look out in the street tomorrow—I shall come!"

Martin woke up, rose from his chair, and rubbed his eyes. He could not tell whether he had heard or dreamt these words. Putting out the lamp, he went to bed.

The next morning, Avdeich got up before dawn, prayed, heated the stove, put on his cabbage soup and *kasha*, lit the samovar, put on his apron, and sat down near the window to work. Avdeich sat and worked, but he kept thinking about what happened on the previous evening. And his thoughts were divided: sometimes he felt he had been dreaming, and sometimes he felt he had actually heard that voice. "Well," he thought, "such things have happened."

Martin sat by the window and did more looking out of the window than working, and whenever anyone came by in unfamiliar shoes, he would stoop and peer out the window to see the face as well as the boots. A house-porter came by in new felt boots; a water carrier passed by. Then an old soldier of Nikolai I's days came even with the window wearing welted old felt boots and carrying a shovel in his hands. Avdeich recognized him by his boots; the old man was called Stepanich, and he lived on charity at the house of a neighboring tradesman; his duties were to help the house-porter. Stepanich began clearing away the snow outside Avdeich's window. Avdeich glanced at him and went back to work.

"See, you've grown stupid with old age," Avdeich thought, laughing at himself. "Stepanich comes to clear away snow, and I think it's Christ come to me. What a stupid old fool I've become."

However, Avdeich had only taken a dozen stitches, when he was again drawn to look out the window. When he looked out, he saw Stepanich leaning his shovel against the wall and trying either to rest or get warm.

"He's an old man; obviously worn out, and not strong enough to shovel snow," thought Avdeich. "Why not give him a little tea? The samovar's just come to a boil anyway."

Avdeich thrust in his awl, got up, put the samovar on the table, fixed the tea, and rapped his fingers on the windowpane. Stepanich turned around and came to the window.

"Come on in and get warm," said Martin. "You're frozen, aren't you?"

"Christ keep you, my bones are aching," said Stepanich.

Stepanich came in, shook off the snow, and carefully wiping his feet, almost fell down.

"Don't bother wiping your feet. I'll mop up; it's all in a day's work. Come in, sit down, and have some tea," said Avdeich.

And Avdeich prepared two glasses of tea, pushed one toward his guest, poured his own in a saucer, and began blowing on it.

Stepanich drank down his glass, turned it bottom up, put the remainder of his sugar lump on top, and thanked him. It was easy to see that he wanted more.

"Have another," Avdeich said, pouring a second glass for his guest and himself.

Avdeich drank his tea, glancing out the window from time to time.

"You waiting for someone?" his guest asked.

"Waiting? I'm ashamed to say who I'm waiting for. I'm waiting, well, not really, but I can't get those words out of my mind. Whether it was a vision or what, I don't know myself. You see, my friend, I was reading the Gospel of our Lord Jesus last night, and how he suffered when he was on earth. I guess you've heard about it?"

"Yes, I've heard," answered Stepanich, "but we're ignorant people and can't read."

"Well, then, I was reading about how He was on earth, and how he came to the Pharisee and how that man did nothing to receive him. Well, then, I was reading along, my friend, and I was thinking about how he didn't receive our Little Father Jesus with honor. If he came to me, for instance, I was thinking, how would I receive him? But the Pharisee did nothing to receive him. So I was thinking like that, and I fell asleep. Fell asleep, my friend, and heard somebody calling me by name; I got up. It was a voice like somebody whispering. 'Wait,' it said, 'tomorrow I shall come.' Twice this happened. Now you see, believe it or not, it's stuck in my mind—I reason with myself, but I still keep waiting for Him, the Little Father!"

Stepanich nodded his head and said nothing. He drank down his glass and put it on its side, but Avdeich picked up the glass and filled it again.

"Drink to your health. You see, I was thinking that when He, the Little Father, was on earth, he scorned nobody, and went about with simple people. He was always among simple people, and he chose his disciples mostly from people like us sinners—workers. 'He who is exalted, shall be humbled, and he who is humble shall be exalted. Ye call me Lord,' He said, 'but I,' He said, 'will wash your feet. Let whoever wants to lead, be the servant of everyone. Because,' He said, 'blessed are the poor, the humble, the meek, and the merciful.' "

Stepanich forgot his tea; he was an old man, and cried easily. He sat, listening, with tears rolling down his face.

"Come, have some more," said Avdeich. But Stepanich crossed himself, thanked him, pushed his glass away, and stood up.

"Thank you, Martin Avdeich," he said, "for inviting me; you have fed my soul as well as my body."

"You are welcome, come again; glad to have a guest," said Avdeich.

When Stepanich had gone, Martin poured himself the last of the tea, drank it, put away the dishes, and sat down again at his window to work. He was stitching a counter on a shoe. Stitching, and still looking out the window all the time—waiting for Christ and thinking about Him and His deeds. And Christ's many sayings ran through his head.

Two soldiers passed by, one in army issued boots, the other in his own; the owner of the neighboring house went past in well-cleaned galoshes; a baker walked by with a basket. They all passed by, and then a woman in woolen stockings and very old shoes came even with the window, passed it, and stopped by the wall next to it. Avdeich looked at her through the window and saw that she was a stranger, badly dressed, standing against the wall with her back to the wind and a child in her arms. She was trying to wrap up the child, but had almost nothing with which to cover it. She wore summer clothes, and ragged ones, at that. Through the window, Avdeich heard the baby crying, and the woman trying to soothe it. Avdeich got up, went out the door and up the steps, calling out, "My good woman!" The woman heard and turned around.

"What are you standing in the cold for with your baby? Come in the room. You can wrap him up better where it's warm. Come on in!"

The woman was surprised to see an old man in an apron with glasses on his nose calling to her, but she followed him.

They went down the steps into the room. The old man led the woman over to the bed.

"Sit down here, my good woman," he said. "It's closer to the stove—warm yourself and feed the little one."

"I've no milk; I haven't eaten since morning myself," said the woman, but she took the child to her breast just the same.

Avdeich nodded his head, went to the table, fetched bread and a bowl; then opening the oven door, he poured cabbage soup in the bowl. He took out the pot of *kasha* too, but it was not ready yet. So he set the soup on the table. He spread a cloth on the table and fetched bread.

"Sit down and eat, good woman; I'll sit with the little one. I've had children of my own—I know how to look after them."

The woman crossed herself, sat down at the table, and started to eat while Avdeich sat on the bed with the baby. Avdeich made clucking noises with his lips, but the sound was not right because he had no teeth. The child kept crying. Then he thought of startling the infant with his fingers, and he waved his finger in front of the child's mouth and whisked it away again, over and over, never letting the child suck it because it was black with cobbler's wax. The child began watching the finger and became quiet; then started to laugh. Avdeich was delighted. Meanwhile, the woman was eating and telling who she was and where she was going.

"They took my soldier husband somewhere eight months ago and I haven't heard since. I worked as a cook till I gave birth—they wouldn't keep me with a child. This is the third month I've been struggling along without work. I've eaten up everything I had. Tried to be a wet nurse—didn't work; too thin, they said. I was going to go to a merchant's wife where a woman I know works, and they promised to take me. I thought I could start at once, but she just told me to come back next week. And she lives far away. I'm starved and the little one's worn out. Thank God the landlady's sorry for us and gives us room for the love of Christ. Otherwise, I don't know how we'd live."

Avdeich sighed and said:

"Don't you have any warm clothes?"

"It would be a fine thing indeed, to have some warm clothing, my dear. Yesterday I pawned my last shawl for twenty kopecks."

The woman went to the bed and picked up the child, while Avdeich got up, went over the the coat hooks on the wall, rummaged around, and got out an old coat.

"Come," he said, "it's an old thing, but it'll do to wrap him in."

The woman looked at the coat, looked at the old man, took the coat, and burst into tears. Avdeich turned away; then he crawled under the bed, dragged out an old truck, groped in it, and sat down again opposite the woman.

And the woman said:

"Christ keep you, Grandfather. It's plain He sent me to your window. Or the child would have frozen. It was warm when I left, but now it's turned cold. And He, the Little Father, made you look out the window and see and take pity on miserable me!"

Avdeich smiled and said:

"He did, it's true. I wasn't looking out the window by accident, my good woman."

And Martin told the soldier's wife about his dream and how he had heard the voice of the Lord promising to come to him that day.

"Take this for the sake of Christ, to get back your shawl," Avdeich said as he gave her twenty kopecks.

The woman crossed herself. Avdeich crossed himself, and went to the door with her. When the woman had gone, Avdeich finished eating his cabbage soup, cleared away the dishes, and sat down to work again. As he worked, he kept thinking of the window—as soon as a shadow crossed it, he looked to see who was passing. People he knew walked by, strangers walked by, but no one unusual. Then Avdeich saw an old woman peddler stopping opposite his window. She was carrying a basket of apples. Few were left; she had evidently sold most of them, but over her shoulder she had a sack of wood chips, which she had probably gathered near a half-finished house. It was obvious that the bag weighed heavily on her shoulder. She stopped to shift it to the other side; putting it down on the sidewalk and setting her apple-basket on a post, she began shaking down the chips in the sack. And while she was shaking the sack, a little boy in a torn cap whirled out of nowhere, snatched an apple out of the basket, and was about to slip off when the woman turned and grabbed him by the sleeve.

The little boy struggled trying to break loose, but the old woman, grasping him with both hands, knocked off his cap and seized him by the hair. The boy shouted; the old woman cursed. Without taking time to thrust in his awl, Avdeich let it fall on the floor as he jumped out the door, dropping his glasses and stumbling on the steps. When he ran out in the street, the old woman was pulling the boy's curls and cursing, threatening to take him to the police; the little boy was parrying her blows and protesting: "I never took it, why hit me? Let me go!" Avdeich separated them, took the boy by the hand, and said:

"Let him go, Grandmother, forgive and forget for the sake of Christ!"

"I'll give him something he won't forget till the cows come home! I'll take the rascal to the police."

Avdeich beseeched the old woman:

"Let him go, Grandmother; he won't do it again. Let him go for the sake of Christ!"

The old woman released him; the boy was about to run off, but Avdeich held him back.

"Ask the Grandmother's pardon! And don't do it again. I saw you take it."

The boy burst into tears and begged her pardon.

"Well, all right. And now here's an apple for you," Avdeich said, taking one out of the basket and giving it to the boy. "I'll pay you for it, Grandmother," he said to the old woman.

"You'll spoil them that way, the thieves," said the old woman. "He should get a reward he wouldn't forget for a week."

"Ah, Grandmother," said Avdeich. "That's our way, but not God's. If he should be whipped for an apple, what should be done to us for our sins?"

The old woman was silent.

And Avdeich told the old woman the parable of how a master released his servant from a large debt, and how the ungrateful servant then went and choked his own debtor. The old woman listened, and the boy stood, listening too.

"God tells us to forgive," said Avdeich, "or we won't be forgiven, and above all, a thoughtless child."

The old woman nodded her head and sighed.

"It's true," she said; "but still, they're very spoiled."

"Then we older ones must teach them," said Avdeich.

"That's what I say," said the old woman. "I had seven of them; one daughter is still living." And the old woman began telling how and where she lived with her daughter, and how many grandchildren she had. "Now," she said, "my strength isn't what it used to be, but I work hard for the sake of my children and grandchildren; and they're good grandchildren. No one greets me like they do. Aksyuta —she won't leave me for anyone. 'Grandma, dear, darling Grandma!' she says . . ." The old woman became very tender and said, nodding at the little boy, "Of course it was child's stuff; God be with you."

The old woman was about to hoist the sack onto her shoulder, when the boy sprang forward and said:

"Let me take it, I'm going that way."

The old woman nodded her head and shifted the sack onto the boy's back. And they went down the road together. The old woman even forgot to ask Avdeich to pay for the apple. Avdeich stood watching and listening to them, walking and talking constantly.

When they were gone, Avdeich turned back home, found his glasses, unbroken, on the steps, picked up his awl, and sat down at his work again. After working a while, he could barely see to thread a bristle, and he noticed that the lamplighter had come to light the street lamps. "I must light the light," he thought, and he trimmed the lamp, hung it up, and began working again. He finished one boot, turned it around, looked at it—it was fine. He put his tools together, swept up the scraps, put away the bristles and threads and awls, took the lamp, put it on the table, and got his Gospel from the shelf. He intended to open his book again at the place he had marked with a bit of leather the day before, but it opened to another spot. As he opened the Gospel, Avdeich remembered his dream. And just as he remembered it, he suddenly heard footsteps, as if there were someone behind him. When he looked around, he thought he saw people standing in the dark corner, but he could not make out who they were. And a voice whispered in his ear:

"Martin, oh Martin, don't you know Me?"

"Who?" murmured Martin.

"Me," said the voice. "It is I."

And old Stepanich stepped, smiling, out of the dark corner; he smiled, then vanished like a cloud, and was no more . . .

"And it is I," said a voice. And the woman with the child came out of the dark corner and smiled; and the child laughed; and they also disappeared.

"And it is I," said a voice. Out stepped the old woman and the boy with the apple, and both smiled and disappeared.

And Avdeich's heart was happy. He crossed himself, put on his glasses, and began reading the Gospel where it had opened. And he read aloud from the top of the page:

"And I hungered and ye gave Me to eat; and thirsted, and ye gave Me to drink; I was a stranger, and ye took Me in . . ."

And at the bottom of the page, he read:

"Inasmuch as ye did this unto one of My brethren, ye did it unto Me." (Matthew, Chapter XXV)

And Avdeich realized that his dream had not deceived him, and that the Saviour had truly come to him that day, and that he had truly received him.

For Discussion

1. Avdeich changed from an unhappy man who wished for death to a truly happy man. What was the cause of this change? How did his attitude toward other people play an important part in this change?

2. One of Tolstoy's favorite themes is how man acts when confronted with death. How did Avdeich act after his son died? What was wrong

with his attitude? What change occurred in Avdeich about this? Did you find this change believable? Why or why not?

3. Point out how every age of human life was represented by the people who came to Avdeich's room. What did all these people have in common? Do you think this revealed anything about Tolstoy's attitude toward people? If so, what?

4. Explain how the theme of this story supports Tolstoy's idea of man's unending search for God. How is the title of the story borne out by the theme?

5. What do you think Tolstoy felt about class distinctions? How was this shown in the choice of his "hero"?

6. The setting for this story is a one-window basement room through which Avdeich saw only the boots of passers-by. What symbolic meaning do you see in Tolstoy's choice of setting? Would the effect have been as great if Avdeich had lived in a room on the street-level? Why or why not?

7. Do you think that the change that occurred in Avdeich was convincing and consistent? Why or why not? Show how he is, or is not, a true-to-life character.

For Composition

1. Write a composition in which you show how these two stories by Tolstoy reveal his basic idea that there is need for suffering in man's life and that he is ultimately dependent on God as the source of his inner strength and peace.

2. Tolstoy had as his stated purpose "to describe the inner consciousness" of his characters. Write a paper in which you show specifically how the two stories you have read illustrate this.

3. Write a composition in which you compare the theme of "Where Love Is, God Is" with that of Dostoyevsky's "An Honest Thief."

The French Symbolists

*I*N the second half of the nineteenth century, a group of French poets reacted against the type of poetry being written at the time, which emphasized perfection of conventional forms and the direct representation of subject matter. This group of poets was also opposed to sentimental and didactic verse, so popular in that period. The "symbolists," as they called themselves, saw poetry as a search for the mystery of reality behind the everyday world perceived through the senses. The main instruments in this search were the music of poetry and the poetic symbol. They believed that an emotional experience was most truthfully expressed through an image or symbol drawn from the external world.

Convinced that each poet had unique experiences and feelings to convey, the symbolists abandoned the old, conventional patterns and symbols and invented new ones specifically related to their personal insights. Unlike the realists and naturalists in vogue at the time, who attempted to present things as they were, the symbolists were preoccupied with the *interpretation of the effect* which things made on the human mind and spirit. Their "revolt" included the use of new subject matter, especially psychological states of mind, which many critics looked upon as "shocking." They also adopted a new technique called "synesthesia," or the description of one sense in terms of another; for example, attributing color to sound, fragrance to color, sound to odors. The purpose was to show the unity behind the diversity of sense experiences.

The chief concern of the symbolists was to capture the essence of a setting or mood and to convey in dreamlike fashion "the vagueness and elusiveness of human experience." As a result, their poetry was suggestive rather than direct in its statement, and the meaning was often difficult to get at immediately. The first members of the new symbolist "school"—Baudelaire and Verlaine—retained the traditional French meters. Later symbolist poets, such as Rimbaud and Mallarmé, employed free verse. All of them emphasized the use of color and sound, striving to capture the rhythms of music. Above all, they wished to express their own personalities without reference to a reading audience.

CHARLES BAUDELAIRE * (1821–1867), often called the "Father of French Symbolism," revolted against romantic pretense and the bourgeois ideas prevalent in his day. Unlike many romantic poets, who found inspiration only in nature, he found beauty and mystery in city life. Most of the poems in his book *Les Fleurs du Mal* (*Flowers of Evil*) reveal his obsession with physical decay and spiritual weariness—attitudes which he admittedly shared with Edgar Allan Poe. Although his poems are sometimes extremely sensuous, he attempted to suffuse them with the ideal. Baudelaire considered this unification of the sensuous with the ideal as the very function of art.

PAUL VERLAINE * (1844–1896), the most lyrical of the symbolist poets, wrote almost exclusively of his states of mind, which he conveyed through the imagery of landscape painted in delicate shades. He was a highly skilled technician, and he worked deliberately to make poetry a purely musical art form. The superb musical effects of his verse combined with a precision and simplicity of language made him one of the most popular French poets of his time. Like Baudelaire, he retained the traditional, poetic forms, but Verlaine gave them a new fluidity as he captured his elusive sensations and emotions in verse.

ARTHUR RIMBAUD * (1854–1891), a brilliant stylist and experimenter with French verse forms, wrote most of his poetry between the ages of sixteen and twenty-one. His work, with its emphasis on dreams and the unconscious, had an important influence on the surrealists of a later period. About one of his most famous poems, "Le Bateau Ivre" ("The Drunken Boat"), he stated that he attempted by a deliberate distortion of the senses, to reach the Absolute. The result was a series of brilliant images, arranged in a dreamlike fashion, without seeming logic.

The French symbolists had a marked effect on modern poets, notably Paul Valéry. In the poetry of today can be found the various characteristics of the symbolists: a concern with psychological states, the preoccupation with city life, the expression of spiritual weariness, private and newly created symbols, the use of free verse, the juxtaposition of seemingly non-logical images, and the use of synesthesia.

* shàrl bō dlâr'   * pôl vâr len'   * àr tür' ran bō'

Charles Baudelaire

Correspondences

Nature is a temple from whose living columns
Commingling voices emerge at times;
Here man wanders through forests of symbols
Which seem to observe him with familiar eyes.

Like long-drawn echoes afar converging   5
In harmonies darksome and profound,
Vast as the night and vast as light,
Colors, scents and sounds correspond.

There are fragrances fresh as the flesh of children,
Sweet as the oboe, green as the prairie,   10
—And others overpowering, rich and corrupt,

Possessing the pervasiveness of everlasting things,
Like benjamin, frankincense, amber, myrrh,
Which the raptures of the senses and the spirit sing.

(tr. Kate Flores)

Landscape

I want, the more chastely to compose my verse,
To sleep close to the sky, like the astrologers,
And, neighbor of steeples, as I dream, to attend
To their grave anthems carried away by the wind.
Chin in hands, from the height of my garret I'll discern   5
The workshop that sings and that gossips in turn,
The pipe-stacks, the steeples, those masts of the city,
And the great skies that foster dreams of eternity.

It is sweet, through the mists, to see begin to glow
The star in azure dark, the lamp at the window,   10
The rivers of coal-smoke ascending to the height
And the moon with enchantment spending her pale light.
I shall witness the Springs, the Summers, the Falls;
And when Winter comes with monotonous snowfalls
I shall close all around me shutters and lattices   15
To build into the night my fairy palaces.

Then I'll dream of horizons the blue of heaven controls,
Of gardens, fountains weeping in alabaster bowls,
Of kisses, of birds singing morning and eve,
And of all that's most childlike the Idyll has to give.   20
The tumult at my window vainly ranging grotesque
Shall not cause me to lift my forehead from my desk;
For I shall be absorbed in that exquisitely still
Delight of evoking the Spring with my will,
Of wresting a sun from my own heart and in calm   25
Drawing from my burning thoughts an atmosphere of balm.

(tr. Vernon Watkins)

The Swan

To Victor Hugo

1

Andromache, I think of you! —This little stream,
Poor wretched mirror resplendent once
With all the grandeur of your widow's grief,
This deceptive Simoïs, heightened with your tears,

Has suddenly, as I wandered through the new Carrousel,   5
Restored a fertile memory of mine.
—Old Paris is no more (the contours of a city
Change, alas! more quickly than a mortal heart);

Only in spirit do I see that regiment of booths,
That array of makeshift capitals and posts,   10

The turf, the rough stones greened by the puddle waters,
And, gleaming in the cases, the jumbled bric-a-brac.

There at one time a menagerie stood;
There I saw one morning, at the hour when, under cold clear skies,
The working world awakes, and the cleaners of the streets   15
Hurl into the quiet air a dismal hurricane,

A swan who had escaped his cage,
And, padding the dry pavement with his webbed feet,
Trailed his snowy plumage along the scraggly ground.
Beside a waterless gutter the creature opened his beak   20

And tremulously bathing his wings in the dust, cried,
His heart full of the lovely lake of his birth:
"Water, when the deluge? Tempests, when do you thunder?"
I can see that hapless one, strange and fatal myth,

Toward the heavens, sometimes, like Ovid's man,   25
Toward the heavens ironical and cruelly blue,
Bend his thirsting head upon his convulsive neck,
As though addressing reproaches unto God!

2

Paris changes! but my melancholy alters not a whit!
New palaces, scaffoldings, stocks,   30
Old neighborhoods to me are all allegory now,
And now my cherished remembrances are heavier than rocks!

Thus before this Louvre an image dejects me:
I think of my glorious swan, with his mad gestures,
Like the exiled, ridiculous and sublime,   35
And wrung by a truceless yearning! and then of you,

Andromache, fallen from a mighty husband's arms,
A lowly creature, beneath the hand of supernal Pyrrhus,
Bending down distraught beside an empty tomb;
Widow of Hector, alas! and wife to Helenus!   40

I think upon the Negress, tubercular and wasted,
Groveling in the mud, and seeking, with haggard eye,
Beyond the massive wall of mist,
Magnificent Africa's absent cocoanut palms;

Of all who have lost what cannot ever be regained, 45
Not ever! of those who drink their fill of tears
And suckle of Sorrow like a good she-wolf!
Of scrawny orphans desiccating like flowers!

Thus in the forest of my spirit's exile
An old Remembrance echoes full blast like a horn! 50
I think upon sailors forgotten on isles,
Of the captured, the defeated! . . . and of so many more!

(tr. Kate Flores)

For Discussion

"Correspondences"

1. What did Baudelaire feel about all the things in the world which appeal to the senses? Why did he call nature "a forest of symbols"?
2. In your opinion, what is this poem in praise of? How does the last line support this? What unity of opposites is praised in this line?
3. Explain the paradox in lines 11 and 12: other fragrances "rich and corrupt" which are like the "pervasiveness of everlasting things."
4. This poem exemplifies the symbolist poets' use of synesthesia, which describes one of the senses in terms of other senses. Which lines in the poem are examples of this?

"Landscape"

1. In this poem, Baudelaire was concerned with his role as poet. What did he consider his role to be? What part did the seasons play in his poetic life?
2. Do you think that this poem indicates that Baudelaire was an "ivory tower" poet? Why or why not? How much did he seem to be interested in the world? Point out lines to support your answer.
3. This poem reveals Baudelaire as a poet of the city. Was his attitude toward the city favorable or unfavorable? Point out lines to support your answer.

4. Note the imagery in the first stanza. What purpose do you think the poet had in choosing places so high up?
5. What opposite emotions did Baudelaire wish to fuse in his poetry, as revealed in the last two lines?

"The Swan"

1. The mood of this poem is one of deep melancholy. What was the cause of this mood? Do you think it was in proportion to its cause? Why or why not?
2. The two images upon which Baudelaire based the poem were those of Andromache and the swan. Andromache, the faithful wife of Hector, the great Trojan warrior, was taken by force from her homeland after her husband's cruel death, and married to Helenus, son of the Greek warrior, Pyrrhus. She never saw Troy again. Both Andromache and the swan, then, represent exile from a former state of happiness. What universal state of exile did they represent for the poet?
3. How did the swan react to its situation? In what way did the swan symbolize mankind?
4. How does the description of contemporary Paris serve as a link between the swan image and that of Andromache? Are the two images consistent? Why or why not?
5. In Part 2, the emphasis is on both Baudelaire's personal feelings and the universality of the condition of exile. Point out images of exile other than those of the swan and Andromache. Discuss their effectiveness.
6. In the first stanza of Part 2, the poet declared that the old neighborhoods he had formerly known were all "allegory" now. An allegory is a story in which characters or happenings represent ideas, usually moral concepts. In what way were the old neighborhoods "allegories" to the poet?
7. How would you evaluate Baudelaire's judgment of mankind's situation? Is the poet's melancholy sufficiently supported artistically in the poem? Is his theme essentially true? Explain. How would you evaluate the poem as a whole, from the Christian viewpoint?

Paul Verlaine

God Said . . .

God said: "My son you must love me. You see
My pierced side, my heart radiant with blood,
And my injured feet bathed by Magdalene's tears,
My arms that ache under the weight of your

Sins, my hands too! You see the cross,   5
You see nails, gall, sponge, and all teach you
To love in this bitter world of flesh
Only my Flesh and Blood, my word and voice.

Oh, have I not loved you even unto death,
Brother in my Father, son in the Holy Ghost,   10
Have I not suffered for you as it was written?

Have I not sobbed for you in your great agony,
Have I not sweated the sweat of your dark nights,
Oh pitiful friend, who seeks me when I am here?"

(tr. Muriel Kittel)

The Sky Above the Roof

The sky above the roof
  Is so blue, so calm!
A tree above the roof
  Sways its fronds.

The bell in the sky we see   5
  Softly chimes.
A bird in the tree we see
  Sings its lament.

203

Dear God, dear God, life is there,
 Simple and still.   10
That peaceful murmur there
 Comes from the town.

What have you done, you who are here,
 Weeping endlessly?
Oh, what have you done, you who are here, 15
 With the days of your youth?
      (*tr. Muriel Kittel*)

Moonlight

Your soul is like a painter's landscape where
charming masks in shepherd mummeries
are playing lutes and dancing with an air
of being sad in their fantastic guise.

Even while they sing, all in a minor key, 5
of love triumphant and life's careless boon,
they seem in doubt of their felicity,
their song melts in the calm light of the moon,

the lovely melancholy light that sets
the little birds to dreaming in the tree 10
and among the statues makes the jets
of slender fountains sob with ecstasy.
      (*tr. C. F. MacIntyre*)

The Art of Poetry

You must have music first of all,
and for that a rhythm uneven is best,
vague in the air and soluble,
with nothing heavy and nothing at rest.

You must not scorn to do some wrong   5
in choosing the words to fill your lines:
nothing more dear than the tipsy song
where the Undefined and Exact combine.

It is the veiled and lovely eye,
the full noon quivering with light;   10
it is, in the cool of an autumn sky,
the blue confusion of stars at night!

Never the Color, always the Shade,
always the nuance is supreme!
Only by shade is the trothal made   15
between flute and horn, of dream with dream!

Epigram's an assassin! Keep
away from him, fierce Wit, and vicious
laughter that makes the Azure weep,
and from all that garlic of vulgar dishes!   20

Take Eloquence and wring his neck!
You would do well, by force and care,
wisely to hold Rhyme in check,
or she's off—if you don't watch—God knows where!

Oh, who will tell the wrongs of Rhyme?   25
What crazy negro or deaf child
made this trinket for a dime,
sounding hollow and false when filed?

Let there be music, again and forever!
Let your verse be a quick-wing'd thing and light—   30
such as one feels when a new love's fervor
to other skies wings the soul in flight.

Happy-go-lucky, let your lines
disheveled run where the dawn winds lure,
smelling of wild mint, smelling of thyme . . .   35
and all the rest is literature.

                         (*tr.* C. F. *MacIntyre*)

For Discussion

"God Said . . ." and "The Sky Above the Roof"

1. At thirty, Paul Verlaine became a convert to the Catholic faith. These two poems are clearly evident of his later preoccupation with religious themes. In "God Said . . ." he carefully listed the images of Christ's passion. What is the relation between these and the last line of the poem?
2. In "The Sky Above the Roof" Verlaine pictured the innocence of the world of nature and the inanimate world as contrasted with the rational world of the human heart. Point out lines which reveal this.
3. Note Verlaine's use of simple diction. Why do you think it is particularly effective in this poem?
4. In the last stanza, there is a complete change in rhythm and meter. Why do you think this occurs? What technical means did Verlaine use to convey the anguish in these lines?

"Moonlight"

1. Verlaine's stated intention was to evoke a mood in his poetry, rather than to communicate an idea. What is the mood of this poem?
2. Point out how the delicate imagery evokes the feeling of longing, regret, the inexpressible, the eternal.
3. What conflict is suggested in the poem? Is there a triumph? Explain.
4. Compare and contrast the mood of this poem with that of Baudelaire's "The Swan." Do you think the emotion in "Moonlight" is either too great or too intense for the situation? Why or why not?

"The Art of Poetry"

1. This poem can be considered a statement of the symbolist poets' creed. Point out lines which show the elements Verlaine considered important in a poem.
2. What elements did he warn poets to avoid? Do you agree or disagree? Why?
3. What contraries did he think poetry should unite? Did he find these contraries united in reality? Explain. Show how Verlaine fused these opposites in his poem "Moonlight."
4. Consult a dictionary for the meaning of the word *nuance*. Point out instances of Verlaine's use of nuances.

Arthur Rimbaud

Morning

. . . .

Yet now I think I have finished the tale of my inferno. And inferno it was: the old one, whose gates the Son of Man flung open.

From the same desert, on the same night, my eyes still awake to the silvery star, still, as the Kings of life, the Three Magi, heart, soul, and mind sleep untroubled. When shall we go beyond shores and mountains, to greet the birth of new labors, the new wisdom, the putting to flight of tyrants and demons, the end of superstition, and worship—the very first! —Noel on earth.

The song of the skies, the march of peoples! Slaves, let us not curse life.

(*tr. William M. Davis*)

My Bohemia

Fists in torn pockets I departed.
My overcoat grew ideal too.
I walked, your knight, O Muse,
And dreamed, O my! what glorious loves.

My only trousers had a hole.   5
Little Tom Thumb, I dropped my dreaming rhymes.
My lodging was the Great Bear Inn,
And in the sky my stars were rustling.

I listened, seated by the road—
In soft September—where the dew   10
Was wine of vigor on my face;

And in weird shadows rhyming, plucked like lyres,
The laces of my martyred shoes,
One foot against my heart.

(*tr. Louise Varèse*)

207

The Drunken Boat

As I descended black, impassive Rivers,
I sensed that haulers were no longer guiding me:
Screaming Redskins took them for their targets,
Nailed nude to colored stakes: barbaric trees.

I was indifferent to all my crews;   5
I carried English cottons, Flemish wheat.
When the disturbing din of haulers ceased,
The Rivers let me ramble where I willed.

Through the furious ripping of the sea's mad tides,
Last winter, deafer than an infant's mind,   10
I ran! And drifting, green Peninsulas
Did not know roar more gleefully unkind.

A tempest blessed my vigils on the sea.
Lighter than a cork I danced on the waves,
Those endless rollers, as they say, of graves: 15
Ten nights beyond a lantern's silly eye!

Sweeter than sourest apple-flesh to children,
Green water seeped into my pine-wood hull
And washed away blue wine stains, vomitings,
Scattering rudder, anchor, man's lost rule.   20

And then I, trembling, plunged into the Poem
Of the Sea, infused with stars, milk-white,
Devouring azure greens; where remnants, pale
And gnawed, of pensive corpses fell from light;

Where, staining suddenly the blueness, delirium,   25
The slow rhythms of the pulsing glow of day,
Stronger than alcohol and vaster than our lyres,
The bitter reds of love ferment the way!

I know skies splitting into light, whirled spouts
Of water, surfs, and currents: I know the night,   30

The dawn exalted like a flock of doves, pure wing,
And I have seen what men imagine they have seen.

I saw the low sun stained with mystic horrors,
Lighting long, curdled clouds of violet,
Like actors in a very ancient play,   35
Waves rolling distant thrills like lattice light!

I dreamed of green night, stirred by dazzling snows,
Of kisses rising to the sea's eyes, slowly,
The sap-like coursing of surprising currents,
And singing phosphors, flaring blue and gold!   40

I followed, for whole months, a surge like herds
Of insane cattle in assault on the reefs,
Unhopeful that three Marys, come on luminous feet,
Could force a muzzle on the panting seas!

Yes, I struck incredible Floridas   45
That mingled flowers and the eyes of panthers
In skins of men! And rainbows bridled green
Herds beneath the horizon of the seas.

I saw the ferment of enormous marshes, weirs
Where a whole Leviathan lies rotting in the weeds!   50
Collapse of waters within calms at sea,
And distances in cataract toward chasms!

Glaciers, silver suns, pearl waves, and skies like coals,
Hideous wrecks at the bottom of brown gulfs
Where giant serpents eaten by red bugs   55
Drop from twisted trees and shed a black perfume!

I should have liked to show the young those dolphins
In blue waves, those golden fish, those fish that sing.
—Foam like flowers rocked my sleepy drifting,
And, now and then, fine winds supplied me wings.   60

When, feeling like a martyr, I tired of poles and zones,
The sea, whose sobbing made my tossing sweet,
Raised me its dark flowers, deep and yellow whirled,
And, like a woman, I fell on my knees . . .

Peninsula, I tossed upon my shores   65
The quarrels and droppings of clamorous, blond-eyed birds.
I sailed until, across my rotting cords,
Drowned men, spinning backwards, fell asleep! . . .

Now I, a lost boat in the hair of coves,
Hurled by tempest into a birdless air,   70
I, whose drunken carcass neither Monitors
Nor Hansa ships would fish back for men's care;

Free, smoking, rigged with violet fogs,
I, who pierced the red sky like a wall
That carries exquisite mixtures for good poets,   75
Lichens of sun and azure mucus veils;

Who, spotted with electric crescents, ran
Like a mad plank, escorted by seahorses,
When cudgel blows of hot Julys struck down
The sea-blue skies upon wild water spouts;   80

I, who trembled, feeling the moan at fifty leagues
Of rutting Behemoths and thick Maelstroms, I,
Eternal weaver of blue immobilities,
I long for Europe with its ancient quays!

I saw sidereal archipelagoes! and isles   85
Whose delirious skies are open to the voyager:
—Is it in depthless nights you sleep your exile,
A million golden birds, O future Vigor?—

But, truly, I have wept too much! The dawns disturb.
All moons are painful, and all suns break bitterly: 90
Love has swollen me with drunken torpors.
Oh, that my keel might break and spend me in the sea!

Of European waters I desire
Only the black, cold puddle in a scented twilight
Where a child of sorrows squats and sets the sails   95
Of a boat as frail as a butterfly in May.

I can no longer, bathed in languors, O waves,
Cross the wake of cotton-bearers on long trips,
Nor ramble in a pride of flags and flares,
Nor swim beneath the horrible eyes of prison ships.

(*tr. Stephen Stepanchev*)

For Discussion

"Morning"

1. Rimbaud frequently used the form of the "prose poem," as in "Morning." What comparison did the poet make between the journey of the Magi to find Christ and man's journey toward true wisdom? Do you think that the details in the poem justify this comparison? Explain.
2. Explain the last two sentences. What is Rimbaud calling for?

"My Bohemia"

1. This is one of Rimbaud's attempts to describe his role as a poet and as a Bohemian. A Bohemian is a person interested in art or intellectual pursuits, who lives and acts with a disregard for the conventional rules of society. In what way was Rimbaud's world his "Bohemia"? What were some of the beauties of this world?
2. Point out evidence which reveals similarities between Rimbaud's world and the Bohemian world of our own time, such as New York's Greenwich Village and elsewhere.
3. To what did Rimbaud compare his shoelaces? In what way is this simile a fusion of the ideal and the real? How does this idea illustrate Rimbaud's role as a symbolist?

"The Drunken Boat"

1. This poem is a series of surrealistic or dreamlike images. As in a dream, the materials used by the poet are drawn from the everyday world, though differently arranged. Point out evidence of this in the poem.
2. Rimbaud had a great struggle in his life reconciling his desire for freedom and his desire for order. Which desire is predominant in this

poem? Explain. How does the title bear this out? Do the final stanzas reveal the opposite desire? Explain.

3. In your opinion, from what did the boat (or Rimbaud) have to be freed to make this trip possible? What was the plight of the boat at the poem's close? What does it symbolize?

4. Point out lines in which the sense of motion is achieved, conveying the experience of the voyage to the reader.

5. The symbolists' use of color and of synesthesia are apparent in this poem. Point out lines which reveal this.

6. Which images do you think are somewhat grotesque? Do you think they mar the beauty of the poem? Why or why not?

For Composition

1. Write a paper on the characteristics of the French symbolist poets. Use specific examples from the poems you have read of Baudelaire, Verlaine, and Rimbaud to support your statements.

2. Read T. S. Eliot's poem, "Journey of the Magi." Write a short critical essay in which you compare this poem with Rimbaud's "Morning." Explain which poem, in your opinion, carries a more profound meaning. Which poem had a greater emotional impact on you? Give reasons to support your answers.

Alphonse Daudet

The Last Class

Alphonse Daudet * (1840–1897), French short-story writer and novelist, is noted for his charming style, his exuberant humor, and his precise observation of life. It is this precise observation which makes him somewhat akin to Emile Zola and other writers of the naturalistic school. The naturalists were extreme realists who believed that life should be recorded scientifically in its most natural and everyday forms, rather than simply interpreted. Daudet, however, was more than a cold, scientific observer. He had a warm, humanitarian, even sentimental view of life which has sometimes been compared to that of Charles Dickens. His humor and fanciful imagination are to be found in two of his most famous works, *Letters from My Mill* and *Tartarin of Tarascon*.

Daudet's most famous short story is "The Last Class," one of a group of tales which he wrote about the Franco-Prussian War. This story reveals his simple and charming style, his careful observation of details, and his emotion about France after she was defeated by the Prussians in 1871.

I was very late for school that morning, and I was terribly afraid of being scolded, especially as Monsieur Hamel had told us that he should examine us on participles, and I did not know the first thing about them. For a moment I thought of staying away from school and wandering about the fields. It was such a warm, lovely day. I could hear the blackbirds whistling on the edge of the wood, and in the Rippert field, behind the sawmill, the Prussians going through their drill. All that was much more tempting to me than the rules concerning participles; but I had the strength to resist, and I ran as fast as I could to school.

As I passed the mayor's office, I saw that there were people gathered about the little board on which notices were posted. For two years all our bad news had come from that board—battles lost, con-

* ål fōns' dō de'

213

scriptions, orders from headquarters; and I thought without stopping:

"What can it be now?"

Then, as I ran across the square, Wachter the blacksmith, who stood there with his apprentice, reading the placard, called out to me:

"Don't hurry so, my boy, you'll get to your school soon enough!"

I thought that he was making fun of me, and I ran into Monsieur Hamel's little yard all out of breath.

Usually, at the beginning of school, there was a great uproar which could be heard in the street, desks opening and closing, lessons repeated aloud in unison, with our ears stuffed in order to learn quicker, and the teacher's stout ruler beating on the desk:

"A little more quiet!"

I counted on all this noise to get to my bench unnoticed; but as it happened, that day everything was quiet, like a Sunday morning. Through the open window I saw my comrades already in their places, and Monsieur Hamel walking back and forth with the terrible iron ruler under his arm. I had to open the door and enter, in the midst of that perfect silence. You can imagine whether I blushed and whether I was afraid!

But no! Monsieur Hamel looked at me with no sign of anger and said very gently:

"Go at once to your seat, my little Frantz; we were going to begin without you."

I stepped over the bench and sat down at once at my desk. Not until then, when I had partly recovered from my fright, did I notice that our teacher had on his handsome blue coat, his plaited ruff, and the black silk embroidered breeches, which he wore only on days of inspection or of distribution of prizes. Moreover, there was something extraordinary, something solemn about the whole class. But what surprised me most was to see at the back of the room, on the benches which were usually empty, some people from the village sitting, as silent as we were; old Hauser with his three-cornered hat, the ex-mayor, the ex-postman, and others besides. They all seemed depressed; and Hauser had brought an old spelling-book with gnawed edges, which he held wide open on his knee, with his spectacles askew.

While I was wondering at all this, Monsieur Hamel had mounted his platform, and in the same gentle and serious voice with which he had welcomed me, he said to us:

"My children, this is the last time that I shall teach you. Orders have come from Berlin to teach nothing but German in the schools of Alsace and Lorraine. The new teacher arrives tomorrow. This is the last class in French, so I beg you to be very attentive."

Those few words overwhelmed me. Ah! the villains! that was what they had posted at the mayor's office.

My last class in French!

And I barely knew how to write! So I should never learn! I must stop short where I was! How angry I was with myself because of the time I had wasted, the lessons I had missed, running about after nests or sliding on the Saar! My books, which only a moment before I thought so tiresome, so heavy to carry—my grammar, my sacred history—seemed to me now like old friends, from whom I should be terribly grieved to part. And it was the same about Monsieur Hamel. The thought that he was going away, that I should never see him again, made me forget the punishments, the blows with the ruler.

Poor man! It was in honor of that last lesson that he had put on his fine Sunday clothes; and I understood now why those old fellows from the village were sitting at the end of the room. It seemed to mean that they regretted not having come oftener to the school. It was also a very good way of thanking our teacher for his forty years of faithful service, and of paying their respects to the fatherland which was vanishing.

I was at that point in my reflections when I heard my name called. It was my turn to recite. What would I not have given to be able to say from beginning to end that famous rule about participles, in a loud distinct voice, without a slip! But I got mixed up at the first words, and I stood there swaying against my bench, with a full heart, afraid to raise my head. I heard Monsieur Hamel speaking to me:

"I will not scold you, my little Frantz; you must be punished enough; that is the way it goes; every day we say to ourselves: 'Pshaw! I have time enough. I will learn tomorrow!' And then you see what happens. Ah! It has been the great misfortune of our Alsace always to postpone its lessons until tomorrow. Now those people are entitled to say to us: 'What! You claim to be French, and you can neither speak nor write your language!' In all this, my poor Frantz, you are not the guiltiest one. We all have our fair share of reproaches to address to ourselves.

"Your parents have not been careful enough to see that you were educated. They preferred to send you to work in the fields or in the factories, in order to have a few more sous. And have I nothing to reproach myself for? Have I not often made you water my garden instead of studying? And when I wanted to go fishing for trout, have I ever hesitated to dismiss you?"

Then, passing from one thing to another, Monsieur Hamel began to talk to us about the French language, saying that it was the most beautiful language in the world, the most clear, the most substantial; that we must always retain it among ourselves, and never forget it, because when a people falls into servitude, "so long as it clings to its language, it is as if it held the key to its prison." Then he took the grammar and read us our lesson. I was amazed to see how readily I understood. Everything that he said seemed so easy to me, so easy. I believed, too, that I had never listened so closely, and that he, for his part, had never been so patient with his explanations. One would have said that, before going away, the poor man desired to give us all his knowledge, to force it all into our heads at a single blow.

When the lesson was at an end we passed to writing. For that day Monsieur Hamel had prepared some entirely new examples, on which was written in a fine, round hand: "France, Alsace, France, Alsace." They were like little flags, waving all about the class, hanging from the rods of our desks. You should have seen how hard we all worked and how silent it was! Nothing could be heard save the grinding of the pens over the paper. At one time some cockchafers flew in; but no one paid any attention to them, not even the little fellows, who were struggling with their straight lines, with a will and conscientious application, as if even the lines were French. On the roof of the schoolhouse pigeons cooed in low tones, and I said to myself as I listened to them:

"I wonder if they are going to compel them to sing in German too!"

From time to time, when I raised my eyes from my paper, I saw Monsieur Hamel sitting motionless in his chair and staring at the objects about him as if he wished to carry away in his glance the whole of his little schoolhouse. Think of it! For forty years he had been there in the same place, with his yard in front of him and his class just as it was! But the benches and desks were polished and rubbed by use: the walnuts in the yard had grown, and the hopvine which he himself had planted now festooned the windows even to the roof. What a heart-rending thing it must have been for that poor man to leave all those things, and to hear his sister walking back and forth in the room overhead, packing their trunks! For they were to go away the next day—to leave the province forever.

However, he had the courage to keep the class to the end. After the writing, we had the lesson in history; then the little ones sang all together the ba, be, bi, bo, bu. Yonder, at the back of the room, old Hauser had put on his spectacles, and, holding his spelling-book in both hands, he spelled out the letters with them. I could see that he too was applying himself. His voice shook with emotion, and it was so funny to hear him, that we all longed to laugh and to cry. Ah! I shall remember that last class.

Suddenly the church clock struck twelve, then the Angelus rang. At the same moment the bugles of the Prussians returning from drill blared under our windows. Monsieur Hamel rose, pale as death, from his chair. Never had he seemed to me so tall.

"My friends," he said, "my friends, I . . . I . . ."

But something suffocated him. He could not finish the sentence.

Thereupon he turned to the blackboard, took a piece of chalk, and, bearing on with all his might, he wrote in the largest letters he could:

"Vive la France!"

Then he stood there, with his head resting against the wall, and without speaking, he motioned to us with his hand:

"That is all; go."

For Discussion

1. What details in the first part of the story created a feeling of suspense, a feeling that something was wrong?
2. When Monsieur Hamel made his announcement, what was Frantz's reaction? Do you see any application to yourself in what Frantz felt? Explain. What universal truth is contained in Monsieur Hamel's speech to Frantz, beginning, "I will not scold you, my little Frantz. . . ." (page 215).

3. During the lesson, Frantz was amazed to find how readily he understood. Why do you think this was so? Is this a common experience? Discuss.
4. The naturalistic school believed that literature should not only record life realistically, but that it should also be a document of society. In what way is this story a social document? Which countries in our own time have been forced to learn a conqueror's language?
5. Point out passages in the story which reveal Monsieur Hamel's humility and self-criticism, his compassion for others, his kindness and dependability, his foresight, and his teaching ability.
6. Although this story has very little plot, there is a conflict present. What is it? Why do you think the author chose a simple schoolroom as the setting for this human experience? What was the author's purpose in having the other people present in the classroom?
7. Why do you think the author chose a little boy as the narrator, rather than one of the adults, such as old Hauser or Monsieur Hamel himself?

For Composition

1. Write a brief character sketch of Frantz. Include what was revealed about him in the way he reacted to the news of the new law passed by the Prussians.
2. Compare or contrast Daudet's style with that of another writer of the naturalistic school, such as Flaubert or Maupassant.

Guy de Maupassant

A Piece of String

Guy de Maupassant * (1850–1893) began his literary career under the personal supervision of his godfather, Gustave Flaubert. The influence of Flaubert can be seen in Maupassant's precise, realistic style, his desire to find the exact word to express what he saw, and his sharp observations of people. His short army career, followed by ten years as a government clerk, enabled him to glimpse closely almost every level of humanity: deposed nobles, bourgeois social climbers, tradesmen, clerks, peasants, and adventurers. All of them found a place in his ironical short stories.

Perhaps the most outstanding characteristic of Maupassant's work is its complete objectivity. While his characters were drawn from his own experiences, he never passed judgment on their deeds or on the motives which led them to act as they did. He preferred to let his characters reveal themselves through how they acted and what they said. Although his people are frequently greedy, miserly, vain men and women, he could write about them with a wry, sharp humor and often with pathos. The story which follows reveals Maupassant's simple, direct style and his ability to observe human nature closely and subtly.

$\mathcal{A}$ LONG all the roads around Goderville the peasants and their wives were coming toward the burgh because it was market day. The men were proceeding with slow steps, the whole body bent forward at each movement of their long twisted legs, deformed by their hard work, by the weight on the plow which, at the same time, raised the left shoulder and swerved the figure, by the reaping of the wheat which made the knees spread to make a firm "purchase," by all the slow and painful labors of the country. Their blouses, blue, "stiff-starched," shining as if varnished, ornamented with a little design in white at the neck and wrists, puffed about their bony bodies, seemed like balloons ready to carry them off. From each of them a head, two arms, and two feet protruded.

Some led a cow or a calf by a cord, and their wives, walking be-

* gē′ də mō′pə-sänt

219

hind the animal, whipped its haunches with a leafy branch to hasten its progress. They carried large baskets on their arms from which, in some cases, chickens and, in others, ducks thrust out their heads. And they walked with a quicker, livelier step than their husbands. Their spare straight figures were wrapped in a scanty little shawl, pinned over their flat bosoms, and their heads were enveloped in a white cloth glued to the hair and surmounted by a cap.

Then a wagon passed at the jerky trot of a nag, shaking strangely, two men seated side by side and a woman in the bottom of the vehicle, the latter holding on to the sides to lessen the hard jolts.

In the public square of Goderville there was a crowd, a throng of human beings and animals mixed together. The horns of the cattle, the tall hats with long nap of the rich peasants, and the headgear of the peasant women rose above the surface of the assembly. And the clamorous, shrill, screaming voices made a continuous and savage din which sometimes was dominated by the robust lungs of some countryman's laugh, or the long lowing of a cow tied to the wall of a house.

All that smacked of the stable, the dairy and the dirt heap, hay and sweat, giving forth that unpleasant odor, human and animal, peculiar to the people of the field.

Maître Hauchecome, of Breaute, had just arrived at Goderville, and he was directing his steps toward the public square, when he perceived upon the ground a little piece of string. Maître Hauchecome, economical like a true Norman, thought that everything useful ought to be picked up, and he bent painfully, for he suffered from rheumatism. He took the bit of thin cord from the ground and began to roll it carefully when he noticed Maître Malandain, the harness-maker, on the threshold of his door, looking at him. They had heretofore had business together on the subject of a halter, and they were on bad terms, being both good haters. Maître Hauchecome was seized with a sort of shame to be seen thus by his enemy, picking a bit of string out of the dirt. He concealed his "find" quickly under his blouse, then in his trousers' pocket; then he pretended to be still looking on the ground for something which he did not find, and he went toward the market, his head forward, bent double by his pains.

He was soon lost in the noisy and slowly moving crowd, which was busy with interminable bargainings. The peasants milked, went and came, perplexed, always in fear of being cheated, not daring to decide, watching the vender's eye, ever trying to find the trick in the man and the flaw in the beast.

The women, having placed their great baskets at their feet, had taken out the poultry which lay upon the ground, tied together by the feet, with terrified eyes and scarlet crests.

They heard offers, stated their prices with a dry air and impassive face, or perhaps, suddenly deciding on some proposed reduction, shouted to the customer who was slowly going away: "All right, Maître Authirne, I'll give it to you for that."

Then little by little the square was deserted, and the Angelus ringing at noon, those who had stayed too long, scattered to their shops.

At Jourdain's the great room was full of people eating, as the big court was full of vehicles of all kinds, carts, gigs, wagons, dump carts, yellow with dirt, mended and patched, raising their shafts to the sky like two arms, or perhaps with their shafts in the ground and their backs in the air.

Just opposite the diners seated at the table, the immense fireplace, filled with bright flames, cast a lively heat on the backs of the row on the right. Three spits were turning on which were chickens, pigeons, and legs of mutton; and an appetizing odor of roast beef and gravy dripping over the nicely browned skin rose from the hearth, increased the jovialness, and made everybody's mouth water.

All the aristocracy of the plow ate there at Maître Jourdain's, tavern keeper and horse dealer, a rascal who had money.

The dishes were passed and emptied, as were the jugs of yellow cider. Everyone told his affairs, his purchases, and sales. They discussed the crops. The weather was favorable for the green things but not for the wheat.

Suddenly the drum beat in the court, before the house. Everybody rose except a few indifferent persons, and ran to the door, or to the windows, their mouths still full and napkins in their hands.

After the public crier had ceased his drum-beating, he called out in a jerky voice, speaking his phrases irregularly:

"It is hereby made known to the inhabitants of Goderville, and in general to all persons present at the market, that there was lost this morning, on the road to Benzeville, between nine and ten o'clock, a black leather pocketbook containing five hundred francs and some business papers. The finder is requested to return same with all haste to the mayor's office or to Maître Fortune Houlbreque of Manneville; there will be twenty francs reward."

Then the man went away. The heavy roll of the drum and the crier's voice were again heard at a distance.

Then they began to talk of this event, discussing the chances that Maître Houlbreque had of finding or not finding his pocketbook.

And the meal concluded. They were finishing their coffee when a chief of the gendarmes appeared upon the threshold.

He inquired:

"Is Maître Hauchecome, of Breaute, here?"

Maître Hauchecome, seated at the other end of the table replied: "Here I am."

And the officer resumed:

"Maître Hauchecome, will you have the goodness to accompany me to the mayor's office? The mayor would like to talk to you."

The peasant, surprised and disturbed, swallowed at a draught his tiny glass of brandy, rose, and, even more bent than in the morning, for the first steps after each rest were especially difficult, set out, repeating: "Here I am, here I am."

The mayor was awaiting him, seated on an armchair. He was the notary of the vicinity, a stout, serious man, with pompous phrases.

"Maître Hauchecome," said he, "you were seen this morning to pick up, on the road to Benzeville, the pocketbook lost by Maître Houlbreque, of Manneville."

The countryman, astounded, looked at the mayor, already terrified by this suspicion resting on him without his knowing why.

"Me? Me? Me pick up the pocketbook?"

"Yes, you, yourself."

"Word of honor, I never heard of it."

"But you were seen."

"I was seen, me? Who says he saw me?"

"Monsieur Malandain, the harness-maker."

The old man remembered, understood, and flushed with anger.

"Ah, he saw me, the clodhopper, he saw me pick up this string, here, M'sieu' the Mayor." And rummaging in his pocket he drew out the little piece of string.

But the mayor, incredulous, shook his head.

"You will not make me believe, Maître Hauchecome, that Monsieur Malandain, who is a man worthy of credence, mistook this cord for a pocketbook."

The peasant, furious, lifted his hand, spat at one side to attest his honor, repeating:

"It is nevertheless the truth of the good God, the sacred truth, M'sieu' the Mayor. I repeat it on my soul and my salvation."

The mayor resumed:

"After picking up the object, you stood like a stilt, looking a long while in the mud to see if any piece of money had fallen out."

The good old man choked with indignation and fear.

"How anyone can tell—how anyone can tell—such lies to take away an honest man's reputation! How can anyone—"

There was no use in his protesting; nobody believed him. He was confronted with Monsieur Malandain, who repeated and maintained his affirmation. They abused each other for an hour. At his own request, Maître Hauchecome was searched, nothing was found on him.

Finally the mayor, very much perplexed, discharged him with the warning that he would consult the public prosecutor and ask for further orders.

The news had spread. As he left the mayor's office, the old man was surrounded and questioned with a serious or bantering curiosity, in which there was no indignation. He began to tell the story of the string. No one believed him. They laughed at him.

He went along, stopping his friends, beginning endlessly his statements and his protestations, showing his pockets turned inside out, to prove that he had nothing.

They said:

"Old rascal, get out!"

And he grew angry, becoming exasperated, hot, and distressed at not being believed, not knowing what to do and always repeating himself.

Night came. He must depart. He started on his way with three neighbors to whom he pointed out the place where he had picked up the bit of string; and all along the road he spoke of his adventure.

In the evening he took a turn in the village of Breaute, in order to tell it to everybody. He only met with incredulity.

It made him ill at night.

The next day about one o'clock in the afternoon, Marius Paumelle, a hired man in the employ of Maître Breton, husbandman at Ymanville, returned the pocketbook and its contents belonging to Maître Houlbreque of Manneville.

This man claimed to have found the object in the road; but not knowing how to read, he had carried it to the house and given it to his employer.

The news spread through the neighborhood. Maître Hauchecome was informed of it. He immediately went the circuit and began to recount his story completed by the happy climax. He was in triumph.

"What grieved me so much was not the thing itself, as the lying. There is nothing so shameful as to be placed under a cloud on account of a lie."

He talked of his adventure all day long, he told it on the highway to people who were passing by, in the wineshop to people who were drinking there, and to persons coming out of church the following Sunday. He stopped strangers to tell them about it. He was calm now, and yet something disturbed him without his knowing exactly what it was. People had the air of joking while they listened. They did not seem convinced. He seemed to feel that remarks were being made behind his back.

On Tuesday of the next week he went to the market at Goderville, urged solely by the necessity he felt of discussing the case.

Malandain, standing at his door, began to laugh on seeing him pass. Why?

He approached a farmer from Crequetot, who did not let him finish, and giving him a thump in the stomach said to his face:

"You big rascal."

Then he turned his back on him.

Maître Hauchecome was confused; why was he called a big rascal?

When he was seated at the table in Jourdain's tavern, he commenced to explain "the affair."

A horse dealer from Monvilliers called to him:

"Come, come, old sharper, that's an old trick; I know all about your piece of string!"

Hauchecome stammered:

"But since the pocketbook was found."

But the other man replied:

"Shut up, papa, there is one that finds, and there is one that reports. At any rate you are mixed with it."

The peasant stood choking. He understood. They accused him of having had the pocketbook returned by a confederate, by an accomplice.

He tried to protest. All the table began to laugh.

He could not finish his dinner and went away, in the midst of jeers.

He went home ashamed and indignant, choking with anger and confusion, the more dejected that he was capable with his Norman cunning of doing what they had accused him of, and even boasting of it as of a good turn. His innocence to him, in a confused way, was impossible to prove, as his sharpness was known. And he was stricken to the heart by the injustice of the suspicion.

Then he began to recount the adventures again, prolonging his history every day, adding each time new reasons, more energetic protestations, more solemn oaths which he imagined and prepared in his hours of solitude, his whole mind given up to the story of the string. He was believed so much the less as his defense was more complicated and his arguing more subtle.

"Those are lying excuses," they said behind his back.

He felt it, consumed his heart over it, and wore himself out with useless efforts. He wasted away before their very eyes.

The wags now made him tell about the string to amuse them, as they make a soldier who has been on a campaign tell about his battles. His mind, touched to the depth, began to weaken.

Toward the end of December he took to his bed.

He died in the first days of January, and in the delirium of his death struggles he kept claiming his innocence, reiterating:

"A piece of string, a piece of string—look—here it is, M'sieu' the Mayor."

For Discussion

1. This story is a satire on the people of Normandy, where Maupassant grew up. What did you find out about these people? Point out sentences or passages to support your answer.

2. In what ways was Hauchecome a typical Norman? What did his picking up the piece of string reveal about him? Do you think his behavior when he noticed Malandain watching him was true to life? Explain.

3. What was ironical about the situation before and after the lost pocket-book was found?

4. The incident of the pocketbook took on the proportions that it did, not because of the accusation against Hauchecome, but because of his insistence on his innocence. Why do you think Hauchecome continued to insist and to be so troubled about people's opinion? Was it only because of the way others acted or because of something in himself? Explain. What was the essential conflict in the story?

5. Did you feel pity for Hauchecome at the end of the story? Why or why not? Point out key passages which characterized Hauchecome and which might account for your emotional reaction to the end of the tale.

6. Would you say that the author was implying that it was fate that drove Hauchecome to his death? Explain.

7. Maupassant described the setting in detail. How important was it to what happened and to the final impact of the story on you?

8. This story has a simple plot based on accidental circumstances, yet it gives the reader a penetrating insight into life and into human behavior. How did the author achieve this?

For Composition

1. Although Maupassant and Tolstoy had very different viewpoints as writers, they both used the idea of a man being accused unfairly. Write a composition in which you contrast "A Piece of String" with "God Sees the Truth, but Waits" (page 175). In what ways did the main characters differ in their reaction to the circumstances in which they found themselves? How did the death scenes in these two stories reveal the difference in viewpoint of these authors regarding man in his relation to God, his fellowmen, and himself?

2. In "A Piece of String," Maupassant used carefully observed details to create a vivid picture of the Norman peasants going to market, bargaining with the venders, and eating in the tavern. Write an essay in which you explain how these descriptions function as genuine helps in giving the reader a picture of the times; that is, how they make this story an authentic "social document."

Anton Chekhov

The Bet

Anton Chekhov (1860–1904) ranks as one of the masters of the Russian short story and the drama. While much of his early writing reveals his humor, his later work shows a deep concern for the complexities of life and an ability to capture the subtle, changing moods of people and the atmosphere in which they move. It is his ability to create an all-pervading mood, often melancholy, which makes his dramas so notable. In his four major plays, *The Sea Gull, Uncle Vanya, The Three Sisters,* and *The Cherry Orchard,* Chekhov demonstrated his ability to reveal the lives of ordinary people through an artistic arrangement of trivial and everyday details. Very little happens in a Chekhov play, but his characters speak for the heart of man.

His stories and one-act plays reveal his humorous and satirical view of life and his awareness of human weakness and foolishness. Yet one feels that Chekhov is essentially a kindly person who cares for people. This was revealed in his own life when, in 1890, he visited the official Russian penal colony near Siberia. He wrote a book about his visit, and so powerful was his description of this place and the conditions there, that he succeeded in bringing about greatly needed reforms in this dreaded place.

"The Bet" is one of Chekhov's many stories which reveals his mastery of the short-story craft and his insight into the deeper values of life. *The Boor* is one of his satirical one-act plays which shows his ability to laugh kindly at people, while dramatizing them in all their contradictory moods.

1

*I*T was a dark autumn night. The old banker was pacing from corner to corner of his study, recalling to his mind the party he gave in the autumn fifteen years before. There were many clever people at the party and much interesting conversation. They talked among other things of capital punishment. The guests, among them not a few scholars and journalists, for the most part disapproved of capital punishment. They found it obsolete as a means of punishment, unfitted to a Christian State, and immoral. Some of them thought that capital punishment should be replaced universally by life imprisonment.

"I don't agree with you," said the host. "I myself have experienced neither capital punishment nor life imprisonment, but if one may judge *a priori*,[1] then in my opinion capital punishment is more moral and more humane than imprisonment. Execution kills instantly; life imprisonment kills by degrees. Who is the more humane executioner, one who kills you in a few seconds or one who draws the life out of you incessantly, for years?"

"They're both equally immoral," remarked one of the guests, "because their purpose is the same, to take away life. The State is not God. It has no right to take away that which it cannot give back, if it should so desire."

Among the company was a lawyer, a young man of about twenty-five. On being asked his opinion, he said:

"Capital punishment and life imprisonment are equally immoral; but if I were offered the choice between them, I would certainly choose the second. It's better to live somehow than not to live at all."

There ensued a lively discussion. The banker, who was then younger and more nervous, suddenly lost his temper, banged his fist on the table, and turning to the young lawyer, cried out:

"It's a lie. I bet you two millions you wouldn't stick in a cell even for five years."

"If you mean it seriously," replied the lawyer, "then I bet I'll stay not five but fifteen."

"Fifteen! Done!" cried the banker. "Gentlemen, I stake two millions."

"Agreed. You stake two millions; I my freedom," said the lawyer.

So this wild, ridiculous bet came to pass. The banker, who at that time had too many millions to count, spoiled and capricious, was beside himself with rapture. During supper he said to the lawyer jokingly:

"Come to your senses, young man, before it's too late. Two millions are nothing to me, but you stand to lose three or four of the best years of your life. I say three or four, because you'll never stick it out any longer. Don't forget either, you unhappy man,

[1] **a priori:** by reasoning rather than by experience (Latin)

that voluntary is much heavier than enforced imprisonment. The idea that you have the right to free yourself at any moment will poison the whole of your life in the cell. I pity you."

And now the banker, pacing from corner to corner, recalled all this and asked himself:

"Why did I make this bet? What's the good? The lawyer loses fifteen years of his life, and I throw away two millions. Will it convince people that capital punishment is worse or better than imprisonment for life? No, no! All stuff and rubbish. On my part, it was the caprice of a well-fed man; on the lawyer's, pure greed of gold."

He recollected further what happened after the evening party. It was decided that the lawyer must undergo his imprisonment under the strictest observation, in a garden wing of the banker's house. It was agreed that during the period he would be deprived of the right to cross the threshold, to see living people, to hear human voices, and to receive letters and newspapers. He was permitted to have a musical instrument, to read books, to write letters, to drink wine and smoke tobacco. By the agreement he could communicate, but only in silence, with the outside world through a little window specially constructed for this purpose. Everything necessary, books, music, wine, he could receive in any quantity by sending a note through the window. The agreement provided for all the minutest details, which made the confinement strictly solitary; and it obliged the lawyer to remain exactly fifteen years from twelve o'clock of November 14, 1870 to twelve o'clock of November 14, 1885. The least attempt on his part to violate the conditions, to escape if only for two minutes before the time, freed the banker from the obligation to pay him the two millions.

During the first year of imprisonment, the lawyer, as far as it was possible to judge from his short notes, suffered terribly from loneliness and boredom. From his wing day and night came the sound of the piano. He rejected wine and tobacco. "Wine," he wrote, "excites desires, and desires are the chief foes of a prisoner; besides, nothing is more boring than to drink good wine alone, and tobacco spoils the air in his room." During the first year the lawyer was sent books of a light character: novels with a complicated love interest, stories of crime and fantasy, comedies, and so on.

In the second year the piano was heard no longer, and the

lawyer asked only for classics. In the fifth year music was heard again, and the prisoner asked for wine. Those who watched him said that during the whole of that year he was only eating, drinking, and lying on his bed. He yawned often and talked angrily to himself. Books he did not read. Sometimes at nights he would sit down to write. He would write for a long time and tear it all up in the morning. More than once he was heard to weep.

In the second half of the sixth year the prisoner began zealously to study languages, philosophy, and history. He fell on these subjects so hungrily that the banker hardly had time to get books enough for him. In the space of four years about six hundred volumes were bought at his request. It was while that passion lasted that the banker received the following letter from the prisoner: "My dear jailer, I am writing these lines in six languages. Show them to experts. Let them read them. If they do not find one single mistake, I beg you to give orders to have a gun fired off in the garden. By the noise I shall know that my efforts have not been in vain. The geniuses of all ages and countries speak in different languages, but in them all burns the same flame. Oh, if you knew my heavenly happiness now that I can understand them!" The prisoner's desire was fulfilled. Two shots were fired in the garden by the banker's order.

Later on, after the tenth year, the lawyer sat immovable before his table and read only the New Testament. The banker found it strange that a man who in four years had mastered six hundred erudite volumes should have spent nearly a year in reading one book, easy to understand and by no means thick. The New Testament was then replaced by the history of religions and theology.

During the last two years of his confinement the prisoner read an extraordinary amount, quite haphazardly. Now he would apply himself to the natural sciences; then he would read Byron or Shakespeare. Notes used to come from him in which he asked to be sent at the same time a book on chemistry, a textbook of medicine, a novel, and some treatise on philosophy or theology. He read as though he were swimming in the sea among broken pieces of wreckage and in his desire to save his life was eagerly grasping one piece after another.

2

The banker recalled all this and thought:

"Tomorrow at twelve o'clock he receives his freedom. Under the agreement, I shall have to pay him two millions. If I pay, it's all over with me. I am ruined forever. . . ."

Fifteen years before he had too many millions to count, but now he was afraid to ask himself which he had more of, money or debts. Gambling on the Stock Exchange, risky speculation, and the recklessness of which he could not rid himself even in old age had gradually brought his business to decay; and the fearless, self-confident, proud man of business had become an ordinary banker, trembling at every rise and fall in the market.

"That cursed bet," murmured the old man, clutching his head in despair. . . . "Why didn't the man die? He's only forty years old. He will take away my last farthing, marry, enjoy life, gamble on the Exchange, and I will look on like an envious beggar and hear the same words from him every day: 'I'm obliged to you for the happiness of my life. Let me help you.' No, it's too much! The only escape from bankruptcy and disgrace—is that the man should die."

The clock had just struck three. The banker was listening. In the house everyone was asleep, and one could hear only the frozen trees whining outside the windows. Trying to make no sound, he took out of his safe the key of the door which had not been opened for fifteen years, put on his overcoat, and went out of the house. The garden was dark and cold. It was raining. A damp, penetrating wind howled in the garden and gave the trees no rest. Though he strained his eyes, the banker could see neither the ground, nor the white statues, nor the garden wing, nor the trees. Approaching the garden wing, he called the watchman twice. There was no answer. Evidently the watchman had taken shelter from the bad weather and was now asleep somewhere in the kitchen or the greenhouse.

"If I have the courage to fulfill my intention," thought the old man, "the suspicion will fall on the watchman first of all."

In the darkness he groped for the steps and the door and entered the hall of the garden wing, then poked his way into a narrow passage, and struck a match. Not a soul was there. Someone's bed, with no bedclothes on it, stood there, and an iron stove loomed dark in the corner. The seals on the door that led into the prisoner's room were unbroken.

When the match went out, the old man, trembling from agitation, peeped into the little window.

In the prisoner's room a candle was burning dimly. The prisoner himself sat by the table. Only his back, the hair on his head, and his hands were visible. Open books were strewn about on the table, the two chairs, and on the carpet near the table.

Five minutes passed, and the prisoner never once stirred. Fifteen years' confinement had taught him to sit motionless. The banker tapped on the window with his finger, but the prisoner made no movement in reply. Then the banker cautiously tore the seals from the door and put the key into the lock. The rusty lock gave a hoarse groan, and the door creaked. The banker expected instantly to hear a cry of surprise and the sound of steps. Three minutes passed, and it was as quiet inside as it had been before. He made up his mind to enter.

Before the table sat a man, unlike an ordinary human being. It was a skeleton, with tight-drawn skin, with long curly hair like a woman's, and a shaggy beard. The color of his face was yellow, of an earthy shade; the cheeks were sunken, the back long and narrow, and the hand upon which he leaned his hairy head was so lean and skinny that it was painful to look upon. His hair was already silvering with gray, and no one who glanced at the senile emaciation of the face would have believed that he was only forty years old. On the table, before his bended head, lay a sheet of paper on which something was written in a tiny hand.

"Poor devil," thought the banker, "he's asleep and probably seeing millions in his dreams. I have only to take and throw this half-dead thing on the bed, smother him a moment with the pillow, and the most careful examination will find no trace of unnatural death. But first, let us read what he has written here."

The banker took the sheet from the table and read:

"Tomorrow at twelve o'clock midnight I shall obtain my freedom and the right to mix with people. But before I leave this room and see the sun, I think it necessary to say a few words to you. On my own clear conscience and before God who sees me I declare to you that I despise freedom, life, health, and all that your books call the blessings of the world.

"For fifteen years I have diligently studied earthly life. True, I saw neither the earth nor the people, but in your books I drank fragrant wine, sang songs, hunted deer and wild boar in the forests, loved women. . . . And beautiful women, like clouds ethereal, created by the magic of your poets' genius, visited me by night and whispered to me wonderful tales which made my head drunken. In your books I climbed the summits of Elburz and Mont Blanc and saw from there how the sun rose in the morning, and in the evening suffused the sky, the ocean, and the mountain ridges with a purple gold. I saw from there how above me lightnings glimmered, cleaving the clouds; I saw green forests, fields, rivers, lakes, cities; I heard sirens singing and the playing of the pipes of Pan;[2] I touched the wings of beautiful devils who came flying to me to speak of God. . . . In your books I cast myself into bottomless abysses, worked miracles, burned cities to the ground, preached new religions, conquered whole countries. . . .

"Your books gave me wisdom. All that unwearying human thought created in the centuries is compressed to a little lump in my skull. I know that I am cleverer than you all.

"And I despise your books, despise all worldly blessings and wisdom. Everything is void, frail, visionary, and delusive as a mirage. Though you be proud and wise and beautiful, yet will death wipe you from the face of the earth like the mice underground; and your posterity, your history, and the immortality of your men of genius will be as frozen slag, burnt down together with the terrestrial globe.

"You are mad and gone the wrong way. You take falsehood for truth and ugliness for beauty. You would marvel if suddenly apple and orange trees should bear frogs and lizards instead of fruit, and if roses should begin to breathe the odor of a sweating horse. So do I marvel at you, who have bartered heaven for earth. I do not want to understand you.

"That I may show you in deed my contempt for that by which you live, I waive the two millions of which I once dreamed as of paradise, and which I now despise. That I may deprive myself of my right to them, I shall come out from here five minutes before the stipulated term and thus shall violate the agreement."

When he had read, the banker put the sheet on the table,

2 **Pan:** Greek god who played alluring music

kissed the head of the strange man, and began to weep. He went out of the wing. Never at any other time, not even after his terrible losses on the Exchange, had he felt such contempt for himself as now. Coming home, he lay down on his bed, but agitation and tears kept him a long time from sleeping. . . .

The next morning the poor watchman came running to him and told him that they had seen the man who lived in the wing climb through the window into the garden. He had gone to the gate and disappeared. The banker instantly went with his servants to the wing and established the escape of his prisoner. To avoid unnecessary rumors he took the paper with the renunciation from the table and, on his return, locked it in his safe.

For Discussion

1. Before the bet was made, the young lawyer stated that "it's better to live somehow than not to live at all." The banker, on the other hand, declared that "life imprisonment kills by degrees." Which was proved right when the experiment had ended?
2. What were the terms of the bet? Do you agree with the author that the bet was "wild" and "ridiculous"? Why or why not? In your opinion, what motivated the two men to make this bet?
3. In the tenth year, the prisoner read only the New Testament, followed by the history of religions and theology. In the last two years, he read a great diversity of books. Reread the last paragraph of Part 1 (page 230). Explain the relation of all these books. Do you think the prisoner was correct in his final opinion about the wisdom learned from books? Why or why not?
4. Why do you think the lawyer had come to despise "freedom, life, health, and all that your books call the blessings of the world"? Think back over his original purpose in accepting this self-imprisonment.
5. In his final letter to the banker, the lawyer implied that he considered himself richer than the banker. Do you agree or disagree with him? Why?
6. After the banker had read the prisoner's note, why did he begin to weep? Why did he feel contempt for himself? Do you think he realized the harm he had done? Explain.
7. Did the story end in the way you thought it would? Point out specific hints Chekhov dropped to prepare the reader for the ending.

8. Chekhov deliberately used the flashback method to delay the action of the story. What is the effect of this delay on the reader?

9. Chekhov's use of realistic details is particularly notable in the passage leading up to the banker's reading of the prisoner's letter. Reread this passage, beginning, "The clock had just struck three. . . ." (page 231). Point out details that contribute to the mood of this scene. What effect is created?

The Boor

Characters

HELENA IVANOVNA POPOV, *a young widow, mistress of a country estate*

GRIGORI STEPANOVITCH SMIRNOV, *proprietor of a country estate*

LUKA, *servant of Mrs. Popov*

A GARDENER

A COACHMAN

SEVERAL WORKMEN

SCENE: *A well-furnished reception room in* MRS. POPOV'S *home.*
MRS. POPOV *is discovered in deep mourning, sitting upon a sofa, gazing steadfastly at a photograph.* LUKA *is also present.*

LUKA. It isn't right, ma'am. You're wearing yourself out! The maid and the cook have gone looking for berries; everything that breathes is enjoying life, even the cat knows how to be happy—slips about the courtyard and catches birds—but you hide yourself here in the house as though you were in a cloister. Yes, truly, by actual reckoning you haven't left this house for a whole year.

MRS. POPOV. And I shall never leave it—why should I? My life is over. He lies in his grave, and I have buried myself within these four walls. We are both dead.

LUKA. There you are again! It's too awful to listen to, so it is! Niko-lai Michailovitch is dead: it was the will of the Lord, and the Lord has given him eternal peace. You have grieved over it and that ought to be enough. Now it's time to stop. One can't weep and wear mourning forever! My wife died a few years ago. I grieved for her, I wept a whole month—and then it was over. Must one be forever singing lamentations? That would be more than your husband was worth! (*He sighs.*) You have forgotten all your neighbors. You don't go out and you receive no one. We live —you'll pardon me—like the spiders, and the good light of day we never see. All the livery is eaten by the mice—as though there weren't any more nice people in the world! But the whole neigh-

borhood is full of gentlefolk. The regiment is stationed in Riblov
—officers—simply beautiful! One can't see enough of them! Every
Friday a ball, and military music every day. Oh, my dear, dear
ma'am, young and pretty as you are, if you'd only let your spirits
live—! Beauty can't last forever. When ten short years are over,
you'll be glad enough to go out a bit and meet the officers—and
then it'll be too late.

MRS. POPOV. (*Resolutely.*) Please don't speak of these things again.
You know very well that since the death of Nikolai Michailovitch
my life is absolutely nothing to me. You think I live, but it only
seems so. Do you understand? Oh, that his departed soul may see
how I love him! I know, it's no secret to you; he was often unjust
toward me, cruel, and—he wasn't faithful, but I shall be faithful
to the grave and prove to him how *I* can love. There, in the
Beyond, he'll find me the same as I was until his death.

LUKA. What is the use of all these words, when you'd so much
rather go walking in the garden or order Tobby or Welikan
harnessed to the trap, and visit the neighbors?

MRS. POPOV. (*Weeping.*) Oh!

LUKA. Madam, dear Madam, what is it? In Heaven's name!

MRS. POPOV. He loved Tobby so! He always drove him to the
Kortschagins or the Vlassovs. What a wonderful horseman he
was! How fine he looked when he pulled at the reins with all
his might! Tobby, Tobby—give him an extra measure of oats
today!

LUKA. Yes, ma'am.

(*A bell rings loudly.*)

MRS. POPOV. (*Shudders.*) What's that? I am at home to no one.

LUKA. Yes, ma'am. (*He goes out, center.*)

MRS. POPOV. (*Gazing at the photograph.*) You shall see, Nikolai,
how I can love and forgive! My love will die only with me—
when my poor heart stops beating. (*She smiles through her
tears.*) And aren't you ashamed? I have been a good, true wife,
I have imprisoned myself and I shall remain true until death,
and you—you—you're not ashamed of yourself, my dear monster!
You quarreled with me, left me alone for weeks—

(LUKA *enters in great excitement.*)

LUKA. Oh, ma'am, someone is asking for you, insists on seeing you—

MRS. POPOV. You told him that since my husband's death I receive no one?

LUKA. I said so, but he won't listen, he says it is a pressing matter.

MRS. POPOV. I receive no one!

LUKA. I told him that, but he's a wildman, he swore and pushed himself into the room; he's in the dining room now.

MRS. POPOV. (*Excitedly.*) Good. Show him in. The impudent—! (LUKA *goes out, center.*)

MRS. POPOV. What a bore people are! What can they want with me? Why do they disturb my peace? (*She sighs.*) Yes, it is clear I must enter a convent. (*Meditatively.*) Yes, a convent. (SMIRNOV *enters, followed by* LUKA.)

SMIRNOV. (*To* LUKA.) Fool, you make too much noise! You're an ass! (*Discovering* MRS. POPOV—*politely.*) Madam, I have the honor to introduce myself: Lieutenant in the Artillery, retired, country gentleman Grigori Stepanovitch Smirnov! I'm compelled to bother you about an exceedingly important matter.

MRS. POPOV. (*Without offering her hand.*) What is it you wish?

SMIRNOV. Your deceased husband, with whom I had the honor to be acquainted, left me two notes amounting to about twelve hundred rubles. Inasmuch as I have to pay the interest tomorrow on a loan from the Agrarian Bank, I should like to request, madam, that you pay me the money today.

MRS. POPOV. Twelve hundred—and for what was my husband indebted to you?

SMIRNOV. He bought oats from me.

MRS. POPOV. (*With a sigh, to* LUKA.) Don't forget to give Tobby an extra measure of oats.

(LUKA *goes out.*)

MRS. POPOV. (*To* SMIRNOV.) If Nikolai Michailovitch is indebted to you, I shall of course pay you, but I am sorry, I haven't the money today. Tomorrow my manager will return from the city and I shall notify him to pay you what is due you, but until then I cannot satisfy your request. Furthermore, today it is just seven months since the death of my husband and I am not in a mood to discuss money matters.

SMIRNOV. And I am in the mood to fly up the chimney with my feet in the air if I can't lay hands on that interest tomorrow. They'll seize my estate!

MRS. POPOV. Day after tomorrow you will receive the money.

SMIRNOV. I don't need the money day after tomorrow, I need it today.

MRS. POPOV. I'm sorry I can't pay you today.

SMIRNOV. And I can't wait until day after tomorrow.

MRS. POPOV. But what can I do if I haven't it?

SMIRNOV. So you can't pay?

MRS. POPOV. I cannot.

SMIRNOV. Hm! Is that your last word?

MRS. POPOV. My last.

SMIRNOV. Absolutely?

MRS. POPOV. Absolutely.

SMIRNOV. Thank you. (*He shrugs his shoulders.*) And they expect me to stand for all that. The toll-gatherer just now met me in the road and asked me why I was always worrying? Why in Heaven's name shouldn't I worry? I need money, I feel the knife at my throat. Yesterday morning I left my house in the early dawn and called on all my debtors. If even one of them had paid his debt! I worked the skin off my fingers! The devil knows in what sort of inn I slept: in a room with a barrel of brandy! And now at last I come here, seventy versts from home, hope for a little money and all you give me is moods! Why shouldn't I worry?

MRS. POPOV. I thought I made it plain to you that my manager will return from town, and then you will get your money.

SMIRNOV. I did not come to see the manager, I came to see you. What the devil—pardon the language—do I care for your manager?

MRS. POPOV. Really, sir, I am not used to such language or such manners. I shan't listen to you any further. (*She goes out, left.*)

SMIRNOV. What can one say to that? Moods! Seven months since her husband died! Do I have to pay the interest or not? I repeat the question, have I to pay the interest or not? The husband is dead and all that; the manager is—the devil with him!—traveling somewhere. Now, tell me, what am I to do? Shall I run away from my creditors in a balloon? Or knock my head against a stone wall? If I call on Grusdev he chooses to be "not at home," Iroschevitch has simply hidden himself, I have quarreled with Kurzin and came near throwing him out of the window, Masutov is ill and this woman has—moods! Not one of them will pay up! And all because I've spoiled them, because I'm an old whiner, dishrag! I'm too tender-hearted with them. But wait! I allow nobody to play tricks with me, the devil with 'em all! I'll stay here and not budge until she pays! Brr! How angry I am, how terribly angry I am! Every tendon is trembling with anger and I can hardly breathe! I'm even growing ill! (*He calls out.*) Servant!

(LUKA *enters.*)

LUKA. What is it you wish?

SMIRNOV. Bring me Kvas or water! (LUKA *goes out.*) Well, what can we do? She hasn't it on hand? What sort of logic is that? A fellow stands with the knife at his throat, he needs money, he is on the point of hanging himself, and she won't pay because she isn't in the mood to discuss money matters. Woman's logic! That's why I never liked to talk to women and why I dislike doing it now. I would rather sit on a powder barrel than talk with a woman. Brr!—I'm getting cold as ice, this affair has made me so angry. I need only to see such a romantic creature from a distance to get so angry that I have cramps in the calves! It's enough to make one yell for help! (*Enter* LUKA.)

LUKA. (*Hands him water.*) Madam is ill and is not receiving.

SMIRNOV. March! (LUKA *goes out.*) Ill and isn't receiving! All right, it isn't necessary. I won't receive, either! I'll sit here and stay until you bring that money. If you're ill a week, I'll sit here a week. If you're ill a year, I'll sit here a year. As Heaven is my witness, I'll get the money. You don't disturb me with your mourning—or with your dimples. We know these dimples! (*He calls out the window.*) Simon, unharness! We aren't going to leave right away. I am going to stay here. Tell them in the stable to give the horses some oats. The left horse has twisted the bridle again. (*Imitating him.*) Stop! I'll show you how. Stop! (*Leaves window.*) It's awful. Unbearable heat, no money, didn't sleep last night and now—mourning dresses with moods. My head aches; perhaps I ought to have a drink. Yes, I must have a drink. (*Calling.*) Servant!

LUKA. What do you wish?

SMIRNOV. Something to drink! (LUKA *goes out.* SMIRNOV *sits down and looks at his clothes.*) Ugh, a fine figure! No use denying that. Dust, dirty boots, unwashed, uncombed, straw on my vest— the lady probably took me for a highwayman. (*He yawns.*) It was a little impolite to come into a reception room with such clothes. Oh, well, no harm done. I'm not here as a guest. I'm a creditor. And there is no special costume for creditors.

LUKA (*Entering with glass.*) You take great liberty, sir.

SMIRNOV. (*Angrily.*) What?

LUKA. I—I—I just—

SMIRNOV. Whom are you talking to? Keep quiet.

LUKA. (*Angrily.*) Nice mess! This fellow won't leave! (*He goes out.*)

SMIRNOV. Lord, how angry I am! Angry enough to throw mud at the whole world! I even feel ill! Servant!

(MRS. POPOV *comes in with downcast eyes.*)

MRS. POPOV. Sir, in my solitude I have become unaccustomed to the human voice and I cannot stand the sound of loud talking. I beg you, please to cease disturbing my rest.

SMIRNOV. Pay me my money and I'll leave.

MRS. POPOV. I told you once, plainly, in your native tongue, that I haven't the money at hand; wait until day after tomorrow.

SMIRNOV. And I also had the honor of informing you in your native tongue that I need the money, not day after tomorrow, but today. If you don't pay me today I shall have to hang myself tomorrow.

MRS. POPOV. But what can I do if I haven't the money?

SMIRNOV. So, you are not going to pay immediately? You're not?

MRS. POPOV. I cannot.

SMIRNOV. Then I'll sit here until I get the money. (*He sits down.*) You will pay day after tomorrow? Excellent! Here I stay until day after tomorrow. (*Jumps up.*) I ask you, do I have to pay that interest tomorrow or not? Or do you think I'm joking?

MRS. POPOV. Sir, I beg of you, don't scream! This is not a stable.

SMIRNOV. I'm not talking about stables, I'm asking you whether I have to pay that interest tomorrow or not?

MRS. POPOV. You have no idea how to treat a lady.

SMIRNOV. Oh, yes, I have.

MRS. POPOV. No, you have not. You are an ill-bred, vulgar person! Respectable people don't speak so to ladies.

SMIRNOV. How remarkable! How do you want one to speak to you? In French, perhaps! Madame, je vous prie! Pardon me for having disturbed you. What beautiful weather we are having today! And how this mourning becomes you! (*He makes a low bow with mock ceremony.*)

MRS. POPOV. Not at all funny! I think it vulgar!

SMIRNOV. (*Imitating her.*) Not at all funny—vulgar! I don't understand how to behave in the company of ladies. Madam, in
the course of my life I have seen more women than you have
sparrows. Three times have I fought duels for women, twelve
I jilted and nine jilted me. There was a time when I played
the fool, used honeyed language, bowed and scraped. I loved,
suffered, sighed to the moon, melted in love's torments. I
loved passionately, I loved to madness, loved in every key,
chattered like a magpie on emancipation, sacrificed half my
fortune in the tender passion, until now the devil knows I've
had enough of it. Your obedient servant will let you lead him
around by the nose no more. Enough! Black eyes, passionate
eyes, coral lips, dimples in cheeks, · moonlight whispers, soft,
modest sighs—for all that, madam, I wouldn't pay a kopeck! I
am not speaking of present company, but of women in general;
from the tiniest to the greatest, they are conceited, hypocritical,
chattering, odious, deceitful from top to toe; vain, petty, cruel
with a maddening logic and (*He strikes his forehead.*) in this
respect, please excuse my frankness, but one sparrow is worth
ten of the aforementioned petticoat-philosophers. When one sees
one of the romantic creatures before him he imagines he is
looking at some holy being, so wonderful that its one breath could
dissolve him in a sea of a thousand charms and delights; but if
one looks into the soul—it's nothing but a common crocodile.
(*He seizes the armchair and breaks it in two.*) But the worst
of all is that this crocodile imagines it is a masterpiece of creation, and that it has a monopoly on all the tender passions. May
the devil hang me upside down if there is anything to love about
a woman! When she is in love, all she knows is how to complain
and shed tears. If the man suffers and makes sacrifices she swings
her train about and tries to lead him by the nose. You have the
misfortune to be a woman, and naturally you know woman's
nature; tell me on your honor, have you ever in your life seen a
woman who was really true and faithful? Never! Only the old and
the deformed are true and faithful. It's easier to find a cat with
horns or a white woodcock, than a faithful woman.

MRS. POPOV. But allow me to ask, who is true and faithful in love?
The man, perhaps?

SMIRNOV. Yes indeed! The man!

MRS. POPOV. The man! (*She laughs sarcastically.*) The man true and faithful in love! Well, that is something *new!* (*Bitterly.*) How can you make such a statement? Men true and faithful! So long as we have gone thus far, I may as well say that of all the men I have known, my husband was the best; I loved him passionately with all my soul, as only a young, sensible woman may love; I gave him my youth, my happiness, my fortune, my life. I worshipped him like a heathen. And what happened? This best of men betrayed me in every possible way. After his death I found his desk filled with love-letters. While he was alive he left me alone for months—it is horrible even to think about it—he made love to other women in my very presence, he wasted my money and made fun of my feelings—and in spite of everything, I trusted him and was true to him. And more than that: he is dead and I am still true to him. I have buried myself within these four walls and I shall wear this mourning to my grave.

SMIRNOV. (*Laughing disrespectfully.*) Mourning! What on earth do you take me for? As if I didn't know why you wore this black domino and why you buried yourself within these four walls. Such a secret! So romantic! Some knight will pass the castle, gaze up at the windows and think to himself: "Here dwells the mysterious Tamara who, for love of her husband, has buried herself within four walls." Oh, I understand the art!

MRS. POPOV. (*Springing up.*) What? What do you mean by saying such things to me?

SMIRNOV. You have buried yourself alive, but meanwhile you have not forgotten to powder your nose!

MRS. POPOV. How dare you speak so?

SMIRNOV. Don't scream at me, please, I'm not the manager. Allow me to call things by their right names. I am not a woman, and I am accustomed to speak out what I think. So please don't scream.

MRS. POPOV. I'm not screaming. It is you who are screaming. Please leave me, I beg of you.

SMIRNOV. Pay me my money and I'll leave.

MRS. POPOV. I won't give you the money.

SMIRNOV. You won't? You won't give me my money?

MRS. POPOV. I don't care what you do. You won't get a kopeck! Leave me!

SMIRNOV. As I haven't the pleasure of being either your husband or your fiancé please don't make a scene. (*He sits down.*) I can't stand it.

MRS. POPOV. (*Breathing hard.*) You are going to sit down?

SMIRNOV. I already have.

MRS. POPOV. Kindly leave the house!

SMIRNOV. Give me the money.

MRS. POPOV. I don't care to speak with impudent men. Leave! (*Pause.*) You aren't going?

SMIRNOV. No.

MRS. POPOV. No?

SMIRNOV. No.

MRS. POPOV. Very well. (*She rings the bell.*)

(*Enter* LUKA.)

MRS. POPOV. Luka, show the gentleman out.

LUKA. (*Going to* SMIRNOV.) Sir, why don't you leave when you are ordered? What do you want?

SMIRNOV. (*Jumping up.*) Whom do you think you are talking to? I'll grind you to powder.

LUKA. (*Puts his hand to his heart.*) Good Lord! (*He drops into a chair.*) Oh, I'm ill, I can't breathe!

MRS. POPOV. Where is Dascha? (*Calling.*) Dascha! Pelageja! Dascha! (*She rings.*)

LUKA. They're all gone! I'm ill! Water!

MRS. POPOV. (*To* SMIRNOV.) Leave! Get out!

SMIRNOV. Kindly be a little more polite!

MRS. POPOV. (*Striking her fists and stamping her feet.*) You are vulgar! You're a boor! A monster!

SMIRNOV. What did you say?

MRS. POPOV. I said you were a boor, a monster!

SMIRNOV. (*Steps toward her quickly.*) Permit me to ask what right you have to insult me?

MRS. POPOV. What of it? Do you think I am afraid of you?

SMIRNOV. And you think that because you are a romantic creature you can insult me without being punished? I challenge you!

LUKA. Merciful heaven! Water!

SMIRNOV. We'll have a duel.

MRS. POPOV. Do you think because you have big fists and a steer's neck I am afraid of you?

SMIRNOV. I allow no one to insult me, and I make no exception because you are a woman, one of the "weaker sex"!

MRS. POPOV. (*Trying to cry him down.*) Boor, boor, boor!

SMIRNOV. It is high time to do away with the old superstition that it is only the man who is forced to give satisfaction. If there is equity at all let there be equity in all things. There's a limit!

MRS. POPOV. You wish to fight a duel? Very well.

SMIRNOV. Immediately.

MRS. POPOV. Immediately. My husband had pistols. I'll bring them. (*She hurries away, then turns.*) Oh, what a pleasure it will be to put a bullet in your impudent head. The devil take you! (*She goes out.*)

SMIRNOV. I'll shoot her down! I'm no fledgling, no sentimental young puppy. For me, there is no weaker sex!

LUKA. Oh, sir! (*Falls to his knees.*) Have mercy on me, an old man, and go away. You have frightened me to death already, and now you want to fight a duel.

SMIRNOV. (*Paying no attention.*) A duel. That's equity, emancipation. That way the sexes are made equal. I'll shoot her down as a matter of principle. What can a person say to such a woman? (*Imitating her.*) "The devil take you. I'll put a bullet in your impudent head." What can one say to that? She was angry, her eyes blazed, she accepted the challenge. On my honor, it's the first time in my life that I ever saw such a woman.

LUKA. Oh, sir, Go away. Go away!

SMIRNOV. That *is* a woman. I can understand her. A real woman. No shilly-shallying, but fire, powder, and noise! It would be a pity to shoot a woman like that.

LUKA. (*Weeping.*) Oh, sir, go away.

(*Enter* MRS. POPOV.)

MRS. POPOV. Here are the pistols. But before we have our duel please show me how to shoot. I have never had a pistol in my hand before!

LUKA. God be merciful and have pity upon us! I'll go and get the gardener and the coachman. Why has this horror come to us? (*He goes out.*)

SMIRNOV. (*Looking at the pistols.*) You see, there are different kinds.

There are special dueling pistols with cap and ball. But these are revolvers, Smith & Wesson, with ejectors; fine pistols! A pair like that cost at least ninety rubles. This is the way to hold a revolver. (*Aside.*) Those eyes, those eyes! A real woman!

MRS. POPOV. Like this?

SMIRNOV. Yes, that way. Then you pull the hammer back—so—then you aim—put your head back a little. Just stretch your arm out, please. So—then press your finger on the thing like that, and that is all. The chief thing is this: don't get excited, don't hurry your aim, and take care that your hand doesn't tremble.

MRS. POPOV. It isn't well to shoot inside; let's go into the garden.

SMIRNOV. Yes. I'll tell you now, I am going to shoot into the air.

MRS. POPOV. That is too much! Why?

SMIRNOV. Because—because. That's my business.

MRS. POPOV. You are afraid. Yes. Ah-h-h! No, no, my dear sir, no flinching! Please follow me. I won't rest until I've made a hole in that head I hate so much. Are you afraid?

SMIRNOV. Yes, I'm afraid.

MRS. POPOV. You are lying. Why won't you fight?

SMIRNOV. Because—because—I—like you.

MRS. POPOV. (*With an angry laugh.*) You like me! He dares to say he likes me! (*She points to the door.*) Go.

SMIRNOV. (*Laying the revolver silently on the table, takes his hat and starts. At the door he stops a moment gazing at her silently, then he approaches her, hesitating.*) Listen! Are you still angry? I was mad as the devil, but please understand me—how can I express myself? The thing is like this—such things are—(*He raises his voice.*) Now, is it my fault that you owe me money? (*Grasps the back of the chair, which breaks.*) The devil knows what breakable furniture you have! I like you! Do you understand? I—I'm almost in love!

MRS. POPOV. Leave! I hate you.

SMIRNOV. Lord! What a woman! I never in my life met one like her. I'm lost, ruined! I've been caught like a mouse in a trap.

MRS. POPOV. Go, or I'll shoot.

SMIRNOV. Shoot! You have no idea what happiness it would be to die in sight of those beautiful eyes, to die from the revolver in this little velvet hand! I'm mad! Consider it and decide immediately, for if I go now, we shall never see each other again.

Decide—speak—I am a noble, a respectable man, have an income of ten thousand, can shoot a coin thrown into the air. I own some fine horses. Will you be my wife?

MRS. POPOV. (*Swings the revolver angrily.*) I'll shoot!

SMIRNOV. My mind is not clear—I can't understand. Servant— water! I have fallen in love like any young man. (*He takes her hand and she cries with pain.*) I love you! (*He kneels.*) I love you as I have never loved before. Twelve women I jilted, nine jilted me, but not one of them all have I loved as I love you. I am conquered, lost, I lie at your feet like a fool and beg for your hand. Shame and disgrace! For five years I haven't been in love; I thanked the Lord for it, and now I am caught, like a carriage tongue in another carriage. I beg for your hand! Yes, or no? Will you?—Good! (*He gets up and goes quickly to the door.*)

MRS. POPOV. Wait a moment!

SMIRNOV. (*Stopping.*) Well?

MRS. POPOV. Nothing. You may go. But—wait a moment. No, go on, go on. I hate you. Or—no: don't go. Oh, if you knew how angry I was, how angry! (*She throws the revolver onto the chair.*) My finger is swollen from this thing. (*She angrily tears her handkerchief.*) What are you standing there for? Get out!

SMIRNOV. Farewell!

MRS. POPOV. Yes, go. (*Cries out.*) Why are you going? Wait—no, go!! Oh, how angry I am! Don't come too near, don't come too near—er—come—no nearer.

SMIRNOV. (*Approaching her.*) How angry I am with myself! Fall in love like a school-boy, throw myself on my knees. I've got a chill! (*Strongly.*) I love you. This is fine—all I needed was to fall in love. Tomorrow I have to pay my interest, the hay harvest has begun, and then you appear! (*He takes her in his arms.*) I can never forgive myself.

MRS. POPOV. Go away! Take your hands off me! I hate you—you— this is—(*A long kiss.*)

(*Enter* LUKA *with an ax, the* GARDENER *with a rake, the* COACHMAN *with a pitchfork, and* WORKMEN *with poles.*)

LUKA. (*Staring at the pair.*) Merciful Heavens! (*A long pause.*)

MRS. POPOV. (*Dropping her eyes.*) Tell them in the stable that Tobby isn't to have any oats.

Curtain

For Discussion

1. Did the play end as you expected it would? How well did the author prepare you for this ending? Do you think it was believable? Give reasons to support your answers.

2. The one-act play, because it usually covers a very brief span of time, must give the background information within the very first lines. How did Chekhov succeed in bringing the reader or audience up to date on the history of Madame Popov's situation?

3. With Smirnov's entrance, the interplay of dramatic forces is put into motion. How did Smirnov progressively get Madame Popov's confession of the truth of things—of the real reason for her drawnout widowhood and her real feelings about her deceased husband?

4. What evidence is there that Smirnov was endeavoring to impress Madame Popov with his manliness and strength of character?

5. What is the crucial moment in the play?

6. With Madame Popov's surprising acceptance of the challenge to duel, there is a complete reversal of roles. What qualities did each of the two main characters reveal? How did the tempo, tone, and mood of the play change to suit the hilariousness of the situation?

7. At what "institutions" or prevailing ideas current at the time was Chekhov poking fun at in this play?

8. A final aspect of Chekhov's skill is seen in the last line of the play. Point out its meaning and what it swiftly revealed about Madame Popov in regard to her "bereavement" and her new-found existence.

For Composition

1. Imagine you are the banker in "The Bet." You have just met the lawyer five years after his escape. Write an entry in your diary in which you describe this meeting. Tell what changes you saw in your friend, physically, mentally, and morally. How has he adapted to the everyday life to which he returned?

2. If Luka were asked what he thought and felt about Smirnov, the proposed duel, and the unexpected outcome, he would probably have quite a tale to tell. Write this tale as you think Luka would tell it, using whatever details in the play that Luka would know, either because he was present or because he couldn't help overhearing what was going on. You might also use bits of the dialogue—what he or another character said—in order to make the tale more dramatic. Use the first-person "I."

August Strindberg

Half a Sheet of Paper

August Strindberg (1849–1912), the Swedish playwright, short-story writer, and novelist, was one of the key people who helped to revolutionize the drama in Europe. Together with Henrik Ibsen, Gerhart Hauptmann, and Maxim Gorky, he brought a new realism to the theater. Some of Strindberg's best-known plays, such as *Miss Julie, The Father,* and *The Spook Sonata,* continue to be produced in America and England, as well as in Europe.

Many of Strindberg's stories and novels, like his plays, reflect the painful effects of his unhappy childhood, his personal difficulties about love and marriage, and his generally turbulent state of mind. His work is colored by bitterness and disillusionment and a fiercely critical attitude toward women. He believed that woman's place was in the home and that she should never seek to dominate men intellectually or spiritually. Despite this viewpoint, he was a brilliant observer and critic of human behavior, as can be seen in his story, "Autumn." He could also achieve a more gentle mood, as in "Half a Sheet of Paper." Something of his attitude toward his work can be seen in his own statement: "People clamor for the joy of life. . . . I find the joy of life in the powerful, cruel struggle of life, and my enjoyment is in discovering something, in learning something. . . ."

*T*HE last moving van had gone; the tenant, a young man with a mourning-band around his hat, wandered through the empty rooms to see if anything had been left behind. No, nothing had been forgotten, nothing. He went out into the corridor, determined never to think again of all he had passed through in this apartment. But there, on the wall, near the telephone, was a slip of paper covered with writing. The entries were in several handwritings; some quite legible, in black ink; some, pencil scrawls in black and red and blue. There stood recorded the whole beautiful romance that had been lived in the short space of two years. All that he had resolved to forget was written there—a bit of human history on half a sheet of paper.

He took the sheet down. It was a piece of sun-yellow scratch paper that casts a sheen. He laid it on the mantel of the fireplace in the living room, and, bending over, he began to read.

First stood her name: Alice—the most beautiful name he knew, because it was the name of his sweetheart. Beside it was a number, 15,111—It looked like a chant number on the hymnboard in church.

Underneath was scribbled: The Bank. It was there his work lay, the sacred work which for him had meant bread, home, family—the foundations of life. A heavy black line had been drawn across the number, for the bank had failed, and he had been taken on at another, after a short period of much anxiety.

Then followed the livery stable and the florist—That was when they were engaged, and he had a pocketful of money.

The furniture dealer—The decorator—They furnish their apartment. Express Bureau—They move in. Opera House Box Office, 50,50—They are newly married and go to the opera on Sunday evenings. Their most delightful hours are those spent there, sitting quietly, while their hearts commune in the beauty and harmony of the fairyland on the other side of the footlights.

Here followed the name of a man (crossed out) a friend who had risen high, but who fell—dazzled by prosperity—fell irremediably, and had to flee the country. So ephemeral is that will-o'-the-wisp, Success!

Now something new came into the lives of the couple. Entered with a pencil in a woman's hand stands The Sister. What sister? Ah! the one with the long gray cloak and the sweet, sympathetic face, who comes so softly and never goes through the drawing room, but takes the corridor way to the bedroom. Below her name is written: Dr. L——

Here first appeared on the list a relative—Mother. That is his mother-in-law, who had discreetly kept away so as not to disturb the newly married. But now she has been called, and comes gladly, since she is needed.

Then came some entries in red and blue pencil. Employment Agency. The maid has left, and a new one must be engaged. The Apothecary—H-m! It begins to look dark. The dairy—Milk is ordered, sterilized milk. The grocer, the butcher, and others. The household affairs are being conducted by telephone. Then the mistress of the house is not at her usual post? No. She is confined to her bed.

That which followed he could not read, for it grew dim before his eyes, as it must for the drowning man at sea who would look through salt water. But there it stood recorded, in plain, black letters: The undertaker.

That tells enough!—a larger and a smaller casket. And in parentheses was written: "Of dust."

There is nothing more. It ended in dust, the way of all flesh.

He took up the sun-yellow paper, kissed it, folded it carefully, and put it in his breast pocket.

In two minutes he had relived two years of his life.

But he was not bowed down as he walked out. On the contrary, he carried his head high, like a proud and happy man, for he knew that to him it had been to hold for a little the best that life can bestow on man. How many there were, alas! who had not had this.

For Discussion

1. In his Preface to *Miss Julie*, Strindberg's most famous play, he wrote, "My souls are conglomerations of past and present stages of culture, scraps of books and newspapers, fragments of men and women, torn shreds of Sunday attire that are now rags such as go to make up a soul." How does "Half a Sheet of Paper" demonstrate Strindberg's conception of true-to-life characters?

2. Point out the young man's reactions to each item that he read. What did they reveal about him? What did the last paragraph reveal about his sense of values? Confronted with his loss, what attitude might he have taken? Would he have been justified? Why or why not?

3. Strindberg's craft as a writer is at its peak in the very first lines of the story. Here, time and place, conditions and mood are depicted in a single, short paragraph. Indicate these elements as they occur.

4. An important element of the short story is suspense. Despite the story's compactness, prove that a certain measure of suspense is achieved. How did the order of the data on the slip of paper help to achieve this?

5. In the history of every human soul, as in that of the young man, events are "interbeaded and knotted in memory." Why is every person, like the hero of this brief story, far richer for these events? Discuss the place and the value of suffering in a person's life, from the point of view of the true Christian imbued with the love of Christ.

Autumn

$\mathcal{T}HEY$ had been married ten years! Happily? As happily as circumstances had permitted. They had pulled along as smoothly and steadily as two bullocks of equal strength, each at its place in the team.

In the first year, naturally, many illusions about marriage were dispelled, that of absolute bliss, for instance. With the next year children began to arrive, and the drudgery of life did not leave much time for reflection.

He was very domestic, extremely domestic, one might say; finding in his family his miniature world, of which he was the middle point. His children were the radii, and his wife sought likewise to be a middle point but never in the center of the circle, since that was where the husband was; for which reason the radii sometimes ran to him, sometimes to her, intersecting each other.

In this tenth year the husband was appointed a secretary of prison inspection, and had therefore to travel about. This was a blow to his domestic habits, and he felt a genuine repugnance at the thought that now he would have to be away a whole month. He could not tell for sure whether it was his wife or the children he should miss most; perhaps it was all of them together.

On the evening before his departure he sat on the sofa watching his wife pack his portmanteau. She was on her knees on the floor putting in his linen. She then dusted off his black clothes and folded them carefully so that they should take as little room as possible; he wasn't very handy at that sort of thing! She had not taken a place in the house as his maid-servant, scarcely as his wife. She was mother, mother to the children and to him. She never felt humiliated at darning his socks and never asked for thanks. Nor did she consider him indebted to her for such things, when he in return gave her and her children both stockings and many other things which she would otherwise have had to go out and get, while her children were left at home alone.

He sat in the corner of the sofa watching her. Now that the departure drew near, small intimations of regret began to stir in him.

252

He surveyed her figure. The shoulder blades had grown more prominent, and the back was bent with work over the cradle, the ironing-board, and the stove. He too was bent with work at his desk, and his eyes needed the help of glasses. But just now he was really not thinking of himself. He saw that her hair was thinner than formerly, and that the part between the braids was growing brighter. Was it for him she had lost her beauty, only for him? No, it was for the little community which consisted of them all, for she had worked for herself too. And his hair had also become thinner on the crown in the fight for them all. He would perhaps have had more youth if there had not been so many mouths to feed, but not for a moment did he wish he had been alone.

"It'll do you good to go about a bit," said his wife; "you that have always sat too much crouched up in the house."

"You're glad to be quit of me, you are," said he, not without a touch of bitterness; "but I shall be missing you a lot."

"You're like the cat, you'll miss your warm corner, but I don't believe you'll miss me so dreadfully."

"And the children?"

"Oh, when you're away; but when you're home you're always picking at them; not seriously of course, but still picking. Oh, you're really fond of them, I believe; I don't mean to be unjust."

At supper he was very gentle and felt in low spirits. He did not read the evening papers but wanted only to talk with his wife. She, however, was so busied with chores that she did not give herself much time to chat, and besides her feelings had been pretty well blunted by her ten years' campaign in the nursery and the kitchen.

He was more emotional than he cared to show, and the disorder about him made him restless. He beheld bits of his daily life, of his existence, tossed higgledy-piggledy on chairs and bureaus, and the black open portmanteau gaped at him like a coffin. White linen was wrapped about black clothes, which still retained the shape of knee and elbow, so that it seemed to him as if he himself were stretched there in his white laying-out shirt ready to have the lid put on and be carried off.

Next morning—an August morning it was—he hurried out of bed, dressed breathlessly and was very nervous. He went into the nursery and kissed all the children, who were rubbing the sleep out of their eyes, and after embracing his wife sat himself in a cab to go to the railway station. The journey in company with his chiefs diverted him, and he felt it was really a good thing to stir himself up a bit. His home behind him seemed like a stuffy bedroom, and he was thoroughly glad when he got to Linköping.

The rest of the day was taken up with a fine prison dinner at the big hotel, where they drank the health of the provincial governor, but not that of the convicts, for whose sake the trip was made. But then came the evening in his lonely room. A bed, two chairs, a table, a washstand and a tallow candle which spread its feeble light on the naked wall-paper. The secretary felt ill at ease. Everything was lacking: slippers, dressing-gown, pipe-rack, desk; all the little things that were the constituents of his life. And his children and wife. How were things with them? Were they well? He grew restless and extremely depressed. When he was going to wind up his watch, he could not find the key. It hung at home on the watch frame his wife had embroidered for him when they were engaged. He went to bed and lighted a cigar. But then he had to get up and hunt for a book in his portmanteau. Everything was so neatly packed that he was afraid to disturb it. But as he dug about he found his slippers. She thought of everything! And then he got hold of the book. But he did not read. He lay and thought of the past, of his wife in the last ten years. With that appeared the picture of old times, and the present vanished in the bluish-brown cigar smoke which rose in spirals toward the rain-splotched ceiling. He was conscious of an infinite remorse. Every hard word since those days came back to him, and he regretted every bitter moment he had caused her. At last he went to sleep.

On the following day, work and another dinner, with healths to the prison governor, but still none for the convicts. In the evening, loneliness, desolation, chill. He ached with the need of talking to her. He therefore got some paper and sat down at a writing table. He paused at the first stroke of the pen. How was he to address her? It was always "Dear Mama" when he sent home a note to say that he should be out for dinner. But now it was not to mama he wrote, it was to his former fiancée, his sweetheart. So he wrote "Lily, my darling," as he used to. At the start it went laboriously, because so many words of endearment had vanished from the dry, dull speech of their common everyday life; but soon he grew ardent, and with that the forgotten melodies rose up in his remembrance: waltz-beats and bits of novels, lilacs and swallows, evening moments of sunset across the mirroring bays; all of life's vernal memories danced out amid golden clouds and grouped themselves about her. At the bottom of the page he put a star, as lovers do, and wrote beside it—just as of old—"Kiss here!" When he had finished and read through his letter, he felt a glow on his cheeks, and was somewhat embarrassed. Why, he could not exactly say. It was like giving out his innermost thoughts to someone who might perhaps not understand them.

Still he sent the letter.

A couple of days passed before the answer came. During the interval of waiting he went about with a feeling of childish discomfort and bashfulness.

But then the answer came. He had struck the right note, and from cooking smells and children's din rose a song, bright and harmonious, warm and pure as that of first love. From now on there began an interchange of love letters. He wrote every evening and sometimes would also send a postcard in the course of the day. His companions did not recognize him. He began to give such attention to his clothes and the details of his outward appearance that he was suspected of a love affair. And he was in love, afresh! He sent her his photograph without spectacles, and she him a lock of her hair. They were childish in their expressions, and he bought tinted writing paper with doves upon it. But at the same time they were persons of middle age not far past forty, though the struggle of life had made them feel older. In the past year he had also given up his conjugal privileges, not so much from coldness as from respect, for he saw in her always the mother of his children.

The end of his trip drew near. He now began to experience a certain unrest at the thought of the reunion. He had corresponded with a sweetheart; should he rediscover her in the mother and the housewife? He feared to find himself disappointed at the homecoming. He did not want to see her with a cook's apron on or with the children at her skirts when he was to embrace her. They ought to meet at another place, alone. Could he bring her into tune with him at Vaxholm, for instance, in the inn where they had spent so many happy hours in their engagement time? That would be an idea! To recapture there in memory for a couple of days the first glad period of their springtime, which would never return.

He sat down and presented his plan in a long glowing letter, which she answered by return mail with her assent, delighted that he had lit upon the same thought as she.

Two days later he was in Vaxholm putting in order their room at the hotel. It was a beautiful day in September. He ate his dinner alone in the big hall, drank a glass of wine, and felt himself young again. It was so bright and airy here. Outside the bays spread shining and blue; only the birches on the shore had changed their color. In the garden the dahlias were still in full bloom, and the mignonette breathed its perfume from the borders. Now and then a bee would still visit the withering blossoms, but would turn back to its hive in disappointment. In the channel there were sailing boats passing in and out before a light breeze. As they came about, the sails would flap and the sheets thresh, while the frightened gulls flew screaming away from the herring-fishers, who sat in their skiffs with rod and float.

He took his coffee on the veranda and began to look forward to the coming of the steamer, which was due at six o'clock.

Restlessly, as if he were going toward an uncertain event, he promenaded up and down the balcony, looking out across the bay and the channel in the direction of the city to catch sight of the boat.

At last a puff of smoke rose across the fir woods of Tenö. His pulse quickened and he drank a liqueur. Then he went down to the shore. The smokestack now appeared in the middle of the channel, and soon he could see the flag at the bow. Was she there, or had she been prevented from coming? It would only need that one of the children should be ailing to keep her at home, and then he would have to spend the night alone at the hotel. The children, who had been in the background during the past weeks, now came forth as something that stood between him and her. In their last letters they had spoken but little of the children, as if they wished to keep out a disturbing element, something they did not want as witness to their present state of feeling.

He paced the landing, which creaked under his feet, till he finally paused irresolutely near a pile, gazing continuously out at the boat, whose hull grew ever larger, while her wake spread a flood of molten gold across the rippling blue expanse of water. He could now see people moving on the upper deck and sailors busy with ropes at the bow.

Then something white flutters beside the pilot house. As he is alone on the dock, no one can well be waving to anybody but himself; and no one can be waving to him but she. He takes out his handkerchief and answers the signal. But he notices that his handkerchief is not white, for he has long since changed to colored ones from motives of economy. . . . The steamboat whistles, and the engine slows down. On up to the landing the vessel glides; and he catches sight of her. They greet with their eyes but cannot as yet exchange words because of the distance. The boat is warped in, and he sees her quietly leaning forward over the gangway. . . . It is she, but it is not she. Ten years are between! The style has changed, the cut of dresses is different. Formerly he saw her dark delicate features half enclosed in the then popular bonnet, which left the forehead free; now it is shaded by a poor imitation of a man's hat. Then her pretty figure was outlined in sportive curves under the graceful drapery of a cloak, that roguishly hid and revealed the roundness of the shoulders and the motions of the arms; now her entire form is distorted by a coachman's ulster which displays the dress but not the figure. And as she takes her last step on the gangway, he sees her little foot, which he had been so fond of when it had been in a buttoned boot that followed its shape, now prolonged in a pointed Chinese slipper which prevents the ball of the foot from rising in those dancing rhythms that had formerly enchanted him so.

It was she, but it was not she! He embraced her and kissed her. They asked each other how they were and how the children were. Then they went up on the shore.

Words came broken, dry, forced. So strange! They were as if shy before each other, and there was no allusion to their correspondence.

At last he took courage and said, "Shall we take a walk before the sun goes down?"

"I should love to," she answered, and took his arm.

They went up the street into the little town. All the places of summer amusement were closed and shuttered up, and the gardens were despoiled. An apple or so that had hidden behind the leaves was still left on the tree, but the beds were stripped of every flower.

The verandas, which had lost their awnings, looked like skeletons, and where faces and happy laughter had been all was silent.

"It has an autumn look," he remarked.

"Yes, it's forlorn to see the summer amusements like this."

And they strolled on.

"We ought to go and see where we used to lodge," she said.

"Yes, that will be nice."

They went along the row of bathhouses.

There lay the little cottage wedged in between the gardener's and the chief pilot's places, with the red fence around it, the veranda and the garden plot.

Memories of the past sprang up. In that room their first child had been born. Jubilation and festivity, song and youth! There stood the rose bush they had planted. There was the strawberry bed they had laid out; but it was there no more, for it was grown over and become a grass plot. There in the cinders were the traces of the swing which had hung there, but was no longer to be seen.

"Thanks for your lovely letters," she said, and pressed his arm.

He blushed and made no answer. Thereupon they turned back to the hotel, while he related the details of his trip.

He had had the table set in the big hall where they used to eat in the old days. They sat down without saying grace.

There they were tête-à-tête again. He took the bread tray and passed it to her. She smiled. It was not yesterday that he had been so polite. But it was very novel and pleasant to eat away from home, and soon they started an eager conversation, as in a duet, each in turn bringing out a memory, and in these memories they lived. Their glances shone, and the little wrinkles were smoothed away. Oh, the rose-and-golden times which we live but once, if live them we may, and which many, many never live! At dessert he whispered to the watiress, who straightway brought in a bottle of champagne.

"My dear Axel, what are you thinking of?" said his wife half reproachfully.

"Of the spring that is gone but will return."

But he did not think of it exclusively, for disturbed by his wife's reproach as if a cat had gone through the room, he had a dark vision of the nursery and the porridge dish.

However, things brightened up again, and the rose-red wine touched again the strings of memory, until they threw themselves once more into the magic intoxication of the past.

The hours flew swiftly. They got up and went into the parlor, where the piano stood, to drink their coffee.

"I wonder how my little ones are," said the wife, awakening for the first time from the enchantment.

"Sit down and sing!" he bade, opening the piano.

"What shall I sing? You know I haven't sung for ever so long."

Oh, he knew that, but now he would have a song.

She sat down and played a prelude. It was a shrill hotel piano that sounded like loose teeth.

"What shall I sing?" she asked, turning around on the stool.

"You know, Lily," he replied, not daring to meet her look.

"Your song! Yes. If I remember it."

And so she sang, "Where lies the happy country Where my true lover dwells."

But alas! the voice was thin and sharp, and emotion made it untrue. At times it was like a scream from the depths of a soul which feels its noon is over and the evening drawing near. The fingers which had been busied with heavy work did not easily find the right keys, and the instrument was played out, the cloth on the hammers being worn so that the bare wood clacked against the metal strings.

When the song was done, she did not dare to turn around for a while, but sat as if waiting for him to come to her and say something. But he did not come, and there was silence in the room. When she turned around on the stool, he was sitting in a corner, weeping. She wanted to run to him, take his head in her hands and kiss him as of old, but she remained sitting motionless, her eyes on the floor.

He held an unlighted cigar between his thumb and forefinger. When he heard that all was quiet, he bit off the end and struck a match.

"Thanks, Lily!" he said, and lighted the cigar. "Will you have coffee now?"

They drank their coffee and talked about summer amusements in general and where they should go next year. But the conversation soon began to lag and repeat itself.

Finally he said in the middle of a long unsuppressible yawn, "I'm going to bed."

"I'll go too," said she, rising. "But I'll go out a little while first—on the balcony."

He went into the bedroom. His wife stopped a while in the dining room to talk to the landlady about pickled onions, from which they digressed into washing woollens, so that the conversation lasted half an hour.

When she returned, she stood at the bedroom door and listened. Everything was quiet within, and her husband's boots were outside. She knocked, but there was no answer. Then she opened the door and went in. He was asleep.

He was asleep!

Next morning they were at coffee together. The husband had a headache, and the wife looked uneasy.

"Bah! what coffee," said he with a grimace.

"It's Brazilian," said she.

"What shall we do today?" he asked, taking out his watch.

"You ought to take some bread and butter instead of fretting over your coffee," opined his wife.

"Yes, I'll do that," said he, "and a little nip to finish with. That champagne, brr!"

He got a bread and butter tray with a brandy flask and brightened up.

"Now we'll go to Pilot's Hill and see the view."

They got up and went out. The weather was splendid, and the promenade went well. But when it came to climbing the hill their pace was slow; the wife was short of breath and the husband stiff in the knees. They drew no comparisons with former times.

They then went out into the meadows.

The fields had been mown long since and afterwards grazed over, so that not a flower was to be seen. They sat down each on a separate stone.

He began to talk about the prison inspection and his work, she about the children.

Next they went on a bit further without talking. He took out his watch.

"It's three hours to dinner," he observed.

At the same time he thought, "I wonder what we shall do tomorrow."

They turned back to the hotel. He began to look for newspapers. She smiled and sat by him without speaking.

Dinner was quite silent. Finally the wife broached the subject of servants.

"Oh, for heaven's sake don't let us start on servants," he burst out.

"Yes, we haven't come here to quarrel," she replied.

"Have I started quarreling, I'd like to know?"

"Or I, either?"

Then came a fearful pause. He would have been glad now if there had been someone to come between them. The children? Oh, by all means. This tête-à-tête began to be tiresome. But with that he felt a pang as he thought of the bright hours yesterday.

"Let's go to Ekbacken and pick wild strawberries," she suggested.

"There are no strawberries this time of the year, my good lady; it's autumn."

"Let's go, anyhow."

So they were walking again. But they found nothing to say to each other. He sought with his glance for an object, a place on the road that they could talk about, but everything was dried out, talked to death. She knew all his opinions on every subject and disapproved of many of them. Furthermore he was now longing for home, home with the house and the children. It was too silly to go about here like a pair of idiots liable any moment to get into a quarrel. At last they stopped, for the wife was tired. He sat down and began to trace on the ground with his stick, only wishing she would give him some opening for an outbreak.

"What are you thinking?" she asked finally.

"I?" he responded as if released from a weight; "why this is what I think: we're old, mama; we've played out our play, and we'd best be content with what has been. If you agree, we'll go home by the evening boat. Eh?"

"That's what I've been thinking all along, dear old boy, but I wanted you to say so first."

"Well, come along, we'll go home then! It's not summer any more, it's autumn."

"Yes, autumn it is."

They went back with lighter steps. He was somewhat abashed at the awkward prosaic turn matters had taken and felt the need of giving a philosophic interpretation to the situation.

"You see, mama," he explained, "my l. . . ." (the word was too strong) "my affection for you has in the course of years undergone an evolution, as they put it nowadays. It has developed, amplified itself, so to speak, so that from concentrating on an individual as in the beginning, it has now broadened itself to include in the family, as it were, a collective object. It refers not to you as a separate person, or to the children, but to the whole combination. . . ."

"As uncle always says, the children are lightning-conductors."

After his philosophic exposition he had become himself again. It was good to get out of the frock-coat attitude and into a dressing gown again.

And as soon as they got back to the hotel, his wife started on the portmanteau, and then she was in her element.

When they boarded the steamer they went down at once to the dining room. To save his face he had first asked if they should watch the sunset, which she had declined. As they ate supper, he helped himself first, and she asked the proprietress what the bread cost.

When he had eaten to his heart's content and was about to put the beer glass to his mouth, he could no longer restrain a thought that had been amusing him for some time:

"Old fools, eh?" he exclaimed, smiling at his wife, who looked up at him in the middle of a bite.

But she did not smile back at his shining fat face. On the contrary, her eyes flashed like lightning for an instant, and then assumed an expression of such withering dignity that he became embarrassed.

The enchantment was now broken, the last trace of the sweetheart had vanished; he was sitting only with the mother of his children, and he felt himself crushed.

"Because I was silly a while, you needn't forget to respect me," she said severely. "But there's a good deal of contempt in a man's affection; it's a funny thing."

"And in a woman's?"

"Much more, that's true. But then she has greater provocation."

"Lord knows, it's about equal, though in different ways. Probably they're both in the wrong. A thing one has overestimated because it is difficult to get may easily become an object of contempt."

"Why should it be overestimated?"

"Why should it be hard to get?"

The steamer's whistle above their heads interrupted the conversation.

They had arrived at their destination.

When they were back in their home, and he saw her in the midst of the children, he soon felt that his "affection" for her had gone through a transformation, and that hers for him had flowed over and been distributed among all these little cry-babies. Perhaps it was only as a means to these that he possessed her affection. His role then was transitory, and he therefore felt himself set to one side. If he was not necessary to provide bread, he would now presumably have been discarded.

He went into his workroom, put on his dressing gown and slippers, lighted a pipe, and felt at home again. Outside the wind-gusts lashed the rain, and there was a whistling in the stovepipe.

His wife came in when she was done with the children.

"This is no weather for strawberry-picking," she remarked.

"No, old lady; the summer's done, and autumn's here."

"Yes, it's autumn," she responded, "but it isn't winter yet, that's one comfort."

"That a comfort! Not much comfort when we only live once."

"Twice, when one has children; three times, if one lives to see one's grandchildren."

"But after that it's really all up."

"Unless there's another life after this."

"There's no being sure of that. Who can tell? I believe in it, but my faith is no proof."

"Yes, but it's nice to believe it, so let's believe, let's believe there may be another spring for us! Let's believe it!"

"All right, we will believe it," said he, putting his arm around her waist.

For Discussion

1. The marriage of the two people in this story may be called "typical." What is the author's chief observation of what has happened to them in ten years?

2. Why do you think the business trip stirred up feelings of regret in the husband? What resentment of his was also stirred up? Was it justified? Why or why not?

3. In the wife's response to her husband's letters, what was revealed about her unspoken hopes? Do you think this exchange of letters was just foolish, or do you think it revealed the desire of two people to see each other freshly? Explain. Do you think that in a dim

way they felt they had been unfair to each other as people? In discussing this, consider how you feel about the way you take people close to you for granted, and the way you feel about being taken for granted.

4. The husband and wife tried to recapture their original feeling of interest and wonder in each other by attempting to relive the past. Point out specific sentences and passages of description, from the time the wife arrives until she and her husband depart, which reveal Strindberg's ironic comments on this attempt.

5. Would you criticize the purpose of the husband and wife, or their method of achieving it? Explain.

6. One of the key passages in this story, which shows what a keen and critical observer of people Strindberg was, is the one beginning " 'Old fools, eh?' he exclaimed. . . ." (page 262). Why did the husband's complacent remark evoke the response it did from his wife? Do you think their observation about the contempt men and women have for each other is true? Why or why not?

7. On their arrival back home, the husband watched his wife with the children and bitterly thought to himself that "if he was not necessary to provide bread, he would now presumably have been discarded." What criticism of the wife is implied here? How is it related to the earlier discussion of contempt?

8. When the wife said passionately, "Let's believe there may be another spring for us!" do you think she was talking only of another life after this? What hope might she have been expressing? How did her attitude toward life differ from that of her husband?

9. Point out Strindberg's symbolic use of the seasons. What was the symbolic and ironic meaning of the fact that the husband was "a secretary of prison inspection"?

10. Why do you think Strindberg did not give the husband and wife a last name and rarely used their first names? Despite this, are the couple fully developed characters? Point out attitudes and actions which make them true-to-life people.

For Composition

1. Using the title "Marriage: Its Meaning for Man and Wife," write a composition in which you show that Strindberg's story, with its critical view of marriage, can have deep and lasting values for the Christian couple.

2. Using the theme that even adults must "grow up," write an essay on the husband's conflict and how he resolved it. Show that it is only by facing reality that man can enjoy true peace.

Henrik Ibsen

A Doll's House

Henrik Ibsen * (1828–1906), the Norwegian playwright, stands as one of the giants of the modern drama, who helped to bring about a revolutionary change in playwriting in the last quarter of the nineteenth century. Previously, plays had been romantic and artificial, with little resemblance to life as people knew it. With Ibsen, the drama became a serious and realistic presentation of the psychological and social problems of ordinary people and the effect their environment had on them. With power and insight, Ibsen attacked the hypocrisy of social conventions, and the selfishness and complacency of people. His plays were compact, swiftly moving dramas, unlike anything that had been seen before on a stage. His bold ideas shocked many people, and for a long time his work could not be produced in England or America. His most famous realistic dramas, such as *A Doll's House*, *Hedda Gabler*, *An Enemy of the People*, and *Ghosts* are constantly revived throughout the world and continue to stir audiences.

A Doll's House, written in 1879, remains one of Ibsen's most powerful plays, despite the fact that some critics have called it "dated." These critics think that women's fight for equality is something of the past because they have won recognition in the fields of business and politics, and achieved equal rights in the home. A wife today, it is true, is far more independent than Nora was in Ibsen's play. A modern wife is not hemmed in by the social and economic conventions of the late nineteenth century. What, then, makes *A Doll's House* so popular with audiences today? What Nora was calling for as a human being has not yet been met satisfactorily by men. That is why this play is still so powerful and meaningful.

As a craftsman, Ibsen raised playwriting to a new level of artistic achievement. As you read this play, note how skillfully he introduces his characters, how he states the "problem" and the issues with economy and immediacy, and, above all, how he creates characters who are alive and real. As Ibsen himself said: "What I wanted to do was to depict human beings, human emotions, and human destinies upon a groundwork of certain social conditions and principles of the present day."

* hen'rik ib's'n

265

Characters

TORVALD HELMER
NORA HELMER
DR. RANK
NILS KROGSTAD
MRS. LINDE
ANNE   ⎫
       ⎬ *servants*
HELEN ⎭
IVAR   ⎫
EMMY ⎬ *the Helmers' children*
BOB   ⎭
NURSE

TIME: The Present; Christmastime.
The action takes place on three consecutive days.

ACT I

SCENE: *A room furnished comfortably and tastefully but not extravagantly. At the back a door to the right leads to the entrance hall; another to the left leads to* HELMER's *study. Between the doors stands a piano. In the middle of the left-hand wall is a door and beyond a window. Near the window are a round table, armchairs and a small sofa. In the right-hand wall, at the farther end, another door, and on the same side, nearer the footlights, a stove, two easy chairs and a rocking chair; between the stove and the door a small table. Engravings on the walls; a cabinet with china and other small objects; a small bookcase with well-bound books. The floors are carpeted, and a fire burns in the stove. It is winter.*

    A bell rings in the hall; shortly afterward the door is heard to open. Enter NORA, *humming a tune and in high spirits. She is in outdoor dress and carries a number of parcels; these she lays on the table to the right. She leaves the outer door open after her, and through it is seen a* PORTER *who is carrying a Christmas tree and a basket, which he gives to the* MAID *who has opened the door.*

NORA. Hide the Christmas tree carefully, Helen. Be sure the children do not see it till this evening, when it is dressed. (*To the* PORTER, *taking out her purse.*) How much?

PORTER. Sixpence.

NORA. There is a shilling. No, keep the change. (*The* PORTER *thanks her and goes out.* NORA *shuts the door. She is laughing to herself as she takes off her hat and coat. She takes a packet of macaroons from her pocket and eats one or two, then goes cautiously to her husband's door and listens.*) Yes, he is in. (*Still humming, she goes to the table on the right.*)

HELMER (*calls out from his room*). Is that my little lark twittering out there?

NORA (*busy opening some of the parcels*). Yes, it is!

HELMER. Is it my little squirrel bustling about?

NORA. Yes!

HELMER. When did my squirrel come home?

NORA. Just now. (*Puts the bag of macaroons into her pocket and wipes her mouth.*) Come in here, Torvald, and see what I have bought.

HELMER. Don't disturb me. (*A little later he opens the door and looks into the room, pen in hand.*) Bought, did you say? All these things? Has my little spendthrift been wasting money again?

NORA. Yes, but, Torvald, this year we really can let ourselves go a little. This is the first Christmas that we have not needed to economize.

HELMER. Still, you know, we can't spend money recklessly.

NORA. Yes, Torvald, we may be a wee bit more reckless now, mayn't we? Just a tiny wee bit! You are going to have a big salary and earn lots and lots of money.

HELMER. Yes, after the new year; but then it will be a whole quarter before the salary is due.

NORA. Pooh! We can borrow till then.

HELMER. Nora! (*Goes up to her and takes her playfully by the ear.*) The same little featherhead! Suppose, now, that I borrowed fifty pounds today and you spent it all in the Christmas week and and then on New Year's Eve a slate fell on my head and killed me and—

NORA (*putting her hands over his mouth*). Oh! don't say such horrid things.

HELMER. Still, suppose that happened—what then?

NORA. If that were to happen, I don't suppose I should care whether I owed money or not.

HELMER. Yes, but what about the people who had lent it?

NORA. They? Who would bother about them? I should not know who they were.

HELMER. That is like a woman! But seriously, Nora, you know what I think about that. No debt, no borrowing. There can be no freedom or beauty about a home life that depends on borrowing and debt. We two have kept bravely on the straight road so far, and we will go on the same way for the short time longer that there need be any struggle.

NORA (*moving toward the stove*). As you please, Torvald.

HELMER (*following her*). Come, come, my little skylark must not droop her wings. What is this! Is my little squirrel out of temper? (*Taking out his purse.*) Nora, what do you think I have got here?

NORA (*turning round quickly*). Money!

HELMER. There you are. (*Gives her some money.*) Do you think I don't know what a lot is wanted for housekeeping at Christmas-time?

NORA (*counting*). Ten shillings—a pound—two pounds! Thank you, thank you, Torvald; that will keep me going for a long time.

HELMER. Indeed it must.

NORA. Yes, yes, it will. But come here and let me show you what I have bought. And all so cheap! Look, here is a new suit for Ivar and a sword, and a horse and a trumpet for Bob, and a doll and dolly's bedstead for Emmy—they are very plain, but anyway she will soon break them in pieces. And here are dress lengths and handkerchiefs for the maids; old Anne ought really to have something better.

HELMER. And what is in this parcel?

NORA (*crying out*). No, no! You mustn't see that till this evening.

HELMER. Very well. But now tell me, you extravagant little person, what would you like for yourself?

NORA. For myself? Oh, I am sure I don't want anything.

HELMER. Yes, but you must. Tell me something reasonable that you would particularly like to have.

NORA. No, I really can't think of anything—unless, Torvald—

HELMER. Well?

NORA (*playing with his coat buttons and without raising her eyes to his*). If you really want to give me something, you might—you might—

HELMER. Well, out with it!

NORA (*speaking quickly*). You might give me money, Torvald. Only just as much as you can afford; and then one of these days I will buy something with it.

HELMER. But, Nora—

NORA. Oh, do! dear Torvald; please, please do! Then I will wrap it up in beautiful gilt paper and hang it on the Christmas tree. Wouldn't that be fun?

HELMER. What are little people called that are always wasting money?

NORA. Spendthrifts—I know. Let us do as I suggest, Torvald, and then I shall have time to think what I am most in want of. That is a very sensible plan, isn't it?

HELMER (*smiling*). Indeed it is—that is to say, if you were really to save out of the money I give you and then really buy something for yourself. But if you spend it all on the housekeeping and any number of unnecessary things, then I merely have to pay up again.

NORA. Oh, but, Torvald—

HELMER. You can't deny it, my dear little Nora. (*Puts his arm around her waist.*) It's a sweet little spendthrift, but she uses up a deal of money. One would hardly believe how expensive such little persons are!

NORA. It's a shame to say that. I do really save all I can.

HELMER (*laughing*). That's very true—all you can. But you can't save anything!

NORA (*smiling quietly and happily*). You haven't any idea how many expenses we skylarks and squirrels have, Torvald.

HELMER. You are an odd little soul. Very like your father. You always find some new way of wheedling money out of me, and as soon as you have got it it seems to melt in your hands. You never know where it has gone. Still, one must take you as you are. It is in the blood; for indeed it is true that you can inherit these things, Nora.

NORA. Ah, I wish I had inherited many of Papa's qualities.

HELMER. And I would not wish you to be anything but just what you are, my sweet little skylark. But, do you know, it strikes me that you are looking rather—what shall I say?—rather uneasy today.

NORA. Do I?

HELMER. You do, really. Look straight at me.

NORA (*looks at him*). Well?

HELMER (*wagging his finger at her*). Hasn't Miss Sweet Tooth been breaking rules in town today?

NORA. No—what makes you think that?

HELMER. Hasn't she paid a visit to the confectioner's?

NORA. No, I assure you, Torvald—

HELMER. Not been nibbling sweets?

NORA. No, certainly not.

HELMER. Not even taken a bite at a macaroon or two?

NORA. No, Torvald, I assure you, really—

HELMER. There, there, of course I was only joking.

NORA (*going to the table on the right*). I should not think of going against your wishes.

HELMER. No, I am sure of that; besides, you gave me your word. (*Going up to her.*) Keep your little Christmas secrets to yourself, my darling. They will all be revealed tonight when the Christmas tree is lit, no doubt.

NORA. Did you remember to invite Doctor Rank?

HELMER. No. But there is no need; as a matter of course he will come to dinner with us. However, I will ask him when he comes in this morning. I have ordered some good wine. Nora, you can't think how I am looking forward to this evening.

NORA. So am I! And how the children will enjoy themselves, Torvald!

HELMER. It is splendid to feel that one has a perfectly safe appointment and a big enough income. It's delightful to think of, isn't it?

NORA. It's wonderful!

HELMER. Do you remember last Christmas? For a full three weeks beforehand you shut yourself up every evening till long after midnight, making ornaments for the Christmas tree and all the other fine things that were to be a surprise to us. It was the dullest three weeks I ever spent!

NORA. I didn't find it dull.

HELMER (*smiling*). But there was precious little result, Nora.

NORA. Oh, you shouldn't tease me about that again. How could I help the cat's going in and tearing everything to pieces?

HELMER. Of course you couldn't, poor little girl. You had the best of intentions to please us all, and that's the main thing. But it is a good thing that our hard times are over.

NORA. Yes, it is really wonderful.

HELMER. This time I needn't sit here and be dull all alone and you needn't ruin your dear eyes and your pretty little hands—

NORA (*clapping her hands*). No, Torvald, I needn't any longer, need I! It's wonderfully lovely to hear you say so! (*Taking his arm.*) Now I will tell you how I have been thinking we ought to arrange things, Torvald. As soon as Christmas is over—(*A bell rings in the hall.*) There's the bell. (*She tidies the room a little.*) There's someone at the door. What a nuisance!

HELMER. If it is a caller, remember I am not at home.

MAID (*in the doorway*). A lady to see you, ma'am—a stranger.

NORA. Ask her to come in.

MAID (*to* HELMER). The doctor came at the same time, sir.

HELMER. Did he go straight into my room?

MAID. Yes sir.

(HELMER *goes into his room. The* MAID *ushers in* MRS. LINDE, *who is in traveling dress, and shuts the door.*)

MRS. LINDE (*in a dejected and timid voice*). How do you do, Nora?

NORA (*doubtfully*). How do you do—

MRS. LINDE. You don't recognize me, I suppose.

NORA. No, I don't know—yes, to be sure, I seem to— (*Suddenly.*) Yes! Christine! Is it really you?

MRS. LINDE. Yes, it is I.

NORA. Christine! To think of my not recognizing you! And yet how could I? (*In a gentle voice.*) How you have altered, Christine!

MRS. LINDE. Yes, I have indeed. In nine, ten long years—

NORA. Is it so long since we met? I suppose it is. The last eight years have been a happy time for me, I can tell you. And so now you have come into the town and have taken this long journey in winter—that was plucky of you.

MRS. LINDE. I arrived by steamer this morning.

NORA. To have some fun at Christmastime, of course. How delightful! We will have such fun together! But take off your things.

You are not cold, I hope. (*Helps her.*) Now we will sit down by the stove and be cozy. No, take this armchair; I will sit here in the rocking chair. (*Takes her hands.*) Now you look like your old self again; it was only the first moment—You are a little paler, Christine, and perhaps a little thinner.

MRS. LINDE. And much, much older, Nora.

NORA. Perhaps a little older; very, very little; certainly not much. (*Stops suddenly and speaks seriously.*) What a thoughtless creature I am, chattering away like this. My poor, dear Christine, do forgive me.

MRS. LINDE. What do you mean, Nora?

NORA (*gently*). Poor Christine, you are a widow.

MRS. LINDE. Yes; it is three years ago now.

NORA. Yes, I knew; I saw it in the papers. I assure you, Christine, I meant ever so often to write to you at the time, but I always put it off and something always prevented me.

MRS. LINDE. I quite understand, dear.

NORA. It was very bad of me, Christine. Poor thing, how you must have suffered. And he left you nothing?

MRS. LINDE. No.

NORA. And no children?

MRS. LINDE. No.

NORA. Nothing at all, then?

MRS. LINDE. Not even any sorrow or grief to live upon.

NORA (*looking incredulously at her*). But, Christine, is that possible?

MRS. LINDE (*smiles sadly and strokes her hair*). It sometimes happens, Nora.

NORA. So you are quite alone. How dreadfully sad that must be. I have three lovely children. You can't see them just now, for they are out with their nurse. But now you must tell me all about it.

MRS. LINDE. No, no; I want to hear about you.

NORA. No, you must begin. I mustn't be selfish today; today I must only think of your affairs. But there is one thing I must tell you. Do you know we have just had a great piece of good luck?

MRS. LINDE. No, what is it?

NORA. Just fancy, my husband has been made manager of the bank!

MRS. LINDE. Your husband? What good luck!

NORA. Yes, tremendous! A barrister's profession is such an uncertain thing, especially if he won't undertake unsavory cases; and nat-

urally Torvald has never been willing to do that, and I quite agree
with him. You may imagine how pleased we are! He is to take
up his work in the bank at the new year, and then he will have a
big salary and lots of commissions. For the future we can live
quite differently—we can do just as we like. I feel so relieved and
so happy, Christine! It will be splendid to have heaps of money
and not need to have any anxiety, won't it?

MRS. LINDE. Yes, anyhow I think it would be delightful to have what
one needs.

NORA. No, not only what one needs but heaps and heaps of money.

MRS. LINDE (*smiling*). Nora, Nora, haven't you learned sense yet?
In our schooldays you were a great spendthrift.

NORA (*laughing*). Yes, that is what Torvald says now. (*Wags her
finger at her.*) But "Nora, Nora" is not so silly as you think. We
have not been in a position for me to waste money. We have both
had to work.

MRS. LINDE. You too?

NORA. Yes; odds and ends, needlework, crochet work, embroidery
and that kind of thing. (*Dropping her voice.*) And other things
as well. You know Torvald left his office when we were married?
There was no prospect of promotion there, and he had to try
and earn more than before. But during the first year he over-
worked himself dreadfully. You see, he had to make money every
way he could; and he worked early and late; but he couldn't stand
it and fell dreadfully ill, and the doctors said it was necessary for
him to go south.

MRS. LINDE. You spent a whole year in Italy, didn't you?

NORA. Yes. It was no easy matter to get away, I can tell you. It was
just after Ivar was born, but naturally we had to go. It was a
wonderfully beautiful journey, and it saved Torvald's life. But it
cost a tremendous lot of money, Christine.

MRS. LINDE. So I should think.

NORA. It cost about two hundred and fifty pounds. That's a lot,
isn't it?

MRS. LINDE. Yes, and in emergencies like that it is lucky to have the
money.

NORA. I ought to tell you that we had it from Papa.

MRS. LINDE. Oh, I see. It was just about that time that he died,
wasn't it?

NORA. Yes; and, just think of it, I couldn't go and nurse him. I was expecting little Ivar's birth every day and I had my poor sick Torvald to look after. My dear, kind father—I never saw him again, Christine. That was the saddest time I have known since our marriage.

MRS. LINDE. I know how fond you were of him. And then you went off to Italy?

NORA. Yes; you see, we had money then, and the doctors insisted on our going, so we started a month later.

MRS. LINDE. And your husband came back quite well?

NORA. As sound as a bell!

MRS. LINDE. But—the doctor?

NORA. What doctor?

MRS. LINDE. I thought your maid said the gentleman who arrived here just as I did was the doctor.

NORA. Yes, that was Doctor Rank but he doesn't come here professionally. He is our greatest friend and comes in at least once every day. No, Torvald has not had an hour's illness since then, and our children are strong and healthy and so am I. (*Jumps up and claps her hands.*) Christine! Christine! It's good to be alive and happy! But how horrid of me; I am talking of nothing but my own affairs. (*Sits on a stool near her and rests her arms on her knees.*) You mustn't be angry with me. Tell me, is it really true that you did not love your husband? Why did you marry him?

MRS. LINDE. My mother was alive then and was bedridden and helpless, and I had to provide for my two younger brothers; so I did not think I was justified in refusing his offer.

NORA. No, perhaps you were quite right. He was rich at that time, then?

MRS. LINDE. I believe he was quite well off. But his business was a precarious one, and when he died it all went to pieces and there was nothing left.

NORA. And then?

MRS. LINDE. Well, I had to turn my hand to anything I could find— first a small shop, then a small school and so on. The last three years have seemed like one long working day, with no rest. Now it is at an end, Nora. My poor mother needs me no more, for she is gone; and the boys do not need me either; they have got situations and can shift for themselves.

NORA. What a relief you must feel it.

MRS. LINDE. No indeed; I only feel my life unspeakably empty. No one to live for any more. (*Gets up restlessly.*) That was why I could not stand the life in my little backwater any longer. I hope it may be easier here to find something which will busy me and occupy my thoughts. If only I could have the good luck to get some regular work—office work of some kind—

NORA. But, Christine, that is so frightfully tiring, and you look tired out now. You had far better go away to some watering place.

MRS. LINDE (*walking to the window*). I have no father to give me money for a journey, Nora.

NORA (*rising*). Oh, don't be angry with me.

MRS. LINDE (*going up to her*). It is you that must not be angry with me, dear. The worst of a position like mine is that it makes one so bitter. No one to work for and yet obliged to be always on the lookout for chances. One must live, and so one becomes selfish. When you told me of the happy turn your fortunes have taken— you will hardly believe it—I was delighted not so much on your account as on my own.

NORA. How do you mean? Oh, I understand. You mean that perhaps Torvald could get you something to do.

MRS. LINDE. Yes, that was what I was thinking of.

NORA. He must, Christine. Just leave it to me; I will broach the subject very cleverly—I will think of something that will please him very much. It will make me so happy to be of some use to you.

MRS. LINDE. How kind you are, Nora, to be so anxious to help me! It is doubly kind in you, for you know so little of the burdens and troubles of life.

NORA. I? I know so little of them?

MRS. LINDE (*smiling*). My dear! Small household cares and that sort of thing! You are a child, Nora.

NORA (*tosses her head and crosses stage*). You ought not to be so superior.

MRS. LINDE. No?

NORA. You are just like the others. They all think that I am incapable of anything really serious—

MRS. LINDE. Come, come.

NORA. —that I have gone through nothing in this world of cares.

MRS. LINDE. But, my dear Nora, you have just told me all your troubles.

NORA. Pooh!—those were trifles. (*Lowering her voice.*) I have not told you the important thing.

MRS. LINDE. The important thing? What do you mean?

NORA. You look down upon me altogether, Christine—but you ought not to. You are proud, aren't you, of having worked so hard and so long for your mother?

MRS. LINDE. Indeed, I don't look down on anyone. But it is true that I am both proud and glad to think that I was privileged to make the end of my mother's life almost free from care.

NORA. And you are proud to think of what you have done for your brothers.

MRS. LINDE. I think I have the right to be.

NORA. I think so too. But now listen to this; I too have something to be proud and glad of.

MRS. LINDE. I have no doubt you have. But what do you refer to?

NORA. Speak low. Suppose Torvald were to hear! He mustn't on any account—no one in the world must know, Christine, except you.

MRS. LINDE. But what is it?

NORA. Come here. (*Pulls her down on the sofa beside her.*) Now I will show you that I too have something to be proud and glad of. It was I who saved Torvald's life.

MRS. LINDE. "Saved"? How?

NORA. I told you about our trip to Italy. Torvald would never have recovered if he had not gone there.

MRS. LINDE. Yes, but your father gave you the necessary funds.

NORA (*smiling*). Yes, that is what Torvald and the others think, but—

MRS. LINDE. But—

NORA. Papa didn't give us a shilling. It was I who procured the money.

MRS. LINDE. You? All that large sum?

NORA. Two hundred and fifty pounds. What do you think of that?

MRS. LINDE. But, Nora, how could you possibly do it. Did you win a prize in the lottery?

NORA (*contemptuously*). In the lottery? There would have been no credit in that.

MRS. LINDE. But where did you get it from, then?

NORA (*humming and smiling with an air of mystery*). Hm, hm! Aha!

MRS. LINDE. Because you couldn't have borrowed it.

NORA. Couldn't I? Why not?

MRS. LINDE. No, a wife cannot borrow without her husband's consent.

NORA (*tossing her head*). Oh, if it is a wife who has any head for business—a wife who has the wit to be a little bit clever—

MRS. LINDE. I don't understand it at all, Nora.

NORA. There is no need you should. I never said I had borrowed the money. I may have got it some other way. (*Lies back on the sofa.*) Perhaps I got it from some other admirers. When anyone is as attractive as I am—

MRS. LINDE. You are a mad creature.

NORA. Now you know you're full of curiosity, Christine.

MRS. LINDE. Listen to me, Nora dear. Haven't you been a little bit imprudent?

NORA (*sits up straight*). Is it imprudent to save your husband's life?

MRS. LINDE. It seems to me imprudent, without his knowledge, to—

NORA. But it was absolutely necessary that he should not know! My goodness, can't you understand that? It was necessary he should have no idea what a dangerous condition he was in. It was to me that the doctors came and said that his life was in danger and that the only thing to save him was to live in the south. Do you suppose I didn't try, first of all, to get what I wanted as if it were for myself? I told him how much I should love to travel abroad like other young wives; I tried tears and entreaties with him; I told him that he ought to remember the condition I was in and that he ought to be kind and indulgent to me; I even hinted that he might raise a loan. That nearly made him angry, Christine. He said I was thoughtless and that it was his duty as my husband not to indulge me in my whims and caprices—as I believe he called them. Very well, I thought, you must be saved—and that was how I came to devise a way out of the difficulty.

MRS. LINDE. And did your husband never get to know from your father that the money had not come from him?

NORA. No, never. Papa died just at that time. I had meant to let him into the secret and beg him never to reveal it. But he was so ill then—alas, there never was any need to tell him.

MRS. LINDE. And since then have you never told your secret to your husband?

NORA. Good heavens, no! How could you think so? A man who has such strong opinions about these things! And besides, how painful and humiliating it would be for Torvald, with his manly independence, to know that he owed me anything! It would upset our mutual relations altogether; our beautiful happy home would no longer be what it is now.

MRS. LINDE. Do you mean never to tell him about it?

NORA (*meditatively and with a half-smile*). Yes—someday, perhaps, after many years, when I am no longer as nice looking as I am now. Don't laugh at me! I mean, of course, when Torvald is no longer as devoted to me as he is now; when my dancing and dressing up and reciting have palled on him; then it may be a good thing to have something in reserve—(*Breaking off.*) What nonsense! That time will never come. Now what do you think of my great secret, Christine? Do you still think I am of no use? I can tell you too, that this affair has caused me a lot of worry. It has been by no means easy for me to meet my engagements punctually. I may tell you that there is something that is called, in business, quarterly interest and another thing called payment in installments, and it is always so dreadfully difficult to manage them. I have had to save a little here and there, where I could, you understand. I have not been able to put aside much from my housekeeping money, for Torvald must have a good table. I couldn't let my children be shabbily dressed; I have felt obliged to use up all he gave me for them, the sweet little darlings!

MRS. LINDE. So it has all had to come out of your own necessaries of life, poor Nora?

NORA. Of course. Besides, I was the one responsible for it. Whenever Torvald has given me money for new dresses and such things I have never spent more than half of it; I have always bought the simplest and cheapest things. Thank heaven any clothes look well on me, and so Torvald has never noticed it. But it was often very hard on me, Christine—because it is delightful to be really well dressed, isn't it?

MRS. LINDE. Quite so.

NORA. Well, then I have found other ways of earning money. Last winter I was lucky enough to get a lot of copying to do, so I locked myself up and sat writing every evening until quite late at night. Many a time I was desperately tired, but all the same it was a tremendous pleasure to sit there working and earning money. It was like being a man.

MRS. LINDE. How much have you been able to pay off in that way?

NORA. I can't tell you exactly. You see, it is very difficult to keep an account of a business matter of that kind. I only know that I have paid every penny that I could scrape together. Many a time I was at my wits' end. (*Smiles.*) Then I used to sit here and imagine that a rich old gentleman had fallen in love with me—

MRS. LINDE. What! Who was it?

NORA. Be quiet!—that he had died and that when his will was opened it contained, written in big letters, the instruction: "The lovely Mrs. Nora Helmer is to have all I possess paid over to her at once in cash."

MRS. LINDE. But, my dear Nora—who could the man be?

NORA. Good gracious, can't you understand? There was no old gentleman at all; it was only something that I used to sit here and imagine, when I couldn't think of any way of procuring money. But it's all the same now; the tiresome old person can stay where he is as far as I am concerned; I don't care about him or his will either, for I am free from care now. (*Jumps up.*) My goodness, it's delightful to think of, Christine! Free from care! To be able to be free from care, quite free from care; to be able to play and romp with the children; to be able to keep the house beautifully and have everything just as Torvald likes it! And, think of it, soon the spring will come and the big blue sky! Perhaps we shall be able to take a little trip—perhaps I shall see the sea again! Oh, it's a wonderful thing to be alive and be happy! (A *bell is heard in the hall.*)

MRS. LINDE (*rising*). There is the bell; perhaps I had better go.

NORA. No, don't go; no one will come in here; it is sure to be for Torvald.

SERVANT (*at the hall door*). Excuse me, ma'am—there is a gentleman to see the master, and as the doctor is with him—

NORA. Who is it?

KROGSTAD (*at the door*). It is I, Mrs. Helmer. (MRS. LINDE *starts, trembles and turns to the window.*)

NORA (*takes a step toward him and speaks in a strained, low voice*). You? What is it? What do you want to see my husband about?

KROGSTAD. Bank business—in a way. I have a small post in the bank, and I hear your husband is to be our chief now.

NORA. Then it is—

KROGSTAD. Nothing but dry business matters, Mrs. Helmer; absolutely nothing else.

NORA. Be so good as to go into the study then. (*She bows indifferently to him and shuts the door into the hall, then comes back and makes up the fire in the stove.*)

MRS. LINDE. Nora—who was that man?

NORA. A lawyer of the name of Krogstad.

MRS. LINDE. Then it really was he.

NORA. Do you know the man?

MRS. LINDE. I used to—many years ago. At one time he was a solicitor's clerk in our town.

NORA. Yes, he was.

MRS. LINDE. He is greatly altered.

NORA. He made a very unhappy marriage.

MRS. LINDE. He is a widower now, isn't he?

NORA. With several children. There now, it is burning up. (*Shuts the door of the stove and moves the rocking chair aside.*)

MRS. LINDE. They say he carries on various kinds of business.

NORA. Really! Perhaps he does; I don't know anything about it. But don't let us think of business; it is so tiresome.

DR. RANK (*comes out of* HELMER's *study. Before he shuts the door he calls to him*). No, my dear fellow, I won't disturb you; I would rather go in to your wife for a little while. (*Shuts the door and see* MRS. LINDE.) I beg your pardon; I am afraid I am disturbing you too.

NORA. No, not at all. (*Introducing him.*) Doctor Rank, Mrs. Linde.

RANK. I have often heard Mrs. Linde's name mentioned here. I think I passed you on the stairs when I arrived, Mrs. Linde?

MRS. LINDE. Yes, I go up very slowly; I can't manage stairs well.

RANK. Ah! Some slight internal weakness?

MRS. LINDE. No, the fact is I have been overworking myself.

RANK. Nothing more than that? Then I suppose you have come to town to amuse yourself with our entertainments?

MRS. LINDE. I have come to look for work.

RANK. Is that a good cure for overwork?

MRS. LINDE. One must live, Doctor Rank.

RANK. Yes, the general opinion seems to be that it is necessary.

NORA. Look here, Doctor Rank—you know you want to live.

RANK. Certainly. However wretched I may feel, I want to prolong the agony as long as possible. All my patients are like that. And so are those who are morally diseased; one of them, and a bad case too, is at this very moment with Helmer—

MRS. LINDE (*sadly*). Ah!

NORA. Whom do you mean?

RANK. A lawyer of the name Krogstad, a fellow you don't know at all. He suffers from a diseased moral character, Mrs. Helmer, but even he began talking of its being highly important that he should live.

NORA. Did he? What did he want to speak to Torvald about?

RANK. I have no idea; I only heard that it was something about the bank.

NORA. I didn't know this—what's his name?—Krogstad had anything to do with the bank.

RANK. Yes, he has some sort of appointment there. (*To* MRS. LINDE.) I don't know whether you find also in your part of the world that there are certain people who go zealously snuffing about to smell out moral corruption and, as soon as they have found some, put the person concerned into some lucrative position where they can keep their eye on him. Healthy natures are left out in the cold.

MRS. LINDE. Still I think the sick are those who most need taking care of.

RANK (*shrugging his shoulders*). Yes, there you are. That is the sentiment that is turning society into a sick house.

(NORA, *who has been absorbed in her thoughts, breaks out into smothered laughter and claps her hands.*)

RANK. Why do you laugh at that? Have you any notion what society really is?

NORA. What do I care about tiresome society? I am laughing at something quite different, something extremely amusing. Tell me, Doctor Rank, are all the people who are employed in the bank dependent on Torvald now?

RANK. Is that what you find so extremely amusing?

NORA (*smiling and humming*). That's my affair! (*Walking about the room.*) It's perfectly glorious to think that we have—that Torvald has so much power over so many people. (*Takes the packet from her pocket.*) Doctor Rank, what do you say to a macaroon?

RANK. What, macaroons? I thought they were forbidden here.

NORA. Yes, but these are some Christine gave me.

MRS. LINDE. What! I?

NORA. Oh well, don't be alarmed! You couldn't know that Torvald had forbidden them. I must tell you that he is afraid they will spoil my teeth. But, bah!—once in a way— That's so, isn't it, Doctor Rank? By your leave! (*Puts a macaroon into his mouth.*) You must have one too, Christine. And I shall have one, just a little one—or at most two. (*Walking about.*) I am tremendously happy. There is just one thing in the world now that I should dearly love to do.

RANK. Well, what is that?

NORA. It's something I should dearly love to say if Torvald could hear me.

RANK. Well, why can't you say it?

NORA. No, I daren't; it's so shocking.

MRS. LINDE. Shocking?

RANK. Well, I should not advise you to say it. Still, with us you might. What is it you would so much like to say if Torvald could hear you?

NORA. I should just love to say— Well, I'm damned!

RANK. Are you mad?

MRS. LINDE. Nora dear!

RANK. Say it, here he is!

NORA (*hiding the packet*). Hush! Hush! Hush!

(HELMER *comes out of his room with his coat over his arm and his hat in his hand.*)

NORA. Well, Torvald dear, have you got rid of him?

HELMER. Yes, he has just gone.

NORA. Let me introduce you—this is Christine, who has come to town.

HELMER. Christine? Excuse me, but I don't know—

NORA. Mrs. Linde, dear; Christine Linde.

HELMER. Of course. A school friend of my wife's, I presume?

MRS. LINDE. Yes, we have known each other since then.

NORA. And just think, she has taken a long journey in order to see you.

HELMER. What do you mean?

MRS. LINDE. No, really, I—

NORA. Christine is tremendously clever at bookkeeping, and she is frightfully anxious to work under some clever man, so as to perfect herself—

HELMER. Very sensible, Mrs. Linde.

NORA. And when she heard you had been appointed manager of the bank—the news was telegraphed, you know—she traveled here as quickly as she could. Torvald, I am sure you will be able to do something for Christine, for my sake, won't you?

HELMER. Well, it is not altogether impossible. I presume you are a widow, Mrs. Linde?

MRS. LINDE. Yes.

HELMER. And have had some experience of bookkeeping?

MRS. LINDE. Yes, a fair amount.

HELMER. Ah well, it's very likely I may be able to find something for you.

NORA (*clapping her hands*). What did I tell you?

HELMER. You have just come at a fortunate moment, Mrs. Linde.

MRS. LINDE. How am I to thank you?

HELMER. There is no need. (*Puts on his coat.*) But today you must excuse me—

RANK. Wait a minute; I will come with you. (*Brings his fur coat from the hall and warms it at the fire.*)

NORA. Don't be long away, Torvald, dear.

HELMER. About an hour, not more.

NORA. Are you going too, Christine?

MRS. LINDE (*putting on her cloak*). Yes, I must go and look for a room.

HELMER. Oh well, then, we can walk down the street together.

NORA (*helping her*). What a pity it is we are so short of space here; I am afraid it is impossible for us—

MRS. LINDE. Please don't think of it! Good-by, Nora dear, and many thanks.

NORA. Good-by for the present. Of course you will come back this evening. And you too, Doctor Rank. What do you say? If you are well enough? Oh, you must be! Wrap yourself up well. (*They go to the door all talking together. Children's voices are heard on the staircase.*)

NORA. There they are. There they are! (*She runs to open the door.*

The NURSE *comes in with the children.*) Come in! Come in!
(*Stoops and kisses them.*) Oh, you sweet blessings! Look at them,
Christine! Aren't they darlings?

RANK. Don't let us stand here in the draught.

HELMER. Come along, Mrs. Linde; the place will only be bearable
for a mother now!

(RANK, HELMER *and* MRS. LINDE *go downstairs. The* NURSE *comes
forward with the children;* NORA *shuts the hall door.*)

NORA. How fresh and well you look! Such red cheeks!—like apples
and roses. (*The children all talk at once while she speaks to
them.*) Have you had great fun? That's splendid! What, you
pulled both Emmy and Bob along on the sledge? Both at once?
That *was* good. You are a clever boy, Ivar. Let me take her for a
little, Anne. My sweet little baby doll! (*Takes the baby from the
NURSE and dances it up and down.*) Yes, yes, Mother will dance
with Bob too. What! Have you been snowballing? I wish I had
been there too! No, no, I will take their things off, Anne; please
let me do it, it is such fun. Go in now, you look half frozen. There
is some hot coffee for you on the stove.

(*The* NURSE *goes into the room on the left.* NORA *takes off the
children's things and throws them about while they all talk to her
at once.*)

NORA. *Really!* Did a big dog run after you? But it didn't bite you?
No, dogs don't bite nice little dolly children. You mustn't look
at the parcels, Ivar. What are they? Ah, I daresay you would like
to know. No, no—it's something nasty! Come, let us have a game!
What shall we play at? Hide and seek? Yes, we'll play hide and
seek. Bob shall hide first. Must I hide? Very well, I'll hide first.

(*She and the children laugh and shout and romp in and out of
the room; at last* NORA *hides under the table; the children rush in
and look for her but do not see her; they hear her smothered
laughter, run to the table, lift up the cloth and find her. Shouts
of laughter. She crawls forward and pretends to frighten them.
Fresh laughter. Meanwhile there has been a knock at the hall door
but none of them has noticed it. The door is half opened and*
KROGSTAD *appears. He waits a little; the game goes on.*)

KROGSTAD. Excuse me, Mrs. Helmer.

NORA (*with a stifled cry turns round and gets up onto her knees*).
Ah! What do you want?

KROGSTAD. Excuse me, the outer door was ajar; I suppose someone
forgot to shut it.

NORA (*rising*). My husband is out, Mr. Krogstad.

KROGSTAD. I know that.

NORA. What do you want here then?

KROGSTAD. A word with you.

NORA. With me? (*To the children, gently.*) Go in to Nurse. What?
No, the strange man won't do Mother any harm. When he has
gone we will have another game. (*She takes the children into the
room on the left and shuts the door after them.*) You want to
speak to me?

KROGSTAD. Yes, I do.

NORA. Today? It is not the first of the month yet.

KROGSTAD. No, it is Christmas Eve, and it will depend on yourself
what sort of a Christmas you will spend.

NORA. What do you want? Today it is absolutely impossible for
me—

KROGSTAD. We won't talk about that till later on. This is something
different. I presume you can give me a moment?

NORA. Yes—yes, I can—although—

KROGSTAD. Good. I was in Olsen's Restaurant and saw your husband
going down the street—

NORA. Yes?

KROGSTAD. With a lady.

NORA. What then?

KROGSTAD. May I make so bold as to ask if it was a Mrs. Linde?

NORA. It was.

KROGSTAD. Just arrived in town?

NORA. Yes, today.

KROGSTAD. She is a great friend of yours, isn't she?

NORA. She is. But I don't see—

KROGSTAD. I knew her too, once upon a time.

NORA. I am aware of that.

KROGSTAD. Are you? So you know all about it; I thought as much.
Then I can ask you, without beating about the bush—is Mrs.
Linde to have an appointment in the bank?

NORA. What right have you to question me, Mr. Krogstad? You, one

of my husband's subordinates! But since you ask, you shall know.
Yes, Mrs. Linde *is* to have an appointment. And it was I who
pleaded her cause, Mr. Krogstad, let me tell you that.

KROGSTAD. I was right in what I thought then.

NORA (*walking up and down the room*). Sometimes one has a tiny
little bit of influence, I should hope. Because one is a woman it
does not necessarily follow that—When anyone is in a subordinate position, Mr. Krogstad, they should really be careful to
avoid offending anyone who—who—

KROGSTAD. Who has influence?

NORA. Exactly.

KROGSTAD (*changing his tone*). Mrs. Helmer, you will be so good
as to use your influence on my behalf.

NORA. What? What do you mean?

KROGSTAD. You will be so kind as to see that I am allowed to keep
my subordinate position in the bank.

NORA. What do you mean by that? Who proposes to take your post
away from you?

KROGSTAD. Oh, there is no necessity to keep up the pretense of ignorance. I can quite understand that your friend is not very anxious to expose herself to the chance of rubbing shoulders with
me, and I quite understand, too, whom I have to thank for being
turned off.

NORA. But I assure you—

KROGSTAD. Very likely; but, to come to the point, the time has come
when I should advise you to use your influence to prevent that.

NORA. But, Mr. Krogstad, I *have* no influence.

KROGSTAD. Haven't you? I thought you said yourself just now—

NORA. Naturally I did not mean you to put that construction on it.
I! What should make you think I have any influence of that kind
with my husband?

KROGSTAD. Oh, I have known your husband from our student days.
I don't suppose he is any more unassailable than other husbands.

NORA. If you speak slightingly of my husband, I shall turn you out
of the house.

KROGSTAD. You are bold, Mrs. Helmer.

NORA. I am not afraid of you any longer. As soon as the New Year
comes I shall in a very short time be free of the whole thing.

KROGSTAD (*controlling himself*). Listen to me, Mrs. Helmer. If necessary, I am prepared to fight for my small post in the bank as if I were fighting for my life.

NORA. So it seems.

KROGSTAD. It is not only for the sake of the money; indeed, that weighs least with me in the matter. There is another reason—well, I may as well tell you. My position is this. I daresay you know, like everybody else, that once, many years ago, I was guilty of an indiscretion.

NORA. I think I have heard something of the kind.

KROGSTAD. The matter never came into court, but every way seemed to be closed to me after that. So I took to the business that you know of. I had to do something; and, honestly, I don't think I've been one of the worst. But now I must cut myself free from all that. My sons are growing up; for their sake I must try and win back as much respect as I can in the town. This post in the bank was like the first step up for me—and now your husband is going to kick me downstairs again into the mud.

NORA. But you must believe me, Mr. Krogstad; it is not in my power to help you at all.

KROGSTAD. Then it is because you haven't the will, but I have means to compel you.

NORA. You don't mean that you will tell my husband that I owe you money?

KROGSTAD. Hm! Suppose I were to tell him?

NORA. It would be perfectly infamous of you. (*Sobbing.*) To think of his learning my secret, which has been my joy and pride, in such an ugly, clumsy way—that he should learn it from you! And it would put me in a horribly disagreeable position.

KROGSTAD. Only disagreeable?

NORA (*impetuously*). Well, do it then!—and it will be the worse for you. My husband will see for himself what a blackguard you are, and you certainly won't keep your post then.

KROGSTAD. I asked you if it was only a disagreeable scene at home that you were afraid of?

NORA. If my husband does get to know of it, of course he will at once pay you what is still owing, and we shall have nothing more to do with you.

KROGSTAD (*coming a step nearer*). Listen to me, Mrs. Helmer. Either you have a very bad memory or you know very little of business. I shall be obliged to remind you of a few details.

NORA. What do you mean?

KROGSTAD. When your husband was ill you came to me to borrow two hundred and fifty pounds.

NORA. I didn't know anyone else to go to.

KROGSTAD. I promised to get you that amount—

NORA. Yes, and you did so.

KROGSTAD. I promisd to get you that amount on certain conditions. Your mind was so taken up with your husband's illness and you were so anxious to get the money for your journey that you seem to have paid no attention to the conditions of our bargain. Therefore it will not be amiss if I remind you of them. Now I promised to get the money on the security of a bond which I drew up.

NORA. Yes, and which I signed.

KROGSTAD. Good, But below your signature there were a few lines constituting your father a surety for the money; those lines your father should have signed.

NORA. Should? He did sign them.

KROGSTAD. I had left the date blank; that is to say your father should himself have inserted the date on which he signed the paper. Do you remember that?

NORA. Yes, I think I remember.

KROGSTAD. Then I gave you the bond to send by post to your father. Is that not so?

NORA. Yes.

KROGSTAD. And you naturally did so at once, because five or six days afterward you brought me the bond with your father's signature. And then I gave you the money.

NORA. Well, haven't I been paying it off regularly?

KROGSTAD. Fairly so, yes. But—to come back to the matter in hand— that must have been a very trying time for you, Mrs. Helmer?

NORA. It was, indeed.

KROGSTAD. Your father was very ill, wasn't he?

NORA. He was very near his end.

KROGSTAD. And died soon afterward?

NORA. Yes.

KROGSTAD. Tell me, Mrs. Helmer, can you by any chance remember what day your father died?—on what day of the month, I mean.

NORA. Papa died on the twenty-ninth of September.

KROGSTAD. That is correct; I have ascertained it for myself. And, as that is so, there is a discrepancy (*taking a paper from his pocket*) which I cannot account for.

NORA. What discrepancy? I don't know—

KROGSTAD. The discrepancy consists, Mrs. Helmer, in the fact that your father signed this bond three days after his death.

NORA. What do you mean? I don't understand.

KROGSTAD. Your father died on the twenty-ninth of September. But look here; your father has dated his signature the second of October. It is a discrepancy, isn't it? (NORA *is silent.*) Can you explain it to me? (NORA *is still silent.*) It is a remarkable thing, too, that the words "second of October," as well as the year, are not written in your father's handwriting but in one that I think I know. Well, of course it can be explained; your father may have forgotten to date his signature and someone else may have dated it haphazardly before they knew of his death. There is no harm in that. It all depends on the signature of the name, and *that* is genuine, I suppose, Mrs. Helmer? It was your father himself who signed his name here?

NORA (*after a short pause, throws her head up and looks defiantly at him*). No, it was not. It was I that wrote Papa's name.

KROGSTAD. Are you aware that is a dangerous confession?

NORA. In what way? You shall have your money soon.

KROGSTAD. Let me ask you a question: why did you not send the paper to your father?

NORA. It was impossible; Papa was so ill. If I had asked him for his signature, I should have had to tell him what the money was to be used for; and when he was so ill himself I couldn't tell him that my husband's life was in danger—it was impossible.

KROGSTAD. It would have been better for you if you had given up your trip abroad.

NORA. No, that was impossible. That trip was to save my husband's life; I couldn't give that up.

KROGSTAD. But did it never occur to you that you were committing a fraud on me?

NORA. I couldn't take that into account; I didn't trouble myself about you at all. I couldn't bear you because you put so many heartless difficulties in my way although you knew what a dangerous condition my husband was in.

KROGSTAD. Mrs. Helmer, you evidently do not realize clearly what it is that you have been guilty of. But I can assure you that my one false step, which lost me all my reputation, was nothing more or nothing worse than what you have done.

NORA. You? Do you ask me to believe that you were brave enough to run a risk to save your wife's life?

KROGSTAD. The law cares nothing about motives.

NORA. Then it must be a very foolish law.

KROGSTAD. Foolish or not, it is the law by which you will be judged if I produce this paper in court.

NORA. I don't believe it. Is a daughter not to be allowed to spare her dying father anxiety and care? Is a wife not to be allowed to save her husband's life? I don't know much about law, but I am certain that there must be laws permitting such things as that. Have you no knowledge of such laws—you who are a lawyer? You must be a very poor lawyer, Mr. Krogstad.

KROGSTAD. Maybe. But matters of business—such business as you and I have had together—do you think I don't understand that? Very well. Do as you please. But let me tell you this—if I lose my position a second time, you shall lose yours with me. (*He bows and goes out through the hall.*)

NORA (*appears buried in thought for a short time, then tosses her head*). Nonsense! Trying to frighten me like that! I am not so silly as he thinks. (*Begins to busy herself putting the children's things in order.*) And yet— No, it's impossible! I did it for love's sake.

THE CHILDREN (*in the doorway on the left*). Mother, the stranger man has gone out through the gate.

NORA. Yes, dears, I know. But don't tell anyone about the stranger man. Do you hear? Not even Papa.

CHILDREN. No, Mother; but will you come and play again?

NORA. No, no—not now.

CHILDREN. But, Mother, you promised us.

NORA. Yes, but I can't now. Run away in; I have such a lot to do. Run away in, my sweet little darlings. (*She gets them into the room by degrees and shuts the door on them, then sits down on the sofa, takes up a piece of needlework and sews a few stitches but soon stops.*) No! (*Throws down the work, gets up, goes to the hall door and calls out.*) Helen! bring the tree in. (*Goes to the table on the left, opens a drawer and stops again.*) No, no! It is quite impossible!

MAID (*coming in with the tree*). Where shall I put it, ma'am?

NORA. Here, in the middle of the floor.

MAID. Shall I get you anything else?

NORA. No, thank you. I have all I want.

(*Exit* MAID.)

NORA (*begins dressing the tree*). A candle here—and flowers here— The horrible man! It's all nonsense—there's nothing wrong. The tree shall be splendid! I will do everything I can think of to please you, Torvald! I will sing for you, dance for you—(HELMER *comes in with some papers under his arm.*) Oh, are you back already?

HELMER. Yes. Has anyone been here?

NORA. Here? No.

HELMER. That is strange. I saw Krogstad going out the gate.

NORA. Did you? Oh yes, I forgot, Krogstad was here for a moment.

HELMER. Nora, I can see from your manner that he has been here begging you to say a good word for him.

NORA. Yes.

HELMER. And you were to appear to do it of your own accord; you were to conceal from me the fact of his having been here; didn't he beg that of you too?

NORA. Yes, Torvald, but—

HELMER. Nora, Nora, and you would be a party to that sort of thing? To have any talk with a man like that and give him any sort of promise? And to tell me a lie into the bargain?

NORA. A lie?

HELMER. Didn't you tell me no one had been here? (*Shakes his finger at her.*) My little songbird must never do that again. A songbird must have a clean beak to chirp with—no false notes! (*Puts his arm around her waist.*) That is so, isn't it? Yes, I am sure it is. (*Lets her go.*) We will say no more about it. (*Sits down by the stove.*) How warm and snug it is here! (*Turns over his papers.*)

NORA (*after a short pause during which she busies herself with the Christmas tree*). Torvald!

HELMER. Yes.

NORA. I am looking forward tremendously to the fancy-dress ball at the Stenborgs' the day after tomorrow.

HELMER. And I am tremendously curious to see what you are going to surprise me with.

NORA. It was very silly of me to want to do that.

HELMER. What do you mean?

NORA. I can't hit upon anything that will do; everything I think of seems so silly and insignificant.

HELMER. Does my little Nora acknowledge that at last?

NORA (*standing behind his chair with her arms on the back of it*). Are you very busy, Torvald?

HELMER. Well—

NORA. What are all those papers?

HELMER. Bank business.

NORA. Already?

HELMER. I have got authority from the retiring manager to undertake the necessary changes in the staff and in the rearrangement of the work, and I must make use of the Christmas week for that, so as to have everything in order for the new year.

NORA. Then that was why this poor Krogstad—

HELMER. Hm!

NORA (*leans against the back of his chair and strokes his hair*). If you hadn't been so busy, I should have asked you a tremendously big favor, Torvald.

HELMER. What is that? Tell me.

NORA. There is no one has such good taste as you. And I do so want to look nice at the fancy-dress ball. Torvald, couldn't you take me in hand and decide what I shall go as and what sort of a dress I shall wear?

HELMER. Aha! So my obstinate little woman is obliged to get someone to come to her rescue?

NORA. Yes, Torvald, I can't get along a bit without your help.

HELMER. Very well, I will think it over; we shall manage to hit upon something.

NORA. That is nice of you. (*Goes to the Christmas tree. A short pause.*) How pretty the red flowers look! But tell me, was it really something very bad that this Krogstad was guilty of?

HELMER. He forged someone's name. Have you any idea what that means?

NORA. Isn't it possible that he was driven to do it by necessity?

HELMER. Yes; or, as in so many cases, by imprudence. I am not so heartless as to condemn a man altogether because of a single false step of that kind.

NORA. No, you wouldn't, would you, Torvald?

HELMER. Many a man has been able to retrieve his character if he has openly confessed his fault and taken his punishment.

NORA. Punishment?

HELMER. But Krogstad did nothing of that sort; he got himself out of it by a cunning trick, and that is why he has gone under altogether.

NORA. But do you think it would—

HELMER. Just think how a guilty man like that has to lie and play the hypocrite with everyone, how he has to wear a mask in the presence of those near and dear to him, even before his own wife and children. And about the children—that is the most terrible part of it all, Nora.

NORA. How?

HELMER. Because such an atmosphere of lies infects and poisons the whole life of a home. Each breath the children take in such a house is full of the germs of evil.

NORA (*coming nearer him*). Are you sure of that?

HELMER. My dear, I have often seen it in the course of my life as a lawyer. Almost everyone who has gone to the bad early in life has had a deceitful mother.

NORA. Why do you only say—mother?

HELMER. It seems most commonly to be the mother's influence, though naturally a bad father's would have the same result. Every lawyer is familiar with the fact. This Krogstad, now, has been persistently poisoning his own children with lies and dissimulation; that is why I say he has lost all moral character. (*Holds out his hands to her.*) That is why my sweet little Nora must promise me not to plead his cause. Give me your hand on it. Come, come, what is this? Give me your hand. There now, that's settled. I assure you it would be quite impossible for me to work with him; I literally feel physically ill when I am in the company of such people.

NORA (*takes her hand out of his and goes to the opposite side of the Christmas tree*). How hot it is in here, and I have such a lot to do.

HELMER (*getting up and putting his papers in order*). Yes, and I must try and read through some of these before dinner, and I must think about your costume too. And it is just possible I may have something ready in gold paper to hang up on the tree. (*Puts his hand on her head.*) My precious little singing bird! (*He goes into his room and shuts the door after him.*)

NORA (*after a pause, whispers*). No, no—it isn't true. It's impossible; it must be impossible.

(*The* NURSE *opens the door on the left.*)

NURSE. The little ones are begging so hard to be allowed to come in to Mamma.

NORA. No, no, no! Don't let them come in to me! You stay with them, Anne.

NURSE. Very well, ma'am. (*Shuts the door.*)

NORA (*pale with terror*). Deprave my little children? Poison my home? (*A short pause. Then she tosses her head.*) It's not true. It can't possibly be true.

Curtain

ACT II

THE SAME SCENE: *The Christmas tree is in the corner by the piano, stripped of its ornaments and with burned-down candle ends on its disheveled branches.* NORA'S *cloak and hat are lying on the sofa. She is alone in the room, walking about uneasily. She stops by the sofa and takes up her cloak.*

NORA (*drops the cloak*). Someone is coming now. (*Goes to the door and listens.*) No—it is no one. Of course no one will come today, Christmas Day—nor tomorrow either. But perhaps— (*Opens the door and looks out.*) No, nothing in the letter box; it is quite empty. (*Comes forward.*) What rubbish! Of course he can't be in earnest about it. Such a thing couldn't happen; it is impossible—I have three little children.

(*Enter the* NURSE *from the room on the left, carrying a big cardboard box.*)

NURSE. At last I have found the box with the fancy dress.

NORA. Thanks; put it on the table.

NURSE (*in doing so*). But it is very much in want of mending.

NORA. I should like to tear it into a hundred thousand pieces.

NURSE. What an idea! It can easily be put in order—just a little patience.

NORA. Yes, I will go and get Mrs. Linde to come and help me with it.

NURSE. What, out again? In this horrible weather? You will catch cold, ma'am, and make yourself ill.

NORA. Well, worse than that might happen. How are the children?

NURSE. The poor little souls are playing with their Christmas presents, but—

NORA. Do they ask much for me?

NURSE. You see, they are so accustomed to having their mamma with them.

NORA. Yes—but, Nurse, I shall not be able to be so much with them now as I was before.

NURSE. Oh well, young children easily get accustomed to anything.

NORA. Do you think so? Do you think they would forget their mother if she went away altogether?

NURSE. Good heavens!—went away altogether?

NORA. Nurse, I want you to tell me something I have often wondered about—how could you have the heart to put your own child out among strangers?

NURSE. I was obliged to if I wanted to be little Nora's nurse.

NORA. Yes, but how could you be willing to do it?

NURSE. What, when I was going to get such a good place by it? A poor girl who has got into trouble should be glad to. Besides, that wicked man didn't do a single thing for me.

NORA. But I suppose your daughter has quite forgotten you.

NURSE. No, indeed she hasn't. She wrote to me when she was confirmed and when she was married.

NORA (*putting her arms round her neck*). Dear old Anne, you were a good mother to me when I was little.

NURSE. Little Nora, poor dear, had no other mother but me.

NORA. And if my little ones had no other mother, I am sure you would— What nonsense I am talking! (*Opens the box.*) Go in

to them. Now I must— You will see tomorrow how charming
I shall look.

NURSE. I am sure there will be no one at the ball so charming as
you, ma'am. (*Goes into the room on the left.*)

NORA (*begins to unpack the box but soon pushes it away from her*).
If only I dared go out. If only no one would come. If only I
could be sure nothing would happen here in the meantime.
Stuff and nonsense! No one will come. Only I mustn't think
about it. I will brush my muff. What lovely, lovely gloves! Out
of my thoughts, out of my thoughts! One, two, three, four, five,
six— (*Screams.*) Ah! there is someone coming. (*Makes a movement toward the door but stands irresolute.*)

(*Enter* MRS. LINDE *from the hall, where she has taken off her
cloak and hat.*)

NORA. Oh, it's you, Christine. There is no one else out there, is there?
How good of you to come!

MRS. LINDE. I heard you were up asking for me.

NORA. Yes, I was passing by. As a matter of fact, it is something
you could help me with. Let us sit down here on the sofa. Look
here. Tomorrow evening there is to be a fancy-dress ball at the
Stenborgs', who live above us, and Torvald wants me to go as a
Neapolitan fishergirl and dance the tarantella that I learnt at
Capri.

MRS. LINDE. I see; you are going to keep up the character.

NORA. Yes, Torvald wants me to Look, here is the dress; Torvald
had it made for me there, but now it is all so torn, and I haven't
any idea—

MRS. LINDE. We will easily put that right. It is only some of the
trimming come unsewn here and there. Needle and thread? Now
then, that's all we want.

MRS. LINDE (*sewing*). So you are going to be dressed up tomorrow,
Nora. I will tell you what—I shall come in for a moment and see
you in your fine feathers. But I have completely forgotten to
thank you for a delightful evening yesterday.

NORA (*gets us and crosses the room*). Well, I don't think yesterday
was as pleasant as usual. You ought to have come down to town
a little earlier, Christine. Certainly Torvald does understand how
to make a house dainty and attractive.

MRS. LINDE. And so do you, it seems to me; you are not your father's daughter for nothing. But tell me, is Doctor Rank always as depressed as he was yesterday?

NORA. No; yesterday it was very noticeable. I must tell you that he suffers from a very dangerous disease. He has consumption of the spine, poor creature. His father was a horrible man who committed all sorts of excesses, and that is why his son was sickly from childhood, do you understand?

MRS. LINDE (*dropping her sewing*). But, my dearest Nora, how do you know anything about such things?

NORA (*walking about*). Pooh! When you have three children you get visits now and then from—from married women who know something of medical matters, and they talk about one thing and another.

MRS. LINDE (*goes on sewing. A short silence*). Does Doctor Rank come here every day?

NORA. Every day regularly. He is Torvald's most intimate friend and a friend of mine too. He is just like one of the family.

MRS. LINDE. But tell me this—is he perfectly sincere? I mean, isn't he the kind of man that is very anxious to make himself agreeable?

NORA. Not in the least. What makes you think that?

MRS. LINDE. When you introduced him to me yesterday he declared he had often heard my name mentioned in this house, but afterward I noticed that your husband hadn't the slightest idea who I was. So how could Doctor Rank—

NORA. That is quite right, Christine. Torvald is so absurdly fond of me that he wants me absolutely to himself, as he says. At first he used to seem almost jealous if I mentioned any of the dear folks at home, so naturally I gave up doing so. But I often talk about such things with Doctor Rank because he likes hearing about them.

MRS. LINDE. Listen to me, Nora. You are still very like a child in many things, and I am older than you in many ways and have a little more experience. Let me tell you this—you ought to make an end of it with Doctor Rank.

NORA. What ought I to make an end of?

MRS. LINDE. Of two things, I think. Yesterday you talked some nonsense about a rich admirer who was to leave you money—

NORA. An admirer who doesn't exist, unfortunately! But what then?

MRS. LINDE. Is Doctor Rank a man of means?

NORA. Yes, he is.

MRS. LINDE. And has no one to provide for?

NORA. No, no one; but—

MRS. LINDE. And comes here every day?

NORA. Yes, I told you so.

MRS. LINDE. But how can this well-bred man be so tactless?

NORA. I don't understand you at all.

MRS. LINDE. Don't prevaricate, Nora. Do you suppose I don't guess who lent you the two hundred and fifty pounds?

NORA. Are you out of your senses? How can you think of such a thing! A friend of ours, who comes here every day! Do you realize what a horribly painful position that would be?

MRS. LINDE. Then it really isn't he?

NORA. No, certainly not. It would never have entered into my head for a moment. Besides, he had no money to lend then; he came into his money afterward.

MRS. LINDE. Well, I think that was lucky for you, my dear Nora.

NORA. No, it would never have come into my head to ask Doctor Rank. Although I am quite sure that if I had asked him—

MRS. LINDE. But of course you won't.

NORA. Of course not. I have no reason to think it could possibly be necessary. But I am quite sure that if I told Doctor Rank—

MRS. LINDE. Behind your husband's back?

NORA. I must make an end of it with the other one, and that will be behind his back too. I *must* make an end of it with him.

MRS. LINDE. Yes, that is what I told you yesterday, but—

NORA (*walking up and down*). A man can put a thing like that straight much easier than a woman.

MRS. LINDE. One's husband, yes.

NORA. Nonsense! (*Standing still.*) When you pay off a debt you get your bond back, don't you?

MRS. LINDE. Yes, as a matter of course.

NORA. And can tear it into a hundred thousand pieces and burn it up—the nasty dirty paper!

MRS. LINDE (*looks hard at her, lays down her sewing and gets up slowly*). Nora, you are concealing something from me.

NORA. Do I look as if I were?

MRS. LINDE. Something has happened to you since yesterday morning. Nora, what is it?

NORA (*going nearer to her*). Christine! (*Listens.*) Hush! There's Torvald come home. Do you mind going in to the children for the present? Torvald can't bear to see dressmaking going on. Let Anne help you.

MRS. LINDE (*gathering some of the things together*). Certainly— but I am not going away from here till we have had it out with one another. (*She goes into the room on the left as* HELMER *comes in from the hall.*)

NORA (*going up to* HELMER). I have wanted you so much, Torvald dear.

HELMER. Was that the dressmaker?

NORA. No, it was Christine; she is helping me to put my dress in order. You will see I shall look quite smart.

HELMER. Wasn't that a happy thought of mine, now?

NORA. Splendid! But don't you think it is nice of me, too, to do as you wish?

HELMER. Nice?—because you do as your husband wishes? Well, well, you little rogue, I am sure you did not mean it in that way. But I am not going to disturb you; you will want to be trying on your dress, I expect.

NORA. I suppose you are going to work.

HEMER. Yes. (*Shows her a bundle of papers.*) Look at that. I have just been in to the bank. (*Turns to go into his room.*)

NORA. Torvald.

HELMER. Yes.

NORA. If your little squirrel were to ask you for something very, very prettily—

HELMER. What then?

NORA. Would you do it?

HELMER. I should like to hear what it is first.

NORA. Your squirrel would run about and do all her tricks if you would be nice and do what she wants.

HELMER. Speak plainly.

NORA. Your skylark would chirp, chirp about in every room, with her song rising and falling—

HELMER. Well, my skylark does that anyhow.

NORA. I would play the fairy and dance for you in the moonlight, Torvald.

HELMER. Nora—you surely don't mean that request you made of me this morning?

NORA (*going near him*). Yes, Torvald, I beg you so earnestly—

HELMER. Have you really the courage to open up that question again?

NORA. Yes, dear, you *must* do as I ask; you *must* let Krogstad keep his post in the bank.

HELMER. My dear Nora, it is his post that I have arranged Mrs. Linde shall have.

NORA. Yes, you have been awfully kind about that, but you could just as well dismiss some other clerk instead of Krogstad.

HELMER. This is simply incredible obstinacy! Because you chose to give him a thoughtless promise that you would speak for him I am expected to—

NORA. That isn't the reason, Torvald. It is for your own sake. This fellow writes in the most scurrilous newspapers; you have told me so yourself. He can do you an unspeakable amount of harm. I am frightened to death of him.

HELMER. Ah, I understand; it is recollections of the past that scare you.

NORA. What do you mean?

HELMER. Naturally you are thinking of your father.

NORA. Yes—yes, of course. Just recall to your mind what these malicious creatures wrote in the papers about Papa and how horribly they slandered him. I believe they would have procured his dismissal if the Department had not sent you over to inquire into it and if you had not been so kindly disposed and helpful to him.

HELMER. My little Nora, there is an important difference between your father and me. Your father's reputation as a public official was not above suspicion. Mine is, and I hope it will continue to be so as long as I hold my office.

NORA. You never can tell what mischief these men may contrive. We ought to be so well off, so snug and happy here in our peaceful home, and have no cares—you and I and the children, Torvald! That is why I beg you so earnestly—

HELMER. And it is just by interceding for him that you make it impossible for me to keep him. It is already known at the bank that I mean to dismiss Krogstad. Is it to get about now that the new manager has changed his mind at his wife's bidding?

NORA. And what if it did?

HELMER. Of course!—if only this obstinate little person can get her way! Do you suppose I am going to make myself ridiculous before my whole staff, to let people think I am a man to be swayed by all sorts of outside influence? I should very soon feel the consequences of it, I can tell you! And besides, there is one thing that makes it quite impossible for me to have Krogstad in the bank as long as I am manager.

NORA. Whatever is that?

HELMER. His moral failings I might perhaps have overlooked if necessary—

NORA. Yes, you could—couldn't you?

HELMER. And I hear he is a good worker too. But I knew him when we were boys. It was one of those rash friendships that so often prove an incubus in afterlife. I may as well tell you plainly, we were once on very intimate terms with one another. But this tactless fellow lays no restraint on himself when other people are present. On the contrary, he thinks it gives him the right to adopt a familiar tone with me, and every minute it is "I say, Helmer, old fellow!" and that sort of thing. I assure you it is extremely painful for me. He would make my position in the bank intolerable.

NORA. Torvald, I don't believe you mean that.

HELMER. Don't you? Why not?

NORA. Because it is such a narrow-minded way of looking at things.

HELMER. What are you saying? Narrow-minded? Do you think I am narrow-minded?

NORA. No, just the opposite, dear—and it is exactly for that reason—

HELMER. It's the same thing. You say my point of view is narrow-minded, so I must be so too. Narrow-minded! Very well—I must put an end to this. (*Goes to the hall door and calls.*) Helen!

NORA. What are you going to do?

HELMER (*looking among his papers*). Settle it. (*Enter* MAID.) Look here; take this letter and go downstairs with it at once. Find a messenger and tell him to deliver it and be quick. The address is on it, and here is the money.

MAID. Very well, sir. (*Exit with the letter.*)

HELMER (*putting his papers together*). Now then, little Miss Obstinate.

NORA (*breathlessly*). Torvald—what was that letter?

HELMER. Krogstad's dismissal.

NORA. Call her back, Torvald! There is still time. Oh, Torvald, call her back! Do it for my sake—for your own sake—for the children's sake! Do you hear me, Torvald? Call her back! You don't know what that letter can bring upon us.

HELMER. It's too late.

NORA. Yes, it's too late.

HELMER. My dear Nora, I can forgive the anxiety you are in, although really it is an insult to me. It is, indeed. Isn't it an insult to think I should be afraid of a starving quill driver's vengeance? But I forgive you nevertheless, because it is such eloquent witness to your great love for me. (*Takes her in his arms.*) And that is as it should be, my own darling Nora. Come what will, you may be sure I shall have both courage and strength if they be needed. You will see I am man enough to take everything upon myself.

NORA (*in a horror-stricken voice*). What do you mean by that?

HELMER: Everything I say.

NORA (*recovering herself*). You will never have to do that.

HELMER. That's right. Well, we will share it, Nora, as man and wife should. That is how it shall be. (*Caressing her.*) Are you content now? There! there!—not these frightened dove's eyes! The whole thing is only the wildest fancy! Now you must go and play through the tarantella and practice with your tambourine. I shall go into the inner office and shut the door, and I shall hear nothing; you can make as much noise as you please. (*Turns back at the door.*) And when Rank comes tell him where he will find me. (*Nods to her, takes his papers and goes into his room and shuts the door after him.*)

NORA (*bewildered with anxiety, stands as if rooted to the spot and whispers*). He was capable of doing it. He will do it. He will do it in spite of everything. No, not that! Never, never! Anything rather than that! Oh, for some help, some way out of it! (*The doorbell rings.*) Doctor Rank! Anything rather than that—anything, whatever it is! (*She puts her hands over her face, pulls herself together, goes to the door and opens it. RANK is standing without, hanging up his coat. During the following dialogue it begins to grow dark.*)

NORA. Good day, Doctor Rank. I knew your ring. But you mustn't go in to Torvald now; I think he is busy with something.

RANK. And you?

NORA (*brings him in and shuts the door after him*). Oh, you know very well I always have time for you.

RANK. Thank you. I shall make use of as much of it as I can.

NORA. What do you mean by that? As much of it as you can?

RANK. Well, does that alarm you?

NORA. It was such a strange way of putting it. Is anything likely to happen?

RANK. Nothing but what I have long been prepared for. But I certainly didn't expect it to happen so soon.

NORA (*gripping him by the arm*). What have you found out? Doctor Rank, you must tell me.

RANK (*sitting down by the stove*). It is all up with me. And it can't be helped.

NORA (*with a sigh of relief*). Is it about yourself?

RANK. Who else? It is no use lying to one's self. I am the most wretched of all my patients, Mrs. Helmer. Lately I have been taking stock of my internal economy. Bankrupt! Probably within a month I shall lie rotting in the churchyard.

NORA. What an ugly thing to say!

RANK. The thing itself is cursedly ugly, and the worst of it is that I shall have to face so much more that is ugly before that. I shall only make one more examination of myself; when I have done that I shall know pretty certainly when it will be that the horrors of dissolution will begin. There is something I want to tell you. Helmer's refined nature gives him an unconquerable disgust at everything that is ugly; I won't have him in my sickroom.

NORA. Oh, but, Doctor Rank—

RANK. I won't have him there. Not on any account. I bar my door to him. As soon as I am quite certain that the worst has come I shall send you my card with a black cross on it, and then you will know that the loathsome end has begun.

NORA. You are quite absurd today. And I wanted you so much to be in a really good humor.

RANK. With death stalking beside me? To have to pay this penalty for another man's sin! Is there any justice in that? And in every single family, in one way or another, some such inexorable retribution is being exacted.

NORA (*putting her hands over her ears*). Rubbish! Do talk of something cheerful.

RANK. Oh, it's a mere laughing matter, the whole thing. My poor innocent spine has to suffer for my father's youthful amusements.

NORA (*sitting at the table on the left*). I suppose you mean that he was too partial to asparagus and pâté de foie gras, don't you?

RANK. Yes, and to truffles.

NORA. Truffles, yes. And oysters too, I suppose?

RANK. Oysters, of course; that goes without saying.

NORA. And heaps of port and champagne. It is sad that all these nice things should take their revenge on our bones.

RANK. Especially that they should revenge themselves on the unlucky bones of those who have not had the satisfaction of enjoying them.

NORA. Yes, that's the saddest part of it all.

RANK (*with a searching look at her*). Hm!

NORA (*after a short pause*). Why did you smile?

RANK. No, it was you that laughed.

NORA. No, it was you that smiled, Doctor Rank!

RANK (*rising*). You are a greater rascal than I thought.

NORA. I am in a silly mood today.

RANK. So it seems.

NORA (*putting her hands on his shoulders*). Dear, dear Doctor Rank, death mustn't take you away from Torvald and me.

RANK. It is a loss you would easily recover from. Those who are gone are soon forgotten.

NORA (*looking at him anxiously*). Do you believe that?

RANK. People form new ties, and then—

NORA. Who will form new ties?

RANK. Both you and Helmer, when I am gone. You yourself are already on the highroad to it, I think. What did that Mrs. Linde want here last night?

NORA. Oho! You don't mean to say that you are jealous of poor Christine?

RANK. Yes, I am. She will be my successor in this house. When I am done for, this woman will—

NORA. Hush! Don't speak so loud. She is in that room.

RANK. Today again. There, you see.

NORA. She has only come to sew my dress for me. Bless my soul, how unreasonable you are! (*Sits down on the sofa.*) Be nice now, Doctor Rank, and tomorrow you will see how beautifully I shall dance, and you can imagine I am doing it all for you—and for Torvald too, of course. (*Takes various things out of the box.*) Doctor Rank, come and sit down here, and I will show you something.

RANK (*sitting down*). What is it?

NORA. Just look at those!

RANK. Silk stockings.

NORA. Flesh colored. Aren't they lovely? It is so dark here now, but tomorrow— No, no, no! You must only look at the feet. Oh well, you may have leave to look at the legs too.

RANK. Hm!

NORA. Why are you looking so critical? Don't you think they will fit me?

RANK. I have no means of forming an opinion about that.

NORA (*looks at him for a moment*). For shame! (*Hits him lightly on the ear with the stockings.*) That's to punish you. (*Folds them up again.*)

RANK. And what other nice things am I to be allowed to see?

NORA. Not a single thing more, for being so naughty. (*She looks among the things, humming to herself.*)

RANK (*after a short silence*). When I am sitting here talking to you as intimately as this I cannot imagine for a moment what would have become of me if I had never come into this house.

NORA (*smiling*). I believe you do feel thoroughly at home with us.

RANK (*in a lower voice, looking straight in front of him*). And to be obliged to leave it all—

NORA. Nonsense, you are not going to leave it.

RANK (*as before*). And not be able to leave behind one the slightest token of one's gratitude, scarcely even a fleeting regret—nothing but an empty place which the firstcomer can fill as well as any other.

NORA. And if I asked you now for a— No!

RANK. For what?

NORA. For a big proof of your friendship—

RANK. Yes, yes!

NORA. I mean a tremendously big favor—

RANK. Would you really make me so happy for once?

NORA. Ah, but you don't know what it is yet.

RANK. No—but tell me.

NORA. I really can't, Doctor Rank. It is something out of all reason; it means advice and help and a favor—

RANK. The bigger a thing it is, the better. I can't conceive what it is you mean. Do tell me. Haven't I your confidence?

NORA. More than anyone else. I know you are my truest and best friend, and so I will tell you what it is. Well, Doctor Rank, it is something you must help me to prevent. You know how devotedly, how inexpressibly deeply Torvald loves me; he would never for a moment hesitate to give his life for me.

RANK (*leaning toward her*). Nora—do you think he is the only one—

NORA (*with a slight start*). The only one—?

RANK. The only one who would gladly give his life for your sake.

NORA (*sadly*). Is that it?

RANK. I was determined you should know it before I went away, and there will never be a better opportunity than this. Now you know it, Nora. And now you know, too, that you can trust me as you would trust no one else.

NORA (*rises deliberately and quietly*). Let me pass.

RANK (*makes room for her to pass him but sits still*). Nora!

NORA (*at the hall door*). Helen, bring in the lamp. (*Goes over to the stove.*) Dear Doctor Rank, that was really horrid of you.

RANK. To have loved you as much as anyone else does? Was that horrid?

NORA. No, but to go and tell me so. There was really no need—

RANK. What do you mean? Did you know? (MAID *enters with lamp, puts it down on the table and goes out.*) Nora—Mrs. Helmer—tell me, had you any idea of this?

NORA. Oh, how do I know whether I had or whether I hadn't? I really can't tell you. To think you could be so clumsy, Doctor Rank! We were getting on so nicely.

RANK. Well, at all events you know that you can command me body and soul. So won't you speak out?

NORA (*looking at him*). After what happened?

RANK. I beg you to let me know what it is.

NORA. I can't tell you anything now.

RANK. Yes, yes. You mustn't punish me in that way. Let me have permission to do for you whatever a man may do.

NORA. You can do nothing for me now. Besides, I really don't need any help at all. You will find that the whole thing is merely fancy on my part. It really is so—of course it is! (*Sits down in the rocking chair and looks at him with a smile.*) You are a nice sort of man, Doctor Rank! Don't you feel ashamed of yourself now the lamp has come?

RANK. Not a bit. But perhaps I had better go—forever?

NORA. No indeed, you shall not. Of course you must come here just as before. You know very well Torvald can't do without you.

RANK. Yes, but you?

NORA. Oh, I am always tremendously pleased when you come.

RANK. It is just that that put me on the wrong track. You are a riddle to me. I have often thought that you would almost as soon be in my company as in Helmer's.

NORA. Yes—you see, there are some people one loves best and others whom one would almost always rather have as companions.

RANK. Yes, there is something in that.

NORA. When I was at home of course I loved Papa best. But I always thought it tremendous fun if I could steal down into the maids' room, because they never moralized at all and talked to each other about such entertaining things.

RANK. I see—it is *their* place I have taken.

NORA (*jumping up and going to him*). Oh, dear, nice Doctor Rank, I never meant that at all. But surely you can understand that being with Torvald is a little like being with Papa—

(*Enter* MAID *from the hall.*)

MAID. If you please, ma'am. (*Whispers and hands her a card.*)

NORA (*glancing at the card*). Oh! (*Puts it in her pocket.*)

RANK. Is there anything wrong?

NORA. No, no, not in the least. It is only something—it is my new dress—

RANK. What? Your dress is lying there.

NORA. Oh yes, that one; but this is another. I ordered it. Torvald mustn't know about it.

RANK. Oho! Then that was the great secret.

NORA. Of course. Just go in to him; he is sitting in the inner room. Keep him as long as—

RANK. Make your mind easy; I won't let him escape. (*Goes into* HELMER'S *room.*)

NORA (*to the* MAID). And he is standing waiting in the kitchen?

MAID. Yes; he came up the back stairs.

NORA. But didn't you tell him no one was in?

MAID. Yes, but it was no good.

NORA. He won't go away?

MAID. No; he says he won't until he has seen you, ma'am.

NORA. Well, let him come in—but quietly. Helen, you mustn't say anything about it to anyone. It is a surprise for my husband.

MAID. Yes, ma'am, I quite understand. (*Exit.*)

NORA. This dreadful thing is going to happen! It will happen in spite of me! No, no, no, it can't happen—it shan't happen! (*She bolts the door of* HELMER's *room. The* MAID *opens the hall door for* KROGSTAD *and shuts it after him. He is wearing a fur coat, high boots and a fur cap.*)

NORA (*advancing toward him*). Speak low—my husband is at home.

KROGSTAD. No matter about that.

NORA. What do you want of me?

KROGSTAD. An explanation of something.

NORA. Make haste then. What is it?

KROGSTAD. You know, I suppose, that I have got my dismissal.

NORA. I couldn't prevent it, Mr. Krogstad. I fought as hard as I could on your side, but it was no good.

KROGSTAD. Does your husband love you so little then? He knows what I can expose you to, and yet he ventures—

NORA. How can you suppose that he has any knowledge of the sort?

KROGSTAD. I didn't suppose so at all. It would not be the least like our dear Torvald Helmer to show so much courage—

NORA. Mr. Krogstad, a little respect for my husband, please.

KROGSTAD. Certainly—all the respect he deserves. But since you have kept the matter so carefully to yourself, I make bold to suppose that you have a little clearer idea than you had yesterday of what it actually is that you have done?

NORA. More than you could ever teach me.

KROGSTAD. Yes, such a bad lawyer as I am.

NORA. What is it you want of me?

KROGSTAD. Only to see how you were, Mrs. Helmer. I have been thinking about you all day long. A mere cashier, a quill driver, a—well, a man like me—even he has a little of what is called feeling, you know.

NORA. Show it then; think of my little children.

KROGSTAD. Have you and your husband thought of mine? But never mind about that. I only wanted to tell you that you need not take this matter too seriously. In the first place there will be no accusation made on my part.

NORA. No, of course not; I was sure of that.

KROGSTAD. The whole thing can be arranged amicably; there is no reason why anyone should know anything about it. It will remain a secret between us three.

NORA. My husband must never get to know anything about it.

KROGSTAD. How will you be able to prevent it? Am I to understand that you can pay the balance that is owing?

NORA. No, not just at present.

KROGSTAD. Or perhaps that you have some expedient for raising the money soon?

NORA. No expedient that I mean to make use of.

KROGSTAD. Well, in any case it would have been of no use to you now. If you stood there with ever so much money in your hand, I would never part with your bond.

NORA. Tell me what purpose you mean to put it to.

KROGSTAD. I shall only preserve it—keep it in my possession. No one who is not concerned in the matter shall have the slightest hint of it. So that if the thought of it has driven you to any desperate resolution—

NORA. It has.

KROGSTAD. If you had it in your mind to run away from your home—

NORA. I had.

KROGSTAD. Or even something worse—

NORA. How could you know that?

KROGSTAD. Give up the idea.

NORA. How did you know I had thought of *that?*

KROGSTAD. Most of us think of that at first. I did too—but I hadn't the courage.

NORA (*faintly*). No more than I.

KROGSTAD (*in a tone of relief*). No, that's it, isn't it—you hadn't the courage either?

NORA. No, I haven't—I haven't.

KROGSTAD. Besides, it would have been a great piece of folly. Once the first storm at home is over— I have a letter for your husband in my pocket.

NORA. Telling him everything?

KROGSTAD. In as lenient a manner as I possibly could.

NORA (*quickly*). He mustn't get the letter. Tear it up. I will find some means of getting money.

KROGSTAD. Excuse me, Mrs. Helmer, but I think I told you just now—

NORA. I am not speaking of what I owe you. Tell me what sum you are asking my husband for, and I will get the money.

KROGSTAD. I am not asking your husband for a penny.

NORA. What do you want then?

KROGSTAD. I will tell you. I want to rehabilitate myself, Mrs. Helmer; I want to get on, and in that your husband must help me. For the last year and a half I have not had a hand in anything dishonorable, and all that time I have been struggling in most restricted circumstances. I was content to work my way up step by step. Now I am turned out, and I am not going to be satisfied with merely being taken into favor again. I want to get on, I tell you. I want to get into the bank again, in a higher position. Your husband must make a place for me—

NORA. That he will never do!

KROGSTAD. He will; I know him; he dare not protest. And as soon as I am in there again with him then you will see! Within a year I shall be the manager's right hand. It will be Nils Krogstad and not Torvald Helmer who manages the bank.

NORA. That's a thing you will never see!

KROGSTAD. Do you mean that you will—

NORA. I have courage enough for it now.

KROGSTAD. Oh, you can't frighten me. A fine, spoilt lady like you—

NORA. You will see, you will see.

KROGSTAD. Under the ice, perhaps? Down into the cold, coal-black water? And then, in the spring, to float up to the surface, all horrible and unrecognizable, with your hair fallen out—

NORA. You can't frighten me.

KROGSTAD. Nor you me. People don't do such things, Mrs. Helmer. Besides, what use would it be? I should have him completely in my power all the same.

NORA. Afterward? When I am no longer—

KROGSTAD. Have you forgotten that it is I who have the keeping of your reputation? (NORA *stands speechlessly looking at him.*) Well, now, I have warned you. Do not do anything foolish. When Helmer has had my letter I shall expect a message from him. And be sure you remember that it is your husband himself who has forced me into such ways as this again. I will never forgive him for that. Good-by, Mrs. Helmer. (*Exit through the hall.*)

NORA (*goes to the hall door, opens it slightly and listens*). He is going. He is not putting the letter in the box. Oh no, no! that's impossible! (*Opens the door by degrees.*) What is that? He is standing outside. He is not going downstairs. Is he hesitating? Can he— (*A letter drops in the box; then* KROGSTAD'S *footsteps are heard, till they die away as he goes downstairs.* NORA *utters a stifled cry and runs across the room to the table by the sofa. A short pause.*)

NORA. In the letter box. (*Steals across to the hall door.*) There it lies —Torvald, Torvald, there is no hope for us now!

(MRS. LINDE *comes in from the room on the left, carrying the dress.*)

MRS. LINDE. There, I can't see anything more to mend now. Would you like to try it on?

NORA (*in a hoarse whisper*). Christine, come here.

MRS. LINDE (*throwing the dress down on the sofa*). What is the matter with you? You look so agitated!

NORA. Come here. Do you see that letter? There, look—you can see it through the glass in the letter box.

MRS. LINDE. Yes, I see it.

NORA. That letter is from Krogstad.

MRS. LINDE. Nora—it was Krogstad who lent you the money!

NORA. Yes, and now Torvald will know all about it.

MRS. LINDE. Believe me, Nora, that's the best thing for both of you.

NORA. You don't know all. I forged a name.

MRS. LINDE. Good heavens!

NORA. I only want to say this to you, Christine—you must be my witness.

MRS. LINDE. Your witness? What do you mean? What am I to—

NORA. If I should go out of my mind—and it might easily happen—

MRS. LINDE. Nora!

NORA. Or if anything else should happen to me—anything, for instance, that might prevent my being here—

MRS. LINDE. Nora! Nora! you are quite out of your mind.

NORA. And if it should happen that there were someone who wanted to take all the responsibility, all the blame, you understand—

MRS. LINDE. Yes, yes—but how can you suppose—

NORA. Then you must be my witness, that it is not true, Christine. I am not out of my mind at all; I am in my right senses now, and I tell you no one else has known anything about it; I, and I alone, did the whole thing. Remember that.

MRS. LINDE. I will, indeed. But I don't understand all this.

NORA. How should you understand it? A wonderful thing is going to happen.

MRS. LINDE. A wonderful thing?

NORA. Yes, a wonderful thing! But it is so terrible. Christine, it *mustn't* happen, not for all the world.

MRS. LINDE. I will go at once and see Krogstad.

NORA. Don't go to him; he will do you some harm.

MRS. LINDE. There was a time when he would gladly do anything for my sake.

NORA. He?

MRS. LINDE. Where does he live?

NORA. How should I know? Yes—(*feeling in her pocket*)—here is his card. But the letter, the letter!

HELMER (*calls from his room, knocking at the door*). Nora!

NORA (*cries out anxiously*). Oh, what's that? What do you want?

HELMER. Don't be so frightened. We are not coming in; you have locked the door. Are you trying on your dress?

NORA. Yes, that's it. I look so nice, Torvald.

MRS. LINDE (*who has read the card*). I see he lives at the corner here.

NORA. Yes, but it's no use. It is hopeless. The letter is lying there in the box.

MRS. LINDE. And your husband keeps the key?

NORA. Yes, always.

MRS. LINDE. Krogstad must ask for his letter back unread, he must find some pretense—

NORA. But it is just at this time that Torvald generally—

MRS. LINDE. You must delay him. Go in to him in the meantime. I will come back as soon as I can. (*She goes out hurriedly through the hall door.*)

NORA (*goes to* HELMER's *door, opens it and peeps in*). Torvald!

HELMER (*from the inner room*). Well? May I venture at last to

come into my own room again? Come along, Rank, now you will
see— (*Halting in the doorway.*) But what is this?

NORA. What is what, dear?

HELMER. Rank led me to expect a splendid transformation.

RANK (*in the doorway*). I understood so, but evidently I was mistaken.

NORA. Yes, nobody is to have the chance of admiring me in my dress
until tomorrow.

HELMER. But, my dear Nora, you look so worn out. Have you been
practicing too much?

NORA. No, I have not practiced at all.

HELMER. But you will need to—

NORA. Yes, indeed I shall, Torvald. But I can't get on a bit without
you to help me; I have absolutely forgotten the whole thing.

HELMER. Oh, we will soon work it up again.

NORA. Yes, help me, Torvald. Promise that you will! I am so nervous
about it—all the people— You must give yourself up to me entirely
this evening. Not the tiniest bit of business—you mustn't even
take a pen in your hand. Will you promise, Torvald dear?

HELMER. I promise. This evening I will be wholly and absolutely at
your service, you helpless little mortal. Ah, by the way, first of all
I will just— (*Goes toward the hall door.*)

NORA. What are you going to do there?

HELMER. Only see if any letters have come.

NORA. No, no! Don't do that, Torvald!

HELMER. Why not?

NORA. Torvald, please don't. There is nothing there.

HELMER. Well, let me look. (*Turns to go to the letter box.* NORA,
at the piano, plays the first bars of the tarantella. HELMER *stops
in the doorway.*) Aha!

NORA. I can't dance tomorrow if I don't practice with you.

HELMER (*going up to her*). Are you really so afraid of it, dear?

NORA. Yes, so dreadfully afraid of it. Let me practice at once; there
is time now, before we go to dinner. Sit down and play for me,
Torvald dear; criticize me and correct me as you play.

HELMER. With great pleasure, if you wish me to. (*Sits down at the
piano.*)

NORA (*takes out of the box a tambourine and a long variegated
shawl. She hastily drapes the shawl round her. Then she springs*

to the middle of the room and calls out). Now play for me! I am going to dance!

(HELMER *plays and* NORA *dances.* RANK *stands by the piano behind* HELMER *and looks on.*)

HELMER (*as he plays*). Slower, slower!

NORA. I can't do it any other way.

HELMER. Not so violently, Nora!

NORA. This is the way.

HELMER (*stops playing*). No, no—that is not a bit right.

NORA (*laughing and swinging the tambourine*). Didn't I tell you so?

RANK. Let me play for her.

HELMER (*getting up*). Yes, do. I can correct her better then.

(RANK *sits down at the piano and plays.* NORA *dances more and more wildly.* HELMER *has taken up a position by the stove and during her dance gives her frequent instructions. She does not seem to hear him; her hair comes down and falls over her shoulders; she pays no attention to it but goes on dancing. Enter* MRS. LINDE.)

MRS. LINDE (*standing as if spellbound in the doorway*). Oh!

NORA (*as she dances*). Such fun, Christine!

HELMER. My dear darling Nora, you are dancing as if your life depended on it.

NORA. So it does.

HELMER. Stop, Rank; this is sheer madness. Stop, I tell you! (RANK *stops playing, and* NORA *suddenly stands still.* HELMER *goes up to her.*) I could never have believed it. You have forgotten everything I taught you.

NORA (*throwing away the tambourine*). There, you see.

HELMER. You will want a lot of coaching.

NORA. Yes, you see how much I need it. You must coach me up to the last minute. Promise me that, Torvald!

HELMER. You can depend on me.

NORA. You must not think of anything but me, either today or tomorrow; you mustn't open a single letter—not even open the letter box—

HELMER. Ah, you are still afraid of that fellow—

NORA. Yes, indeed I am.

HELMER. Nora, I can tell from your looks that there is a letter from him lying there.

NORA. I don't know; I think there is; but you must not read anything of that kind now. Nothing horrid must come between us till this is all over.

RANK (*whispers to* HELMER). You mustn't contradict her.

HELMER (*taking her in his arms*). The child shall have her way. But tomorrow night, after you have danced—

NORA. Then you will be free. (*The* MAID *appears in the doorway to the right.*)

MAID. Dinner is served, ma'am.

NORA. We will have champagne, Helen.

MAID. Very good, ma'am. (*Exit.*)

HELMER. Hullo!—are we going to have a banquet?

NORA. Yes, a champagne banquet till the small hours. (*Calls out.*) And a few macaroons, Helen—lots, just for once!

HELMER. Come, come, don't be so wild and nervous. Be my own little skylark, as you used.

NORA. Yes, dear, I will. But go in now, and you too, Doctor Rank. Christine, you must help me to do up my hair.

RANK (*whispers to* HELMER *as they go out*). I suppose there is nothing—she is not expecting anything?

HELMER. Far from it, my dear fellow; it is simply nothing more than this childish nervousness I was telling you of. (*They go into the right-hand room.*)

NORA. Well!

MRS. LINDE. Gone out of town.

NORA. I could tell from your face.

MRS. LINDE. He is coming home tomorrow evening. I wrote a note for him.

NORA. You should have let it alone; you must prevent nothing. After all, it is splendid to be waiting for a wonderful thing to happen.

MRS. LINDE. What is it that you are waiting for?

NORA. Oh, you wouldn't understand. Go in to them, I will come in a moment. (MRS. LINDE *goes into the dining room.* NORA *stands still for a little while, as if to compose herself. Then she looks at her watch.*) Five o'clock. Seven hours till midnight; and then four-and-twenty hours till the next midnight. Then the tarantella will be over. Twenty-four and seven? Thirty-one hours to live.

HELMER (*from the doorway on the right*). Where's my little sky-lark?

NORA (*going to him with her arms outstretched*). Here she is!

Curtain

ACT III

THE SAME SCENE: *The table has been placed in the middle of the stage with chairs round it. A lamp is burning on the table. The door into the hall stands open. Dance music is heard in the room above.* MRS. LINDE *is sitting at the table idly turning over the leaves of a book; she tries to read but does not seem able to collect her thoughts. Every now and then she listens intently for a sound at the outer door.*

MRS. LINDE (*looking at her watch*). Not yet—and the time is nearly up. If only he does not— (*Listens again.*) Ah, there he is. (*Goes into the hall and opens the outer door carefully. Light footsteps are heard on the stairs. She whispers.*) Come in. There is no one here.

KROGSTAD (*in the doorway*). I found a note from you at home. What does this mean?

MRS. LINDE. It is absolutely necessary that I should have a talk with you.

KROGSTAD. Really? And it is absolutely necessary that it should be here?

MRS. LINDE. It is impossible where I live; there is no private entrance to my rooms. Come in; we are quite alone. The maid is asleep, and the Helmers are at the dance upstairs.

KROGSTAD (*coming into the room*). Are the Helmers really at a dance tonight?

MRS. LINDE. Yes, why not?

KROGSTAD. Certainly—why not?

MRS. LINDE. Now, Nils, let us have a talk.

KROGSTAD. Can we two have anything to talk about?

MRS. LINDE. We have a great deal to talk about.

KROGSTAD. I shouldn't have thought so.

MRS. LINDE. No, you have never properly understood me.

KROGSTAD. Was there anything else to understand except what was obvious to all the world—a heartless woman jilts a man when a more lucrative chance turns up?

MRS. LINDE. Do you believe I am as absolutely heartless as all that? And do you believe it with a light heart?

KROGSTAD. Didn't you?

MRS. LINDE. Nils, did you really think that?

KROGSTAD. If it were as you say, why did you write to me as you did at the time?

MRS. LINDE. I could do nothing else. As I had to break with you, it was my duty also to put an end to all that you felt for me.

KROGSTAD (*wringing his hands*). So that was it. And all this—only for the sake of money!

MRS. LINDE. You mustn't forget that I had a helpless mother and two little brothers. We couldn't wait for you, Nils; your prospects seemed hopeless then.

KROGSTAD. That may be so, but you had no right to throw me over for anyone else's sake.

MRS. LINDE. Indeed, I don't know. Many a time did I ask myself if I had the right to do it.

KROGSTAD (*more gently*). When I lost you it was as if all the solid ground went from under my feet. Look at me now—I am a ship-wrecked man clinging to a bit of wreckage.

MRS. LINDE. But help may be near.

KROGSTAD. It *was* near, but then you came and stood in my way.

MRS. LINDE. Unintentionally, Nils. It was only today that I learned it was your place I was going to take in the bank.

KROGSTAD. I believe you, if you say so. But now that you know it, are you not going to give it up to me?

MRS. LINDE. No, because that would not benefit you in the least.

KROGSTAD. Oh, benefit, benefit—I would have done it whether or no.

MRS. LINDE. I have learned to act prudently. Life and hard, bitter necessity have taught me that.

KROGSTAD. And life has taught me not to believe in fine speeches.

MRS. LINDE. Then life has taught you something very reasonable. But deeds you must believe in.

KROGSTAD. What do you mean by that?

MRS. LINDE. You said you were like a shipwrecked man clinging to some wreckage.

KROGSTAD. I had good reason to say so.

MRS. LINDE. Well, I am like a shipwrecked woman clinging to some wreckage—no one to mourn for, no one to care for.

KROGSTAD. It was your own choice.

MRS. LINDE. There was no other choice—then.

KROGSTAD. Well, what now?

MRS. LINDE. Nils, how would it be if we two shipwrecked people could join forces?

KROGSTAD. What are you saying?

MRS. LINDE. Two on the same piece of wreckage would stand a better chance than each on his own.

KROGSTAD. Christine!

MRS. LINDE. What do you suppose brought me to town?

KROGSTAD. Do you mean that you gave me a thought?

MRS. LINDE. I could not endure life without work. All my life, as long as I can remember, I have worked, and it has been my greatest and only pleasure. But now I am quite alone in the world—my life is so dreadfully empty and I feel so forsaken. There is not the least pleasure in working for one's self. Nils, give me someone and something to work for.

KROGSTAD. I don't trust that. It is nothing but a woman's overstrained sense of generosity that prompts you to make such an offer of yourself.

MRS. LINDE. Have you ever noticed anything of the sort in me?

KROGSTAD. Could you really do it? Tell me—do you know all about my past life?

MRS. LINDE. Yes.

KROGSTAD. And do you know what they think of me here?

MRS. LINDE. You seemed to me to imply that with me you might have been quite another man.

KROGSTAD. I am certain of it.

MRS. LINDE. Is it too late now?

KROGSTAD. Christine, are you saying this deliberately? Yes, I am sure you are. I see it in your face. Have you really the courage, then—

MRS. LINDE. I want to be a mother to someone, and your children need a mother. We two need each other. Nils, I have faith in your real character—I can dare anything with you.

KROGSTAD (*grasps her hands*). Thanks, thanks, Christine! Now I shall find a way to clear myself in the eyes of the world. Ah, but I forgot—

MRS. LINDE (*listening*). Hush! The tarantella! Go, go!

KROGSTAD. Why? What is it?

MRS. LINDE. Do you hear them up there? When that is over we may expect them back.

KROGSTAD. Yes, yes—I will go. But it is all no use. Of course you are not aware what steps I have taken in the matter of the Helmers.

MRS. LINDE. Yes, I know all about that.

KROGSTAD. And in spite of that have you the courage to—

MRS. LINDE. I understand very well to what lengths a man like you might be driven by despair.

KROGSTAD. If I could only undo what I have done!

MRS. LINDE. You cannot. Your letter is lying in the letter box now.

KROGSTAD. Are you sure of that?

MRS. LINDE. Quite sure, but—

KROGSTAD (*with a searching look at her*). Is that what it all means?— that you want to save your friend at any cost? Tell me frankly. Is that it?

MRS. LINDE. Nils, a woman who has once sold herself for another's sake doesn't do it a second time.

KROGSTAD. I will ask for my letter back.

MRS. LINDE. No, no.

KROGSTAD. Yes, of course I will. I will wait here till Helmer comes; I will tell him he must give me my letter back—that it only concerns my dismissal—that he is not to read it—

MRS. LINDE. No, Nils, you must not recall your letter.

KROGSTAD. But, tell me, wasn't it for that very purpose that you asked me to meet you here?

MRS. LINDE. In my first moment of fright it was. But twenty-four hours have elapsed since then, and in that time I have witnessed incredible things in this house. Helmer must know all about it. This unhappy secret must be disclosed; they must have a complete understanding between them, which is impossible with all this concealment and falsehood going on.

KROGSTAD. Very well, if you will take the responsibility. But there is one thing I can do in any case, and I shall do it at once.

MRS. LINDE (*listening*). You must be quick and go! The dance is over; we are not safe a moment longer.

KROGSTAD. I will wait for you below.

MRS. LINDE. Yes, do. You must see me back to my door.

KROGSTAD. I have never had such an amazing piece of good fortune in my life! (*Goes out through the outer door. The door between the room and the hall remains open.*)

MRS. LINDE (*tidying up the room and laying her hat and cloak ready*). What a difference! What a difference! Someone to work for and live for—a home to bring comfort into. That I will do, indeed. I wish they would be quick and come. (*Listens.*) Ah, there they are now. I must put on my things. (*Takes up her hat and cloak.* HELMER's *and* NORA's *voices are heard outside; a key is turned, and* HELMER *brings* NORA *almost by force into the hall. She is in an Italian costume with a large black shawl round her; he is in evening dress and a black domino which is flying open.*)

NORA (*hanging back in the doorway and struggling with him*). No, no, no!—don't take me in. I want to go upstairs again; I don't want to leave so early.

HELMER. But, my dearest Nora—

NORA. Please, Torvald dear—please, *please*—only an hour more.

HELMER. Not a single minute, my sweet Nora. You know that was our agreement. Come along into the room; you are catching cold standing there. (*He brings her gently into the room in spite of her resistance.*)

MRS. LINDE. Good evening.

NORA. Christine!

HELMER. You here so late, Mrs. Linde?

MRS. LINDE. Yes, you must excuse me; I was so anxious to see Nora in her dress.

NORA. Have you been sitting here waiting for me?

MRS. LINDE. Yes; unfortunately I came too late—you had already gone upstairs—and I thought I couldn't go away again without having seen you.

HELMER (*taking off* NORA's *shawl*). Yes, take a good look at her. I think she is worth looking at. Isn't she charming, Mrs. Linde?

MRS. LINDE. Yes, indeed she is.

HELMER. Doesn't she look remarkably pretty? Everyone thought so at the dance. But she is terribly self-willed, this sweet little person. What are we to do with her? You will hardly believe that I had almost to bring her away by force.

NORA. Torvald, you will repent not having let me stay, even if it were only for half an hour.

HELMER. Listen to her, Mrs. Linde! She had danced her tarantella, and it had been a tremendous success, as it deserved—although possibly the performance was a trifle too realistic—a little more so, I mean, than was strictly compatible with the limitations of art. But never mind about that! The chief thing is, she had made ·a success—she had made a tremendous success. Do you think I was going to let her remain there after that and spoil the effect? No indeed! I took my charming little Capri maiden—my capricious little Capri maiden, I should say—on my arm, took one quick turn round the room, a curtsey on either side, and, as they say in novels, the beautiful apparition disappeared. An exit ought always to be effective, Mrs. Linde; but that is what I cannot make Nora understand. Pooh! this room is hot. (*Throws his domino on a chair and opens the door of his room.*) Hullo! it's all dark in here. Oh, of course—excuse me. (*He goes in and lights some candles.*)

NORA (*in a hurried and breathless whisper*). Well?

MRS. LINDE (*in a low voice*). I have had a talk with him.

NORA. Yes, and—

MRS. LINDE. Nora, you must tell your husband all about it.

NORA (*in an expressionless voice*). I knew it.

MRS. LINDE. You have nothing to be afraid of as far as Krogstad is concerned, but you must tell him.

NORA. I won't tell him.

MRS. LINDE. Then the letter will.

NORA. Thank you, Christine. Now I know what I must do. Hush!

HELMER (*coming in again*). Well, Mrs. Linde, have you admired her?

MRS. LINDE. Yes, and now I will say good night.

HELMER. What, already? Is this yours, this knitting?

MRS. LINDE (*taking it*). Yes, thank you. I had very nearly forgotten it.

HELMER. So you knit?

MRS. LINDE. Of course.

HELMER. Do you know, you ought to embroider.

MRS. LINDE. Really? Why?

HELMER. Yes, it's far more becoming. Let me show you. You hold the embroidery thus in your left hand and use the needle with the right—like this—with a long easy sweep. Do you see?

MRS. LINDE. Yes, perhaps—

HELMER. Yes, but in the case of knitting—that can never be anything but ungraceful; look here—the arms close together, the knit-

ting needles going up and down—it has a sort of Chinese effect.
. . . That was really excellent champagne they gave us.

MRS. LINDE. Well—good night, Nora, and don't be self-willed any
more.

HELMER. That's right, Mrs. Linde.

MRS. LINDE. Good night, Mr. Helmer.

HELMER (*accompanying her to the door*). Good night, good night.
I hope you will get home all right. I should be very happy to—
But you haven't any great distance to go. Good night, good night.
(*She goes out; he shuts the door after her and comes in again.*)
Ah!—at last we have got rid of her. She is a frightful bore, that
woman.

NORA. Aren't you very tired, Torvald?

HELMER. No, not in the least.

NORA. Nor sleepy?

HELMER. Not a bit. On the contrary I feel extraordinarily lively.
And you?—you really look both tired and sleepy.

NORA. Yes, I am very tired. I want to go to sleep at once.

HELMER. There, you see it was quite right of me not to let you stay
there any longer.

NORA. Everything you do is quite right, Torvald.

HELMER (*kissing her on the forehead*). Now my little skylark is
speaking reasonably. Did you notice what good spirits Rank was
in this evening?

NORA. Really? Was he? I didn't speak to him at all.

HELMER. And I very little, but I have not for a long time seen him
in such good form. (*Looks for a while at her and then goes
nearer to her.*) It is delightful to be at home by ourselves again,
to be all alone with you—you fascinating, charming little darling!

NORA. Don't look at me like that, Torvald.

HELMER. Why shouldn't I look at my dearest treasure?—at all the
beauty that is mine, all my very own?

NORA (*going to the other side of the table*). You mustn't say things
like that to me tonight.

HELMER (*following her*). You have still got the tarantella in your
blood, I see. And it makes you more captivating than ever. Listen
—the guests are beginning to go now. (*In a lower voice.*) Nora—
soon the whole house will be quiet.

NORA. Yes, I hope so.

HELMER. Yes, my own darling Nora. Do you know that when I am out at a party with you like this why I speak so little to you, keep away from you and only send a stolen glance in your direction now and then?—do you know why I do that? It is because I make believe to myself that we are secretly in love and you are my secretly promised bride and that no one suspects there is anything between us.

NORA. Yes, yes—I know very well your thoughts are with me all the time.

HELMER. And when we are leaving and I am putting the shawl over your beautiful young shoulders—on your lovely neck—then I imagine that you are my young bride and that we have just come from our wedding and I am bringing you, for the first time, into our home—to be alone with you for the first time—quite alone with my shy little darling! All this evening I have longed for nothing but you. When I watched the seductive figures of the tarantella my blood was on fire; I could endure it no longer, and that was why I brought you down so early—

NORA. Go away, Torvald! You must let me go. I won't—

HELMER. What's that? You're joking, my little Nora! You won't—you won't? Am I not your husband? (A *knock is heard at the outer door.*)

NORA (*starting*). Did you hear—

HELMER (*going into the hall*). Who is it?

RANK (*outside*). It is I. May I come in for a moment?

HELMER (*in a fretful whisper*). Oh, what does he want now? (*Aloud.*) Wait a minute. (*Unlocks the door.*) Come, that's kind of you not to pass by our door.

RANK. I thought I heard your voice, and I felt as if I should like to look in. (*With a swift glance round.*) Ah yes!—these dear familiar rooms. You are very happy and cosy in here, you two.

HELMER. It seems to me that you looked after yourself pretty well upstairs too.

RANK. Excellently. Why shouldn't I? Why shouldn't one enjoy everything in this world?—at any rate as much as one man and as long as one can. The wine was capital—

HELMER. Especially the champagne.

RANK. So you noticed that too? It is almost incredible how much I managed to put away!

NORA. Torvald drank a great deal of champagne tonight too.

RANK. Did he?

NORA. Yes, and he is always in such good spirits afterward.

RANK. Well, why should one not enjoy a merry evening after a well-spent day?

HELMER. Well-spent? I am afraid I can't take credit for that.

RANK (*clapping him on the back*). But I can, you know!

HELMER. Exactly.

NORA. Doctor Rank, you must have been occupied with some scientific investigation today.

HELMER. Just listen!—little Nora talking about scientific investigations!

NORA. And may I congratulate you on the result?

RANK. Indeed you may.

NORA. Was it favorable, then?

RANK. The best possible, for both doctor and patient—certainty.

NORA (*quickly and searchingly*). Certainty?

RANK. Absolute certainty. So wasn't I entitled to make a merry evening of it after that?

NORA. Yes, you certainly were, Doctor Rank.

HELMER. I think so too, so long as you don't have to pay for it in the morning.

RANK. Oh well, one can't have anything in this life without paying for it.

NORA. Doctor Rank—are you fond of fancy-dress balls?

RANK. Yes, if there is a fine lot of pretty costumes.

NORA. Tell me—what shall we two wear at the next?

HELMER. Little featherbrain!—are you thinking of the next already?

RANK. We two? Yes, I can tell you. You shall go as a good fairy—

HELMER. Yes, but what do you suggest as an appropriate costume for that?

RANK. Let your wife go dressed just as she is in everyday life.

HELMER. That was really very prettily turned. But can't you tell us what you will be?

RANK. Yes, my dear friend, I have quite made up my mind about that.

HELMER. Well?

RANK. At the next fancy-dress ball I shall be invisible.

HELMER. That's a good joke!

RANK. There is a big black hat—have you ever heard of hats that make you invisible? If you put one on, no one can see you.

HELMER (*suppressing a smile*). Yes, you are quite right.

RANK. But I am clean forgetting what I came for. Helmer, give me a cigar—one of the dark Havanas.

HELMER. With the greatest pleasure. (*Offers him his case.*)

RANK (*takes a cigar and cuts off the end*). Thanks.

NORA (*striking a match*). Let me give you a light.

RANK. Thank you. (*She holds the match for him to light his cigar.*) And now good-by!

HELMER. Good-by, good-by, dear old man!

NORA. Sleep well, Doctor Rank.

RANK. Thank you for that wish.

NORA. Wish me the same.

RANK. You? Well, if you want me to sleep well! And thanks for the light. (*He nods to them both and goes out.*)

HELMER (*in a subdued voice*). He has drunk more than he ought.

NORA (*absently*). Maybe. (HELMER *takes a bunch of keys out of his pocket and goes into the hall.*) Torvald! What are going to do there?

HELMER. Empty the letter box; it is quite full; there will be no room to put the newspaper in tomorrow morning.

NORA. Are you going to work tonight?

HELMER. You know quite well I'm not. What is this? Someone has been at the lock.

NORA. At the lock?

HELMER. Yes, someone has. What can it mean? I should never have thought the maid— Here is a broken hairpin. Nora, it is one of yours.

NORA (*quickly*). Then it must have been the children.

HELMER. Then you must get them out of those ways. There, at last I have got it open. (*Takes out the contents of the letter box and calls to the kitchen.*) Helen! Helen, put out the light over the front door. (*Goes back into the room and shuts the door into the hall. He holds out his hand full of letters.*) Look at that—look what a heap of them there are. (*Turning them over.*) What on earth is that?

NORA (*at the window*). The letter— No! Torvald, no!

HELMER. Two cards—of Rank's.

NORA. Of Doctor Rank's?

HELMER (*looking at them*). Doctor Rank. They were on the top. He must have put them in when he went out.

NORA. Is there anything written on them?

HELMER. There is a black cross over the name. Look there—what an uncomfortable idea! It looks as if he were announcing his own death.

NORA. It is just what he is doing.

HELMER. What? Do you know anything about it? Has he said anything to you?

NORA. Yes. He told me that when the cards came it would be his leave-taking from us. He means to shut himself up and die.

HELMER. My poor old friend. Certainly I knew we should not have him very long with us. But so soon! And so he hides himself away like a wounded animal.

NORA. If it has to happen, it is best it should be without a word—don't you think so, Torvald?

HELMER (*walking up and down*). He had so grown into our lives. I can't think of him as having gone out of them. He, with his sufferings and his loneliness, was like a cloudy background to our sunlit happiness. Well, perhaps it is best so. For him, anyway. (*Standing still.*) And perhaps for us too, Nora. We two are thrown quite upon each other now. (*Puts his arms round her.*) My darling wife, I don't feel as if I could hold you tight enough. Do you know, Nora, I have often wished that you might be threatened by some great danger, so that I might risk my life's blood and everything for your sake.

NORA (*disengaging herself and speaking firmly and decidedly*). Now you must read your letters, Torvald.

HELMER. No, no; not tonight. I want to be with you, my darling wife.

NORA. With the thought of your friend's death—

HELMER. You are right; it has affected us both. Something ugly has come between us—the thought of the horrors of death. We must try and rid our minds of that. Until then—we will each go to our own room.

NORA (*hanging on his neck*). Good night, Torvald—good night!

HELMER (*kissing her on the forehead*). Good night, my little singing bird. Sleep sound, Nora. Now I will read my letters through.

(*He takes his letters and goes into his room, shutting the door after him*).

NORA (*gropes distractedly about, seizes* HELMER's *domino, throws it about her, speaking in quick, hoarse, spasmodic whispers*). Never to see him again. Never! Never! (*Puts her shawl over her head.*) Never to see my children again either—never again. Never! Never! Ah! the icy black water—the unfathomable depths—if only it were over! He has got it now—now he is reading it. Good-by, Torvald and my children! (*She is about to rush out through the hall when* HELMER *opens his door hurriedly and stands with an open letter in his hand.*)

HELMER. Nora!

NORA. Ah!

HELMER. What is this? Do you know what is in this letter?

NORA. Yes, I know. Let me go! Let me get out!

HELMER (*holding her back*). Where are you going?

NORA (*trying to get free*). You shan't save me, Torvald!

HELMER (*reeling*). True? Is this true, that I read here? Horrible! No, no—it is impossible that it is true.

NORA. It is true. I have loved you above everything else in the world.

HELMER. Oh, don't let us have any silly excuses.

NORA (*taking a step toward him*). Torvald!

HELMER. Miserable creature—what have you done?

NORA. Let me go. You shall not suffer for my sake. You shall not take it upon yourself.

HELMER. No tragedy airs, please. (*Locks the hall door.*) Here you shall stay and give me an explanation. Do you understand what you have done? Answer me! Do you understand what you have done?

NORA (*looking steadily at him and speaking with a growing look of coldness in her face*). Yes, now I am beginning to understand thoroughly.

HELMER (*walking about the room*). What a horrible awakening! All these eight years—she who was my joy and pride—a hypocrite, a liar—worse, worse—a criminal! The unutterable ugliness of it all! For shame! For shame! (NORA *is silent and looks steadily at him. He stops in front of her.*) I ought to have suspected that something of the sort would happen. I ought to have foreseen it. All your father's want of principle—be silent!—all your father's want of principle has come out in you. No religion, no morality, no sense of duty— How I am punished for having winked at what he did! I did it for your sake, and this is how you repay me.

NORA. Yes, that's just it.

HELMER. Now you have destroyed all my happiness. You have ruined all my future. It is horrible to think of! I am in the power of an unscrupulous man; he can do what he likes with me, ask anything he likes of me, give me any orders he pleases—I dare not refuse. And I must sink to such miserable depths because of a thoughtless woman!

NORA. When I am out of the way you will be free.

HELMER. No fine speeches, please. Your father had always plenty of those ready too. What good would it be to me if you were out of the way, as you say? Not the slightest. He can make the affair known everywhere; and if he does, I may be falsely suspected of having been a party to your criminal action. Very likely people will think I was behind it all—that it was I who prompted you! And I have to thank you for all this—you whom I have cherished during the whole of our married life. Do you understand now what it is you have done for me?

NORA (*coldly and quietly*). Yes.

HELMER. It is so incredible that I can't take it in. But we must come to some understanding. Take off that shawl. Take it off, I tell you. I must try and appease him in some way or another. The matter must be hushed up at any cost. And as for you and me, it must appear as if everything between us were just as before —but naturally only in the eyes of the world. You will still remain in my house, that is a matter of course. But I shall not allow you to bring up the children; I dare not trust them to you. To think that I should be obliged to say so to one whom I have loved so dearly and whom I still— No, that is all over. From this moment happiness is not the question; all that concerns us is to save the remains, the fragments, the appearance—

(A *ring is heard at the front doorbell.*)

HELMER (*with a start*). What is that? So late! Can the worst—can he— Hide yourself, Nora. Say you are ill.

(NORA *stand motionless.* HELMER *goes and unlocks the hall door.*)

MAID (*half dressed, comes to the door*). A letter for the mistress.

HELMER. Give it to me. (*Takes the letter and shuts the door.*) Yes, it is from him. You shall not have it; I will read it myself.

NORA. Yes, read it.

HELMER (*standing by the lamp*). I scarcely have the courage to do it. It may mean ruin for the both of us. No, I must know. (*Tears open the letter, runs his eye over a few lines, looks at a paper enclosed and gives a shout of joy.*) Nora! (*She looks at him questioningly.*) Nora! No, I must read it once again. Yes, it is true! I am saved! Nora, I am saved!

NORA. And I?

HELMER. You too, of course; we are both saved, both you and I. Look, he sends you your bond back. He says he regrets and re-pents—that a happy change in his life— Never mind what he says! We are saved, Nora! No one can do anything to you. Oh, Nora, Nora— No, first I must destroy these hateful things. Let me see. (*Takes a look at the bond.*) No, no, I won't look at it. The whole thing shall be nothing but a bad dream to me. (*Tears up the bond and both letters, throws them all into the stove and watches them burn.*) There—now it doesn't exist any longer. He says that since Christmas Eve you— These must have been three dreadful days for you, Nora.

NORA. I have fought a hard fight these three days.

HELMER. And suffered agonies and seen no way out, but— No, we won't call any of the horrors to mind. We will only shout with joy and keep saying, "It's all over! It's all over!" Listen to me, Nora. You don't seem to realize that it is all over. What is this?— such a cold, set face! My poor little Nora, I quite understand; you don't feel as if you could believe that I have forgiven you. But it is true, Nora, I swear it; I have forgiven you everything. I know that what you did you did out of love for me.

NORA. That is true.

HELMER. You have loved me as a wife ought to love her husband. Only you had not sufficient knowledge to judge of the means you used. But do you suppose you are any the less dear to me be-cause you don't understand how to act on your own responsibility? No, no; only lean on me; I will advise and direct you. I should not be a man if this womanly helplessness did not just give you a double attractiveness in my eyes. You must not think any more about the hard things I said in my first moment of consternation, when I thought everything was going to overwhelm me. I have forgiven you, Nora! I swear to you I have forgiven you.

NORA. Thank you for your forgiveness. (*She goes out through the door to the right.*)

HELMER. No, don't go. (*Looks in.*) What are you doing in there?

NORA (*from within*). Taking off my fancy dress.

HELMER (*standing at the open door*). Yes, do. Try and calm yourself and make your mind easy again, my frightened little singing bird. Be at rest and feel secure; I have broad wings to shelter you under. (*Walks up and down by the door.*) How warm and cosy our home is, Nora. Here is shelter for you; here I will protect you like a hunted dove that I have saved from a hawk's claws; I will bring peace to your poor beating heart. It will come, little by little, Nora, believe me. Tomorrow morning you will look upon it all quite differently; soon everything will be just as it was before. Very soon you won't need me to assure you that I have forgiven you; you will yourself feel the certainty that I have done so. Can you suppose I should ever think of such a thing as repudiating you or even reproaching you? You have no idea what a true man's heart is like, Nora. There is something so indescribably sweet and satisfying, to a man, in the knowledge that he has forgiven his wife—forgiven her freely and with all his heart. It seems as if that had made her, as it were, doubly his own; he has given her a new life, so to speak, and she has in a way become both wife and child to him. So you shall be for me after this, my little scared, helpless darling. Have no anxiety about anything, Nora; only be frank and open with me, and I will serve as will and conscience both to you— What is this? Not gone to bed? Have you changed your things?

NORA (*in everyday dress*). Yes, Torvald, I have changed my things now.

HELMER. But what for?—so late as this.

NORA. I shall not sleep tonight.

HELMER. But, my dear Nora—

NORA (*looking at her watch*). It is not so very late. Sit down here, Torvald. You and I have much to say to one another. (*She sits down at one side of the table.*)

HELMER. Nora—what is this?—this cold, set face?

NORA. Sit down. It will take some time; I have a lot to talk over with you.

HELMER (*sits down at the opposite side of the table*). You alarm
me, Nora!—and I don't understand you.

NORA. No, that is just it. You don't understand me, and I have
never understood you either—before tonight. No, you mustn't
interrupt me. You must simply listen to what I say. Torvald, this
is a settling of accounts.

HELMER. What do you mean by that?

NORA (*after a short silence*). Isn't there one thing that strikes you
as strange in our sitting here like this?

HELMER. What is that?

NORA. We have been married now eight years. Does it not occur
to you that this is the first time we two, you and I, husband and
wife, have had a serious conversation?

HELMER. What do you mean, serious?

NORA. In all these eight years—longer than that—from the very
beginning of our acquaintance we have never exchanged a word
on any serious subject.

HELMER. Was it likely that I would be continually and forever telling
you about worries that you could not help me to bear?

NORA. I am not speaking about business matters. I say that we have
never sat down in earnest together to try and get at the bottom
of anything.

HELMER. But, dearest Nora, would it have been any good to you?

NORA. That is just it; you have never understood me. I have been
greatly wronged, Torvald—first by Papa and then by you.

HELMER. What! By us two—by us two who have loved you better
than anyone else in the world?

NORA (*shaking her head*). You have never loved me. You have only
thought it pleasant to be in love with me.

HELMER. Nora, what do I hear you saying?

NORA. It is perfectly true, Torvald. When I was at home with Papa
he told me his opinion about everything, and so I had the same
opinions; and if I differed from him I concealed the fact, because
he would not have liked it. He called me his doll child, and he
played with me just as I used to play with my dolls. And when
I came to live with you—

HELMER. What sort of an expression is that to use about our marriage?

NORA (*undisturbed*). I mean that I was simply transferred from
Papa's hands to yours. You arranged everything according to your

own taste, and so I got the same tastes as you—or else I pretended to. I am really not quite sure which—I think sometimes the one and sometimes the other. When I look back on it it seems to me as if I have been living here like a poor woman—just from hand to mouth. I have existed merely to perform tricks for you, Torvald. But you would have it so. You and Papa have committed a great sin against me. It is your fault that I have made nothing of my life.

HELMER. How unreasonable and how ungrateful you are, Nora! Have you not been happy here?

NORA. No, I have never been happy. I thought I was, but it has never really been so.

HELMER. Not—not happy!

NORA. No, only merry. And you have always been so kind to me. But our home has been nothing but a playroom. I have been your doll wife, just as at home I was Papa's doll child; and here the children have been my dolls. I thought it great fun when you played with me, just as they thought it great fun when I played with them. That is what our marriage has been, Torvald.

HELMER. There is some truth in what you say—exaggerated and strained as your view of it is. But for the future it shall be different. Playtime shall be over and lesson time shall begin.

NORA. Whose lessons? Mine or the children's?

HELMER. Both yours and the children's, my darling Nora.

NORA. Alas, Torvald, you are not the man to educate me into being a proper wife for you.

HELMER. And you can say that!

NORA. And I—how am I fitted to bring up the children?

HELMER. Nora!

NORA. Didn't you say so yourself a little while ago—that you dare not trust me to bring them up?

HELMER. In a moment of anger! Why do you pay any heed to that?

NORA. Indeed, you were perfectly right. I am not fit for the task. There is another task I must undertake first. I must try and educate myself—you are not the man to help me in that. I must do that for myself. And that is why I am going to leave you now.

HELMER (springing up). What do you say?

NORA. I must stand quite alone if I am to understand myself and everything about me. It is for that reason that I cannot remain with you any longer.

HELMER. Nora, Nora!

NORA. I am going away from here now, at once. I am sure Christine will take me in for the night.

HELMER. You are out of your mind! I won't allow it! I forbid you!

NORA. It is no use forbidding me anything any longer. I will take with me what belongs to myself. I will take nothing from you, either now or later.

HELMER. What sort of madness is this?

NORA. Tomorrow I shall go home—I mean to my old home. It will be easiest for me to find something to do there.

HELMER. You blind, foolish woman!

NORA. I must try and get some sense, Torvald.

HELMER. To desert your home, your husband and your children! And you don't consider what people will say!

NORA. I cannot consider that at all. I only know that it is necessary for me.

HELMER. It's shocking. This is how you would neglect your most sacred duties.

NORA. What do you consider my most sacred duties?

HELMER. Do I need to tell you that? Are they not your duties to your husband and your children?

NORA. I have other duties just as sacred.

HELMER. That you have not. What could those be?

NORA. Duties to myself.

HELMER. Before all else you are a wife and a mother.

NORA. I don't believe that any longer. I believe that before all else I am a reasonable human being just as you are—or, at all events, that I must try and become one. I know quite well, Torvald, that most people would think you right and that views of that kind are to be found in books; but I can no longer content myself with what most people say or with what is found in books. I must think over things for myself and get to understand them.

HELMER. Can you understand your place in your own home? Have you not a reliable guide in such matters as that?—have you no religion?

NORA. I am afraid, Torvald, I do not exactly know what religion is.

HELMER. What are you saying?

NORA. I know nothing but what the clergyman said when I went to be confirmed. He told us that religion was this and that and the other. When I am away from all this and am alone I will look into that matter too. I will see if what the clergyman said is true, or at all events if it is true for me.

HELMER. This is unheard of in a girl of your age! But if religion cannot lead you aright, let me try and awaken your conscience. I suppose you have some moral sense? Or—answer me—am I to think you have none?

NORA. I assure you, Torvald, that is not an easy question to answer. I really don't know. The thing perplexes me altogether. I only know that you and I look at it in quite a different light. I am learning, too, that the law is quite another thing from what I supposed; but I find it impossible to convince myself that the law is right. According to it a woman has no right to spare her old dying father or to save her husband's life. I can't believe that.

HELMER. You talk like a child. You don't understand the conditions of the world in which you live.

NORA. No, I don't. But now I am going to try. I am going to see if I can make out who is right, the world or I.

HELMER. You are ill, Nora; you are delirious; I almost think you are out of your mind.

NORA. I have never felt my mind so clear and certain as tonight.

HELMER. And is it with a clear and certain mind that you forsake your husband and your children?

NORA. Yes, it is.

HELMER. Then there is only one possible explanation.

NORA. What is that?

HELMER. You do not love me any more.

NORA. No, that is just it.

HELMER. Nora!—and you can say that?

NORA. It gives me great pain, Torvald, for you have always been so kind to me, but I cannot help it. I do not love you any more.

HELMER (*regaining his composure*). Is that a clear and certain conviction too?

NORA. Yes, absolutely clear and certain. That is the reason why I will not stay here any longer.

HELMER. And can you tell me what I have done to forfeit your love?

NORA. Yes, indeed I can. It was tonight, when the wonderful thing did not happen; then I saw you were not the man I had thought you.

HELMER. Explain yourself better—I don't understand you.

NORA. I have waited so patiently for eight years; for, goodness knows, I knew very well that wonderful things don't happen every day. Then this horrible misfortune came upon me, and then I felt quite certain that the wonderful thing was going to happen at last. When Krogstad's letter was lying out there never for a moment did I imagine that you would consent to accept this man's conditions. I was so absolutely certain that you would say to him: Publish the thing to the whole world. And when that was done—

HELMER. Yes, what then?—when I had exposed my wife to shame and disgrace?

NORA. When that was done I was so absolutely certain you would come forward and take everything upon yourself and say: I am the guilty one.

HELMER. Nora!

NORA. You mean that I would never have accepted such a sacrifice on your part? No, of course not. But what would my assurances have been worth against yours? That was the wonderful thing which I hoped for and feared, and it was to prevent that that I wanted to kill myself.

HELMER. I would gladly work night and day for you, Nora—bear sorrow and want for your sake. But no man would sacrifice his honor for the one he loves.

NORA. It is a thing hundreds of thousands of women have done.

HELMER. Oh, you think and talk like a heedless child.

NORA. Maybe. But you neither think nor talk like the man I could bind myself to. As soon as your fear was over—and it was not fear for what threatened me but for what might happen to you—when the whole thing was past, as far as you were concerned it was exactly as if nothing at all had happened. Exactly as before, I was your little skylark, your doll, which you would in the future treat with doubly gentle care because it was so brittle and fragile. (*Getting up.*) Torvald—it was then it dawned upon me that for eight years I had been living here with a strange man and had borne him three children. Oh, I can't bear to think of it! I could tear myself into little bits!

HELMER (*sadly*). I see, I see. An abyss has opened between us— there is no denying it. But, Nora, would it not be possible to fill it up?

NORA. As I am now, I am no wife for you.

HELMER. I have it in me to become a different man.

NORA. Perhaps—if your doll is taken away from you.

HELMER. But to part—to part from you! No, no, Nora; I can't understand that idea.

NORA (*going out to the right*). That makes it all the more certain that it must be done. (*She comes back with her cloak and hat and a small bag which she puts on a chair by the table.*)

HELMER. Nora. Nora, not now! Wait till tomorrow.

NORA (*putting on her cloak*). I cannot spend the night in a strange man's room.

HELMER. But can't we live here like brother and sister?

NORA (*putting on her hat*). You know very well that would not last long. (*Puts the shawl round her.*) Good-by, Torvald. I won't see the little ones. I know they are in better hands than mine. As I am now, I can be of no use to them.

HELMER. But someday, Nora—someday?

NORA. How can I tell? I have no idea what is going to become of me.

HELMER. But you are my wife, whatever becomes of you.

NORA. Listen, Torvald. I have heard that when a wife deserts her husband's house, as I am doing now, he is legally freed from all obligations toward her. In any case I set you free from all your obligations. You are not to feel yourself bound in the slightest way, any more than I shall. There must be perfect freedom on both sides. See, here is your ring back. Give me mine.

HELMER. That too?

NORA. That too.

HELMER. Here it is.

NORA. That's right. Now it is all over. I have put the key here. The maids know all about everything in the house—better than I do. Tomorrow, after I have left her, Christine will come here and pack up my own things that I brought with me from home. I will have them sent after me.

HELMER. All over! All over! Nora, shall you never think of me again?

NORA. I know I shall often think of you and the children and this house.

HELMER. May I write to you, Nora?

NORA. No—never. You must not do that.

HELMER. But at least let me send you—

NORA. Nothing—nothing.

HELMER. Let me help you if you are in want.

NORA. No. I can receive nothing from a stranger.

HELMER. Nora—can I never be anything more than a stranger to you?

NORA (*taking her bag*). Ah, Torvald, the most wonderful thing of all would have to happen.

HELMER. Tell me what that would be!

NORA. Both you and I would have to be so changed that— Oh, Torvald, I don't believe any longer in wonderful things happening.

HELMER. But I will believe in it. Tell me. So changed that—

NORA. That our life together would be a real wedlock. Good-by. (*She goes out through the hall.*)

HELMER (*sinks down on a chair at the door and buries his face in his hands*). Nora! Nora! (*Looks round and rises.*) Empty! She is gone. (*A hope flashes across his mind.*) The most wonderful thing of all—?

(*The sound of a door shutting is heard from below.*)

Curtain

For Discussion

Act I

1. Ibsen gets the audience or reader into the center of the situation at the opening of the first scene. At the same time, he begins to reveal the kinds of people his characters are. Point out some of the endearing terms Helmer called his wife. What did they reveal about his attitude toward her? What did Nora's reaction reveal about her? How would you describe the relationship of Helmer and Nora in the first act?

2. What purpose did Mrs. Linde's arrival serve? Tell why you think it did, or did not, seem too much of a coincidence.

3. With the entrance of Krogstad, the suspense begins to build. Why? What was revealed that showed that Nora was not "just a child"?

4. In your opinion, was Nora justified in what she secretly did for her husband? Why or why not? What else might she have done? What did her attitude toward what she had done reveal about Nora?

5. Describe Nora's attitude toward her children. What did this show about her?
6. What crime had Krogstad committed in the past? Why was this ironical? What was Helmer's attitude toward Krogstad? Why did this frighten Nora?

Act II

1. What part did Dr. Rank play in Nora's life? What did this reveal about her relationship with Helmer? Why was Dr. Rank's confession to Nora both touching and dramatic, coming when it did in the play? Compare and contrast Dr. Rank's attitude toward Nora with that of Helmer's.
2. How did Nora's "dressing up" for the fancy-dress ball symbolize her marriage to Helmer? What significance did you see in the fact that Helmer chose her costume for her?
3. In her second interview with Krogstad, what new aspect of Nora was revealed? In your opinion, was Krogstad a completely unsympathetic character in this scene? Why or why not?
4. Can you guess what Nora meant when she said to Mrs. Linde, "A wonderful thing is going to happen . . . but . . . it mustn't happen for all the world." What effect did this statement have on you?
5. Point out the irony of Helmer's last line in this act, "Where's my little skylark?" How had Nora changed from Act I?
6. In a modern three-act play, which Ibsen did so much to establish, the conflict reaches its greatest moment of suspense at the end of the second act. What is the conflict in this play? What important question is the audience, or reader, left with at the end of the act?

Act III

1. In the first two acts, a relationship in the past between Mrs. Linde and Krogstad was hinted at. This relationship was revealed in Act III. What was it? In your opinion, was Mrs. Linde right in what she did many years before? Why or why not?
2. What part had circumstances, or environment, played in the lives of both Mrs. Linde and Krogstad? What reasons do you have for believing that their relationship in the future will be different from the kind that Nora and Helmer have had?
3. Why did Mrs. Linde refuse to allow Krogstad to get back his letter from Helmer, even though it would save Nora? What general criticism of marriage was Ibsen making at this point?
4. Just before Helmer opened his mail, he said, "Do you know, Nora, I have often wished that you might be threatened by some great danger,

so that I might risk my life's blood and everything for your sake."
Why was this particularly ironical in the light of what occurred a few
moments later? What was the great shock Nora received in listening
to Helmer's furious outburst?

5. In what Helmer said, what was revealed about his notions of heredity?
What attitude did he take toward society and the opinions of other
people? What do you think Ibsen felt about these matters?

6. What was so shocking about Helmer's reaction after he read the letter
from Krogstad in which he returned Nora's bond? Was this reaction
consistent with his attitude toward Nora throughout the play? Why
or why not?

7. In the final scene between Nora and Helmer, many things were brought
to light. Why did Nora feel she had been "greatly wronged"? What
part had her father played in this? How had her education and religious background contributed to her ignorance of the meaning of life
and marriage? What was it Nora felt she had to do in the future?

8. How did Helmer's reaction to Nora's decision reveal that he still did
not understand his wife or the real issue at stake?

Discussing the Play as a Whole

1. A *Doll's House* ends on a highly dramatic note. What emotion did
you experience at the play's ending? Explain why you felt as you did.

2. Was Nora right in clinging to her decision to leave Helmer? Did the
"unhappy" ending add to or detract from the effectiveness of the play
for you? Explain.

3. Do you think that the final words in the play, "The sound of a door
shutting is heard from below," symbolically represented defeat or
hope? Explain. Why do you think most contemporary critics have
said that the shutting of the door at the end of A *Doll's House* was
the beginning of the modern drama?

4. What is the fundamental problem of the play? Is it the conflict arising from Nora's early sacrifice for her husband and the ensuing results, or does it go deeper than that? Discuss fully.

5. What was the climax of the play? On what did you base your decision?
What purpose was served by the denouement which followed?

6. Show where Ibsen employed foreshadowing at various points in the
play to give the reader hints of what was to come.

7. What dramatic change did Nora undergo in the course of the play?
What other characters also changed? What characters seemed to develop rather than change? Explain.

8. In its time, this play was a dramatic and daring criticism of marriage in the nineteenth century. Summarize Ibsen's criticisms, including those concerning the attitudes of husbands and wives, the economic basis for middle-class marriages, and the rights of women. If this play were written today, which aspects of the play would remain as they are? Which would be different?
9. Do you think *A Doll's House* is dated? Why or why not? Why might audiences be stirred by the play today? Explain.

For Composition

1. In a short essay, compare and contrast the relationship of Nora and Helmer to that of the husband and wife in Strindberg's story, "Autumn."
2. "A play should lift the audience, or reader, intellectually, spiritually, and morally." Using this as your topic sentence, write a composition in which you show how *A Doll's House* does, or does not, fulfill this requirement.
3. Eric Bentley has said that Ibsen's characters lead lives that, under the pressure of dramatic events, reveal "not unexpected depths, but unexpected shallows." Is this true of the main characters in *A Doll's House*? Present your views in a well-organized paper, citing passages from the play to support your answer.
4. From a Catholic viewpoint, do you consider Nora's actions as a wife and mother ethically sound? Write a composition that is reasonable and clear, in which you express your views on this question.

GLOSSARY OF LITERARY TERMS

action: the series of incidents or happenings that occur in a work of fiction or play. *Rising action* is the incidents or happenings that lead to the climax of a story or play. *Falling action*, see *denouement*.

allegory: the use of characters, objects, or events in fiction or drama to represent moral, spiritual, or abstract ideas. Two famous allegories are *Everyman* and *Pilgrim's Progress*. See also: *parable, fable, morality play, personification, symbol*.

alliteration: the use of the same initial letter or sound in a group of two or more words that occur close together; for example, The *l*ittle *l*ady *l*oved to *l*isten to his stories.

antagonist: the character who directly opposes the main character in a play or work of fiction.

art-for-art's-sake: a literary and artistic movement of the late nineteenth and early twentieth centuries to which works of art were created and judged solely for their aesthetic values. This movement arose as a reaction against didactic art and literature that attempted to teach or moralize.

assonance: a partial rhyme that results from the use of the same stressed vowel sound in two or more words or syllables whose consonants differ; for example, *fate* and *sake*.

atmosphere: the over-all mood of a play or work of fiction; for example, the "eerie" atmosphere of a story by Poe.

blank verse: unrhymed verse in iambic pentameter.

caesura: a pause or break in the rhythm of a line of poetry that usually occurs near the middle of the line; for example,

"To be, or not to be, || that is the question."—Shakespeare

character, dynamic: a character that grows or develops during the action of a play or work of fiction. A *static* character is one that remains the same during the action.

characterization: the creation of characters in a literary work.

classicism: the principles of literature and art of the ancient Greeks and Romans. Classicism is characterized by attention to form, balance, proportion, regularity, simplicity, and emotional control.

341

Neoclassicism was the revival of classicism in literature and art in the seventeenth and eighteenth centuries.

climax: the highest point of interest, usually the decisive turning point of the main action in a drama or work of fiction.

conflict: the struggle between opposing forces, ideas, or significant characters that forms the basis of the plot of a story or a play. *Internal conflict* is the struggle that occurs within the heart and mind of a significant character. *External conflict* is the struggle between a significant character and an outside force.

connotation: the implied or suggested meanings that are associated with a word or expression.

couplet: two successive lines of verse that rhyme and are usually equal in length.

denouement: the final unraveling and resolution of the main conflict and minor complications in a play or story. The denouement is also called the *falling action*.

dialogue: the conversation between two or more characters in a literary work.

diction: the author's choice and arrangement of words, and the power and accuracy with which he uses them.

didactic: concerned with teaching a lesson, frequently a moral lesson.

elegy: a poem of meditation or lament about death that is usually written as an expression of personal grief.

essay: a short prose composition in which the author expresses his opinions on a particular subject. An *informal essay* is an essay that is written in a conversational and entertaining style. A *formal essay* is an essay that is usually serious, informative, thought-provoking, and objective.

euphemism: a mild, inoffensive word or expression that is used instead of one that is harsh or blunt, for example, "to pass away" is a euphemism for "to die."

exposition: a piece of writing in which a subject is explained. *Dramatic exposition* is the background information that the reader or audience must know in order to understand the motives and actions of the characters in a play.

figure of speech: an expression in which words are used in a non-literal way in order to convey a forceful or vivid mental picture.

For examples of figures of speech, see *simile, metaphor, personification, hyperbole, irony*.

flashback: a device by which an author interrupts a play or story to reveal events that occurred at an earlier time.

foot: a specific number of syllables in a definite pattern that forms a unit of rhythm in a line of verse; for example, an iambic foot consists of one unaccented syllable and one accented syllable ($\cup/$). Other frequently used poetic feet are the trochee ($/\cup$), the anapest ($\cup\cup/$), and the dactyl ($/\cup\cup$).

foreshadowing: the dropping of important hints by the author of a play or work of fiction to prepare the reader for the events that are to come.

free verse: poetry that consists of unrhymed lines with irregular rhythmic patterns.

hyperbole: a figure of speech in which obvious exaggeration is used; for example, Before he reached the dentist's office he died a thousand deaths.

imagery: the use of words to create mental pictures of sense impressions.

irony: a mode of expression in which the author says one thing but means the opposite. Irony is also an outcome of events that is contrary to what would normally be hoped for or expected.

legend: a story that has come down from the past that may have some historical basis. A second, though obsolete, meaning of legend is: the story of the life of a saint.

locale: the particular place in which the action of a work of fiction occurs.

lyric: a poem that has the form and musical quality of a song in which the poet expresses an intense personal feeling.

metaphor: a figure of speech in which two things are identified with each other, without using *like* or *as*; for example, The fog was a gray veil through which I viewed the city.

meter: the rhythm of a line of poetry that is created by the regular repetition of similar accent patterns or feet; for example,

"If músǐc bé thě foód ǒf lové, pľay ón."—Shakespeare

miracle play: a medieval religious drama about the life of a saint or a miracle performed by a saint.

monologue: a long speech in a play in which one character speaks alone.

mood: the state of feeling created by a literary work, such as a *sentimental* mood or a *whimsical* mood. See *atmosphere.*

moral: the lesson to be learned from a literary work.

morality play: a medieval religious play in which the characters are personifications of abstract virtues and vices, such as Honesty and Greed. The conflict in a morality play is between the forces of good and evil for the soul of Man.

motivation: the cause or reason that compels a character to act as he does.

mystery play: a religious play of the Middle Ages that is based upon stories from the Bible. A mystery play often includes comic elements.

narration: the recounting of an event or series of events. In a *simple narrative,* the details are arranged chronologically, as in a newspaper report of a robbery. In a *narrative with plot,* the details are arranged artistically rather than chronologically. A *narrative poem* is a poem in which a story is told.

naturalism: an extreme form of realism; a manner of writing which applied scientific concepts and methods to such problems as plot development and characterization. Naturalistic writers emphasized the minute and often sordid details of everyday life.

ode: a lengthy, dignified lyric poem of exaltation and praise about someone or something worthy of esteem.

onomatopoea: a word or phrase that imitates the sound of the thing it describes; for example, *buzz, clash, sizzle, hiss.*

paradox: a seemingly contradictory statement which may actually be true.

pathetic fallacy: the human traits and emotions attributed to nature; for example, The wind moaned.

personification: a figure of speech in which human form or characteristics are given to animals, objects, or ideas; for example,

"But look, the morn in russet mantle clad

Walks o'er the dew of yon high eastward hill."—Shakespeare

plot: the series of interrelated events that makes up the total action of a play or work of fiction.

point of view: the outlook or position from which a short story or novel is presented by the author. *First person point of view* is the telling of the story by one of the characters, frequently the main character. *Omniscient point of view* is the telling of the story by an outside observer who has complete knowledge and understanding of the characters and their actions.

protagonist: the main character in a story, novel, or play.

realism: a manner of writing in which things are presented as they actually exist in real life without romantic or idealistic coloring.

rhyme: the use in poetry of words whose final sounds are in agreement. *Internal rhyme* is the use of rhyme in the middle of lines of poetry, as well as at the end of lines. *Rhyme scheme* is the arrangement of lines in a poem so that their rhyming final sounds form a definite pattern.

rhythm: the regular rise and fall of sound; the uniform recurrence of an accent pattern in prose and poetry.

romanticism: a nineteenth-century movement in which writers and artists were concerned with their emotional reactions to the wonders of nature and to personal experience. The romantic writers exalted the primitive and common man, defended the downtrodden, and supported humanitarian causes. Romanticism arose as a reaction against neoclassic art and literature in which reason, intellect, and classical forms were stressed.

satire: the use of ridicule to expose, denounce, or poke fun at individuals, customs, or social and political institutions.

setting: the background for the action of a drama or work of fiction.

simile: a figure of speech in which two things are compared and shown to have at least one thing in common. The comparison is usually introduced by the word *like* or *as*; for example, The moon shone like a new silver dollar.

soliloquy: a speech in a play that is made by a character when he is alone, as if he were talking to himself. The purpose of a soliloquy is to inform the audience of the character's thoughts.

sonnet: a fourteen-line poem that deals with a single idea or emotion. The *Italian* or *Petrarchian sonnet* is divided into two parts. The first eight lines, or *octave*, has the rhyme scheme *abbaabba*. The last six lines, or *sestet*, has the rhyme scheme *cdcdcd*. The *English* or *Shakespearean sonnet* is divided into three *quatrains* and a final rhymed *couplet*. It has the rhyme scheme *abab, cdcd, efef, gg*.

style: the distinctive manner in which a writer chooses and arranges words.

surrealism: a movement in literature and art during the twentieth century, in which ideas and images are expressed in a seemingly non-logical order, as in a dream. Surrealistic writers give freedom to the imagination in an attempt to bridge the gap between the conscious and unconscious.

suspense: a feeling of excitement, intense curiosity, or expectation about the outcome of a play or work of fiction.

symbol: an object that represents an idea; for example, a dove represents peace; a pair of scales represents justice. The *symbolist poets* of the nineteenth and twentieth centuries, notably in France, used symbols extensively in their attempt to present the mystery of reality behind the everyday world.

synesthesia: the description of one of the senses in terms of another; for example, attributing color to sound, fragrance to color, sound to odors.

theme: the central thought or idea in a story, novel, or play. A *theme* is also a composition written about a single topic.

tone: the writer's attitude toward his subject that affects his style of writing and choice of words; for example, a *satirical* tone.

tragedy: a form of drama in which the protagonist undergoes a significant struggle and is defeated, sometimes because of a flaw in his own character, more often because he is unable to overcome the force, or forces, that oppose him.